# Lecture Notes in Computer Science    14150

Founding Editors

Gerhard Goos
Juris Hartmanis

The series Lecture Notes in Computer Science (LNCS), including its subseries Lecture Notes in Artificial Intelligence (LNAI) and Lecture Notes in Bioinformatics (LNBI), has established itself as a medium for the publication of new developments in computer science and information technology research, teaching, and education.

LNCS enjoys close cooperation with the computer science R & D community, the series counts many renowned academics among its volume editors and paper authors, and collaborates with prestigious societies. Its mission is to serve this international community by providing an invaluable service, mainly focused on the publication of conference and workshop proceedings and postproceedings. LNCS commenced publication in 1973.

Maciej Koutny · Robin Bergenthum ·
Gianfranco Ciardo
Editors

# Transactions on Petri Nets and Other Models of Concurrency XVII

*Editors-in-Chief*
Maciej Koutny ⓘ
School of Computing Science
Newcastle University
Newcastle upon Tyne, UK

*Guest Editors*
Robin Bergenthum
Fakultät Zentralbereich
FernUniversität in Hagen
Hagen, Nordrhein-Westfalen, Germany

Gianfranco Ciardo
Dept of Computer Science
Iowa State University
Ames, IA, USA

ISSN 0302-9743        ISSN 1611-3349 (electronic)
Lecture Notes in Computer Science
ISSN 1867-7193        ISSN 1867-7746 (electronic)
Transactions on Petri Nets and Other Models of Concurrency
ISBN 978-3-662-68190-9        ISBN 978-3-662-68191-6 (eBook)
https://doi.org/10.1007/978-3-662-68191-6

This Springer imprint is published by the registered company Springer-Verlag GmbH, DE,
part of Springer Nature
The registered company address is: Heidelberger Platz 3, 14197 Berlin, Germany

Paper in this product is recyclable.

# Preface by Editor-in-Chief

The 17th issue of LNCS *Transactions on Petri Nets and Other Models of Concurrency* (ToPNoC) contains revised and extended versions of a selection of the best papers from the workshops held at the 43rd International Conference on Application and Theory of Petri Nets and Concurrency (Petri Nets 2022, Bergen, Norway, 22–24 June 2022).

I would like to thank the two guest editors of this special issue: Robin Bergenthum and Gianfranco Ciardo. Moreover, I would like to thank all authors, reviewers, and organizers of the Petri Nets 2022 satellite workshops, without whom this issue of ToPNoC would not have been possible.

August 2023                                                                                   Maciej Koutny

# LNCS Transactions on Petri Nets and Other Models of Concurrency: Aims and Scope

ToPNoC aims to publish papers from all areas of Petri nets and other models of concurrency ranging from theoretical work to tool support and industrial applications. The foundations of Petri nets were laid by the pioneering work of Carl Adam Petri and his colleagues in the early 1960s. Since then, a huge volume of material has been developed and published in journals and books as well as presented at workshops and conferences.

The annual International Conference on Application and Theory of Petri Nets and Concurrency started in 1980. For more information on the international Petri net community, see: http://www.informatik.uni-hamburg.de/TGI/PetriNets/.

All issues of ToPNoC are LNCS volumes. Hence they appear in all main libraries and are also accessible on SpringerLink (electronically).

- Revised versions of a selection of the best papers from workshops and tutorials concerned with Petri nets and concurrency
- Special issues related to particular subareas (similar to those published in the *Advances in Petri Nets* series)
- Other papers invited for publication in ToPNoC
- Papers submitted directly to ToPNoC by their authors

Like all other journals, ToPNoC has an Editorial Board, which is responsible for the quality of the journal. The members of the board assist in the reviewing of papers submitted or invited for publication in ToPNoC. Moreover, they may make recommendations concerning collections of papers for special issues. The Editorial Board consists of prominent researchers within the Petri net community and in related fields.

## Topics

The topics covered include: system design and verification using nets; analysis and synthesis; structure and behavior of nets; relationships between net theory and other approaches; causality/partial order theory of concurrency; net-based semantical, logical and algebraic calculi; symbolic net representation (graphical or textual); computer tools for nets; experience with using nets, case studies; educational issues related to nets; higher-level net models; timed and stochastic nets; and standardization of nets.

Also included are applications of nets to: biological systems; security systems; e-commerce and trading; embedded systems; environmental systems; flexible manufacturing systems; hardware structures; health and medical systems; office automation; operations research; performance evaluation; programming languages; protocols and networks; railway networks; real-time systems; supervisory control; telecommunications; cyber physical systems; and workflow.

## Submission of Manuscripts

Manuscripts should follow LNCS formatting guidelines, and should be submitted as PDF or zipped PostScript files to ToPNoC@ncl.ac.uk. All queries should be addressed to the same e-mail address.

# Preface by Guest Editors

This volume of ToPNoC contains an extended version of a selected paper from the 43th International Conference on Application and Theory of Petri Nets and Concurrency (Petri Nets 2022):

- *A Toolchain to Compute Concurrent Places of Petri Nets*, by Nicolas Amat, Pierre Bouvier, and Hubert Garavel, presents a toolchain to revisit and tackle the concurrent-place problem. While the formulation of this problem is simple, its complexity is PSPACE-complete, making it a challenge for large inputs. The paper shows promising experimental results introducing a tool chain of five tools that combine various techniques to tackle nets from the Model Checking Contest.

and affiliated workshops, specifically, the International Workshop on Petri Nets and Software Engineering (PNSE 2022):

- *Development and Verification of a Microservice Architecture for a Fire Risk Notification System*, by Ruben Dobler Strand, Lars M. Kristensen, and Laure Petrucci, presents a Coloured Petri Net model specifying the software architecture of a microservice-based predictive fire risk notification system. The model captures the set of microservices provided via REST APIs as well as the interaction between all service components. The authors show how to use simulation and state-space exploration to verify key behavioral properties of the notification system.
- *Computing a Parametric Reveals Relation for Bounded Equal-Conflict Petri Nets*, by Federica Adobbati, Luca Bernardinello, Görkem Kılınç Soylu, and Lucia Pomello, revisits the "reveals" relation for Petri nets. If a Petri net contains both hidden and observable actions, it is of importance to check whether the occurrence of an observable action can reveal the occurrence of a hidden one. The paper presents a new and more efficient algorithm to tackle this problem.
- *Analysing Adaption Processes of Hornets*, by Michael Köhler-Bußmeier and Heiko Rölke, studies adaptive multi-agent systems modeled by HORNETs, which follow the net-within-nets paradigm where tokens of nets are nets. The paper presents key measures to capture the adaptive behavior of the system. The authors highlight their approach by applying it to Axelrod's tournament.

the International Health Data Workshop (HEDA 2022):

- *A Validated Learning Approach to Healthcare Process Analysis through Contextual and Temporal Filtering*, by Bahareh Fatemi, Fazle Rabbi, and Wendy MacCaull, introduces a validated learning approach for healthcare process analysis that uses a mix of data mining and formal methods techniques to generate and capture contextual and temporal insights. The approach is demonstrated on a healthcare event log analyzing comorbidity patterns.
- *A Case Study on Data Protection for a Cloud-and AI-based Homecare Medical Device*, by Philipp Bende, Olga Vovk, David Caraveo, Ludwig Pechmann, and Martin

Leucker, discusses the current state of data protection of homecare medical devices. The paper compares the risks of an attack to one's patients' data between using a homecare OCT device and a clinical OCT system in a secure hospital environment. Analyzing this case study, the paper advocates measures to mitigate the risks of a successful attack.

and the Algorithms and Theories for the Analysis of Event Data workshop (ATAED 2022):

- *Strategies for Minimising the Synthesised ENL-systems*, by Aishah Ahmed and Marta Pietkiewicz-Koutny, presents strategies to minimize Elementary Net Systems with Localities synthesized from step transition systems. The paper discusses properties of minimal regions and presents reduction rules to eliminate redundant ones. Besides the theoretical results, the approach is implemented and evaluated in the workcraft framework.
- *Implementable Strategies for a Two-Player Asynchronous Game on Petri Nets*, by Federica Adobbati, Luca Bernardinello, Lucia Pomello, and Riccardo Stramare, introduces a two-player game on Petri nets. One of the players follows a strategy that is implementable if there is a Petri net where all the runs are justified by the players' strategy. Using region theory, the paper presents an algorithm to decide whether a strategy is implementable or not.

In addition, the following papers were submitted directly to ToPNoC:

- *Confusion-Tolerant Computation of Probability in Acyclic Nets*, by Anirban Bhattacharyya and Maciej Koutny, presents a solution to the issue of how to compute probabilities in nets with confusion, where confusion is interference between concurrent choices of which enabled transition to perform.
- *An Efficient State Space Construction for a Class of Timed Automata*, by Johan Arcile, Raymond Devillers, and Hanna Klaudel, proposes a timed abstraction, called acceleration, for a class of networks of timed automata tailored to model systems composed out of non-deterministic cyclic agents updating shared variables.
- *Compositional Techniques for Boolean Networks and Attractor Analysis*, by Hanin Abdulrahman and Jason Steggles, extends recently proposed compositional framework for constructing and analysing Boolean networks based on merging entities using Boolean connectives, by developing a new general structure for compositions and by providing new techniques for compositionally identifying the attractors of a Boolean network.

We would like to thank the members of the Program Committees of these events, and especially the Program Committee Chairs, for assisting us in the initial selection of the papers for this special issues of ToPNoC. We invited the authors of the selected papers to submit extended versions of these papers, and we managed an anonymous review process where each paper was thoroughly reviewed by at least two reviewers, both to evaluate their intrinsic quality and to assess their additional contribution with respect to the original version. We are thus extremely grateful to the reviewers, who helped us evaluate each extended paper and provided valuable feedback to the respective authors.

Most importantly, we would like to recognize the authors themselves, whose work is the reason for this special issue of ToPNoC.

Finally, on a personal note, we would like to thank Maciej Koutny, editor-in-chief of ToPNoC, for his guidance in helping us perform our guest editor duties.

August 2023                                                    Robin Bergenthum
                                                               Gianfranco Ciardo

# Organization of This Issue

## Guest Editors

Robin Bergenthum — FernUniversität in Hagen, Germany
Gianfranco Ciardo — Iowa State University, USA

## Workshop Co-chairs

Michael Köhler-Bussmeier — University of Applied Science Hamburg, Germany
Yngve Lamo — Western Norway University of Applied Sciences, Norway
Robert Lorenz — University of Augsburg, Germany
Daniel Moldt — Universität Hamburg, Germany
Heiko Rölke — University of Applied Sciences Graubünden, Switzerland
Jan-Martin van der Werf — Utrecht University, The Netherlands
Sebastiaan J. van Zelst — Fraunhofer FIT/RWTH Aachen University, Germany

## Reviewers

Robin Bergenthum
Gianfranco Ciardo
José Manuel Colom
Philipp Czerner
Jörg Desel
Boudewijn van Dongen
Lisa Ehrlinger
Sabine Folz-Weinstein
Stefan Haar
Ekkart Kindler
Maciej Koutny
Jakub Kovar
Lars Kristensen
Yngve Lamo

Elena Gómez-Martínez
Lukasz Mikulski
Andrew Miner
Laure Petrucci
Gunnar Piho
Pascal Poizat
Ashur Rafiev
Andrey Rivkin
Wallapak Tavanapong
Yann Thierry-Mieg
Eric Verbeek
Alex Yakovlev
Wensheng Zhang

# Contents

# A Toolchain to Compute Concurrent Places of Petri Nets

Nicolas Amat[1]([✉])(iD), Pierre Bouvier[2], and Hubert Garavel[2]

[1] LAAS-CNRS, Université de Toulouse, CNRS, INSA, Toulouse, France
nicolas.amat@laas.fr
[2] Univ. Grenoble Alpes, INRIA, CNRS, Grenoble INP LIG, Grenoble, France

**Abstract.** The concurrent places of a Petri net are all pairs of places that may simultaneously have a token in some reachable marking. Concurrent places generalize the usual notion of dead places and are particularly useful for decomposing a Petri net into synchronized automata executing in parallel. We present a state-of-the-art toolchain to compute the concurrent places of a Petri net. This is achieved by a rich combination of various techniques, including: state-space exploration using BDDs, structural rules for concurrent places, quadratic over- and underapproximation of reachable markings, and polyhedral abstraction of the state space based on structural reductions and linear arithmetic constraints on markings. We assess the performance of our toolchain on a large collection of 850 nets originating from the 2022 edition of the Model Checking Contest.

**Keywords:** Petri nets · Nested-unit Petri nets · Model checking · Reachability problems · Concurrency theory · Abstraction techniques · Structural reductions · State-space exploration

## 1 Introduction

There is a rich corpus of scientific literature on the analysis of concurrent systems, which is a difficult topic, as most algorithms have a high complexity that increases with the size of the systems under study. Besides the usual properties expressing safety and liveness features of concurrent systems, the present article focuses on a less known property that fundamentally characterizes where parallelism is present in such systems. To present this property, a few preliminary definitions are necessary.

### 1.1 Petri Nets

Petri nets [31,32] are one of the oldest techniques for modelling concurrent systems. In this article, the full generality of Petri nets is not required and we can merely consider nets that are *ordinary* (i.e., all arcs have multiplicity one) and *one-safe* (i.e., all reachable markings contain at most one token per place).

M. Koutny et al. (Eds.): TPNOMCXVII, LNCS 14150, pp. 1–26, 2024.
https://doi.org/10.1007/978-3-662-68191-6_1

Formally, we define here a Petri net as a 4-tuple $(P, T, F, M_0)$, where $P$ is a finite, non-empty set (the elements of $P$ are called *places*); $T$ is a finite set such that $P \cap T = \varnothing$ (the elements of $T$ are called *transitions*); $F$ is a subset of $P \times T \cup T \times P$ (the elements of $F$ are called *arcs*); $M_0$ is a subset of $P$ ($M_0$ is called the *initial marking*). Figure 1 gives an example of a Petri net having 13 places (two of which being initial places), 11 transitions, and 26 arcs.

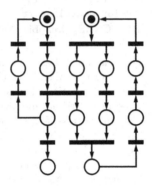

**Fig. 1.** An ordinary, one-safe Petri Net.

Given a transition $t \in T$, the *pre-set* of $t$ (noted ${}^\bullet t$) and the *post-set* of $t$ (noted $t^\bullet$) are the two sets of places defined as follows: ${}^\bullet t = \{p \in P \mid (p, t) \in F\}$ and $t^\bullet = \{p \in P \mid (t, p) \in F\}$.

A *marking* is a subset of $P$. A transition $t$ can fire from some marking $M_1$ to some other marking $M_2$ (noted $M_1 \xrightarrow{t} M_2$) iff ${}^\bullet t \subseteq M_1$ and $M_2 = (M_1 \setminus {}^\bullet t) \cup t^\bullet$. A marking $M$ is *reachable* from the initial marking $M_0$ iff $M = M_0$ or there exist $n \geq 1$ transitions $t_1, t_2, ..., t_n$ and $(n-1)$ markings $M_1, M_2, ..., M_{n-1}$ such that $M_0 \xrightarrow{t_1} M_1 \xrightarrow{t_2} M_2 ... M_{n-1} \xrightarrow{t_n} M$. To simplify the presentation, we denote by $(N, M_0)$ a marked net, which is a pair composed of a net $N \triangleq (P, T, F)$ and an initial marking $M_0$.

## 1.2   Nested-Unit Petri Nets

Nested-Unit Petri Nets (NUPNs, for short) [12,13] are a widespread extension of Petri nets for expressing *locality* and *hierarchy* properties of concurrent systems. The concept of NUPN is not recent (see, e.g., [18]), but it has been adopted by many recent Petri-net analysis tools, which significantly increase their performance by exploiting NUPN information about locality and hierarchy.

Formally, a NUPN is defined as a 8-tuple $(P, T, F, M_0, U, u_0, \sqsubseteq, \text{unit})$, where: $(P, T, F, M_0)$ is a Petri net (as defined in Sect. 1.1); $U$ is a finite, non-empty set such that $U \cap T = U \cap P = \varnothing$ (the elements of $U$ are called *units*); $u_0$ is an element of $U$ ($u_0$ is called the *root unit*); $\sqsubseteq$ is a binary relation over $U$ such that $(U, \sqsupseteq)$ is a tree with a single root $u_0$, where $(\forall u_1, u_2 \in U)$ $u_1 \sqsupseteq u_2$ is defined as $u_2 \sqsubseteq u_1$ ($\sqsubseteq$ is thus a reflexive, antisymmetric, and transitive relation that expresses that a unit is transitively included in another unit, the root unit $u_0$ being the maximal element for $\sqsubseteq$, i.e., the unit that transitively contains all other units); unit is a function $P \rightarrow U$ such that $(\forall u \in U \setminus \{u_0\})\ (\exists p \in P)$ unit $(p) = u$ (intuitively, unit $(p) = u$ expresses that unit $u$ directly contains place $p$). The *height* of a NUPN is the height of its unit tree, not counting the root unit if it contains no place directly (i.e., for each $p \in P$, unit $(p) \neq u_0$). The *width* of a NUPN is the number of leaf units in its unit tree.

The token game for NUPNs is exactly the same as for Petri nets, meaning that the rules for firing transitions and the set of reachable markings are not modified by the introduction of units.

A key property of NUPNs is the notion of *unit safeness* [13, Sect. 3], which generalizes the one-safeness property of Petri nets. Formally, two units $u_1$ and $u_2$ are *disjoint* iff $(u_1 \not\sqsubseteq u_2) \wedge (u_2 \not\sqsubseteq u_1)$, meaning that both units are neither equal nor contained one in the other. A NUPN is *unit-safe* iff each of its reachable markings (including $M_0$) only contains pairs of places located into disjoint units, meaning that each unit, or two transitively nested units, may not contain two tokens at the same time. This property enables logarithmic reductions in the number of bits or Boolean variables needed to represent reachable markings [13, Sect. 6].

In practice, the unit-related information, namely $(U, u_0, \sqsubseteq, \text{unit})$, is directly obtained when the NUPN is produced from a higher-level model [13, Sect. 4]. For instance, if the NUPN is generated from a process-calculus language such as LOTOS [21] or LNT [16], the unit tree can be deduced from the parallel composition operators present in the source specifications; if the NUPN is generated from a network of automata, the unit tree represents the various automata that execute concurrently; etc.

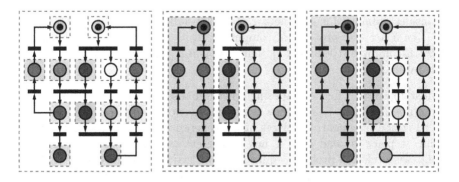

**Fig. 2.** Petri Net of Fig. 1 decomposed either into a trivial NUPN (left), a flat NUPN (middle) or a hierarchical NUPN (right).

Any unit-safe NUPN can be converted to an ordinary, one-safe Petri net by erasing unit-related information. Reciprocally, any ordinary, one-safe Petri net can be easily converted to a unit-safe NUPN by putting each of its places into a separate unit and having a root unit $u_0$ encapsulating all the other units; such a NUPN (whose width is equal to its number of places) is called *trivial* (see Fig. 2 (left)). Unfortunately, this easy transformation brings no gain for state-space exploration. However, an ordinary, one-safe Petri net may have various corresponding unit-safe NUPNs, which may be either *flat* if their height is one (see Fig. 2 (middle)) or *hierarchical* if their height is greater than one (see Fig. 2 (right)). Converting an ordinary, one-safe Petri net into a non-trivial unit-safe NUPN is an involved task (see [11] for insights on the decomposition into flat NUPNs), but may bring significant benefits for further analyses conducted with tools that take advantage of NUPN information.

### 1.3   Concurrent Places

We now introduce the notion of concurrent places, which is central to the present article. Given a net (Petri net or NUPN), two places $p$ and $p'$ are *concurrent* iff there exists a reachable marking $M$ such that both $p$ and $p'$ have a token in $M$. This relation is symmetric and quasi-reflexive; it is reflexive iff the net has no dead place (i.e., no place that has no token in any reachable marking) [10, Sect. 2.4].

This relation characterizes those parts of the net that can be simultaneously active. It is mentioned in many publications under various names, such as: *coexistency defined by markings* [23, Sect. 9], *concurrency graph* [24] [35], or *concurrency relation* [27, 29, 33] [17, 28], etc. These definitions slightly differ by minor details, such as the kind of Petri nets considered, or the handling of reflexivity, i.e., whether and when a place is concurrent or not with itself.

In general, this relation is relevant only for one-safe, ordinary Petri nets, since the presence of multiple tokens in the same places often implies that most pairs of places are concurrent [10, Sect. 2.4]. This retrospectively justifies our choice to consider ordinary, one-safe nets, rather than full-fledged P/T nets.

Given a net, the problem of computing all its pairs of concurrent places is PSPACE-complete [10, Sect. 2.5]. This problem is practically useful [14] for, at least, two reasons:

- Most approaches for decomposing a net into a set of concurrent automata or into a NUPN [11] require knowledge about concurrent places.
- The notion of concurrent places nicely generalizes the notion of dead places, since a place is dead iff it is not concurrent with itself. Determining dead places is a relevant problem, equivalent, for Petri nets, to dead-code removal in software engineering. Indeed, many global properties of a net can be changed to true or to false just by adding or removing dead places; also, the memory cost of verification is likely to be increased by the presence of dead places. For instance, the Grafcet specification [20] used in industrial automation prohibits Sequential Function Charts containing "unreachable" branches (i.e., Petri nets with dead places or dead transitions).

### 1.4   Outline

This article presents a toolchain that efficiently computes the concurrent places of a given net (Petri net or NUPN). Although such computation could be done by reusing some existing Petri-net model checker, this approach would not be efficient, as the number of temporal-logic formulas to be evaluated would be quadratic in the number of places: a more "global" algorithm should be preferred. To this aim, our toolchain integrates various tools implementing a combination of complementary analysis techniques, such as: state-space exploration using Binary Decision Diagrams (BDDs), structural rules for concurrent places, quadratic over- and under-approximation of reachable markings, and polyhedral abstraction of the state space based on structural reductions and linear arithmetic constraints on markings.

The remainder of the present article is organized as follows. Section 2 gives an overview of our toolchain from the user's point of view, by describing the software components as well as the supported formats for input and output data. Sections 3 and 4 present in detail the two main software components of the toolchain, CÆSAR.BDD and KONG, respectively. Section 5 provides experimental results obtained by applying the toolchain to a large collection of 850 nets used in the 2022 edition of the Model Checking Contest; the validation of the toolchain outputs is also discussed. Finally, Sect. 6 gives concluding remarks.

## 2   Overview of the Toolchain

This section presents our toolchain for computing the concurrent places of a given net. We adopt the point of view of an end user, by first introducing the main software components of the toolchain (Sect. 2.1), and then defining the format of its input data (Sect. 2.2) and output data (Sect. 2.3).

### 2.1   Software Components of the Toolchain

Our toolchain consists of five different tools:

1. CÆSAR.BDD (developed in Grenoble, France) is one of the many components of the CADP toolbox [15] and can be obtained as part of this toolbox[1]. CÆSAR.BDD is written in C and its principles are detailed below in Sect. 3. For our experiments, we used version 3.7 of CÆSAR.BDD, available with CADP version 2022-j *"Kista"* of October 2022. CÆSAR.BDD internally uses the most recent version 3.1.0 of Fabio Somenzi's CUDD library for BDDs.
2. CONCNUPN (developed in Grenoble, France) is a 830-line Python 3.7 program for checking one-safeness and unit-safeness, and cross-checking the results provided by CÆSAR.BDD. The command-line options of CONCNUPN are compatible with those of CÆSAR.BDD. Information about the use of CONCNUPN is given in Sect. 5.4.

---

[1] https://cadp.inria.fr.

3. KONG (developed in Toulouse, France) is a verification tool for Petri nets. Written in Python, it is available on GitHub[2] under the GPLv3 license. The principles and software architecture of KONG are presented in Sect. 4. For our experiments, we used version 3.0 of this tool.

4. PNML2NUPN (developed in Paris, France) is a translator that converts Petri nets to NUPNs. This tool can be downloaded from the Web[3]. We used version 4.0 of PNML2NUPN (February 2022).

5. REDUCE (developed in Toulouse, France) is a tool for computing polyhedral reductions. This tool is invoked by KONG, and is also used by the TINA.TEDD [9] and SMPT [4] model-checkers, which participate in the Model Checking Contest [7,25,26]. We use version 3.7 of REDUCE (January 2022), which has been recently added to the TINA model-checking toolbox[4].

For the end user, CÆSAR.BDD and KONG are the two main entry points of our toolchain. Both tools can be invoked separately on a net to compute the pairs of concurrent places. Yet, KONG uses CÆSAR.BDD and REDUCE as auxiliary tools, meaning that, if KONG is used, it will automatically invoke CÆSAR.BDD under the hood, thus delivering results always equal or better than those provided by CÆSAR.BDD. The user can also invoke CÆSAR.BDD directly but, in such case, will not benefit from the enhancements brought by the reduction techniques implemented in KONG.

## 2.2   Input Formats for Petri Nets

Our toolchain takes as input nets (Petri nets or NUPNs) that are expected to be ordinary and one-safe (or even unit-safe, in the case of NUPNs). Concretely, these models can be provided in two different formats:

- The PNML (Petri Net Markup Language) format [22], which is a standard, XML-based representation adopted by most Petri-net tools; PNML can also describe NUPNs, as it is equipped with a "tool-specific" extension[5] for encoding all unit-related information present in NUPNs.
- The NUPN format[6], which is a concise, human-readable representation of NUPNs; this format supports a "`!unit_safe`" pragma certifying that the NUPN is unit-safe[7], a "`!multiple_arcs`" pragma indicating that the NUPN was obtained from a non-ordinary P/T net, and a "`!multiple_initial_tokens`" pragma indicating that the NUPN was obtained from a non-safe P/T net, the initial marking of which contains places with several tokens.

---

[2] https://github.com/nicolasAmat/Kong.

[3] https://pnml.lip6.fr/pnml2nupn.

[4] https://projects.laas.fr/tina.

[5] https://mcc.lip6.fr/2022/nupn.php.

[6] https://cadp.inria.fr/man/nupn.html.

[7] When unit-safeness is known by construction, or if it has been proven later.

Depending on their format, the input files given to the toolchain should end with a suffix ".pnml" or ".nupn". It is worth noticing that CÆSAR.BDD and KONG are able to exploit the unit-related information present in their input files.

Conversion between both formats is easy: NUPN files can be translated to PNML files by invoking CÆSAR.BDD with its "-pnml" option, while PNML files can be translated to NUPN files by invoking either PNML2NUPN or the NDRIO tool[8] from the TINA toolbox.

The KONG tool supports both input formats, whereas CÆSAR.BDD only accepts the NUPN format. PNML files given to CÆSAR.BDD should therefore be pre-processed by PNML2NUPN. In practice, we observed that the depth-first-search order in which PNML2NUPN encodes the unit tree gives good results, while attempts at using other orders statistically degrade the performance of BDD calculations performed by CÆSAR.BDD.

## 2.3   Output Format for Concurrent Places

Given a net with $n$ places, our toolchain displays information about concurrent places using a dedicated file format that was carefully designed:

– We opt for a unique format, excluding the coexistence of two distinct formats, namely a compressed binary format to minimize disk space, and a textual format intended for humans. Indeed, the problem addressed by our toolchain does not justify the definition of two separate formats, the development of conversion tools between these formats, and the tedious manipulations to perform such conversions.
– The format should be concise and readable by humans; it is therefore a textual format, not based on XML. Given that the concurrent-place relation is symmetric, it can be represented as a lower triangular matrix (named *concurrency matrix*) containing $n(n + 1)/2$ characters. The $(i, j)$-th element of this matrix is equal to "1" if the corresponding places are concurrent, or to "0" if they are not. Each diagonal element of this matrix is "0" if the corresponding place is dead, or "1" otherwise.
   As a side note, CÆSAR.BDD may use "synonymous" characters for "0", in order to explain why two places are not concurrent. For instance, if the net is known to be unit-safe, any pair of places directly contained in the same unit cannot be concurrent, which is noted "=" rather than "0"; similarly, any pair of places contained in two nested units cannot be concurrent, which is noted "<" or ">"—see here[9] for details.
– Since the determination of concurrent places is PSPACE-complete, it may fail on large nets, by lack of memory or upon timeout, leaving a concurrency matrix that is not entirely computed. Instead of aborting the computation with no output at all, it is practically better to deliver a result that is a concurrency matrix with unknown values, which can later be replaced by

---

[8] https://projects.laas.fr/tina/manuals/ndrio.html.
[9] https://cadp.inria.fr/man/caesar.bdd.html.

either "0" or "1", based upon pessimistic assumptions (see, e.g., [11]). Such a matrix is called *partial* or *incomplete* and the file format uses the notation "." (a dot) for those elements corresponding to pairs of places where the concurrency relation is undecided. A concurrency matrix is *complete* iff it contains no "." element.

– Being quadratic in the number of places, the size of the concurrency matrix may get large. For instance, the nets used as benchmarks in Sect. 5 have an average number of places equal to 2665, leading to 3.4-Mbyte matrices, and the largest of these nets has 78,643 places, leading to a 2.9-Gbyte matrix. To ensure that large matrices can be stored in computer files of manageable sizes, our file format introduces a simple, yet effective run-length compression [14] on the lines of the concurrency matrix. Measured on 12,600+ examples, this compression reduces file sizes by a factor of 214 (mean value) up to 4270 (maximal value). The compression and decompression algorithms, together with an example of compressed matrix, are given in Appendix A.

## 3    Presentation of Caesar.bdd

### 3.1    Overview of Caesar.bdd

CÆSAR.BDD has been part of the CADP toolbox since 2004. Originally, it was introduced as an auxiliary tool for detecting dead transitions in the interpreted Petri nets generated by the LOTOS compiler [18] present in CADP; to this aim, symbolic methods (based on BDDs) were found to be more effective than explicit-state methods, and thus implemented in CÆSAR.BDD.

The tool was also capable of computing *concurrent units* in NUPNs (i.e., pairs of units that may simultaneously have a token in some reachable marking), a notion that is required to perform data-flow analyses on interpreted Petri nets [17].

As from 2013, CÆSAR.BDD has progressively been extended with new functionalities, such as the conversion of the NUPN file format to PNML (see Sect. 2.2) and the computation of 20 structural and behavioural properties of Petri nets (liveness, reversibility, etc.); the latter feature is routinely used by the organization team of the Model Checking Contest to check the properties of the models used during the competition.

The tool was further modified to enrich the NUPN file format with pragmas, place labels, transition labels, unit labels, and more stringent syntax and static-semantics constraints. Many new options were added to CÆSAR.BDD to query NUPN models: number of places, number of transitions, arc density, unit-tree height, etc.

CÆSAR.BDD was then extended with new algorithms for computing dead places, dead transitions, and concurrent places [10], which are useful notions when decomposing Petri nets into flat NUPNs (i.e., automata networks) [11] or hierarchical NUPNs.

Recently, the tool was enriched with new options that help detecting isomorphic Petri nets and NUPNs, a major issue when building and managing large benchmarks with tens or hundreds of thousands of nets, which are generated automatically and potentially contain many "duplicates".

## 3.2 Command-Line Invocation of Caesar.bdd

CÆSAR.BDD is a command-line tool with many (currently, 54) options[10]. Computing the concurrent places is done by invoking CÆSAR.BDD with its "-concurrent-places" option. The name of the input NUPN file is given on the command line and, if the file is correct, the concurrency matrix is displayed on the standard output. Environment variables (in the POSIX style) can be set to control the state-space exploration performed by CÆSAR.BDD; they will be presented in the next section.

## 3.3 Principles of Caesar.bdd

To compute the concurrent places, CÆSAR.BDD uses dedicated data structures (which also serve for its other options) and implements four methods, which are detailed in [10, Sect. 5] and used in combination:

1. *Marking graph exploration* performs a forward traversal of the state space, starting from the initial marking. The visited markings are stored symbolically using BDDs, as implemented in the CUDD library. The user can bound the exploration either by setting the environment variable `CAESAR_BDD_TIMEOUT` to a maximal number of seconds, or by setting the environment variable `CAESAR_BDD_ITERATIONS` to a maximal depth. Once the exploration terminates, the BDD containing all visited markings is queried repeatedly to decide whether a given pair of places belongs or not to at least one visited marking. If the exploration was fully done, the concurrency matrix is complete; otherwise, only a subset of concurrent pairs of places can be inferred from the visited markings.
2. *Structural rules* are a collection of 7 theorems that enable one to conclude that certain pairs of places are concurrent (or not concurrent) by examining only their local context. In particular, if the net is a unit-safe NUPN, this information is exploited to conclude that two places belonging to the same unit or to two nested units are not concurrent. Structural rules are applied repeatedly until saturation.
3. *Quadratic under-approximation* explores an abstraction of the marking graph by approximating a reachable marking $M$ by the set of all pairs[11] of places having a token in $M$. This is an under-approximation because the algorithm may miss exploring certain pairs of places that are actually reachable and concurrent. The exploration progresses forwards, starting from the initial marking (or, better, from all pairs of places already known to be concurrent), and produces a subset of concurrent pairs of places.

---

[10] https://cadp.inria.fr/man/caesar.bdd.html.
[11] In this method, singletons are also considered as pairs $\{p, p\}$.

4. *Quadratic over-approximation* also does a forward exploration of the marking graph, again abstracted away using a set of pairs of places, but performs (improving the prior approach of [29]) an over-approximation instead of an under-approximation. Indeed, the algorithm explores all markings that it assumes to be potentially reachable because all the pairs of places in each of these markings are potentially concurrent. If the exploration completes, it produces a subset of non-concurrent pairs of places.

CÆSAR.BDD applies these four complementary methods in sequence, in the specified order 1-2-3-4. The execution may terminate earlier, as soon as the concurrency matrix does not contain unknown values any more.

# 4  Presentation of Kong

## 4.1  Overview of Kong

KONG, the *Koncurrent places Grinder*, is an open-source[12] formal verification tool for Petri nets. It can take advantage of structural reductions to accelerate the verification of reachability properties.

KONG is written in Python and requires version 3.5 or higher. Scripts and models included in the GitHub repository are used for benchmarking and for continuous testing. KONG is intended to be as understandable as possible; the code is heavily documented, and we provide many tracing and debugging options that can help a user understand its inner workings.

The main application [5,6] of KONG is to accelerate the computation of the *concurrency relation* of a Petri net using polyhedral reductions, that is computing the concurrency relation on a reduced version of the input net, and then tracing back the result to the original net (more details in Sect. 4.4). But KONG is not only designed for this problem, as well as for one-safe and ordinary Petri nets. It also provides procedures to check if a given marking is reachable, without any constraints on the bound of places.

## 4.2  Command-Line Invocation of Kong

KONG offers a command-line interface with various subcommands to expose its different features. The tool provides several options, which are described in the documentation using "--help".

The main subcommands of KONG are "conc" and "dead" for, respectively, computing the concurrency relation and the list of dead places in a net.

KONG can be executed as a Python script or converted into a standalone executable using cx_Freeze. Each subcommand only requires the path to the input Petri net (with a .pnml or .nupn extension). Hence a typical call to KONG is of the form "./kong.py conc model.pnml". We also provide two main options to limit the exploration performed by CÆSAR.BDD: "--bdd-timeout" to set a

---

[12] https://github.com/nicolasAmat/Kong.

time limit and "`--bdd-iterations`" to limit the number of iterations. Debugging options are described in Sect. 4.6.

A call to "`kong.py conc`" delegates the computation of the concurrency relation on the reduced net to the tool CÆSAR.BDD. It can also take as input a precomputed concurrency matrix of the reduced net, using option "`--reduced-matrix`". Likewise, the "`dead`" subcommand provides such option if we have a precomputed list of dead places for the reduced net.

For the sake of readability, it is possible to disable the run-length encoding of the concurrency matrix produced by KONG or to print the place ordering.

### 4.3  Auxiliary Tools Invoked by Kong

When computing a concurrency matrix, KONG relies on an external tool, such as CÆSAR.BDD, to compute the concurrency matrix of the reduced net.

In our approach, the computation of polyhedral reductions is delegated to the tool REDUCE. We can also reuse a precomputed reduced net with the option "`--reduced-net`".

### 4.4  Principles of Kong

In a nutshell, KONG can compute a reduced Petri net, $(N', M')$, from an initial one, $(N, M)$, and prove properties about the initial net by exploring only the state space of the reduced one. A difference with previous works on structural reductions [8,30], is that our approach is not tailored to a particular class of properties—such as safety or the absence of deadlocks—but could be applied to more general problems.

The correctness of our tool relies on two main theoretical notions. First, a new state space abstraction method, that we called *polyhedral abstraction* in [1, 2], which involves a combination of structural reductions and linear arithmetic constraints between the marking of places. Second, a new data structure, called *Token Flow Graph* (TFG) in [5,6], that can be used to compute properties based on a polyhedral abstraction. We give a short overview of these two notions in this paper. Nonetheless, our main objective here is to describe the features implemented in our tool.

The basic operation involved in our approach is to compute reductions of the form $(N, M) \triangleright_E (N', M')$ where: $N$ is an initial Petri net (that we want to analyse); $N'$ is a residual net (hopefully simpler than $N$); and $E$ is a system of linear equations. The goal is to preserve enough information in $E$ so that we can rebuild the reachable markings of $N$ knowing only those of $N'$. We say in this case that $N$ and $N'$ are $E$-equivalent. While there are many examples of the benefits of structural reductions when model-checking Petri nets, the use of an equation system ($E$) for tracing back the effect of reductions is new.

A TFG is a Directed Acyclic Graph (DAG) that can be built from an $E$-equivalence statement, $(N, M) \triangleright_E (N', M')$, capturing the specific structure of the equations in $E$, that allows us to reason about the reachable markings by

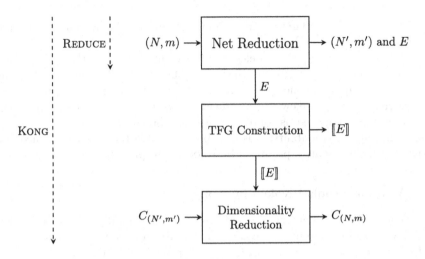

**Fig. 3.** KONG's architecture.

playing a token game on this graph. KONG can build a TFG from sequences of reductions computed using REDUCE, and use it to symbolically explore the state space of the initial net.

### 4.5    Software Architecture of Kong

Our tool is basically composed of three modules: `kong.py` the front-end program in charge of parsing command-line options; `pt.py` a Petri net parser; and `tfg.py` the data structure and computational module based on Token Flow Graphs. We illustrate the architecture of KONG in Fig. 3, where we describe the different steps involved during a typical computation. The first step is to reduce the input Petri net, say $(N, M)$, using the REDUCE tool. REDUCE outputs a reduced net $(N', M')$ and a system of linear equations $E$. We display in Fig. 4 a sequence of structural reductions, with their equations, computed using REDUCE. By construction, the result of this first stage is guaranteed to be a polyhedral abstraction. Then we build a Token Flow Graph, $[\![E]\!]$, from the set of linear equations in $E$.

If the initial net has some non-trivial NUPN information, we are able to project the decomposition on the reduced net. This can be done using the graph structure of the TFG.

At this stage, we must distinguish two possible cases. First, the net could be fully reduced, meaning the resulting net is "empty"; it has no remaining places. In this case, the set of markings of $(N, M)$ gives exactly the solutions of the linear system $E$. Hence, the TFG is enough to compute the concurrency matrix using an algorithm that we call *dimensionality reduction*. Otherwise, we have a non-trivial reduced net, in which case we need to compute the concurrency matrix of $(N', M')$.

## 4.6  Net Reduction on a Concrete Example

The simplest way to illustrate the usage of KONG is to look at a concrete example. This is also a good opportunity to show the debugging options provided by our tool. Assume $(N, M)$ is the net in top left position in Fig. 4.

Structural reduction is performed iteratively, until no new reductions are possible. We display, Fig. 4, a sequence of three reductions that leads to the result computed with REDUCE; the marked net at the bottom-right. Each row is an example of reduction, and its associated equation. First, it is always safe to remove a *redundant place*, e.g., a place with the same pre and post conditions than another one. This is the case with places $p_4, p_5$. Redundant places can sometimes be found by looking at the structure of the net, but we can use more elaborate methods to find redundant places by solving an integer linear programming problem [34]. After the removal of $p_5$, we obtain the equation $p_4 = p_5$, and we are left with the residual net at the left part of row 2. In this case, we can use an agglomeration rule, which states that we can fuse places inside a "deterministic sequence" of transitions. For instance, places $p_1$ and $p_2$ can be fused into a new place, $a_1$, and $p_3$, $p_4$ can be fused into $a_2$. Similar situations, where we can aggregate several places together, can be found by searching patterns in the net. After this step, we conclude with a new opportunity to reduce a redundant place, based on the structural invariant $a_1 = a_2$.

At the end of this process, we obtain the reduced net, $(N', M')$, with only 3 places instead of 6. We also obtain a system of four linear equations $E \triangleq (p_5 = p_4), (a_1 = p_1 + p_2), (a_2 = p_3 + p_4), (a_1 = a_2)$.

KONG provides an option, "`--save-reduced-net`", to save the reduced net into a specific file. Additionally, we can print the reduction equations with the option "`--show-equations`".

## 4.7  Token Flow Graph Construction

KONG can build the TFG associated with the linear system $E$; see Fig. 5. It is possible to output a graphical version of the TFG using option "`--draw-graph`", which requires the `graphviz` Python library. The TFG is a DAG where the vertices are the places of the input and reduced net, in addition to the free variables from $E$. The set of roots (nodes with no predecessor) is exactly the set of places of the reduced net $N'$. Arcs in the TFG are used to depict the relation induced by equations in $E$.

A TFG includes two different kinds of arcs. Arcs for *redundancy equations*, $q \twoheadrightarrow p$, represent equations of the form $p = q$ (or $p = q + r + \ldots$ in which case we also have $r \twoheadrightarrow p, \ldots$), corresponding to redundant places. In this case, we say that place $p$ is *removed* by arc $q \twoheadrightarrow p$, because the marking of $q$ may influence the marking of $p$, but not necessarily the other way round.

The second kind of arcs, $a \rightarrowtail p$, is for *agglomeration equations*. It represents equations of the form $a = p + q$, generated when we agglomerate several places into a new one. In this case, we expect that if we can reach a marking with $k$ tokens in $a$, then we can certainly reach a marking with $k_1$ tokens in $p$ and $k_2$

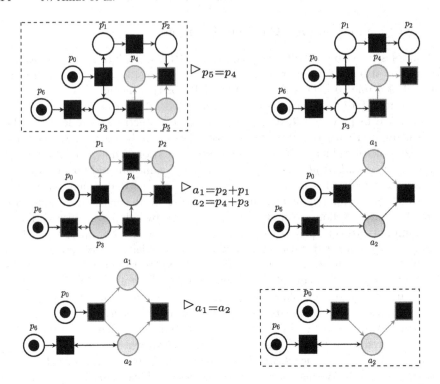

**Fig. 4.** Example of sequence of three reductions leading from the net $N$ to $N'$.

tokens in $q$ when $k = k_1 + k_2$. Hence, information flows in reverse order compared to the case of redundancy equations. This is why, in this case, we say that places $p$ and $q$ are removed. We also say that node $a$ is *inserted*; it does not appear in $N$ but may appear as a new place in $N'$. We can have more than two places in an agglomeration.

The idea is that each relation $X \twoheadrightarrow v$ or $v \circ\rightarrow X$ corresponds to one equation $v = \sum_{v_i \in X} v_i$ in $E$, and that all the equations in $E$ should be reflected in the TFG. We also want to avoid situations where the same place is removed more than once, or where some place occurs in the TFG but is never mentioned in $N$, $N'$ or $E$. All these constraints can be expressed using a suitable notion of well-formed graph built from $E$ in [5,6].

We can use the TFG to reason about the reachable markings of a net by playing a "token game" on this DAG. Basically, we can put tokens on the roots of the graph (given a marking of $N'$) then propagate them downwards while respecting the constraints dictated by the $\twoheadrightarrow$ and $\circ\rightarrow$ arcs. The result observed on the $\circ\rightarrow$-leaf nodes (the places of $N$) is guaranteed to be reachable in $(N, M)$.

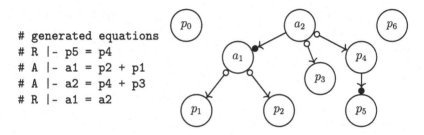

```
# generated equations
# R |- p5 = p4
# A |- a1 = p2 + p1
# A |- a2 = p4 + p3
# R |- a1 = a2
```

**Fig. 5.** Equations generated from net $N$, in Fig. 4, and associated TFG $[\![E]\!]$.

### 4.8   Dimensionality Reduction Algorithm

The final stage is to compute the concurrency matrix of the input net, $C_{(N,M)}$, from the one of the reduced net, $C_{(N',M')}$. Currently, KONG uses CÆSAR.BDD to compute $C_{(N',M')}$. But we could adapt KONG to use any other tool that can compute the concurrency relation, such as [36]. It is possible to output this matrix with option "`--show-reduced-matrix`".

We can give an intuition for our *Dimensionality Reduction* algorithm using our example. For instance, we have that place $a_2$, in the reduced net $N'$ of Fig. 4, is non-dead (because we can fire both input transitions). As a consequence, all the successors nodes of $a_2$ in the TFG (that are also places in $N$) must also be non-dead, meaning $C[p_i, p_i] = 1$ for all $i$ in 1..5. Also, we can deduce that $p_4$ is concurrent to $p_5$ (meaning $C[p_4, p_5] = 1$), because of the redundancy $p_5 = p_4$, and $p_1, p_2$ are concurrent to $p_3, p_4, p_5$. A detailed description of our algorithm can be found in [5,6].

## 5   Experiments with the Toolchain

We now report about the assessment of our integrated toolchain to large benchmarks of significant complexity. We first describe our benchmarks, and how they were produced (Sect. 5.1), then present the results of experiments on these benchmarks (Sects. 5.2 and 5.3), and finally discuss the validation of these results (Sect. 5.4).

### 5.1   Benchmarks for Experiments

We have chosen to base our assessment on the collection of Petri nets provided by the Model Checking Contest (MCC) [7,26], a yearly international competition devoted to the evaluation of formal verification tools. This collection grows every year and has been constructed by gathering complex models provided by the Petri-net community. Given that the challenge of computing concurrent places is not covered by the MCC, we are confident that this collection provides an unbiased ground for our experiments.

The 2022 edition of the MCC[13] provides 128 (potentially parameterized) models, which amount to a total of 1628 individual nets. After excluding colored nets, this total drops down to 1387 nets, available in both PNML and NUPN formats. We opted for the NUPN format, taking as is any model natively provided in this format, while converting all other models from PNML to NUPN using the PNML2NUPN translator. Since our experiments require unit-safe NUPNs (keeping in mind that one-safe, ordinary nets are trivial, unit-safe NUPNs), we proceeded in two (independent) steps:

– Among these 1387 nets, we kept those that were ordinary and whose initial marking was one-safe; this was done by discarding all NUPN files containing "`!multiple_arcs`" or "`!multiple_initial_tokens`" pragmas. This resulted in 777 nets, from which we selected those that were provably unit-safe, either because they contained a "`!unit_safe`" pragma, or by invoking CÆSAR.BDD or CONCNUPN to check unit-safeness[14]. This led to 705 nets, from which we further excluded 3 nets that were found to be (potentially) isomorphic to 3 other nets according to structural signatures computed using CÆSAR.BDD with its "`-signature`" option. We therefore obtained 702 unit-safe, non-isomorphic NUPNs.

– Among these 1387 nets, we also considered the 610 ones containing "`!multiple_arcs`" and/or "`!multiple_initial_tokens`" pragmas. By deleting these pragmas, we obtained "new" nets, in which each arc has multiplicity one and each place contains at most one token initially. Again, we retained only those nets that were provably unit-safe, using CÆSAR.BDD and/or CONCNUPN, followed by a manual verification of the safeness indications given by the authors of these models. This resulted in 439 nets, from which we eliminated all (potentially) isomorphic nets, still using structural signatures; doing so, many nets were rejected, because a fraction of MCC nets are just derived from each other by changing the number of tokens in the initial marking. This left us with 148 unit-safe, non-isomorphic NUPNs.

By gathering both sets of 702 and 148 nets, we obtained a collection of 850 nets. We made sure that all of them have distinct structural signatures, so that the collection contains no isomorphic duplicates. Notice that this collection is twice as large as that used in our earlier work [3], which used 424 nets taken from the 2021 edition of the MCC. Table 1 summarizes statistical properties about our collection, highlighting its diversity of models.

To assess the performance of our toolchain on "traditional" Petri nets (as in our earlier work [3]), we built a second collection of 850 nets obtained by removing all unit-related information from the NUPNs of the collection described in Table 1. Notice that 18.6% of the first collection (i.e., 158 trivial NUPNs) are also present in the second collection, and that the second collection contains a pair of isomorphic duplicates, originating from two NUPNs that only differ by their unit trees.

---

[13] https://mcc.lip6.fr/2022/models.php.

[14] This succeeded for all the nets considered here, although, in general, unit-safeness may be difficult to determine for large nets.

**Table 1.** Structural, behavioural, and numerical properties of the 850 NUPNs.

| property | yes | no | property | yes | no |
|---|---|---|---|---|---|
| pure | 57.3% | 42.7% | connected | 94.5% | 5.5% |
| free-choice | 2.4% | 97.6% | strongly connected | 20.2% | 79.8% |
| extended free-choice | 2.4% | 97.6% | conservative | 9.3% | 90.7% |
| marked graph | 0.0% | 100.0% | sub-conservative | 16.6% | 83.4% |
| state machine | 0.7% | 99.3% | trivial | 18.6% | 81.4% |

| feature | min value | max value | average | median | std deviation |
|---|---|---|---|---|---|
| #places | 4 | 78 643 | 2 665.2 | 403 | 7 712 |
| #transitions | 1 | 1 070 836 | 10 479.5 | 677 | 48 460 |
| #arcs | 4 | 25 615 632 | 106 034 | 2 760 | 1 023 467 |
| arc density | 0 | 50 | 1.7 | 0.5 | 3.6 |
| #units | 4 | 78 644 | 1 317 | 67 | 5 800 |
| height | 1 | 2 891 | 24.4 | 2 | 164.6 |
| width | 3 | 78 643 | 1 273.7 | 56 | 5 799 |

## 5.2 Experiments on Nested-Unit Petri Nets

We assessed the performance of our toolchain by separately running CÆSAR.BDD and KONG (which itself invokes REDUCE to compute net reductions, and CÆSAR.BDD to compute the concurrency matrices of reduced nets) on each of the 850 NUPNs of our first collection. Each run was made using two different wallclock timeout values: 10 min (corresponding to the patience of a human user waiting for the result computed by a tool) and one hour (corresponding to the duration granted by the MCC to each of its examinations). In order to vary the computation time allocated to the marking-graph-exploration phase of CÆSAR.BDD, we set the environment variable CAESAR_BDD_TIMEOUT to three possible values: 25%, 50%, and 75% of the wallclock timeout. To perform our experiments, we used the machine clusters (Intel x64 processors) of the French GRID'5000 testbed[15]; further details about the experimental setting are given in Sect. 5.4.

Table 2 summarizes the outcome of these experiments, focussing on three types of results: (i) the percentage of complete matrices generated by a tool during a specified timeout; (ii) the average percentage of known values (i.e., "0" or "1") in all the matrices generated from the 850 NUPNs; and (iii) the average computation time taken by the tool to generate these matrices.

Finally, we present supplementary data to address potential biases that could affect the average computation time in our performance evaluation due to the significant difference between general computation time and the timeout value.

---

[15] https://www.grid5000.fr.

**Table 2.** Performance results of the toolchain on the first collection.

| observed results | tool | timeout | |
|---|---|---|---|
| | | 10 min | 1 h |
| complete matrices | CÆSAR.BDD | 62.7% | 66.6% |
| | KONG | 64.5% | 67.6% |
| average matrix completion | CÆSAR.BDD | 72.1% | 76.2% |
| | KONG | 74.4% | 77.4% |
| average computation time | CÆSAR.BDD | 3 min 36 s | 17 min 44 s |
| | KONG | 3 min 14 s | 16 min 40 s |
| average computation time, considering only those matrices fully computed by both tools | CÆSAR.BDD | 46 s | 3 min 26 s |
| | KONG | 33 s | 2 min 26 s |

We calculate the average time based solely on matrices that are successfully computed by both tools (525 and 527 respectively, with timeouts of 10 min and 1 h). By excluding partial matrices, we ensure a more accurate representation of the acceleration achieved when KONGis used in conjunction with CÆSAR.BDD.

In this table, CAESAR_BDD_TIMEOUT is set to 50% of the wallclock timeout (i.e., 5 and 30 min); our experiments show that, when CAESAR_BDD_TIMEOUT increases, the number of complete matrices slightly increases (by 1.7% maximum) but matrix completion decreases (by −4.8% maximum), as BDD calculations take most of the time, preventing later approaches (structural rules, quadratic under- and over-approximations) from being applied.

The key finding of Table 2 is that our toolchain can entirely solve 64.5% of our first collection in less than ten minutes.

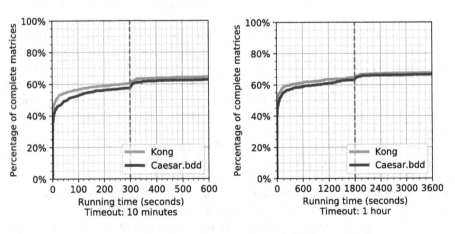

**Fig. 6.** Percentage of complete matrices on the first collection.

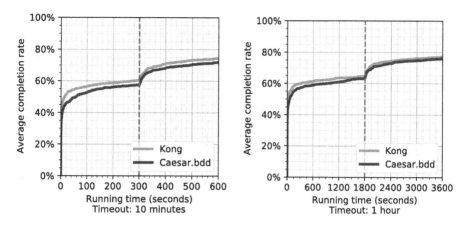

**Fig. 7.** Average matrix completion on the first collection.

Figures 6 and 7 provide additional information about the speed of the tools by showing the growth, as time elapses, of the number of complete matrices generated and the matrix completion rate. The red dotted vertical line corresponds to the 50% value given to `CAESAR_BDD_TIMEOUT` (5 and 30 min, respectively). These figures show very fast progress during the first minutes, which progressively slows down, followed by a rebound upon expiration of the BDD timeout, as other techniques (structural rules, under- and over-approximations) are executed and show their effectiveness. Despite the impression given by these figures, there is no horizontal asymptote, as infinite CPU time should allow the results to reach 100%.

### 5.3   Experimental Results on Petri Nets

We did the same experiments as in Sect. 5.2 on our second collection, which contains Petri nets without unit-related information. Table 3 presents the results of these experiments. Compared to Table 2, all percentages are significantly lower, since the symbolic exploration of reachable markings becomes more demanding once unit-related information has been dropped, thereby increasing the number of BDD variables: this confirms the practical importance of the NUPN concept. In Table 3, the value of `CAESAR_BDD_TIMEOUT` is set to 50%; our experiments show that, when `CAESAR_BDD_TIMEOUT` increases, the number of complete matrices slightly increases (by 3.8% maximum) but matrix completion decreases (by −6.3% maximum); these observations are in line with those of Sect. 5.2, the influence of `CAESAR_BDD_TIMEOUT` being somewhat greater when unit-related information is not present.

Figures 8 and 9 show the effectiveness of our toolchain as time elapses. Together with Table 3, these figures illustrate the added value of the structural reductions performed by KONG, especially when state-space exploration is time-intensive.

**Table 3.** Performance results of the toolchain on the second collection.

| observed results | tool | timeout | |
|---|---|---|---|
| | | 10 min | 1 h |
| complete matrices | CÆSAR.BDD | 52.5% | 59.9% |
| | KONG | 59.6% | 63.4% |
| average matrix completion | CÆSAR.BDD | 62.1% | 68.1% |
| | KONG | 69.8% | 73.7% |
| average computation time | CÆSAR.BDD | 4 min 30 s | 23 min 28 s |
| | KONG | 3 min 39 s | 19 min 16 s |
| average computation time, considering only those matrices fully computed by both tools | CÆSAR.BDD | 50 s | 5 min 18 s |
| | KONG | 29 s | 2 min 34 s |

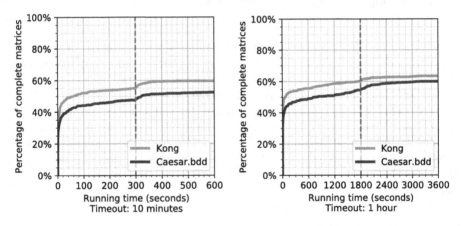

**Fig. 8.** Percentage of complete matrices on the second collection.

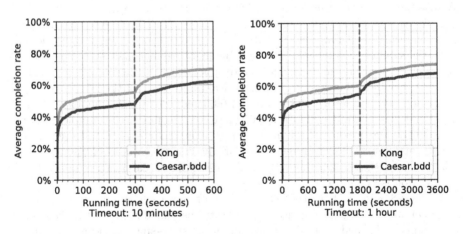

**Fig. 9.** Average matrix completion on the second collection.

## 5.4   Validation of Results

Beforehand, the algorithms of CÆSAR.BDD for computing concurrent places had been intensively validated on a test suite of 13,116 nets [10, Sect. 5.6]. When bringing together the software components of our toolchain, we also did a preliminary validation of KONG on roughly 7 200 "small" nets (having less than 20 places each), and brought enhancements to ensure plain interoperability between the components of the toolchain.

For the validation of results, we also used CONCNUPN, which implements the quadratic under- and over-approximations of Sect. 3.3. This tool can be invoked exactly in the same way as CÆSAR.BDD, but ignores the `CAESAR_BDD_TIMEOUT` and `CAESAR_BDD_ITERATIONS` environment variables, as it does not perform any BDD-based marking graph exploration.

On each x64 machine of the GRID'5000 testbed, we decided to run only two experiments in parallel, in order to benefit from the highest clock frequency of the processor, and to avoid dividing the 96-Gbyte RAM between too many tasks. The exit status and the standard error stream of each tool invoked to compute concurrency matrices was systematically recorded and analysed. This enabled us to proactively detect crashes, unexpected interrupts, and other run-time errors (e.g., memory shortage arising from two memory-intensive benchmarks concurrently running on the same machine). When there was a doubt about an execution, it was systematically restarted as a single task on a machine. All experiments were repeated to ensure that their results, including execution times and matrix completion rates, were consistent across executions.

We checked that each concurrency matrix generated by our experiments was syntactically correct, i.e., that the matrix after decompression was indeed triangular, only contained valid characters, and was not truncated (having as many rows as places of the corresponding net).

We developed a script that checks whether two matrices generated from the same net are *compatible*, which is defined as follows: for each "0" element in one matrix, the corresponding element in the other matrix should be "0" or ".", and for each "1" element in one matrix, the corresponding element in the other matrix should be "1" or ".". In particular, two complete matrices are compatible iff they are identical.

For each of the 850 benchmarks of Sect. 5.1, we generated many matrices by invoking our tools with various options: (i) CÆSAR.BDD was invoked with several BDD-timeout values, including 0, which means that the marking graph exploration (see Sect. 3.3) is turned off, and $+\infty$ (actually, the value of the global timeout), which means that structural rules and the quadratic under- and over-approximations are never invoked; (ii) KONG was invoked with three different back-ends: CÆSAR.BDD (invoked with several timeout values), CONCNUPN, and a "dummy" tool that always gives KONG a reduced matrix containing only unknown values; (iii) CONCNUPN was invoked too. For each non-trivial NUPN, we also generated these matrices for the Petri net obtained by removing all unit-related information from the NUPN. In total, this gave 17 matrices for each trivial NUPN and 34 matrices for each non-trivial NUPN; we cross-checked all these matrices two by two to make sure that they are compatible, and did not find any problem.

## 6  Conclusion

The concurrent-place problem is an old issue, which can be traced back at least to the 80 s [23, Sect. 9]. It is of practical importance, as it subsumes the dead-place problem and seems unavoidable for decomposing a net into a flat or hierarchical NUPN. The formulation of this problem is extremely simple, but its complexity (PSPACE-complete) makes it difficult, especially on large nets, for which the solution may require too much memory or time, unless one is ready to accept partial solutions only (namely, incomplete concurrency matrices).

The present article proposes a toolchain that addresses this fascinating problem. The toolchain combines different tools that implement a wealth of complementary techniques: state-space exploration using BDDs, structural rules for concurrent places, quadratic over- and under-approximation of reachable markings, and polyhedral abstraction of the state space based on structural reductions and linear arithmetic constraints on markings.

When applied to a collection of 850 nets from the Model Checking Contest, our toolchain was able to determine all concurrent places for roughly 55% of the nets in less than one minute, and 65% in less than ten minutes. Building this toolchain enabled us to improve the individual tools, e.g., by making sure that KONG introduces no performance overhead when directly invoking CÆSAR.BDD on input nets that cannot be reduced.

Concerning future work, the clearest objective would be to improve the toolchain and its components to better address the challenging nets of our benchmark. For instance:

- CÆSAR.BDD could be enhanced with heuristics to keep the dynamic reordering of BDDs under control (avoiding situations where, on large nets, most of the CPU time is spent in reordering) and by implementing more compact BDD encodings for the markings of unit-safe, hierarchical NUPNs (so as to reduce the number of BDD variables).
- KONG is also destined to evolve. We plan to explore new reduction rules, and we are particularly interested in reachability queries expressed using a Boolean combination of constraints over place markings. Another interesting problem would be the verification of generalized mutual exclusion constraints, as in [19], that amount to invariants $\sum_{p \in P} w_p.m(p) \leqslant k$ involving weighted sums over the marking of places, with $w_1, \ldots, w_n$, and $k$ constants in $\mathbb{Z}$.

Finally, we believe that the concurrent-place problem should become part of the Model Checking Contest, so as to foster the development of new algorithms and tools for this problem. Such an evolution could take place after a few preliminary changes, such as replacing Boolean queries (e.g., *does the net contain dead places?*) by more precise ones (e.g., *what are the dead places of the net?*).

**Acknowledgements.** Experiments presented in this paper were carried out using the GRID'5000 testbed, supported by a scientific interest group hosted by INRIA and including CNRS, RENATER, and several Universities as well as other organizations. We are grateful to Lom Messan Hillah for his PNML2NUPN translator, to Fabio Somenzi for providing us with the latest version 3.1.0 of CUDD, to Bernard Berthomieu for providing the tool REDUCE, and to Silvano Dal Zilio and Didier Le Botlan for their contributions to KONG.

# A     Run-Length-Encoding Compression

As mentioned in Sect. 2.3, each line of the concurrency matrix is compressed using a simple run-length-encoding scheme: any sequence of $n > 3$ consecutive identical characters is replaced by a single character followed by the value of $n$ enclosed between parentheses. For instance, the following sequence of 18 characters: "10000.........001" is replaced by a sequence of 13 characters: "10(4).(10)001". Table 4 illustrates the compression of an entire matrix, and Table 5 gives an implementation in C of the compression and decompression algorithms (which we also implemented in Awk, Python, and Bourne shell).

This scheme enjoys three nice properties: (i) the size (in characters) of the compressed output is always less or equal to the size of the input; in practice, we observed a reduction factor of 214 (mean value) up to 4270 (maximal value) measured on 12,671 NUPNs; (ii) compressing an already compressed input has no effect; (iii) compression and decompression can operate on the fly (e.g., using coroutines, pipes, or data streams), meaning that it is not mandatory to generate a matrix entirely before starting to compress it, and that one can compare two (or more) compressed matrices without having to decompress them entirely in advance.

**Table 4.** Sample uncompressed matrix (left) and its compressed version (right).

| | |
|---|---|
| 1 | 1 |
| 01 | 01 |
| 001 | 001 |
| 0001 | 0001 |
| 0000. | 0(4). |
| 00000. | 0(5). |
| 0000001 | 0(6)1 |
| 0.0000.. | 0.0(4).. |
| 010000.01 | 010(4).01 |
| 010000.001 | 010(4).001 |
| 010000.0001 | 010(4).0001 |
| 0010.0000001 | 0010.0(6)1 |
| 00010.0000001 | 00010.0(6)1 |
| 010000.0000001 | 010(4).0(6)1 |
| 01..000......11 | 01..000.(6)11 |
| 0.00000.0000000. | 0.0(5).0(7). |
| 0000.........001 | 0(4).(10)001 |

**Table 5.** Decompression (left) and compression (right) algorithms.

```c
#include <assert.h>
#include <stdbool.h>
#include <stdio.h>

int uncompress () {
    char c, previous = '\0';
    int repeat = 0;
    while (true) {
        if (repeat > 0) {
            assert (previous != '\0');
            assert (previous != '\n');
            putchar (previous);
            -- repeat;
        } else {
            c = getchar ();
            if (c == EOF)
                return 0;
            if (c != '(') {
                putchar (c);
                previous = c;
            } else {
                scanf ("%d)", &repeat);
                assert (repeat > 3);
                -- repeat;
            }
        }
    }
}
```

```c
int compress () {
    char c, previous = '\0';
    int n, repeat = 0;
    while (true) {
        c = getchar ();
        if (c == previous) {
            assert (c != '\0');
            assert (c != EOF);
            assert (c != '\n');
            ++ repeat;
        } else {
            // flush repetition buffer, if any
            if (repeat > 3) {
                printf ("(%d)", repeat);
            } else if (repeat > 0) {
                for (n = 1; n < repeat; ++ n)
                    putchar (previous);
            }
            if (c == EOF)
                return 0;
            putchar (c);
            if (c == '0') {
                previous = '\0';
                repeat = 0;
            } else {
                previous = c;
                repeat = 1;
            }
        }
    }
}
```

# References

1. Amat, N., Berthomieu, B., Dal Zilio, S.: On the combination of polyhedral abstraction and SMT-based model checking for Petri nets. In: Buchs, D., Carmona, J. (eds.) PETRI NETS 2021. LNCS, vol. 12734, pp. 164–185. Springer, Cham (2021). https://doi.org/10.1007/978-3-030-76983-3_9

2. Amat, N., Berthomieu, B., Dal Zilio, S.: A polyhedral abstraction for Petri Nets and its application to SMT-based model checking. Fund. Inform. **187**(2–4), 103–138 (2022). https://doi.org/10.3233/FI-222134, publisher: IOS Press

3. Amat, N., Chauvet, L.: Kong: a tool to squash concurrent places. In: Bernardinello, L., Petrucci, L. (eds.) PETRI NETS 2022. LNCS, vol. 13288, pp. 115–126. Springer, Cham (2022). https://doi.org/10.1007/978-3-031-06653-5_6

4. Amat, N., Dal Zilio, S.: SMPT: a testbed for reachabilty methods in generalized Petri nets. In: Chechik, M., Katoen, J.P., Leucker, M. (eds.) FM 2023. LNCS, vol. 14000, pp. 445–453. Springer, Cham (2023). https://doi.org/10.1007/978-3-031-27481-7_25

5. Amat, N., Dal Zilio, S., Le Botlan, D.: Accelerating the computation of dead and concurrent places using reductions. In: Laarman, A., Sokolova, A. (eds.) SPIN 2021. LNCS, vol. 12864, pp. 45–62. Springer, Cham (2021). https://doi.org/10.1007/978-3-030-84629-9_3

6. Amat, N., Dal Zilio, S., Le Botlan, D.: Leveraging polyhedral reductions for solving Petri net reachability problems. Int. J. Softw. Tools Technol. Transfer (2022). https://doi.org/10.1007/s10009-022-00694-8

7. Amparore, E., et al.: Presentation of the 9th edition of the model checking contest. In: Beyer, D., Huisman, M., Kordon, F., Steffen, B. (eds.) TACAS 2019. LNCS, vol. 11429, pp. 50–68. Springer, Cham (2019). https://doi.org/10.1007/978-3-030-17502-3_4

8. Berthelot, G.: Transformations and decompositions of nets. In: Brauer, W., Reisig, W., Rozenberg, G. (eds.) ACPN 1986. LNCS, vol. 254, pp. 359–376. Springer, Heidelberg (1987). https://doi.org/10.1007/978-3-540-47919-2_13

9. Berthomieu, B., Ribet, P.O., Vernadat, F.: The tool TINA - construction of abstract state spaces for Petri nets and time Petri nets. Int. J. Prod. Res. **42**(14) (2004).https://doi.org/10.1080/00207540412331312688

10. Bouvier, P., Garavel, H.: Efficient algorithms for three reachability problems in safe Petri nets. In: Buchs, D., Carmona, J. (eds.) PETRI NETS 2021. LNCS, vol. 12734, pp. 339–359. Springer, Cham (2021). https://doi.org/10.1007/978-3-030-76983-3_17

11. Bouvier, P., Garavel, H., Ponce-de-León, H.: Automatic decomposition of Petri nets into automata networks – a synthetic account. In: Janicki, R., Sidorova, N., Chatain, T. (eds.) PETRI NETS 2020. LNCS, vol. 12152, pp. 3–23. Springer, Cham (2020). https://doi.org/10.1007/978-3-030-51831-8_1

12. Garavel, H.: Nested-unit Petri nets: a structural means to increase efficiency and scalability of verification on elementary nets. In: Devillers, R., Valmari, A. (eds.) PETRI NETS 2015. LNCS, vol. 9115, pp. 179–199. Springer, Cham (2015). https://doi.org/10.1007/978-3-319-19488-2_9

13. Garavel, H.: Nested-unit Petri nets. J. Logical Algebraic Methods Program. **104**, 60–85 (2019)

14. Garavel, H.: Proposal for adding useful features to Petri-net model checkers. Technical report, abs/2101.05024, arXiv Computing Research Repository, December 2020. https://hal.inria.fr/hal-03087421

15. Garavel, H., Lang, F., Mateescu, R., Serwe, W.: CADP 2011: a toolbox for the construction and analysis of distributed processes. Springer Int. J. Softw. Tools Technol. Transf. (STTT) **15**(2), 89–107 (2013)

16. Garavel, H., Lang, F., Serwe, W.: From LOTOS to LNT. In: Katoen, J.-P., Langerak, R., Rensink, A. (eds.) ModelEd, TestEd, TrustEd. LNCS, vol. 10500, pp. 3–26. Springer, Cham (2017). https://doi.org/10.1007/978-3-319-68270-9_1

17. Garavel, H., Serwe, W.: State space reduction for process algebra specifications. Theoret. Comput. Sci. **351**(2), 131–145 (2006)

18. Garavel, H., Sifakis, J.: Compilation and verification of LOTOS specifications. In: Logrippo, L., Probert, R.L., Ural, H. (eds.) Proceedings of the 10th IFIP International Symposium on Protocol Specification, Testing and Verification (PSTV'90), Ottawa, Canada, pp. 379–394. North-Holland, June 1990

19. Giua, A., DiCesare, F., Silva, M.: Generalized mutual exclusion constraints on nets with uncontrollable transitions. In: IEEE International Conference on Systems, Man, and Cybernetics. IEEE (1992). https://doi.org/10.1109/ICSMC.1992.271666

20. IEC: GRAFCET specification language for sequential function charts. International Standard 60848:2013, International Electrotechnical Commission, Geneva, February 2013

21. ISO/IEC: LOTOS - A Formal Description Technique Based on the Temporal Ordering of Observational Behaviour. International Standard 8807, International Organization for Standardization - Information Processing Systems - Open Systems Interconnection, Geneva, September 1989

22. ISO/IEC: High-level Petri Nets - Part 2: Transfer Format. International Standard 15909-2:2011, International Organization for Standardization - Information Technology - Systems and Software Engineering, Geneva (2011)

23. Janicki, R.: Nets, sequential components and concurrency relations. Theoret. Comput. Sci. **29**, 87–121 (1984)

24. Karatkevich, A.: Conditions of SM-coverability of Petri nets, September 2012. https://www.researchgate.net/publication/267508814_Conditions_of_SM-Coverability_of_Petri_Nets

25. Kordon, F., et al.: Complete Results for the 2021 Edition of the Model Checking Contest, June 2021. http://mcc.lip6.fr/2021/results.php

26. Kordon, F., et al.: Complete Results for the 2022 Edition of the Model Checking Contest, June 2022. https://mcc.lip6.fr/2022/results.php

27. Kovalyov, A.V.: Concurrency relations and the safety problem for Petri nets. In: Jensen, K. (ed.) ICATPN 1992. LNCS, vol. 616, pp. 299–309. Springer, Heidelberg (1992). https://doi.org/10.1007/3-540-55676-1_17

28. Kovalyov, A.: A polynomial algorithm to compute the concurrency relation of a regular STG. In: Yakovlev, A., Gomes, L., Lavagno, L. (eds.) Hardware Design and Petri Nets, pp. 107–126. Springer, Boston (2000). https://doi.org/10.1007/978-1-4757-3143-9_6

29. Kovalyov, A., Esparza, J.: A polynomial algorithm to compute the concurrency relation of free-choice signal transition graphs. In: Proceedings of the 3rd Workshop on Discrete Event Systems (WODES'96), Edinburgh, Scotland, UK, pp. 1–6 (1996)

30. Murata, T., Koh, J.: Reduction and expansion of live and safe marked graphs. IEEE Trans. Circuits Syst. **27**(1) (1980). https://doi.org/10.1109/TCS.1980.1084711

31. Murata, T.: Petri nets: analysis and applications. Proc. IEEE **77**(4), 541–580 (1989)

32. Peterson, J.L.: Petri nets. ACM Comput. Surv. **9**(3), 223–252 (1977)

33. Semenov, A., Yakovlev, A.: Combining partial orders and symbolic traversal for efficient verification of asynchronous circuits. In: Ohtsuki, T., Johnson, S. (eds.) Proceedings of the 12th International Conference on Computer Hardware Description Languages and their Applications (CHDL'95), Makuhari, Chiba, Japan. IEEE, August–September 1995

34. Silva, M., Terue, E., Colom, J.M.: Linear algebraic and linear programming techniques for the analysis of place/transition net systems. In: Reisig, W., Rozenberg, G. (eds.) ACPN 1996. LNCS, vol. 1491, pp. 309–373. Springer, Heidelberg (1998). https://doi.org/10.1007/3-540-65306-6_19

35. Wiśniewski, R., Karatkevich, A., Adamski, M., Kur, D.: Application of comparability graphs in decomposition of Petri nets. In: Proceedings of the 7th International Conference on Human System Interactions (HSI'14), Costa da Caparica, Portugal, pp. 216–220. IEEE, June 2014

36. Wiśniewski, R., Wiśniewska, M., Jarnut, M.: C-exact hypergraphs in concurrency and sequentiality analyses of cyber-physical systems specified by safe Petri nets. IEEE Access **7** (2019). https://doi.org/10.1109/ACCESS.2019.2893284

# Development and Verification of a Microservice Architecture for a Fire Risk Notification System

Ruben Dobler Strand[1]([✉])(iD), Lars M. Kristensen[2](iD), and Laure Petrucci[3](iD)

[1] Department of Safety, Chemistry, and Biomedical Laboratory Sciences, Western Norway University of Applied Sciences, Haugesund, Norway
rds@hvl.no

[2] Department of Computer Science, Electrical Engineering and Mathematical Sciences, Western Norway University of Applied Sciences, Bergen, Norway

[3] LIPN, CNRS UMR 7030, Université Sorbonne Paris Nord, Villetaneuse, France

**Abstract.** Long periods of dry and cold weather conditions significantly increase fire risks for wooden buildings. Recent advances in predictive fire risk models combined with publicly available cloud-based weather data services have enabled the development of smart software systems for location-oriented fire risk notification. We have developed a Coloured Petri Net (CPN) model specifying the software architecture of a microservice-based predictive fire risk notification system. The CPN model captures the set of micro-services provided via REST APIs and the interaction between the constituent services for location tracking and subscription, fire risk computation and data harvesting. As part of the work, we have applied an agile-oriented implementation-first modelling approach and developed a general pattern for REST-based APIs. We apply simulation and state space exploration to validate and verify key behavioural properties of the predictive fire risk notification system.

**Keywords:** Coloured Petri Nets · Modelling · Verification · Microservices and REST APIs · Software Architecture · Fire risk prediction

## 1 Introduction

The pervasive presence of cloud-based data services provides access to a wide range of data sources that enable the development of data-driven applications supporting decision making and control. Prominent examples of such data sources include weather data measurements and weather forecasts which can be used by authorities in the context of early warning systems, including smart systems for fire risk predictions.

The winter period in certain regions of Norway is characterised by long periods with dry and cold weather conditions which combined with the high density

M. Koutny et al. (Eds.): TPNOMCXVII, LNCS 14150, pp. 27–53, 2024.
https://doi.org/10.1007/978-3-662-68191-6_2

of wooden houses poses a significant threat to many cities in Norway. An example of this was the incident on January 18th 2014, when at that date, the largest fire in Norway since World War II developed in the village of Lærdalsøyri at night-time [13]. Forty buildings were lost, including four historic buildings, in a fire that only developed between houses [6].

It is generally known that the winter in cold climate regions brings along increased fire frequencies [13,24]. This was originally identified by Pirsko and Fons [22] suggesting ambient dew point as an explanation for the increased fire frequency in buildings. More recently, Log [14] proposed indoor relative humidity as a fire risk indicator and developed a mathematical model [15] that predicts indoor fuel moisture content (FMC) for a wooden house. The model correlates the FMC with the time to flash-over (TTF) [12], resulting in the possibility of indicating a relative rate of fire development. Combined with forecast weather data, the TTF can be predicted for the upcoming days, enabling proactive emergency planning. Further, by combining the TTF with the influence of wind, a combined fire risk can be expressed, as presented in [18]. The basic idea underlying the model of Log is to use outdoor temperature and relative humidity to estimate (compute) indoor relative humidity which in turn enables computation of the wooden fuel moisture content (FMC). In Norway, measured weather data and weather forecast data (including temperature and relative humidity) are available via cloud-based REST APIs of the Norwegian Meteorological Institute (MET) [16,17].

The work presented in this paper is conducted in the context of the DYNAMIC research project [5] which has as a main objective to develop a cloud-based predictive fire risk indication system based upon the recent fire risk prediction models. In earlier work, we have validated the predictive fire risk indication model [29] demonstrating that it can provide trustworthy fire risk indications, that a combination of weather measurements and forecast data can be used, and that the weather data available from MET [16,17] can be used to obtain fire risk indications of the correct order of magnitude (minutes).

The contribution of this paper is three-fold: Firstly, to develop a formal specification of the software system architecture and the constituent micro-services, as well as presenting our modelling methodology; Secondly, to develop some general modelling patterns for REST-based micro-services; and thirdly to verify the system services and the behavioural interaction between the micro-services. A main benefit of the constructed CPN model is that it provides an implementation independent specification of the fire risk notification system. An advantage of our implementation-first approach followed by formal modelling is the implication that we base our work upon initial prototyping which in turn ensures the implementability of the system.

*Overview.* The rest of this paper is organised as follows. Section 2 gives an overview of the fire risk notification system by presenting the top-level modules of the CPN model and exemplifying the interaction between the micro-services. Section 3 introduces our modelling methodology and the modelling patterns developed for REST APIs. Sections 4–6 present our modelling of the three micro-services (business logic, fire risk computation, and data harvesting) based upon our general approach to modelling REST-based APIs. In Sect. 7, we formulate key behavioural properties for the fire risk notification system and explain how they have been validated and verified using simulation and state space exploration. Section 8 contains a further discussion of related work, and in Sect. 9 we sum up conclusions and outline directions for future work. We assume that the reader is familiar with the basic concepts of high-level Petri Nets. The present paper is an extended version of our earlier workshop paper [28].

## 2 Fire Risk Notification System and Model Overview

The main system to be modelled is the fire risk notification system, which is the name of the aforementioned predictive cloud-based fire risk indication system. The system computes fire risk indications by using an implemented fire risk indication model and weather data harvested from external sources. Fire risk indications are computed for specific locations and clients may subscribe to these locations in order to receive fire risk notifications during days of high fire risk. Clients may also request fire risk for locations existing within the system, without subscribing.

The top-level CPN module is presented in Fig. 1. It consists of the substitution transitions *Client Applications*, *Fire Risk Notification System* (FRNS), *External Weather Data Services* and connecting socket places. The substitution transition *Fire Risk Notification System* represents the notification system that we are developing. It is composed of 22 CPN sub-modules. The substitution transition *External Weather Data Services* represents the cloud-based weather data sources, providing historical and forecast weather data services. This is the data that the FRNS uses as input to the fire risk computation model in order to compute fire risks. The *Client Applications* represent any front-end service used by the clients to communicate with the FRNS, *e.g.* a web browser or a mobile application.

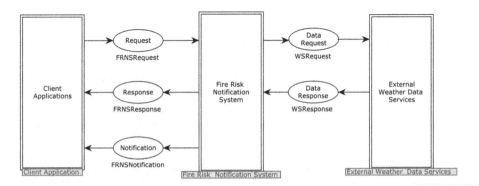

**Fig. 1.** Top-level CPN module, with the front-end client applications (left), the main software component FRNS (middle), and the external weather data services (right).

The services communicate by producing and consuming tokens on the connected socket places representing data transferred between the services. Each place is associated with a specific colour set, allowing only a certain type or combination of data to be present. Considering a request from the *Client Applications*, a token is produced onto the place *Request*, connecting this application with the FRNS. Then, the FRNS consumes the token, processes the request and responds by producing a token onto the place *Response*. The FRNS either responds to a request from the *Client Applications*, or it notifies subscribed clients through scheduled services. Scheduled services result in tokens being produced at the place *Notification*. The remaining two places in Fig. 1 are the *Data Request* and *Data Response*. These are the places connecting the *Fire Risk Notification System* and the *External Weather Data Services*. Tokens are produced at these places whenever the FRNS needs historical data (measurements) or forecasts weather data for fire risk computations.

Expanding on the system, Fig. 2 shows the *Fire Risk Notification System* module which is the submodule of the accordingly named substitution transition in Fig. 1. The module consists of three substitution transitions and associated socket places representing the constituent micro-services of the software system. The *Business Logic Controller Service* (BLCS) represents the front-end service that the user client interacts with in order to use the FRNS. The *Fire Risk Computation Service* is the service where the fire risk computation takes place. The *Data Harvesting Service* (DHS) is responsible for retrieving the required weather data from the external weather data sources. The services are modelled as loosely coupled micro-services, communicating through defined REST API endpoints. The BLCS and DHS micro-services are connected to the overall system in Fig. 1 through port-socket assignments of correspondingly named places. Services are only aware of the existence of directly connected services.

The BLCS is the middleware, separating the *Client Applications* and the *Fire Risk Computation Service* (FRCS). It processes and responds to requests from the clients, either directly or by further requesting services from the FRCS. In addition to the RESTful services, it also handles the fixed interval process of notifying clients in case of high estimated fire risks. To receive a notification for a location, a client must be subscribed to that location. The subscription database, handled by the BLCS, keeps track of these subscriptions.

The FRCS is responsible for estimating the fire risk for the locations being tracked, which is primarily a scheduled service. Upon computing the fire risks, the FRCS requests historic (measurements) and predicted weather data from the DHS. Provided that the weather data is received, the FRCS predicts the upcoming fire risks and updates the local fire risk database. When requested by the BLCS, the FRCS can return updated fire risk estimates. The DHS implements a weather database containing locations and associated weather data. The database is subject to scheduled updates, similar to the FRCS. When the FRCS requests weather data, the DHS can respond with recently fetched forecasts and measurements for all the locations within the database. The existence of locations is synchronised between the databases.

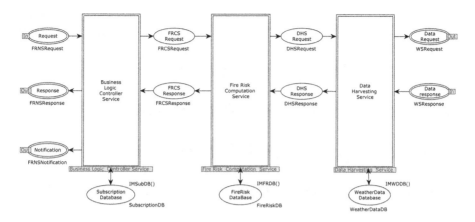

**Fig. 2.** The FRNS submodule, with the BLCS (left), the FRCS (middle) and the DHS (right). The left-most and right-most port places are connected via port-socket assignments to the accordingly named places in Fig. 1. The three places at the bottom represent the databases associated with each of the micro-services.

Figure 3 presents a sequence diagram for the services of the system and their interaction. In general, clients may: (1) start or stop tracking a new location; (2) subscribe or unsubscribe to existing locations to receive notifications; or (3) request fire risk for locations existing within the system. In order to provide fire risk notifications, the system needs to continuously monitor the current and future fire risk of the tracked locations. This is achieved by the aforementioned scheduled updates, running every six hours. It starts by an update of the weather database at DHS, then the FRCS requests the recently fetched weather data, and recomputes all fire risks and updates the fire risk database. Then, the BLCS requests all recently computed fire risks and determines which clients to notify, if any, based on certain fire risk criteria.

## 3   Modelling Methodology and Patterns

In this section we introduce the methodology that we have followed when developing the CPN model and the implementation of the fire risk notification system. Furthermore, we describe the key abstractions made in the CPN model and the general modelling pattern adopted for REST micro-services.

### 3.1   Modelling Methodology

Formal modelling traditionally follows a model-first-implementation-last approach, where a formal specification of the system is first constructed and then followed by an implementation based on the specification. In our work, we have adopted a more agile-oriented implementation-first-model-last approach, where the implementation was developed in parallel with developing the CPN model.

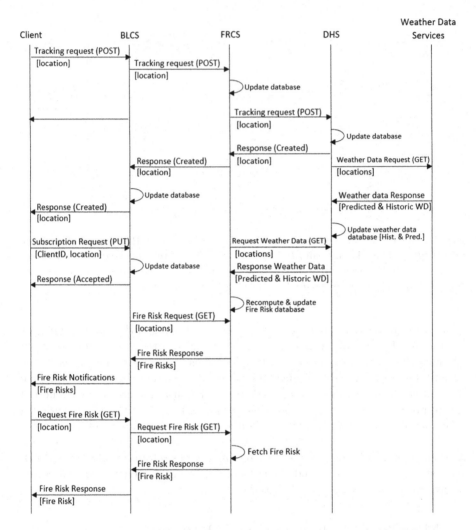

**Fig. 3.** Time sequence diagram for selected requests and processes, exemplifying location tracking, subscription and fire risk requests, as well as the scheduled update of databases and associated notifications.

Both developments have been using an agile approach with on-demand communication between developments, occasionally resulting in short iterative sessions. The approach is illustrated in Fig. 4.

The basic principle is that the (continuous) on-demand communication continuously updates the CPN model so as to reflect the current system implementation. The construction of the model will typically identify design problems, pitfalls, and possible design improvements which are then fed back to update the prototype implementation. This means that the development of the CPN model is being based on the prototype system, and hence is developed a bit behind

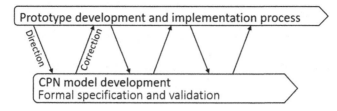

**Fig. 4.** The agile-oriented development approach combining prototype development (direction) and CPN modelling (formal specification) (correction).

of the prototype. The result is a supportive direction-correction development process where the CPN modelling continuously impacts the implementation. A main aim of the approach is to assure a robust and complete development of the system, in particular ensuring the practical implementability of the system design. Furthermore, the prototype system and the CPN model were developed by different people, which was also considered to strengthen the development process.

In initial work [29], we implemented a simple first version of the system, which served as a basis for the development of a prototype of the fire risk notification system based on a micro-service software architecture. The prototype implementation associated with the CPN model presented in this paper was achieved using the Heroku [10] and Amazon EC2 cloud platforms and the Spring Boot framework [27] in combination with MongoDB noSQL databases to realise the micro-services. In addition, a web-based front-end application was prototyped using the React single-page web application framework, and a mobile front-end was prototyped using the Xamarin cross-platform application framework [9].

The current paper reports on version two of the CPN model, which was constructed based on the Spring Boot-based implementation. This CPN model is intended to serve as basis for the final system implementation. This means that we have had two iterations on the implementation and the CPN model. The most important aspects that were identified through CPN modelling during the development process and where the modelling resulted in either direct changes or highly affected the implementation (system) were: (1) aided to define constituent microservices and their extent; (2) database synchronization, revealed synchronization errors; (3) missing system functions, identified missing scheduled services for location monitoring; (4) splitting of main system functions, herein separated functions initially triggered by a single client request; (5) status codes, distinguished between non-existing locations and existing locations with unavailable data; and (6) user permissions, especially deleting of locations.

It is worth mentioning that the CPN model developed in parallel with the system implementation, was a first low fidelity version of the model. Then, the second version improved several aspects by introducing more advanced functions, robust use of guards and a more streamlined modelling pattern for REST APIs.

## 3.2   Service Modelling Pattern and Abstractions

The microservices in the FRNS are provided as REST APIs [8] which is an architectural style for web services based on the HTTP protocol. This means that access to the web services are based on the HTTP request-response pattern where the operation to be performed on resources is specified using HTTP verbs. For the FRNS we consider GET (safe and idempotent operation to retrieve a resource), POST (unsafe and non-idempotent operation to create a resource), PUT (unsafe and idempotent operation to update a resource), and DELETE (unsafe and idempotent operation to delete a resource). The resources on which the operations are to be performed are identified based on URI/URLs which provide unique, stable and global identifiers for resources. Representation of resources are based on XML and JSON. The resources being manipulated by the FRNS are locations, subscriptions, fire risks, and weather data.

The modelling of the REST micro-services follows a general pattern which we introduce below prior to presenting the modelling of the concrete micro-services in the subsequent sections. Figure 5 lists the basis declarations associated with the pattern while Fig. 6 shows the modelling structure. The colour sets *Method* and *StatusCode* are used for representing the HTTP verbs and returning the status of request processing. The colour sets *Request* and *Response* are in accordance with the HTTP standard and are used to represent the HTTP requests and responses, respectively. Both request and responses hold identification of resources which are generically represented via the colour set *R*. The definition of *R* will depend on the concrete resources being manipulated by the service.

Considering Fig. 6, the port places *Request* and *Response* represent the interface to the service and tokens on these places will represent incoming requests and outgoing responses, respectively. The processing related to reception of an incoming request and an outgoing response is modelled by the two transitions. The internal state of the service is modelled via the places *LocalData*, *Idle*, and *Process*. The latter two places represent the control flow, while *LocalData* is used to model data/information which is locally stored in the service. The colour set of the place *Request* is *ServiceRequest* and may contain a consumer and/or provider component. The components can be included if the origin of a request is needed. The place *Idle* is a port place as a service may have multiple end-points, *i.e.* additional modules modelled according to the pattern presented in Fig. 6. The reception of a request and the sending of a response may involve interaction with other services, and would be modelled with additional structures in the right-hand side of Fig. 6. This is, however, not shown as it depends on the concrete service as will be evident from the instances of the modelling pattern to be presented in the following sections.

*Abstraction of Data.* Abstractions are made to the model and in the modelling pattern to arrive at an appropriate level of detail. Although some details in data are useful for simulation purposes, they are not necessarily relevant when doing verification. The included data need only to correspond with the modelling objective concerned with capturing the software architecture, constituent

```
1 colset Method      = with GET |   PUT   |   POST   | DELETE;
2 colset StatusCode = with  OK | CREATED | ACCEPTED | NOTFOUND;
3
4 (* constructors for resources *)
5 colset Resource = union R;
6
7 colset Request  = record method   : Method *
8                          resource : Resource;
9 var     request : Request;
10
11 colset Response = record status : StatusCode *
12                          body   : Resource;
13 var     reponse : Response;
14
15 (* constructors for consumer components *)
16 colset CComponent = union CC;
17 var     cc : CComponent;
18
19 (* constructors for provider components *)
20 colset PComponent = union PC;
21 var     pc : PComponent;
22
23 colset ServiceRequest = product CComponent * PComponent *
24                                 Request;
25
26 colset ServiceResponse = product CComponent * Response;
```

**Fig. 5.** Colour sets definitions for the service modelling pattern.

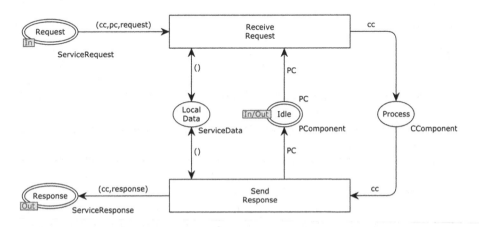

**Fig. 6.** Modelling pattern for the micro-services.

micro-services, service end-points, and the interaction between services. Further, abstraction of unnecessary data is important to reduce the size of the state space, ensuring a finite space and allowing a more exhaustive verification.

The abstractions made to the CPN model primarily relate to the payload of the HTTP messages. When the different services communicate, the purpose of the communication is more important than the content, *e.g.* the verification only requires to distinguish between the absence of a notification of fire risk or its sending, but not on the actual levels of risk. Hence, risk levels are abstracted and emphasis is given to properly capture the purpose of the interactions between the constituent services. A consequence of this is that we also abstract from the actual values related to weather data and only consider the absence or presence of weather data for locations. It can also be seen that we have abstracted from several of the header fields of the HTTP messages which are not important for modelling the interaction of the services.

## 4   Business Logic Controller Service

The BLCS transition from Fig. 2 consists of two substitution transitions and associated sub-modules, as well as the subscription database. The two modules represent: (1) the processing of client requests; and (2) the scheduled update and associated notifications. Figure 7 shows the *BLCS Handle Request* module responsible for the processing of client requests. It contains three transitions representing the different kinds of incoming client requests, that is, tracking, subscription and single fire risk request. A request either results in an immediate response in the case of a subscription request, or the requesting of further information from the FRCS in the case of tracking or single fire risk request, as partly evident from Fig. 7.

Considering a request from the *Client Applications*, a token is produced onto the place *Request*, connecting the client applications with the BLCS. The colour set associated with this place is *FRNSRequest*, which is a product colour set combining the index set *Client* with the record set *frnsRequest*, as can be seen from Fig. 8 which lists the colour sets used for the BLCS modelling. The general structure can be seen to follow the modelling pattern from Sect. 3. The resources are modelled through a union colour set, defining the REST API endpoints (constructors) and the associated data (arguments). The resources are service specific, defined for all interactions associated with the service. Similarly, the colour set *FRNSResponse* is associated with the place *Response*. Here, the record colour set *frnsResponse* includes a *status* and a *body*, associated with the colour sets *StatusCode* and the service specific resource, respectively. The *status* is used to indicate the status post processing the request, while the *body* embeds response data, if any.

If the BLCS needs to request the FRCS, a token is produced at the place *FRCSRequest*, while in response, a token will be received at *FRCSResponse*. Associated colour sets follow the same general structure as previously described. However, these colour sets make use of the aforementioned *Component* to identify

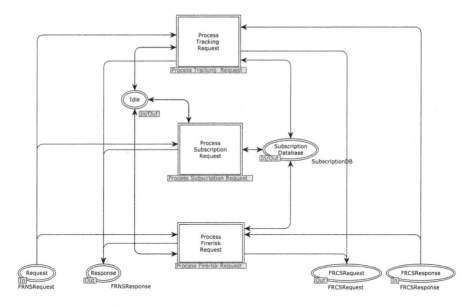

**Fig. 7.** The *BLCS Handle Request* sub-module responsible for handling requests within the BLCS. The handling of tracking (top), subscription (middle) and single fire risk requests (bottom) are represented through substitution transitions.

the type of request and from where it originates, allowing any response to be returned to the requesting component. It is also useful when performing visual single-step and interactive simulations.

To illustrate how a specific request is handled, Fig. 9 presents the sub-module of *Process Tracking Request* from Fig. 7. Any client request, regardless of its type, will arrive as a token at the top left place *Request*. However, only the POST requests associated with *FRNSLocation* will be considered within this module as ensured by the arc inscriptions. POST requests are associated with clients requesting tracking of new locations, hence the location (*loc*) carried by *FRNSLocation*. A requested location tracking may either contain an unconsidered location or an existing location. Guards at the transitions connected to the place *Request* check whether the requested location exists or not by use of the *hasLoc* (has location) function. If the function evaluates to true, it means the requested location exists within the subscription database and only the transition *Request Location Exist* becomes enabled. If this is the case, a token is produced at the place *Response*, containing an ACCEPTED *response* and the location in question. Similarly, the transition *Process New Location* only becomes enabled if *hasLoc* is not true and there is an available token at place *Idle*. The idle-token is introduced to ensure the full consideration of a request or process, before engaging in the next (flow control). This is in accordance with the prototyped system as well as contributing to a reduced state space. When fired, the transition produces a token at *FRCSRequest*. As can be seen from the arc

```
 1 colset Component   = union BLCSTracking
 2                            + BLCSUpdate
 3                            + BLCSRequest;
 4 val Cn = 2;
 5 val Ln = 5;
 6
 7 colset Client        = index   Client with 1..Cn;
 8 colset Location      = index   Loc    with 1..Ln;
 9 colset Locations     = list    Location;
10 colset ClientxLocation = product Client * Location;
11
12 colset FireRisk      = with    Risk | NA;
13 colset LocxFireRisk  = product Location * FireRisk;
14 colset FireRisks     = list    LocxFireRisk;
15
16 colset FRNSResource  = union FRNSLocation     : Location
17                            + FRNSFirerisk     : Location
18                            + FRNSSubscription : Location
19                            + FRNSFirerisks    : FireRisks;
20
21 colset FRCSResource  = union FRCSLocation   : Location
22                            + FRCSFirerisk   : Location
23                            + FRCSFirerisks  : FireRisks
24                            + FRCSAllRisks;
25
26 colset frnsRequest   =   record  method   : Method *
27                                   resource : FRNSResource;
28 colset frnsResponse  =   record  status   : StatusCode *
29                                   body     : FRNSResource;
30 colset frcsRequest   =   record  method   : Method *
31                                   resource : FRCSResource;
32 colset frcsResponse  =   record  status   : StatusCode *
33                                   body     : FRCSResource;
34
35 colset FRNSRequest   = product Client    * frnsRequest;
36 colset FRNSResponse  = product Client    * frnsResponse;
37 colset FRCSRequest   = product Component * frcsRequest;
38 colset FRCSResponse  = product Component * frcsResponse;
```

**Fig. 8.** Colour sets definitions used to model the BLCS.

inscription, the token consists of the component *BLCSTracking*, as well as the specified POST method and *FRCSLocation*.

When a tracking response (new location) is received at place *FRCSResponse* it contains the *response* CREATED and a body with the specific location. Together with the wait-token produced upon the firing of *Process New Location*, the *FRCSResponse* token enables the transition *Process Response*, which in turn may update the subscription database through the function *AddLocation*,

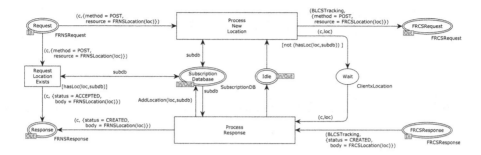

**Fig. 9.** The *Process POST Request* submodule. Presenting the BLCS handling of a tracking (POST) request.

as well as produce a response to the place *Response*. Note that it is evident from the *component* that the response originates from a tracking request.

## 5   Fire Risk Computation Service

The FRCS is responsible for the computation of fire risks and the handling of the *FireRisk DataBase*. Fire risks are computed by use of weather data received from the DHS and computed values are stored within the risk database, for later retrieval. The FRCS either responds to requests from the BLCS or performs scheduled recomputations of the fire risks within the database. Figure 10 presents the FRCS submodule, where the two substitution transitions *FRCSProcessRequest* and *RecomputeFireRisks* represent the processing of requests and scheduled recomputations, respectively. The place *FireRisk DataBase* is associated with the colour set *FireRiskDB*, which is a list of entries consisting of the combination of *location* and *FireRisk*. The places *DHSRequest* and *DHSResponse* are constructed in accordance with presented modelling pattern, see Fig. 11.

Expanding the substitution transition of *FRCSProcessRequest* gives the submodule presented in Fig. 12. The module consists of two substitution transitions, representing the processing of tracking requests (*Process Tracking Request*) and fire risk requests (*Process GET Request*). These are the only two types of requests processed by the FRCS, as the subscription requests were limited to within the BLCS. The recently considered tracking request (new location) from Fig. 9 would appear at the place *FRCSRequest* and be processed in a similar manner within *Process Tracking Request*.

The handling of the scheduled update of the *FireRisk DataBase* is presented in Fig. 13 and is the sub-module of the transition *Recompute FireRisks*. When firing, transition *Send Request* requests weather data from the DHS, for all locations kept within the fire risk database. The response received is a *status* OK and a list of locations and associated weather data. The latter resources are represented by *DHSWD* and the variable *wd*, as can be seen from the arc inscription and declarations in Fig. 11. The received response results in the update of the *FireRisk DataBase* through the *updateFRDB* function.

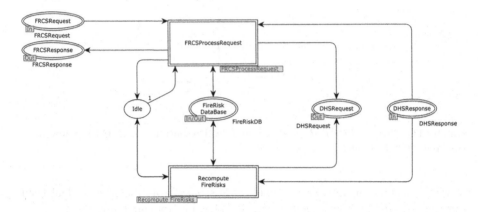

**Fig. 10.** The *FireRisk Computation Service* submodule and associated substitution transitions and database.

```
1 colset WeatherData = with FORECAST    |
2                            MEASUREMENT |
3                            NOTPRESENT;
4
5 colset LocxWDxWD = product Location * WeatherData *
6                            WeatherData;
7
8 colset LocsxWDs  = list    LocxWDxWD;
9 var     wd : LocsxWDs;
10
11 colset DHSResource = union DHSLocation  : Location
12                          + DHSLocations : Locations
13                          + DHSWD        : LocsxWDs;
14
15 colset DHSRequest = record method    : Method
16                            * resource  : DHSResource;
17
18 colset DHSResponse = record status : StatusCode
19                             * body   : DHSResource;
```

**Fig. 11.** Colour set definitions used to model the state of the FRCS.

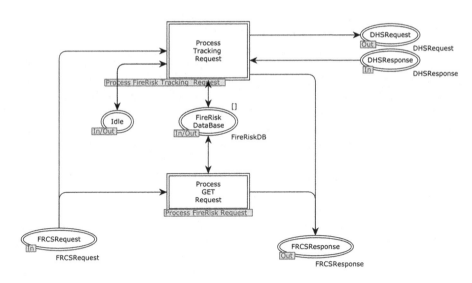

**Fig. 12.** The sub-module of *FRCS Process Request*. It can be seen that the FRCS handles tracking (POST) and single fire risk (GET) requests only.

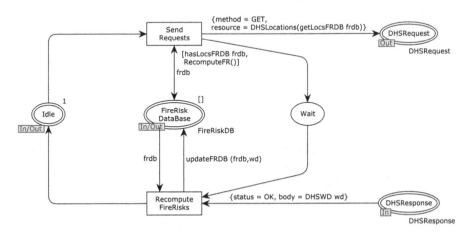

**Fig. 13.** The sub-module *Recompute FireRisks* responsible for the scheduled update of the *FireRisk DataBase*.

## 6   Data Harvesting Service

The DHS is responsible for retrieving weather data from external sources and handling the *Weather Data DataBase*. The DHS either responds to requests from the FRCS or performs scheduled updates of the weather data in the database by requesting external services. The data fetched by the DHS is both historic and predicted weather data, requested from the FROST and MET APIs of the Norwegian Meteorological Institute, respectively. Figure 14 presents the DHS sub-module for processing requests. The three substitution transitions are *Process POST Request*, *Process GET Request* and *Process DELETE Request*. The POST request is related to the initiation of location tracking and involves updating the local database, as previously described. The GET request is a request for service specific data, in this case weather data needed by the FRCS to perform fire risk computations. In general, a DELETE request may be related to a subscription or a location tracking. Within the DHS, the DELETE request is only related to the termination of a tracking, hence the deletion of a location within the weather database.

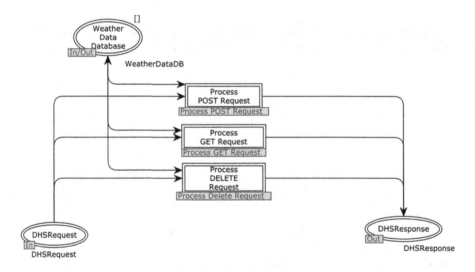

**Fig. 14.** The sub-module responsible for handling requests within the DHS. The DHS either POST or DELETE a location from its database, or fetches weather data from the *Weather Data DataBase* (GET).

The DHS is responsible for harvesting weather data from the external services. Figure 15 presents the modelling of the weather data harvesting, through a single harvesting module. The requesting of weather data from the two external services of FROST and MET, is modelled through a single combined weather data request. In turn, this means that the weather data response is a combined response, containing both historical and forecast weather data. The involved places *Data Request* and *Data Response* have the colour sets *WSRequest* and *WSResponse* and follow the presented design pattern. The service specific resource is *WSResource* and represent both forecast and historic weather data for one or more locations, as can be seen from Fig. 16. A weather data response results in the update of weather data within the database, which in turn can be requested by the FRCS.

# 7   Model Validation and Verification

To validate the constructed CPN model, we initially performed single-step execution combined with interactive and automatic simulation. The overall aim of using simulation first was to confirm that the detailed basic behaviour of the CPN model was as intended, including the interaction between micro-services. In particular, we wanted to eliminate as many modelling errors as possible (if any) before proceeding with state space exploration. Modelling errors often lead

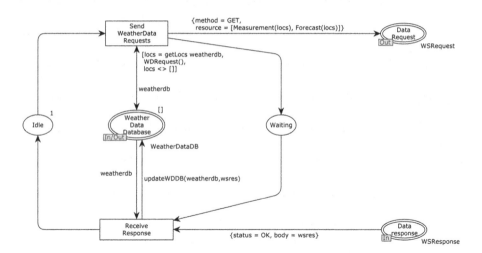

**Fig. 15.** The sub-module *Harvest Weather Data*, within the DHS, responsible for the harvesting of weather data from external services. The modelling combines the requesting from two external services into a single combined request.

```
1 colset WSResource   = union Forecast     : Locations +
2                             Measurement  : Locations;
3
4 colset WSRequest    = record method      : Method       *
5                             resource     : WSResource;
6 colset WSResponse   = record status      : StatusCode *
7                             body         : WSResource;
```

**Fig. 16.** Colour set definitions used to model the state of the DHS.

to excessively large state spaces. Hence, the initial application of simulation will provide a more solid foundation for undertaking the state space exploration. In interactive simulation the user (modeller) selects which enabled transition is to occur in each step, and the user may observe and inspect the intermediate markings. In automatic simulation the CPN Tools simulator executes the model by randomly selecting the enabling transition to occur in each step, for a number of steps and only the end (resulting) marking is shown to the user. Testing the CPN model using simulation identified a number of smaller modelling errors related to the arc inscriptions and associated functions, which could easily be corrected.

To perform a more exhaustive verification of the CPN model, we report in this section on how we have used the state space exploration facilities of CPN Tools in conjunction with the state- and action-oriented ASK-CTL library [3,4] to verify key behavioural properties of the fire risk notification system using temporal logic. We adopted an incremental verification approach similar to the one developed in [23], where we gradually verified the services of the fire risk notification system. In particular, we started with the verification of the location tracking service and then incrementally enabled subscription, fire risk computation, and data harvesting until we finally considered the verification of some system-wide behavioural properties.

In the following paragraphs we present the behavioural properties considered for the different services. We derived the set of CTL properties to be verified by going systematically through each of the REST API service endpoints and formulate associated CTL properties based on their functionality. In addition, the micro-service architecture and associated databases were used as a basis for the formulation of inter-service properties.

We assume that the reader is familiar with the basic CTL temporal operators **AG** (always/globally), **EF** (reachable/exists future), and **AF** (eventually/always future). For properties related to the processing of requests, we initially specify these on the form **AG** ((request) $\Rightarrow$ **EF** ($l$ processed)), *i.e.* when making a request to a service there exists a future state in which the response has been processed. In particular, we do not consider the stronger property **AG** ((request) $\Rightarrow$ **AF** ($l$ processed)), *i.e.* that the request is eventually processed. The reason for this is that there exists multiple sources of cyclic behaviour in the model which implies that without any fairness assumptions progress on the processing of a request cannot in general be guaranteed. As an example, we may want to verify that when a client requests the tracking of a location, then eventually the location is being tracked. However, because all services run independently in parallel without any progress/fairness assumptions, we have an infinite execution after the request for tracking has been made comprised of the data harvesting service continuously sending requests and receiving responses from the weather data service. Hence, there is no guarantee that the tracking request is eventually handled. At the end of this section we use the fairness properties of transitions to characterise the possible infinite behaviour that may cause a request to not be processed. Based on this characterisation, we then show that processing of request is indeed guaranteed under the assumption that such unfair executions are not possible.

In the specification of the CTL properties below, we use $L$ to denote the set of locations and $C$ to denote the set of clients.

*Tracking Properties.* Clients send requests to start and stop the tracking of locations which in turn determines the locations for which weather data is being harvested and for which fire risks are being computed. For tracking we consider the following properties.

**T-P1** $\forall c \in C, l \in L : \mathbf{AG}\,\mathbf{EF}\,(c$ requests tracking of $l)$. This property states that it is always possible for any client to initiate the tracking of any location. The proposition $c$ *requests tracking of* $l$ can be implemented by considering the binding of the transition in the *Client* module corresponding to the event of requesting a location to be tracked.

**T-P2** $\forall c \in C, l \in L : \mathbf{AG}\,((c$ requests tracking of $l) \Rightarrow \mathbf{EF}\,(l$ is tracked$))$. This property states that if a client requests tracking of a location, then there exists a future state in which this location is being tracked. Checking that a location is being tracked can be implemented by considering the tokens present on the places representing the databases of the three micro-services.

**T-P3** $\forall c \in C, l \in L : \mathbf{AG}\,\mathbf{EF}\,(c$ stops tracking of $l)$. This is the dual property of T-P1 for stopping the tracking of locations.

**T-P4** $\forall c \in C, l \in L : \mathbf{AG}\,(c$ stops tracking of $l) \Rightarrow \mathbf{EF}\,(l$ is not tracked$)$. This is the dual property of T-P2 for stopping the tracking of locations.

*Subscription Properties.* Clients subscribe to a location in order to receive fire risk notifications for that location. For subscription we consider the following properties.

**S-P1** $\forall c \in C, l \in L : \mathbf{AG}\,\mathbf{EF}\,(c$ requests subscription to $l)$. This property states that it is always possible for any client to request subscription to any location. The proposition $c$ *requests subscription to* $l$ can be implemented by considering the binding of the transition in the *Client* module corresponding to the event of requesting a subscription.

**S-P2** $\forall c \in C, l \in L : \mathbf{AG}\,((c$ requests subscription to $l) \Rightarrow \mathbf{EF}\,(c$ is subscribed to $l))$. This property states that if a client requests subscription to a location, then there exists a future state in which the client is subscribed to that location. Checking the client subscription to the location can be implemented by considering the tokens present on the *Subscription Database* place (see Fig. 2).

**S-P3** $\forall c \in C, locs \subseteq L : \mathbf{AG}\,\mathbf{EF}\,(c$ is subscribed to all locations in $locs)$. This property states that it is always possible for a client to be subscribed to any subset of locations.

**S-P4** $\forall c \in C : \mathbf{AG}\,(c$ is subscribed to a subset of $L)$. This property ensures that a client cannot have multiple subscriptions to the same location.

**S-P5** $\forall c \in C, l \in L : \mathbf{AG}\,\mathbf{EF}\,(c$ unsubscribes to $l)$. This is the dual property of S-P1 but for unsubscribing to a location.

**S-P6**

$\forall c \in C, l \in L :$ **AG** $((c$ unsubscribes to $l) \Rightarrow$ **EF** $(c$ is not subscribed to $l))$. This is the dual property of S-P2 but for unsubscribing to a location.

*Fire Risk Properties.* Fire risk is to be computed by the fire risk computation service for a given location when this location is being tracked. For the fire risk computation service, we consider the following properties.

**F-P1** $\forall l \in L :$ **AG EF** (risk is computed for $l$). This property states that for any location it is always possible to compute the fire risk. The fire risk being computed for a given location can be checked from the *Firerisk Database* place.

**F-P2** $\forall l \in l :$ **AG EF** (risk recompute). This property states that it is always possible to recompute the fire risk for any given location, and hence that fire risk can be periodically recomputed. Re-computation of fire risks corresponds to the occurrence of the *Recompute FireRisks* transition in Fig. 13.

**F-P3** $\forall c \in C, l \in L :$ **AG** (c requests risk for $l \Rightarrow$ **EF** (c receives risk response for $l$)). This property states that if a client $c$ requests a fire risk for a given location $l$, then it is possible for $c$ to obtain the response.

*Data Harvesting Properties.* The data harvesting service is to retrieve weather data periodically for the currently tracked locations in order for the fire risk computation service to be able to compute fire risks. For data harvesting we consider the following properties.

**W-P1** $\forall l \in L :$ **AG EF** (weather data is stored for $l$). This property states that for any location it is always possible to store weather data. That the weather data has been stored for a given location can be checked from the *Weatherdata Database* place.

**W-P2** $\forall l \in L :$ **AG EF** (weather data requested for $l$). This property states that it is always possible to harvest data for a given location. The harvesting of data for a location corresponds to an occurrence of the *SendWeatherDataRequests* transition in Fig. 15.

*Inter-service Properties.* In addition to the properties related to specific services above, we also consider the following properties which rely on the collaboration between all micro-services in the system.

**A-P1 AG** (no pending client requests $\Rightarrow$ consistent data bases). This property states that if no client is currently executing requests against the service, then the databases of the micro-services are consistent in terms of storing information for the same set of locations. That the databases are consistent can be checked by considering the markings of the three places representing information stored in the databases (see Fig. 2).

```
1 (* check whether location exists in subscription database *)
2 fun hasLoc (l,subsrcDB) =
3     List.exists (fn (l',_) => l' = l) subsrcDB;
4
5 (* add location to the subscription database *)
6 fun AddLocation (l,subsrcDB) =
7   if (not (hasLoc (l,subsrcDB)))
8   then sort
9             (fn ((Loc(i),_),(Loc(j),_)) => i<=j)
10         ((l,[])::subsrcDB)
11   else subsrcDB;
12
13 (* delete location from the subscription database *)
14 fun DelLocation (l',subsrcDB) =
15     List.filter (fn (l,_) => l <> l') subsrcDB;
16
17 (* add a subscriber for a given location *)
18 fun AddSubscriber (l',u',subsrcDB) =
19     List.map
20         (fn (l,subs) =>
21             if ((l = l') andalso (not (mem subs u')))
22             then (l,sort (fn (Client(i),Client(j)) => (i<=j))
23                         (u'::subs))
24             else (l,subs))
25         subsrcDB;
26
27 (* delete a subscriber for a given location *)
28 fun DelSubscriber (l',u',subsrcDB) =
29     List.map
30         (fn (l,subs) =>
31             if (l = l')
32             then (l,List.filter (fn u => u <> u') subs)
33             else (l,subs))
34         subsrcDB
```

**Fig. 17.** Functions definitions used to add or delete subscriptions.

**A-P2** $\forall c \in C, l \in L : \mathbf{AG} \, (c$ subscribed to $l) \Rightarrow \mathbf{EF} \, (c$ receives risk notification for $l)$. This property states that if a client is subscribed to a location, then it is possible for the client to receive fire risks for that location. That a client is subscribed to a location can be retrieved from the place representing the subscription database while the reception of a notification is represented by the occurrence of the corresponding transition in the *Client* module.

*Property Correct by Construction.* Property S-P4 can easily be proven correct by construction. Indeed, we can observe that the place *Subscription Database*, initially containing an empty list, is accessed by transitions:

– that only read the value of its content, *i.e.* takes and puts back the very same token, which does not alter the property;
– which take a token and return it with a value updated by one of the functions `AddLocation`, `DelLocation`, `AddSubscriber` or `DelSubscriber`. These are detailed in Fig. 17. It is obvious that: `DelLocation` and `DelSubscriber` cannot insert a value in the list; `AddLocation` does not insert a client; and `AddSubscriber` checks whether the client is already registered for the location before adding it.

*Experimental Results.* We verified the properties presented above for selected configurations of the CPN model in terms of locations, clients, tracked locations, and subscriptions.

Table 1 summarises the statistics for the state space exploration and verification of properties. The *States* and *Arcs* columns give the number of states and edges, respectively, in the state space. The *G-Time* column provides the time (in seconds) used to generate the state space for the given configuration while the *V-Time* column lists the time (in seconds) used for verification of properties. The verification was undertaken on i5-PC 2.4 GHz PC with a 16 Gb memory.

We use $Cx - Ly$ to denote a configuration with $x$ clients and $y$ locations. A $*$ indicates that we have fixed the tracking and subscription such that all locations

**Table 1.** State space statistics for configurations considered in the verification.

| Configuration | States | Arcs | G-Time | V-Time |
|---|---|---|---|---|
| C1-L1 | 3,435 | 11,901 | < 1 s | < 1 s |
| C1-L2 | 215,181 | 739,797 | 2,093 s | 555 s |
| C2-L1 | 274,581 | 1,238,395 | 9,100 s | 1,404 s |
| C2-L2-* | 14,556 | 62,535 | 27.7 s | 26.6 s |
| C2-L3-*-Request | 5,151 | 21,138 | 4 s | 10.5 s |
| C2-L3-*-Notify | 216 | 687 | < 1 s | < 1 s |
| C2-L4-*-Notify | 216 | 687 | < 1 s | < 1 s |
| C2-L5-*-Notify | 216 | 687 | < 1 s | < 1 s |
| C3-L2-*-Request | 18,654 | 91,596 | 49.5 s | 67.0 s |
| C3-L2-*-Notify | 372 | 1,311 | < 1 s | < 1 s |
| C3-L3-*-Request | 54,894 | 276,378 | 480.9 s | 339.8 s |
| C3-L3-*-Notify | 372 | 1,311 | < 1 s | < 1 s |
| C3-L4-*-Notify | 372 | 1,311 | < 1 s | < 1 s |
| C3-L5-*-Notify | 372 | 1,311 | < 1 s | < 1 s |
| C4-L1-*-Request | 14,121 | 75,762 | 26.3 s | 38.9 s |
| C4-L5-*-Notify | 684 | 2,715 | < 1 s | 2.9 s |
| C5-L1-*-Request | 58,014 | 355,518 | 566.1 s | 339.4 s |
| C5-L5-*-Notify | 1,308 | 5,835 | < 1 s | 9.5 s |

are tracked and all clients subscribe to all locations. We use *Request* to specify configurations where we only consider single requests from clients and *Notify* to specify configurations where we consider only the system initiated notifications (and not individual client requests). It can be observed that for configurations with only notification, the size of the state space does not grow when increasing the number of locations. This is due to the subscriptions being fixed and the fact that a client is notified about all subscribed locations in one single message.

The verification of the model revealed an error related to the notification of clients with respect to fire risks which was not identified during simulation. This demonstrates the added value of undertaken state space exploration of the CPN model, in order to perform more exhaustive verification of properties.

*Fairness and Eventual Processing of Requests.* The properties T-P2, T-P4, S-P2, S-P6, F-P3, and A-P2 are all of the form **AG** (request $\Rightarrow$ **EF** request processed) and concerned with establishing that whenever (**AG**) making a service request (*e.g.* for tracking, subscription, and fire risk computation), then there exists a future state (**EF**) in which the request has been processed. Ideally, we would like to establish the stronger property **AG** (request $\Rightarrow$ **AF** request processed) which would guarantee that the request will eventually (**AF**) be processed. However, as there may be independent cyclic (infinite) behaviour not related to the processing of the requests in question, then this cannot immediately be guaranteed.

When a property of the form **AG** (request $\Rightarrow$ **AF** request processed) does not immediately hold it means that there must be a cycle (representing an infinite execution) in the state space that can be reached from a state where the request has been made, but where there is no state on this cycle where the request has been processed. This is essentially the counter example being the cause of the property not holding. Hence, if we are able to characterise the set of transitions that must occur on such cycles in the state space, then we have identified the circumstances under which a request may not eventually be processed. Based on this we can then conclude that when considering only (fair) executions where such transitions do not repeatedly occur, then **AG** (request $\Rightarrow$ **AF** request processed) does hold.

A set of transitions is said to be *impartial* if transitions in the set occur infinitely often on any infinite execution. Hence, if the state space is finite (as in the case here), then the definition of impartiality implies that any cycle in the state space contains at least one transition from this set. Formulated differently, if we only consider executions with a finite number of transitions from the set, then these will all be finite.

For the CPN model of the fire risk notification system, we are able to verify from the state space using the fairness query functions in CPN Tools that the set containing the following transitions are impartial:

**Start Tracking and Stop Tracking Request** in the client application module corresponding to sending request for start and stopping tracking of locations.

**Request Subscribe and Request Unsubscribe** in the client application module corresponding to sending request for subscribing and unsubscribing to locations.

**Send Request** in the client application module corresponding to sending a request for obtaining a fire risk for a given location.

**Request Fire Risks** in the *Scheduled Update* module corresponding periodic request for updated fire risks for tracked locations.

**Recompute Fire Risks** in the *Recompute Fire Risk* module corresponding to the periodic re-computation of the fire risks for tracked locations (see Fig. 13).

**Send Weather Data Requests** corresponding to the periodic requests for updated weather data from the data harvesting service (see Fig. 15).

It can be seen that all these transitions are related to the sending of requests to the different micro-services. Hence, if we only consider fair executions where we have only a finite number of occurrences of transitions in this set corresponding to other requests, then if a property of the form **AG** (request ⇒ **EF** request processed) holds, this implies that also **AG** (request ⇒ **AF** request processed) holds as explained above.

## 8   Related Work

Several works in the recent literature have addressed formal modelling of (micro) services. Most of these works do not benefit from the data handling offered by Coloured Petri Nets nor provide a structured hierarchical design. In [2], services are modelled using Timed Petri Nets (TPNs), thus focusing on the process flow and discarding the data exchanges. An automatically generated TPN then allows for verifying properties of an input microservice specified in the CONDUCTOR orchestration language. A similar approach for self-adaptive systems using high-level Petri nets was conveyed in [1].

The Saga patterns are extended with concurrency features in [25] via workflow nets. They are further translated into reference nets embedded in the RENEW tool which provides simulation features. It also considers only the restricted data representation and analysis capabilities. Services are organised using simple Petri net patterns in [26]. In [11], the authors propose a Coloured Petri net model for RESTful services, with a particular focus on composition issues. However, it does not exhibit a hierarchical model nor a general architecture for micro-service modelling.

A CPN-based case-study verification of a cloud-based information integration architecture was presented in [20]. Although modelling the different layers of the cloud-based architecture and verifying specific model properties, emphasis was not given to the communication and data exchange between the layers. However, [21] presents a structuring of data and colour sets which has similarities with the general communication between the REST-based micro-services presented in this paper. In their work, they considered the automatic generation of a CPN model for a distributed automation architecture.

# 9    Conclusions and Future Work

In this paper we have presented a formal specification of the micro-service based architecture for the fire risk notification system being developed in the DYNAMIC research project. Our modelling patterns represent a general app-roach to modelling REST APIs using CPNs. In addition, we have formally vali-dated the system services and the interaction between the micro-services using state space exploration and model checking.

The design of the fire risk notification system has been following an implementation-first approach where two prototypes were implemented and tested. The purpose has been to first validate the fire risk model itself, as to better understand the functional requirements and software technology capa-bilities in the technical solution space. The final step has then been to specify the software architecture and micro-services in an implementation-independent manner using a CPN model. The CPN model presented in this paper will then serve as basis for implementing a final version of the fire risk notification system.

In the present work we have considered only a limited number of system configurations as we have reached the limit for what is feasible to verify with CPN Tools using full state spaces. Future work includes verification of a more complete set of system configurations using the incremental methodology presented in [23]. In order to tackle systems with more instances of clients and locations and explore the scalability of the verification, it will be necessary to use state space reduction techniques such as symbolic approaches, partial order reductions, symmetries, or parametric approaches. These are not supported by CPN Tools, but other coloured Petri nets tools could be experimented with, such as Helena [7] or CPN-AMI [19]. The scope of colours and functions might be limited in these, and therefore a careful transformation of our model must be achieved first. The CPN model constructed by our approach may potentially be used to generate test-cases for the implementation using the model-based approach presented in [30]. Extraction of test cases combined with monitoring and run-time verification may also provide a direction forward for establishing a more formal relationship between the CPN model and the implementation of the fire risk notification system.

**Acknowledgements.** This study was partly funded by the Research Council of Nor-way, grant no 298993, Reducing fire disaster risk through *dynamic risk assessment and management* (DYNAMIC). The study was also supported by Haugaland Kraft Nett, Norwegian Directorate for Cultural Heritage and Stavanger municipality. Part of this work was achieved while Lars M. Kristensen was visiting Université Sorbonne Paris Nord as invited professor.

# References

1. Camilli, M., Bellettini, C., Capra, L.: A high-level Petri net-based formal model of distributed self-adaptive systems. In: Proceedings of the 12th European Conference on Software Architecture: Companion Proceedings, ECSA, pp. 40:1–40:7. ACM (2018). https://doi.org/10.1145/3241403.3241445

2. Camilli, M., Bellettini, C., Capra, L., Monga, M.: A formal framework for specifying and verifying microservices based process flows. In: Cerone, A., Roveri, M. (eds.) SEFM 2017. LNCS, vol. 10729, pp. 187–202. Springer, Cham (2018). https://doi.org/10.1007/978-3-319-74781-1_14

3. Cheng, A., Christensen, S., Mortensen, K.H.: Model checking coloured Petri nets - exploiting strongly connected components. DAIMI Report Series **26**(519) (1997). https://doi.org/10.7146/dpb.v26i519.7048, https://tidsskrift.dk/daimipb/article/view/7048

4. Christensen, S., Mortensen, K.H.: Design/CPN ASK-CTL Manual, Version 0.9 (1996)

5. DYNAMIC Research Project: Reducing fire disaster risk through dynamic risk assessment and management (2022). https://www.hvl.no/en/project/2495578/. Accessed 27 Mar 2022

6. DSB: Brannene i Lærdal, Flatanger og på Frøya Vinteren 2014 (The fires at Lærdal, Flatanger and Frøya, winter 2014). Technical report, Norwegian Directorate for Civil Protection (2014). in Norwegian

7. Evangelista, S.: The Helena Petri net tool (2022). https://lipn.univ-paris13.fr/~evangelista/helena/. Accessed 10 Nov 2022

8. Fielding, R.: Architectural styles and the design of network-based software architectures. Technical report, University of California, Irvine (2000). Doctoral dissertation

9. Framework, X.: Xamarin framework (2022). https://dotnet.microsoft.com/en-us/apps/xamarin. Accessed 28 Mar 2022

10. Heroku:   Heroku   (2022).   https://devcenter.heroku.com/articles/heroku-cli. Accessed 28 Mar 2022

11. Kallab, L., Mrissa, M., Chbeir, R., Bourreau, P.: Using colored Petri nets for verifying RESTful service composition. In: Panetto, H., et al. (eds.) OTM 2017. LNCS, vol. 10573, pp. 505–523. Springer, Cham (2017). https://doi.org/10.1007/978-3-319-69462-7_32

12. Kraaijeveld, A., Gunnarshaug, A., Schei, B., Log, T.: Burning rate and time to flashover in wooden 1/4 scale compartments as a function of fuel moisture content. In: Proceedings of the 14th International Fire Science and Engineering Conference. Interflam, Windsor, UK, pp. 553–558, 4–6 July 2016

13. Log, T.: Cold climate fire risk; a case study of the Lærdalsøyri fire. Fire Technol. **52**, 1815–1843 (2014)

14. Log, T.: Indoor relative humidity as a fire risk indicator. Build. Environ. **111**, 238–248 (2017)

15. Log, T.: Modeling indoor relative humidity and wood moisture content as a proxy for wooden home fire risk. Sensors **19**(22) (2019)

16. Norwegian Meteorological Services: Frost API (2022). https://frost.met.no/index.html. Accessed 27 Mar 2022

17. Norwegian Meteorological Services: MET Norway Weather API (2022). https://api.met.no/. Accessed 27 Mar 2022

18. Metallinou, M., Log, T.: Cold climate structural fire danger rating system? Challenges **9**(1), 12 (2018)

19. Move team: CPN-AMI web site (2022). https://move.lip6.fr/software/CPNAMI/. Accessed 10 Nov 2022

20. Narayanan, M., Cherukuri, A.K.: Verification of cloud based information integration architecture using colored Petri nets. Int. J. Comput. Netw. Inf. Secur. **2**, 1–11 (2018). https://doi.org/10.5815/ijcnis.2018.02.01

21. Ndiaye, M., Pétin, J.F., Georges, J.P., Camerini, J.: Practical use of coloured Petri nets for the design and performance assessment of distributed automation architectures. In: Cabac, L., Kristensen, L.M., Rölke, H. (eds.) Proceedings of the International Workshop on Petri Nets and Software Engineering 2016, pp. 113–131 (2016)
22. Pirsko, A.R., Fons, W.L.: Frequency of urban building fires as related to daily weather conditions. Technical report 866, US Department of Agriculture (1956)
23. Rodríguez, A., Kristensen, L.M., Rutle, A.: Formal modelling and incremental verification of the MQTT IoT protocol. Trans. Petri Nets Other Model. Concurr. **14**, 126–145 (2019)
24. Rohrer-Mirtschink, S., Forster, N., Giovanoli, P., Guggenheim, M.: Major burn injuries associated with Christmas celebrations: a 41-year experience from Switzerland. Ann. Burns Fire Disasters **28**(1), 71–75 (2015)
25. Röwekamp, J.H., Buchholz, M., Moldt, D.: Petri net sagas. In: Proceedings of the International Workshop on Petri Nets and Software Engineering 2021 co-located with the 42nd International Conference on Application and Theory of Petri Nets and Concurrency (PETRI NETS. CEUR Workshop Proceedings, vol. 2907, pp. 65–84. CEUR-WS.org (2021). http://ceur-ws.org/Vol-2907/paper4.pdf
26. Sakai, M., Takahashi, K., Kondoh, S.: Method of constructing Petri net service model using distributed trace data of microservices. In: 22nd Asia-Pacific Network Operations and Management Symposium, APNOMS, pp. 214–217. IEEE (2021). https://doi.org/10.23919/APNOMS52696.2021.9562589
27. Spring Boot Framework (2022). https://spring.io/projects/spring-boot. Accessed 28 Mar 2022
28. Strand, R.D., Kristensen, L.M., Petrucci, L.: Formal specification and validation of a data-driven software system for fire risk prediction. In: Proceedings of Petri Nets and Software Engineering 2022. CEUR Workshop Proceedings, vol. 3170, pp. 1–20 (2022)
29. Strand, R.D., Stokkenes, S., Kristensen, L.M., Log, T.: Fire risk prediction using cloud-based weather data services. J. Ubiquit. Syst. Pervasive Netw. **16**(1) (2021). https://doi.org/10.5383/JUSPN.16.01.005
30. Wang, R., Kristensen, L.M., Stolz, V.: MBT/CPN: a tool for model-based software testing of distributed systems protocols using coloured Petri nets. In: Atig, M.F., Bensalem, S., Bliudze, S., Monsuez, B. (eds.) VECoS 2018. LNCS, vol. 11181, pp. 97–113. Springer, Cham (2018). https://doi.org/10.1007/978-3-030-00359-3_7

# Computing a Parametric Reveals Relation For Bounded Equal-Conflict Petri Nets

Federica Adobbati[1,3] , Luca Bernardinello[1(✉)] , Görkem Kılınç Soylu[2] ,
and Lucia Pomello[1]

[1] Dipartimento di Informatica, Sistemistica e Comunicazione, Università degli Studi
di Milano - Bicocca, viale Sarca 336 U14, Milano, Italy
`f.adobbati@campus.unimib.it`, {`luca.bernardinello,lucia.pomello`}`@unimib.it`
[2] Department of Computing Engineering, Izmir Institute of Technology, Gülbahçe,
Urla, İzmir, Turkey
`gorkemkilinc@iyte.edu.tr`
[3] National Institute of Oceanography and Applied Geophysics - OGS, Trieste, Italy

**Abstract.** In a distributed system, in which an action can be either
"hidden" or "observable", an unwanted information flow might arise
when occurrences of observable actions give information about occurrences of hidden actions. A collection of relations, i.e. reveals and its
variants, is used to model such information flow among transitions of
a Petri net. This paper recalls the reveals relations defined in [3], and
proposes an algorithm to compute them on bounded equal-conflict PT
systems, using a smaller structure than the one defined in [3].

**Keywords:** Information flow · Noninterference · Bounded
equal-conflict Petri nets · Reveals relations · Distributed systems

## 1 Introduction

In distributed systems, it is often the case that some actions are confidential,
and it is not desired that a user is able to deduce information about occurrences
of these confidential actions, while still being able to interact with the system.
This kind of unwanted information flow can form a security concern for systems.
*Noninterference* is a formal notion which guarantees that a system does not
suffer from such information flow.

The concept of noninterference was introduced by Goguen and Meseguer for
deterministic state machines in [21]. In this concept, a system is viewed as consisting of components at two distinct levels of confidentiality: *high* (hidden) and
*low* (observable). A system is then said to be secure with respect to noninterference if a user, who knows the structure of the system, cannot deduce information
about high actions by interacting only via low actions. Sutherland and McCullough moved the concept to the nondeterministic and concurrent systems in
[29,33]. Since then, various noninterference properties have been proposed in

M. Koutny et al. (Eds.): TPNOMCXVII, LNCS 14150, pp. 54–83, 2024.
https://doi.org/10.1007/978-3-662-68191-6_3

the literature based on different system models, e.g. [13, 20, 27, 30]. An overview on information-flow security and noninterference is provided in [28].

Busi and Gorrieri moved the notion of noninterference to 1-safe Petri nets by studying observational equivalences and structural properties in [14]. In [15], the authors investigate structural properties, such as absence of certain places, for defining noninterference in elementary net systems. In [11], Best et al. study the decidability of noninterference in Petri nets. In [7], Baldan and Carraro give a characterisation of noninterference in terms of causalities and conflicts on unfoldings of 1-safe Petri nets. In [8], the authors work on the minimal solutions for enforcing noninterference on bounded Petri nets.

The work presented in [10, 26] distinguish two kinds of information flow in Petri nets, i.e. positive and negative information flow. The first one arises when the occurrence of a low transition gives information about the occurrence of a high transition whereas the second arises when the occurrence of a low transition allows one to deduce the non-occurrence of a high transition. The authors introduce two families of relations, namely *reveals* and *excludes*, to model positive and negative information flow among transitions of a Petri net. The reveals relation was originally defined for the events of an occurrence net by Haar in [23] to be used in fault diagnosis [24]. The reveals relation was then redefined for the transitions of Petri nets in [10, 26] and was used, together with its variants and the excludes relation, to define various noninterference properties for distributed systems modelled with Petri nets.

In [5], a formal basis is provided for modelling and analysing information flow with 1-safe free-choice Petri nets by computing reveals and excludes relations. The authors introduce a notion of *maximal-step computation tree*, which represents the behaviour of a 1-safe free-choice net under maximal-step semantics. They define a finite prefix, named *full prefix*, on the tree and provide methods for computing reveals and excludes relations on the prefix.

In [3], we extended the results of [5] to bounded equal-conflict Petri nets, which are a weighted generalisation of (extended) free-choice nets and were introduced in [34]. We introduced two new parametric reveals relations, formalised the maximal-step computation tree and its full prefix for bounded equal-conflict PT systems, and provided methods for computing reveals relations on the full prefix.

The maximal step computation tree can be seen as an unfolding of the marking graph corresponding to the maximal step semantics, denoted MaxMg. This is the graph containing only the markings which are reachable by maximal steps, and the arcs labelled by maximal steps.

Even if the reachable markings in MaxMg may be much less than the ones in the sequential marking graph, the full prefix of the derived tree of maximal step computations, as in [3], may have a huge amount of nodes; for this reason, in this paper, we extend paper [3] by proposing a method to compute the new parametric reveals relations starting from a reduced version of the maximal step marking graph and based on an algorithm which constructs a prefix of the infinite tree unfolding the reduction of MaxMg.

We implemented this method and carried on some experiments, comparing the results with those obtained by the algorithm in [3].

The paper is organised as follows. Section 2 provides the necessary background on Petri nets. Section 3 recalls some definitions based on the reveals relation in the context of information flow and presents the new parametric variants, as introduced in [3]. Section 4 deals with the computation of the parametric reveals relations on bounded equal-conflict nets. Section 5 gives information on the implementation and discusses some experiments. Section 6 concludes the paper and discusses some possible future work.

## 2 Petri Nets

In this section we recall basic definitions concerning Petri nets and net unfoldings that will be useful in the rest of the paper, see also [12, 17, 18, 22, 31].

A *net* is a triple $N = (P, T, F)$, where $P$ and $T$ are disjoint sets. The elements of $P$ are called *places* and are represented by circles, the elements of $T$ are called *transitions* and are represented by squares, $F \subseteq (P \times T) \cup (T \times P)$ is the *flow relation*, represented by directed arcs. The *pre-set* of an element $x \in P \cup T$ is the set $^\bullet x = \{y \in P \cup T : (y, x) \in F\}$; the *post-set* of $x$ is the set $x^\bullet = \{y \in P \cup T : (x, y) \in F\}$. Let $X \subseteq P \cup T$ be a subset of elements, its pre-set is defined as $^\bullet X = \{y \in P \cup T : \exists x \in X : (y, x) \in F\}$, and its post-set as $X^\bullet = \{y \in P \cup T : \exists x \in X : (x, y) \in F\}$.

A net $(P, T, F)$ is a *subnet* of another net $(P', T', F')$ if $P \subseteq P'$, $T \subseteq T'$ and $F$ is the restriction of $F'$ to $(P \times T) \cup (T \times P)$.

A net is *finite* if $P \cup T$ is finite, and *infinite* otherwise. A net is *T-restricted* if for any $t \in T$, $^\bullet t \neq \emptyset$ and $t^\bullet \neq \emptyset$.

A Place Transition (PT) *system*, $\Sigma = (P, T, F, W, m_0)$ is defined by a finite net $(P, T, F)$, a map $W : F \to \mathbb{N}$ which assigns a positive *weight* to each arc, and an *initial marking* $m_0 : P \to \mathbb{N}$. We write $W(x, y) = 0$ when $(x, y) \notin F$. The tuple $(P, T, F, W)$ will be called *PT net*. In graphical representations, arcs are inscribed by their weights, if the weight is greater than one, and markings $m$ are represented by $m(p)$ dots, called tokens, in each place $p$.

Let $\Sigma$ be a PT net and $m : P \to \mathbb{N}$ be a marking. A transition $t$ is *enabled* at $m$, denoted $m[t\rangle$, if, for any $p \in P$, $m(p) \geq W(p, t)$. Let $t$ be enabled at $m$; then, $t$ can *occur* (or *fire*) in $m$ producing the new marking $m'$, denoted $m[t\rangle m'$ and defined as follows: $\forall p \in P$, $m'(p) = m(p) - W(p, t) + W(t, p)$.

A finite or infinite sequence of transitions $t_1 t_2 \ldots t_k \ldots$ is an *occurrence sequence* enabled at $m_0$, denoted $m_0[t_1 \ldots t_k \ldots \rangle$, if there are intermediate markings $m_1 \ldots m_k \ldots$ such that: $m_0[t_1\rangle m_1 \ldots [t_k\rangle m_k \ldots$.

Let $m$ be a marking of $\Sigma$, the set $[m\rangle$ is the smallest set of markings such that: $m \in [m\rangle$, and if $m' \in [m\rangle$ and $m'[t\rangle m''$, then $m'' \in [m\rangle$. The set $[m_0\rangle$, also denoted $M_\Sigma$, is the set of *reachable markings* of $\Sigma$.

A *multiset* of transitions $U : T \to \mathbb{N}$ is *concurrently enabled* at $m \in [m_0\rangle$, denoted $m[U\rangle$, and called *step*, iff $\forall p \in P$, $\sum_{t \in T} U(t) \cdot W(p, t) \leq m(p)$; if $U$ is enabled at $m$, it can occur producing the new marking $m'$, denoted $m[U\rangle m'$ and defined as follows: $\forall p \in P$, $m'(p) = m(p) - \sum_{t \in T} U(t) \cdot W(p,t) + \sum_{t \in T} U(t) \cdot W(t,p)$.

A multiset $U : T \to \mathbb{N}$ is a *maximal-step* at $m \in [m_0\rangle$ iff $m[U\rangle$ and $\forall t' \in T$, $\exists p \in P$ such that: $m(p) < \sum_{t \in T} U(t) \cdot W(p,t) + W(p,t')$.

The set of possible steps in $\Sigma$ is $U_\Sigma = \{U : T \to \mathbb{N} \mid \exists m, m' \in M_\Sigma : m[U\rangle m'\}$.

Analogously to occurrence sequences, a finite or infinite sequence of steps (or maximal-steps) $U_1 U_2 ... U_k...$ is a *step sequence* (or a *maximal-step sequence*) enabled at $m_0$, denoted $m_0[U_1...U_k...\rangle$, if there are intermediate markings $m_1...m_k...$ such that: $m_0[U_1\rangle m_1...[U_k\rangle m_k...$.

The behaviour of a PT system $\Sigma = (P,T,F,W,m_0)$ can be described by its *marking graph* $MG(\Sigma) = (M_\Sigma, U_\Sigma, A, m_0)$, that is a labelled transition system where the states are the reachable markings $M_\Sigma$, with $m_0$ the initial one, and each arc in $A$ is labelled by the step leading from the source marking to the target one, $A = \{(m, U, m') \mid m, m' \in M, U \in U_\Sigma, and\ m[U\rangle m'\}$. In the case in which we consider only the arcs which are labelled by single transitions, we get the *sequential marking graph*. In general a labelled transition system TS $= (Q, L, A, q_0)$ is a tuple where $Q$ is the set of states, $L$ is the set of labels, $A$ is the set of transitions, and $q_0$ is the initial state.

Two transitions $t_1$ and $t_2$ are in *conflict at a marking* $m \in [m_0\rangle$ iff they are both enabled at $m$, $m[t_1\rangle$ and $m[t_2\rangle$, however they are not concurrently enabled at $m$, $\neg(m[\{t_1, t_2\}\rangle)$, the occurrence of one of them disables the other one.

In some situations concurrency and conflicts overlap in such a way that it is not clear if in the execution of concurrent transitions a conflict has been solved or not. This is a so called situation of 'confusion' which has been introduced by C.A. Petri and discussed in several papers as for example in [32,35], and which can be formalised in the following way. Let $m \in [m_0\rangle$, $t_1, t_2 \in T$ such that: $m[\{t_1, t_2\}\rangle$, then $(m, t_1, t_2)$ is a *confusion* at $m$ if $\mathrm{cfl}(t_1, m) \neq \mathrm{cfl}(t_1, m_2)$, where $\mathrm{cfl}(t_1, m) = \{t' \in T : m[t'\rangle \wedge \neg(m[\{t_1, t'\}\rangle)\}$, and $m_2$ is such that $m[t_2\rangle m_2$. In Fig. 1, the two main situations of confusion are illustrated, namely *asymmetric* confusion, on the left side, and *symmetric* confusion, on the right side. In the particular case of asymmetric confusion, the occurrence of the step $\{t_1, t_2\}$ hides the information whether the conflict in-between $t_1$ and $t_3$ has been solved or not; moreover, in this case, maximal-step semantics is not equivalent to step semantics, since transition $t_3$ will never occur in any sequence of maximal steps, whereas the step sequence $m_0[\{t_2\}\rangle\{b_1, b_3, b_4\}[\{t_3\}\rangle$ may occur.

The relation between step semantics and maximal-step semantics has been studied for example in [25], where it is shown that they are equivalent in the case of systems without asymmetric confusion. A general class of nets in which confusion cannot arise is the class of equal-conflict PT nets, a generalisation of (extended) free-choice nets [16] to nets with arc weights, studied by various authors, see for example [34]. A PT net $(P, T, F, W)$ is an *equal-conflict PT net*, also called *EC PT net*, iff $\forall t, t' \in T$, $^\bullet t \cap ^\bullet t' \neq \emptyset \Rightarrow (^\bullet t = ^\bullet t' \wedge \forall p \in ^\bullet t, W(p,t) = W(p,t'))$.

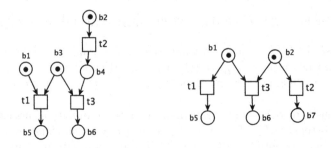

**Fig. 1.** Asymmetric confusion (on the left) and symmetric confusion (on the right side).

From the definition, it follows that in EC PT systems, if two transitions share a pre-place, then any given marking enables either both transitions or neither. All the figures in this paper, except for Fig. 1, provide examples of EC PT systems.

A PT system $\Sigma$ is *bounded* if there is a finite number $n$ such that: for any reachable marking $m \in [m_0\rangle$ and for any place $p$, $m(p) \leq n$. If $\Sigma$ is bounded, its set of reachable markings $[m_0\rangle$ is finite. A marking $m$ is a *deadlock* if no transition is enabled in $m$. $\Sigma$ is *1-live* if for all $t \in T$ there exists $m \in [m_0\rangle$ such that $m[t\rangle$.

In the rest of the paper, we will consider finite, bounded, and 1-live PT systems, whose underlying nets are T-restricted.

We now introduce two technical relations that will be useful to define the partial order semantics of PT systems. The $\prec$ relation on the elements of a net $N$ is the transitive closure of $F$ and $\preceq$ is the reflexive closure of $\prec$. Let $x, y \in P \cup T$, $x \# y$, iff there exist $t_1, t_2 \in T : t_1 \neq t_2$, $t_1 \preceq x$, $t_2 \preceq y$ and there exists $p \in {}^\bullet t_1 \cap {}^\bullet t_2$.

A net $N = (B, E, F)$, possibly infinite, is an *occurrence net* if the following restrictions hold:

1. $\forall x \in B \cup E : \neg(x \prec x)$
2. $\forall x \in B \cup E : \neg(x \# x)$
3. $\forall e \in E : \{x \in B \cup E \mid x \preceq e\}$ is finite
4. $\forall b \in B : |{}^\bullet b| \leq 1$

In an occurrence net, the elements of $B$ are called *conditions* and the elements of $E$ are called *events*; the transitive and reflexive closure of $F$, $\preceq$, forms a *partial order*. The set of minimal elements of an occurrence net $N$ with respect to $\preceq$ will be denoted by $\min(N)$. Since we only consider T-restricted nets the elements of $\min(N)$ are conditions.

A *configuration* of an occurrence net $N = (B, E, F)$ is a, possibly infinite, set of events $C \subseteq E$ which is causally closed (for every $e \in C$, $e' \preceq e \Rightarrow e' \in C$) and free of conflicts ($\forall e_1, e_2 \in C$, $\neg(e_1 \# e_2)$). $C$ is *maximal* if it is maximal with respect to set inclusion.

On the elements of an occurrence net the relation of concurrency, **co**, is defined as follows: let $x, y \in B \cup E$, $x$ **co** $y$, if neither $(x \prec y)$ nor $(y \prec x)$ nor $(x \# y)$.

A *B-cut* of $N$ is a maximal set of pairwise concurrent elements of $B$, and can be intuitively seen as a global state of the net in a certain moment. An *E-cut* of $N$ is a maximal set of pairwise concurrent elements of $E$, that corresponds to a maximal step on $N$.

A *branching process* of a bounded 1-live PT system $\Sigma = (P, T, F, W, m_0)$, whose underlying net is T-restricted, is a pair $(O, \lambda)$, where $O = (B, E, F')$ is an occurrence net, and $\lambda$ is a map from $B \cup E$ to $P \cup T$ such that:

1. $\lambda(B) \subseteq P$; $\lambda(E) \subseteq T$
2. $\forall e \in E$, $\forall p \in P$, $W(p, \lambda(e)) = |\lambda^{-1}(p) \cap {}^{\bullet}e|$ and $W(\lambda(e), p) = |\lambda^{-1}(p) \cap e^{\bullet}|$
3. $\forall p \in P \; m_0(p) = |\lambda^{-1}(p) \cap \min(O)|$
4. $\forall x, y \in E$, if ${}^{\bullet}x = {}^{\bullet}y$ and $\lambda(x) = \lambda(y)$, then $x = y$

We extend the definition of $\lambda$ to the set of configurations of the branching process: for each configuration $C$, $\lambda(C)$ is the multiset of the transitions whose occurrences are recorded in $C$ and is called the *footprint* of $C$; formally $\lambda(C) = \sum_{e_i \in C} \lambda(e_i)$. If a transition $t$ belongs to the support set of $\lambda(C)$, i.e. at least an occurrence of $t$ is in $C$, $\lambda(C)(t) \geq 1$, then we use the notation $t \in \lambda(C)$. If $C$ is infinite, it records the infinite occurrence of some transitions, and the multiset $\lambda(C)$ is such that the multiplicity of those transitions is infinite, whereas its support set is obviously finite, being a subset of $T$.

A branching process $(O_1, \lambda_1)$ is a *prefix* of a branching process $(O_2, \lambda_2)$ if $O_1$ is a subnet of $O_2$ containing all minimal elements $(\min(O_2))$ and such that: if $e \in E_1$ and $(b, e) \in F_2$ or $(e, b) \in F_2$ then $b \in B_1$; if $b \in B_1$ and $(e, b) \in F_2$ then $e \in E_1$; and $\lambda_1$ is the restriction of $\lambda_2$ to $B_1 \cup E_1$.

Any finite PT system $\Sigma = (P, T, F, W, m_0)$ has a unique branching process which is maximal with respect to the prefix relation. This maximal branching process, called the *unfolding* of $\Sigma$, will be denoted by $\mathrm{Unf}(\Sigma) = ((B, E, F'), \lambda)$, where $\lambda$ is the map from $B \cup E$ to $P \cup T$.

A *run* records a possible non sequential behaviour of the system, it is a branching process, whose occurrence net is free of conflicts, i.e., its set of events is a configuration. A run is *maximal* if the corresponding configuration is maximal. Let $\rho$ be a run, its footprint, denoted $\lambda(\rho)$, is the footprint of its set of events.

*Example 1.* Figure 2 represents an equal-conflict PT system $\Sigma$ and a branching process, which is a prefix of the unfolding of $\Sigma$. A maximal run of the branching process is the labelled subnet whose elements are grey, the set of its events is the configuration $C = \{e_1, e_2, e_3, e_4, e_5, e_6\}$, The footprint of $C$ is the multiset $\lambda(C) = \{a, e, f, g, 2.h\}$.

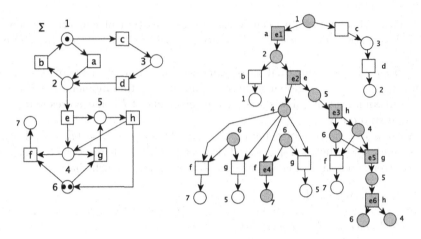

**Fig. 2.** A bounded equal-conflict PT system and a branching process of it (a prefix of Unf($\Sigma$)).

## 3   Formal Relations for the Analysis of Information Flow

In [10, 26], a family of relations, i.e., *reveals* and its variants, were introduced to express information flow among transitions of a Petri net. These relations were then used to define several noninterference properties for specification of security requirements. In [3] we introduced two new parametric relations generalising those in [10, 26]. In this section, we recall the definitions of all these relations.

Let $\Sigma = (P, T, F, W, m_0)$ be a PT system (bounded, 1-live PT system with T-restricted underlying net) and Unf($\Sigma$) = $((B, E, F), \lambda)$ be its unfolding. In the following, $C_{max}$ will denote the set of all maximal configurations of Unf($\Sigma$). The set of events of Unf($\Sigma$) corresponding to a specific transition $t$ of a given PT system $\Sigma$ will be denoted by $E_t = \{e \in E : \lambda(e) = t\}$. We will assume *progress* of the system, i.e., an enabled transition either fires or gets disabled by another transition in conflict with it; the set of configurations satisfying this assumption coincides with $C_{max}$.

The reveals relation was originally introduced for events of an occurrence net in [23], and in [24] it was applied in the field of fault diagnosis. In [10], the reveals relation was redefined for the transitions of a 1-live Petri net in order to express positive information flow: transition $t_1$ reveals transition $t_2$ if each maximal configuration which contains an occurrence of $t_1$ also contains at least one occurrence of $t_2$. This means that the occurrence of $t_1$ implies the occurrence of $t_2$, either in the past or in the future. Hence, if a low transition reveals a high transition, this might cause a positive information flow endangering the security of the system.

**Definition 1.** *Let $t_1, t_2 \in T$ be two transitions; $t_1$ reveals $t_2$, denoted $t_1 \rhd t_2$, iff $\forall C \in C_{max}$   $t_1 \in \lambda(C) \implies t_2 \in \lambda(C)$.*

Since we consider 1-live nets, there is at least one maximal configuration in which $t_1$ occurs. If there exists a maximal configuration in which $t_1$ occurs and $t_2$ does not occur, then $t_1 \not\triangleright t_2$.

Sometimes, even if a transition alone does not give much information about the occurrence of another transition, a set of transitions together might imply the occurrence of some transitions in another set. This relation was originally defined for the events of an occurrence net in [6], and later in [10] was redefined for the transitions of a Petri net in order to be used in information-flow analysis. Set $X$ extended reveals set $Y$ if each maximal configuration which has all the transitions of $X$ also has at least one transition of $Y$. It can violate the security of a system if a group of low transitions extended reveals a group of high transitions.

**Definition 2.** *Let $X, Y \subseteq T$. If there is at least one maximal configuration in which all transitions of $X$ appear, then we say $X$ extended reveals $Y$, denoted $X \twoheadrightarrow Y$, iff $\quad \forall\, C \in C_{max}$*

$$\bigwedge_{t_i \in X} t_i \in \lambda(C) \implies \bigvee_{t_j \in Y} t_j \in \lambda(C).$$

Note that $X \twoheadrightarrow Y$ is not defined if the transitions of $X$ never appear together.

*Remark 1.* The extended reveals relation between two singletons coincides with the reveals relation.

The next relation takes the repeated occurrences of a transition into account. In some cases, the occurrence of a transition does not give information while several occurrences of the transition imply the occurrence of another transition. This relation was defined in [10] without progress assumption, thus considering all configurations. Here, we alter the definition for the setting in which maximal configurations are considered. We say that $t_1$ $n$-repeated reveals $t_2$ if each maximal configuration which has at least $n$ occurrences of $t_1$, also has at least one occurrence of $t_2$. It can violate the security of a system if a number of occurrences of a low transition imply occurrence of a high transition.

**Definition 3.** *Let $t_1, t_2 \in T$ be two transitions, and $C_{max}$ be the set of all maximal configurations of $\mathrm{Unf}(\Sigma)$. Let $n$ be a positive integer. If there exists a maximal configuration in which $t_1$ occurs at least $n$ times, then we say $t_1$ $n$-repeated reveals $t_2$, denoted $n.t_1 \triangleright t_2$, iff*

$$\forall C \in C_{max} \quad |C \cap E_{t_1}| \geq n \implies C \cap E_{t_2} \neq \emptyset.$$

Note that $n$-repeated reveals is not defined if there is no maximal configuration in which $t_1$ occurs at least $n$ times.

The following statements are direct consequences of Definition 3.

*Remark 2.* The reveals relation (as in Definition 1) coincides with 1-repeated reveals.

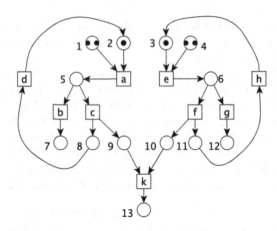

**Fig. 3.** A bounded equal-conflict PT system.

*Remark 3.* If $n.t_1 \triangleright t_2$ and $\exists C \in C_{max}$ such that $|C \cap E_{t_1}| \geq n + 1$ then $(n + 1).t_1 \triangleright t_2$.

*Remark 4.* $n.t_1 \not\triangleright t_2 \implies (n - 1).t_1 \not\triangleright t_2$.

*Example 2.* A bounded equal-conflict PT system is illustrated in Fig. 3. In this system, the occurrence of $b$ implies the occurrence of $a$ since every maximal configuration which has $b$ also has $a$. However, vice versa is not correct since there is a maximal configuration in which $a$ occurs without $b$. Thus, $b \triangleright a$ and $a \not\triangleright b$. Some other reveals relations are $c \triangleright d$, $d \triangleright c$, $f \triangleright h$, $h \triangleright f$, $d \triangleright a$ and $h \triangleright e$.

Examples of extended reveals are as follows. The occurrence of $c$ alone or $f$ alone is not sufficient to say something about the occurrence of $k$, but the occurrence of $c$ and $f$ together implies the occurrence of $k$, i.e., $\{c, f\} \twoheadrightarrow \{k\}$. Although $a \not\triangleright c$ and $a \not\triangleright b$, the occurrence of $a$ implies the occurrence of either $b$ or $c$, i.e., $\{a\} \twoheadrightarrow \{b, c\}$. Similarly, $\{e\} \twoheadrightarrow \{f, g\}$.

Examples of repeated reveals are as follows. Only one occurrence of $a$ does not give information about $d$, hence $a \not\triangleright d$, however, if $a$ occurs twice, this implies the occurrence of $d$, i.e.: $2.a \triangleright d$. Similarly, one occurrence of $e$ does not imply the occurrence of $h$, however, two occurrences of $e$ imply the occurrence of $h$, i.e.: $e \not\triangleright h$ and $2.e \triangleright h$. Considering the PT system in Fig. 2, a single occurrence of $h$ does not reveal $g$, but two occurrence do, i.e.: $h \not\triangleright g$ and $2.h \triangleright g$.

The following variant of the reveals relation is parametric and it generalises all the variants above. This relation is more expressive and allows one to specify the expected security requirements in a more tailored fashion.

**Definition 4.** *Let* $i, k \geq 1$ *and* $\{n_1, ..., n_k\}$ *be positive integers. Let* $\{t_1, ..., t_k\}, Y \subseteq T$. *If there is at least one maximal configuration in which each transition* $t_i$ *of* $\{t_1, ..., t_k\}$ *occurs at least* $n_i$ *times, then we say* $\{n_1.t_1, ..., n_k.t_k\}$

extended-repeated reveals $Y$ *denoted* $\{n_1.t_1, ..., n_k.t_k\} \rightarrow Y$ *iff* $\forall\, C \in C_{max}$

$$\bigwedge_{t_i \in \{t_1, ..., t_k\}} (|C \cap E_{t_i}| \geq n_i) \implies \bigvee_{t \in Y} (C \cap E_t \neq \emptyset).$$

Note that $\{n_1.t_1, ..., n_k.t_k\}$ extended-repeated reveals $Y$ is not defined if there is no maximal configuration in which each transition $t_i$ of $\{t_1, ..., t_k\}$ occurs at least $n_i$ times.

*Remark 5.* Reveals, extended reveals and repeated reveals can be expressed by Definition 4.

$$t_1 \rhd t_2 \iff \{1.t_1\} \rightarrow \{t_2\},$$

$$\{t_1, t_2\} \rightarrow \{t_3, t_4\} \iff \{1.t_1, 1.t_2\} \rightarrow \{t_3, t_4\},$$

$$n.t_1 \rhd t_2 \iff \{n.t_1\} \rightarrow \{t_2\}.$$

*Example 3.* In the system net illustrated in Fig. 3, let us examine the relation between the transitions $a, e$ and $k$. Neither $a$ nor $e$ reveals $k$ alone. There is no extended reveals or repeated reveals relation between them either. However, there is still some information flow. Two occurrences of $a$ together with two occurrences of $e$ extended-repeated reveal $k$, i.e., $\{2.a, 2.e\} \rightarrow \{k\}$. This might cause a security violation in a system where the occurrence of $k$ is supposed to be a secret.

Let us consider a case in which the total number of occurrences of a set of transitions gives information about another set of transitions. In other words, if the total number of occurrences of the transitions in the first set is more than a certain number, this implies that at least one transition of the second set must have occurred or will occur inevitably. The next relation defines such situation. If a set of low transitions collectively reveal some high transitions this might cause a security violation.

**Definition 5.** *Let* $n \geq 1$ *and* $X, Y \subseteq T$*. If there is at least one maximal configuration in which the total number of occurrences of the transitions in set* $X$ *is at least* $n$*, then we say* $X$ *$n$-collective reveals* $Y$*, denoted* $n.X \rightarrow Y$*, iff* $\forall\, C \in C_{max}$

$$\sum_{t \in X} |C \cap E_t| \geq n \implies \bigvee_{t \in Y} (C \cap E_t \neq \emptyset).$$

Note that $X$ $n$-collective reveals $Y$ is not defined if there is no maximal configuration in which the total number of occurrences of the transitions in set $X$ is at least $n$.

*Remark 6.* Reveals and repeated reveals can be expressed by Definition 5.

$$t_1 \rhd t_2 \iff 1.\{t_1\} \rightarrow \{t_2\},$$

$$n.t_1 \rhd t_2 \iff n.\{t_1\} \rightarrow \{t_2\}.$$

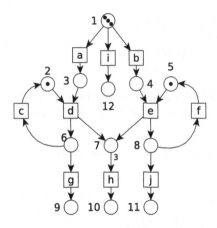

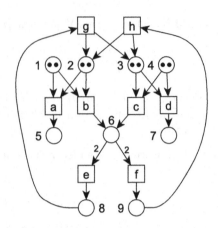

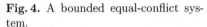

**Fig. 4.** A bounded equal-conflict system.

**Fig. 5.** A bounded equal-conflict system.

*Example 4.* In the net in Fig. 4, if the total number of occurrences of $d$ and $e$ is at least 3, this implies the occurrence of $h$, i.e., $3.\{d, e\} \twoheadrightarrow \{h\}$.

In the net in Fig. 5, if the total number of occurrences of $b$ and $c$ is at least 2, this implies occurrence of either $e$ or $f$, i.e., $2.\{b, c\} \twoheadrightarrow \{e, f\}$.

## 4  Computing Information Flow on Bounded Equal-Conflict Nets

In this section, we consider bounded equal-conflict PT systems and show how to compute the relations introduced in Sect. 3 by exploiting the equal-conflict structure of the net.

The relations in Sect. 3 consider the unfolding of a system $\mathrm{Unf}(\Sigma)$ and analyse their maximal configurations checking footprints, the multisets of transitions occurring in maximal configurations. Here, we consider maximal-step semantics, since, as recalled in Sect. 2, it is equivalent to step semantics in the case of equal-conflict systems, where there is no asymmetric confusion [25].

Moreover, thanks to the results in [12], it is possible to show a strict relation between footprints of step sequences of a system $\Sigma$ and footprints of configurations of $\mathrm{Unf}(\Sigma)$.

In fact, in [12], the authors studied the relationships between various classes of non-sequential processes (runs of an unfolding), occurrence sequences and step sequences. They showed that, in the special case of countable, T-restricted nets of finite synchronisation (i.e., where any transition has a finite set of pre- and post-places) with finite initial marking, and then also in the case of the nets here considered, the distinction between occurrence sequences and step sequences disappears. Moreover, for the same class of nets, they showed that it is possible to consider equivalence relations both on the set of occurrence sequences and on the set of processes such that there is a bijection between the induced equivalence classes.

In the case of occurrence sequences, the equivalence relation abstracts w.r.t. the total order arbitrarily chosen when transitions are concurrent; in the case of processes, the equivalence abstracts from the distinction among several tokens on the same place.

From the construction of the equivalence classes both of occurrence sequences and of processes, it is possible to observe that the elements in each class have the same footprints, i.e., the same multiset of transitions which can be observed through the corresponding behaviour, and that elements of an equivalence class in bijective correspondence with a class of the other sort have the same footprint too. In conclusion, since for the previous motivations, footprints of maximal configurations correspond to footprints of maximal sequences of maximal steps, in order to verify the reveal relations we need to know indifferently either the footprints of maximal configurations or the footprints of maximal sequences of maximal steps.

In order to compute these footprints, we could start from the marking graph. However, a maximal path on it, namely a maximal sequence of states and transitions starting in the initial marking, is not necessarily associated with maximal configurations in the unfolding, as shown in Example 5. More efficiently, we consider the marking graph corresponding to the maximal step semantics, here denoted MaxMg($\Sigma$), or just MaxMg, if $\Sigma$ is clear from the context. It contains only the markings which are reachable by maximal steps, and its arcs are labelled by maximal steps.

*Example 5.* Consider the P/T system in Fig. 6 and its marking graph. The path repeating infinite times the sequence $\{1,3\}d\{1,4\}c$ is maximal, but it is not associated to any maximal configuration on the unfolding, since transition $b$ is always available but never taken. When we consider maximal steps this does not happen, as illustrated on the right of Fig. 6.

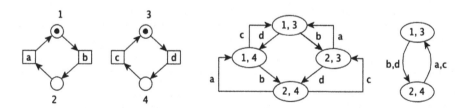

**Fig. 6.** A P/T system with two concurrent component on the left, its marking graph in the centre, and its marking graph with maximal step semantics on the right.

Figure 7 recalls the bounded equal-conflict PT system already presented in Fig. 2, and shows its marking graph and its maximal-step marking graph.

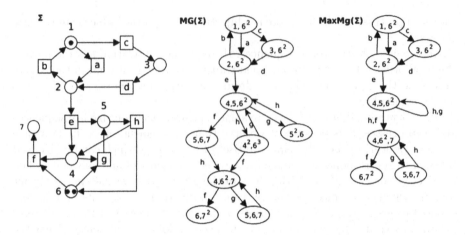

**Fig. 7.** A bounded equal-conflict PT system, its marking graph, and its maximal-step marking graph.

Given MaxMg, the computation of the maximal sequences of maximal steps is performed by considering the different cycles on the graph and in particular their possible unfoldings.

In the next subsections, we propose an algorithm to compute a collective reveals relation (Definition 5) starting from a reduced version of MaxMg. The algorithm constructs a prefix of the infinite tree unfolding of the reduction of MaxMg. We show that this prefix is sufficient to compute the collective reveals relation. Finally, we discuss how the algorithm can be adapted to compute an extended-repeated reveals relation (Definition 2), or multiple instances of them.

### 4.1 Reduction of MaxMg Based on an Instance of Collective Reveals

Let $\Sigma = (P, T, F, W, m_0)$ be a bounded equal-conflict PT net system, $X, Y \subseteq T$ and $n \geq 1$, and assume that we need to verify $n.X \rightarrow Y$. This relation does not hold if, and only if, there is a maximal run with $n$ occurrences of $X$ and none of $Y$. While finding a run with $n$ occurrences of $X$ and at least an occurrence of $Y$ does not give us any information, finding a run with $n$ occurrences of $X$ and none of $Y$ is sufficient to conclude that the relation does not hold. For this reason, while checking collective reveals, we can consider only the runs with no occurrence of $Y$, and check if there is one with at least $n$ occurrences of $X$ among them.

Note that in this way we do not detect the case in which the relation is not defined. However, it is reasonable to assume that in practical cases, users may be interested in verifying a relation which they already know to be defined on the system. If this is not the case, in [3] we present a version of this algorithm discriminating also the undefined case. The difference between that algorithm and the one proposed in this paper are discussed in Sect. 4.4 and Sect. 4.5.

The relation discussed above between maximal step sequences and footprints of the runs of the unfolding, allows us to reduce $\text{MaxMg}(\Sigma)$ by keeping only the sequences of maximal steps without occurrences of $Y$, and to check on them whether $n.X \twoheadrightarrow Y$ does not hold. We denote such a reduction of MaxMg with respect to $Y$ as $\text{RMG}_Y$.

Given $\Sigma$ and $Y$, the construction of $\text{RMG}_Y$ is presented in Algorithm 1. The construction start with procedure RMG. During its execution, the algorithm constructs a reduction of MaxMg, where the arcs labelled with an occurrence of $Y$ have been removed. At the same time, it stores in *remove* the list of markings that are not deadlock in $\Sigma$, but have no outgoing arc in the reduction of MaxMg. The paths crossing these markings need to be removed from the final result, since a sequence ending on them would not be associated to any maximal sequence in MaxMg. This further reduction is carried out by procedure UPDATE_RMG, that takes the list *remove* and the reduced marking graph constructed so far as input. This is a recursive procedure that removes from the marking graph all the arcs having a marking in *remove* as final point, and constructs another list of markings (*new_bad*) that have no outgoing arcs at the end of the procedure. The procedure calls recursively itself until the list of nodes to remove is empty. This must happen at some point, since the number of markings is finite, and once that a marking has been removed, it can never be added again.

*Example 6.* Figure 8 shows three reductions of the MaxMg of the PT system in Fig. 7. The first graph is reduced for the set $\{b\}$, the second is reduced for the set $\{h\}$, and the third for the set $\{g\}$. Considering set $\{b\}$, only one arc is removed from the original MaxMg since there is only one arc labelled with $b$. Since this arc arrives in the node labelled $1, 6^2$, that is still reachable in the $\text{RMG}_{\{b\}}$ (being the initial node) and has two outgoing arcs, no other element is removed from $\text{RMG}_{\{b\}}$. Similarly, when we construct $\text{RMG}_{\{g\}}$, we only remove one node and three arcs from MaxMg. Instead, when we consider the set $\{h\}$, the size of $\text{RMG}_{\{h\}}$ is much smaller than the one of MaxMg. This happens also because Algorithm 1 does not only remove all the arcs labelled with $h$ from MaxMg, but also the nodes that are not deadlocks in MaxMg, but have no outgoing arcs after removing the occurrences of $h$ from MaxMg, and the arcs pointing to these nodes. The graph resulting from this procedure, exactly produces all the maximal runs of the PT system which do not have any occurrence of $h$.

## 4.2   The Tree of Maximal-Step Computations

In this section, we define a tree which unfolds the maximal sequences of a labelled transition system. Given a PT system $\Sigma$ and an instance of collective reveals $n.X \twoheadrightarrow Y$, we can use the tree constructed from $\text{RMG}_Y$ to compute the relations defined in Sect. 3.

A first version of the tree was introduced in [5] for computing reveals and extended reveals on 1-safe free-choice systems, and then adapted to the class of bounded equal-conflict PT systems in [3]. Here, the construction of the tree is generalised to any labelled transition system, therefore also including those representing the marking graph of bounded PT systems.

---

**Algorithm 1** Computing the reduction $RMG_Y$ of $MaxMg(\Sigma)$

---

**procedure** RMG($\Sigma$: net, $Y \subseteq T$)
    pending = $[m_0]$
    RMG.markings = $\{\Sigma.m_0\}$
    RMG.trans = $\emptyset$
    remove = $[]$
    **while** pending $\neq []$ **do**
        $m$ = pending.pop()
        steps = compute_max_steps($m$)
        **if** steps $== \emptyset$ **then**
            new_dead = False
        **else**
            new_dead = True
        **end if**
        **for** step $\in$ steps **do**
            **if** step $\cap Y == \emptyset$ **then**
                new_dead = False
                m_next = compute_next_mrk($m$, step)
                **if** m_next $\notin$ RMG.markings **then:**
                    RMG.markings.add(m_next)
                    pending.append(next_mrk)
                **end if**
                RMG.trans.add(($m$, step, m_next))
            **end if**
        **end for**
        **if** new_dead $==$ True **then**
            remove.append($m$)
        **end if**
    **end while**
    **return** update_RMG(RMG, remove)
**end procedure**

**procedure** UPDATE_RMG(RMG, remove)
    **if** remove $== []$ **then:**
        **return** RMG
    **end if**
    new_bad = $[]$
    **for** $m \in$ remove **do**
        RMG.markings.remove($m$)
        **for** $t \in$ RMG.trans **do**
            **if** $t[2] == m$ **then**
                RMG.trans.remove($t$)
            **end if**
            **if** $\nexists t' \in$ RMG.trans $: t'[0] = t[0]$ **then**
                new_bad.add($t[0]$)
            **end if**
        **end for**
    **end for**
    **return** update_RMG(RMG, new_bad)
**end procedure**

---

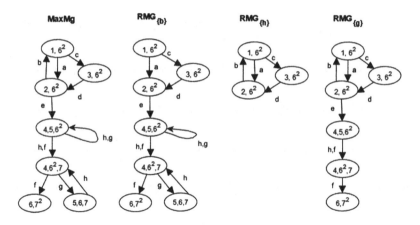

**Fig. 8.** The MaxMg of the PT system in Fig. 7, and three of its reductions.

**Definition 6.** *Let* $\mathrm{TS} = (Q, U, A, q_0)$ *be a labelled transition system on alphabet* $T$, *where* $U$ *is the set of labels of the transitions in* $A$, *and it is the set of multisets of the elements in* $T$. *The* unfolding tree *of* $\mathrm{TS}$, *denoted as* $\mathrm{TS}$-*tree, is a tree defined as follows.*

- *Each node of the tree is labelled with a state in* $Q$.
- *The root of the tree is labelled with the initial state* $q_0$.
- *From each node labelled with state* $q$ *in the tree, for each transition* $(q, u, q')$ *in the TS, there is exactly an arc in the tree, labelled with* $u$, *and leading to a node labelled with* $q'$.

A *path* in a TS-tree is a sequence $\pi = v_1 u_1 v_2 u_2 \cdots$, such that, for each $i$, there is an arc from $v_i$ to $v_{i+1}$, labelled with $u_i$. A path is *initial* if it starts in the root of the tree. A path can be either finite or infinite An (initial) path is *maximal* if it cannot be prolonged any more. Let $v$, $r$ be two nodes on the same path $\pi$, $v < r$ iff $v$ is closer to the root than $r$. The *footprint* of the path $\pi$, denoted $\lambda(\pi)$, is the (multiset) union of all the labels occurring in $\pi$.

We define an inclusion relation between footprints: let $\pi_1$ and $\pi_2$ be paths on a TS-tree; then $\lambda(\pi_1) \subseteq \lambda(\pi_2)$ iff $\forall t \in T$, $\lambda(\pi_1)(t) \leq \lambda(\pi_2)(t)$, i.e., for each element $t$, the number of occurrences in the footprint of $\pi_1$ is less than or equal to that in the footprint of $\pi_2$.

To simplify the notation, we will write $t \in \lambda(\pi)$ when $\lambda(\pi)(t) \geq 1$, namely when $t$ occurs in some step of path $\pi$.

Let $\Sigma$ be a PT system and $Y \subseteq T$. In the special case in which the labelled transition system is the MaxMg (resp. the $\mathrm{RMG}_Y$) of $\Sigma$, we also call the MaxMg-tree (resp. $\mathrm{RMG}_Y$-tree) *tree of (reduced) maximal-step computation* of $\Sigma$, since, in this case, all the arcs are labelled with maximal steps of $\Sigma$. From the considerations in the first part of Sect. 4, each maximal path in MaxMg-tree and in $\mathrm{RMG}_Y$-tree can be associated to at least one maximal configuration of the unfolding, with the same footprint. The vice versa holds for MaxMg-tree: each configuration of Unf($\Sigma$) is represented in the MaxMg-tree by a path with the same footprint. In RMG$_Y$-tree this is not true, since all the paths with an occurrence of $Y$ have been removed; still, the vice versa holds when we consider only the maximal configurations on the unfolding without any occurrence of $Y$.

*Remark 7.* If $Y = \emptyset$, MaxMg coincides with RMG$_Y$, therefore, if a property holds on RMG$_Y$-tree for any $Y$, it holds also on MaxMg-tree.

*Example 7.* Figure 9 illustrates a prefix of the MaxMg($\Sigma$)-tree, a prefix of the RMG$_{\{b\}}(\Sigma)$-tree, a prefix of the RMG$_{\{h\}}(\Sigma)$-tree, and a prefix of the RMG$_{\{g\}}(\Sigma)$-tree, where $\Sigma$ is the system net illustrated in Fig. 7. In the trees, the markings are represented as multisets of places. In each marking, if a place

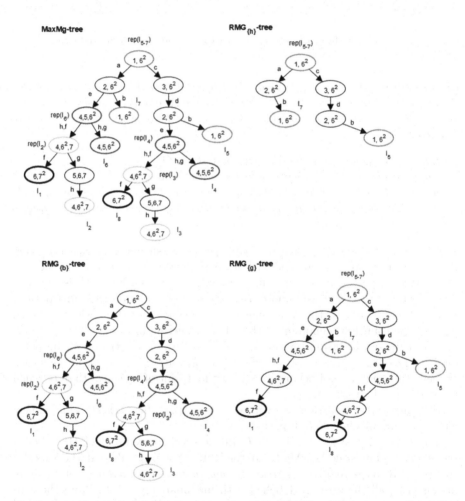

**Fig. 9.** A prefix of MaxMg($\Sigma$)-tree, a prefix of the RMG$_{\{b\}}(\Sigma)$-tree, a prefix of the RMG$_{\{h\}}(\Sigma)$-tree, and a prefix of the RMG$_{\{g\}}(\Sigma)$-tree, where $\Sigma$ is the system net illustrated in Fig. 7.

appears only once, its multiplicity is omitted; if a place $p$ appears $n$ times, for the sake of clarity in the figure, it is denoted with $p^n$. For example, the initial marking of the net is represented with $1, 6^2$.

Let $V = \{v_1, v_2, ..., v_n, ...\}$ be the set of nodes in the TS-tree, and $\mu : V \to Q$ the labelling function, mapping to each node the corresponding state. Two nodes $v_1$ and $v_2$ are equivalent if $\mu(v_1) = \mu(v_2)$. Let $\pi_1 = v_1 u_1 v_2 u_2 ... v_n u_n ...$ and $\pi_2 = v'_1 u'_1 v'_2 u'_2 ... v'_n u'_n ...$ be two paths on the tree, where the elements $v_j$ represent nodes of the tree, and the elements $u_j$ represent the labels of the arcs. The path $\pi_1$ is isomorphic to the path $\pi_2$ (in symbols $\pi_1 \simeq \pi_2$) iff for each $j$, $\mu(v_j) = \mu(v'_j)$, and $\lambda(u_j) = \lambda(u'_j)$. Finally, two subtrees $L_1$ and $L_2$ are isomorphic iff for each maximal path $\pi$ on $L_1$ there is a maximal path $\pi'$ in $L_2$ such that $\pi \simeq \pi'$, and vice versa.

Let $\pi$ be a maximal path on the tree, and $v_n$ one of its nodes. We denote with $\downarrow \pi(v_n)$ the path from the root to $v_n$, and with $\uparrow \pi(v_n)$ the subpath of $\pi$ starting from $v_n$.

**Lemma 1.** *Let $v_n$ and $v_k$ be two nodes of a TS-tree such that $\mu(v_n) = \mu(v_k)$. The subtree with $v_n$ as root and the one with $v_k$ as root are isomorphic.*

*Proof.* Since $\mu(v_n) = \mu(v_k)$, the arcs leaving from $v_n$ and from $v_k$ have the same labels. Then, by construction the children of $v_n$ are equivalent to the children of $v_k$, and the same reasoning can be applied to each of them. □

On the maximal paths of the TS-tree, we can define a *peeling* operation as follows [5,24]. Let $\pi = v_1 u_1 v_2 u_2 \cdots$ be a maximal path on the TS-tree, $v_n$ and $v_k$ be two nodes in $\pi$ with $n < k$ and $\mu(v_n) = \mu(v_k)$. Let $\pi_{n,k}$ be the subpath between $v_{n+1}$ and $v_k$. The peeling of $\pi$ with respect to $\pi_{n,k}$ is the path $\pi' = peel(\pi, \pi_{n,k})$ such that $\downarrow (\pi(v_n)) = \downarrow (\pi'(v_n))$, $\pi_{n,k}$ is deleted from $\pi$, and $\uparrow (\pi(v_k))$ is equivalent to $\uparrow (\pi'(v_n))$. In words, peeling $\pi$ means to consider the execution in which the cycle $\pi_{n,k}$ has not been executed. The path $\pi'$ constructed in this way is also maximal in the TS-tree.

### 4.3   The Full Prefix of the TS-Tree

In this section we adapt the definition of full prefix given in [5] and we recall some results that will be useful when presenting the algorithm.

**Definition 7.** *Let* $TS = (Q, U, A, q_0)$ *be a labelled transition system on alphabet $T$, where $U$ is the multiset of the elements in $T$. The full prefix of the TS-tree, denoted fp(TS), is a labelled rooted tree defined by the following clauses.*

1. *The root of* fp(TS) *is the root of the TS-tree.*
2. *Let $v$ be a node of* fp(TS). *If there is no $v'$ such that $v' < v$ and $\mu(v') = \mu(v)$, then all the children of $v$ in the TS-tree are nodes in* fp(TS); *otherwise $v$ is a leaf in* fp(TS).

Let $\Sigma$ be a bounded equal-conflict PT system. If the TS in Definition 7 is MaxMg, the definition of fp(MaxMg) coincides with the definition of fp($\Sigma$) given in [3].

*Example 8.* The trees in Fig. 9 are full prefixes of the MaxMg($\Sigma$)-tree, the RMG$_{\{b\}}(\Sigma)$-tree, the RMG$_{\{h\}}(\Sigma)$-tree, and the RMG$_{\{g\}}(\Sigma)$-tree. Each node is labelled with a marking, and each arc is labelled with a multiset of transitions. The leaves are either deadlocks, and in this case they are denoted with a black thick line, or repeated markings, and in this case the leaves are in the same colour of the node that they repeat. Moreover, some nodes have a second label: in particular, the leaves are labelled with $l_i$, $i \in \{1, ..., 8\}$, and, for each leaf corresponding to a repeated marking labelled with $l_i$, its repetition is labelled rep($l_i$).

The full prefix fp(TS) is finite, since the length of a path cannot exceed the number of states $Q$ in the TS, and every node has a finite number of children.

For each maximal path $\pi$ on $L = $ fp(TS), we will denote with $l(\pi)$ the leaf of the path, and, if $l(\pi)$ is not a deadlock, we will denote as rep($l(\pi)$) the node preceding $l(\pi)$ and such that $\mu(l(\pi)) = \mu(\text{rep}(l(\pi)))$. In addition, we will denote as $L_{\text{rep}(l(\pi))}$ the subtree of $L$ with root rep($l(\pi)$).

**Lemma 2.** *Let $\pi$ be a path on the TS-tree, and $t \in T$ an element of the alphabet of TS. If $n \leq \lambda(\pi)(t)$, but $t \notin \pi \cap $ fp(TS), then there is another path $\pi'$ in the TS-tree such that $\lambda(\pi') \subseteq \lambda(\pi)$, $n \leq \lambda(\pi')(t)$, and $t \in \pi' \cap $ fp(TS).*

*Proof.* Let $l(\pi_1)$ be the leaf of $\pi_1 = \pi \cap $ fp(TS) and rep($l(\pi_1)$) its repetition in the prefix. We can construct the path $\pi'_1 = peel(\pi, \pi_{\text{rep}(l(\pi_1)),l(\pi_1)})$. If $t \in \pi_2 = \pi'_1 \cap $ fp(TS) we can stop the construction, otherwise we repeat the procedure by considering $l(\pi_2)$. Since the distance between the root and the first occurrence of $t$ is finite, and every step of the peeling reduces it, after a finite number of peeling operations the thesis must be satisfied. $\square$

Let $\pi'$ be a maximal path on the TS-tree, and $\pi$ its prefix on fp(TS). If $l(\pi)$ is not a deadlock, there must be a prefix of $\pi'$ extending $\pi$ with a segment isomorphic to another segment in fp(TS) starting from rep($l(\pi)$) and arriving to a leaf of fp(TS). Let $\pi_1$ be such a segment; we denote with $\pi + \pi_1$ the prefix of $\pi'$ obtained by concatenating $\pi$ with a segment isomorphic to $\pi_1$. If $l(\pi_1)$ is not a deadlock, then $\pi + \pi_1$ can be extended further by looking in fp(TS) which segments start from rep($l(\pi_1)$). Among them, there must be a segment $\pi_2$ such that $\pi + \pi_1$ can be extended with a segment isomorphic to $\pi_2$, obtaining a longer prefix of $\pi'$: $\pi + \pi_1 + \pi_2$.

Proceeding in this way, we can obtain an arbitrarily long prefix of $\pi'$ from fp(TS).

Let $\Sigma = (P, T, F, W, m_0)$ be a bounded equal-conflict PT system, and $Y \subseteq T$. We discussed in Sect. 4.2 that RMG$_Y$-tree represents all the maximal paths on RMG$_Y$, i.e.: all the maximal paths on MaxMg without any occurrence of $Y$. The considerations above show that considering fp(RMG$_Y$) is sufficient to construct any prefix of the paths in RMG$_Y$-tree, and therefore it can be used to compute the collective reveals relation.

### 4.4   An Algorithm for the Collective Reveals Relation

In this section, given a bounded equal-conflict PT system $\Sigma = (P, T, F, W, m_0)$, $n \in \mathbf{N}$, and $X, Y \subseteq T$, we propose an algorithm to check if the relation $n.X \rightarrowtail Y$, as defined in Definition 5, holds on $\Sigma$, through the full prefix $\text{fp}(\text{RMG}_Y)$. Its pseudo-code is presented in Algorithm 2. Since reveals (Definition 1) and repeated reveals (Definition 3) can be expressed as special cases of collective reveals (see Remark 6), the algorithm allows to compute also these relations. In Sect. 4.5, we will discuss how to modify it to compute also extended-repeated reveals (Definition 4).

Algorithm 2 takes as input the full prefix $L = \text{fp}(\text{RMG}_Y)$, the set of transitions $X$, and the positive number $n$. If there is no path in the $\text{RMG}_Y$ with at least $n$ occurrences of transitions of $X$, then the algorithm returns *true*, otherwise it returns *false*. The main function of the algorithm is *repex*. The variable 'Paths' includes all the prefixes of the paths of the $\text{RMG}_Y$-tree on which we need to verify the relation. Initially, it includes all the paths in $\text{fp}(\text{RMG}_Y)$ with at least an occurrence of a transition of $X$ (this is justified by Lemma 2). 'Paths' is also the input arguments of the function *extendPaths*. This function checks which input paths already include at least $n$ occurrences of transitions of $X$, and, if it finds a path with $n$ occurrences of $X$, it sets the value of 'stop' to true, and stops the execution. In this case, also the main function will stop, and return false, since the path could be extended to a maximal path of the $\text{RMG}_Y$-tree without adding any new transition label. Since such a path does not have any occurrence of $Y$ by construction, and it is also a maximal path of the MaxMg-tree, then $n.X \not\rightarrowtail Y$.

Let $\pi$ be a path with less than $n$ occurrences of $X$; then the algorithm needs to check which extensions could be useful to add more occurrences of transitions of $X$. If $\pi$ ends with a deadlock, it is not possible to extend it further, and since there are no $n$ occurrences of $X$ we are not interested in it. Otherwise, $\text{rep}(l(\pi))$ is well defined, and all the paths extending $\pi$ are labelled as one of the paths starting from $\text{rep}(l(\pi))$. Let *ext* be any path starting from $\text{rep}(l(\pi))$. If *ext* does not have any occurrence of $X$ and ends with a deadlock, then we do not need to consider it, since the concatenation $\pi + ext$ of $\pi$ and *ext* does not have $n$ occurrences of $X$. Also, we do not consider the extension of $\pi$ with no occurrence of $X$, and such that $\text{rep}(l(\pi)) \leq \text{rep}(l(ext))$, since each path with such a prefix and $n$ occurrences of $X$ can be peeled removing *ext* and still have $n$ occurrences of $X$. All the other extensions are put in the variable 'newPaths', and will be considered in the next round. If there are no paths left to analyse, then the algorithm returns true.

*Example 9.* Consider the PT system $\Sigma$ in Fig. 7. Assume that we want to check the relation $2.\{a, c\} \rightarrowtail \{b\}$. Given the PT system $\Sigma$ and the set $\{b\}$, Algorithm 1 computes the reduced marking graph $\text{RMG}_{\{b\}}(\Sigma)$ which is also illustrated in Fig. 8. This procedure results in a marking graph which only produces the maximal runs without an occurrence of $\{b\}$. Then the full prefix of the reduced graph $(\text{fp}(\text{RMG}_{\{b\}}(\Sigma))$ is constructed as defined in Definition 7 and is illustrated in Fig. 9. Algorithm 2 takes $\text{fp}(\text{RMG}_{\{b\}}(\Sigma))$, the set $\{a, c\}$ and number 2 as input.

**Algorithm 2** Computing collective reveals

---

**procedure** REPEX($L$ : fp(RMG$_Y$), $X \subseteq T, n \in \mathbf{N}$)
    Paths = The list of maximal paths in $L$ with at least an element of $X$
    **while** Paths $\neq$ [] **do**
        Paths, stop = extendPaths(Paths)
        **if** stop == True **then**
            **return** False
        **end if**
    **end while**
    **return** True
**end procedure**

**procedure** EXTENDPATHS(Paths)
    # returns a pair $(x, y)$, where $x$ is a list of paths, and $y$ is a boolean value
    newPaths = []
    **for** $\pi \in$ Paths **do**
        **if** $|\pi \cap X| \geq n$ **then**
            **return** [], True
        **else if** $l(\pi)$ is not a deadlock **then**
            **for** $ext \in L_{rep(l(\pi))}$ **do**
                **if** $ext \cap X \neq \emptyset \vee (rep(l(ext)) < rep(l(\pi)))$ **then**
                    newPaths.append($\pi + ext$)
                **end if**
            **end for**
        **end if**
    **end for**
    **return** newPaths, False
**end procedure**
# $|\pi \cap X|$ is equivalent to $\sum_{t \in X} \lambda(\pi)(t)$

---

When the algorithm runs, it detects that there is no maximal path with at least two occurrences of $\{a, c\}$. Knowing that the relation is defined for the net system $\Sigma$, this means that $2.\{a, c\} \twoheadrightarrow \{b\}$.

Now let us assume that we want to check the relation $f \triangleright h$ which is equivalent to $1.\{f\} \twoheadrightarrow \{h\}$. We can follow the same procedure as above. Given the net system $\Sigma$ and the set $\{h\}$, Algorithm 1 produces the reduced marking graph RMG$_{\{h\}}(\Sigma)$ which is also illustrated in Fig. 8. The full prefix fp(RMG$_{\{h\}}(\Sigma)$) is illustrated in Fig. 9. Algorithm 2 takes fp(RMG$_{\{h\}}(\Sigma)$), the set $\{f\}$ and number 1 as input. When the algorithm runs, it detects that there is no maximal path with at least an occurrence of $f$. Knowing that the relation is defined for the net system $\Sigma$, this means that $f \triangleright h$.

To check the relation $2.\{a, c\} \twoheadrightarrow \{h\}$, we call Algorithm 2 with fp(RMG$_{\{h\}}(\Sigma)$), the set $\{a, c\}$ and number 2 as input. The algorithm finds a maximal run such that $h$ does not occur but the number of occurrences of $\{a, c\}$ is 2. In fact, the prefix of RMG$_{\{h\}}(\Sigma)$-tree illustrated in Fig. 9 can be extended to produce many of such maximal runs, e.g., the maximal run which repeats the sequence $abcdbab$, as well as $abab$ or $abcdb$. With these given inputs, Algorithm 2 returns *false* meaning that $2.\{a, c\} \not\rightarrow \{h\}$.

Finally, consider the relations $h \triangleright g$ and $2.\{h\} \rightarrow \{g\}$. The first relation holds, as we can easily see from the $\text{RMG}_{\{g\}}$-tree, where there is a path with an occurrence of $h$, whereas the second does not. In order to check that $2.\{h\} \not\rightarrow \{g\}$, the algorithm starts from the $\text{RMG}_{\{g\}}$-tree and checks whether the paths with at least an occurrence of $h$ can be extended in order to have a second occurrence. Since in the $\text{RMG}_{\{g\}}$-tree all the leaves following an occurrence of $h$ are associated to deadlocks, we cannot elongate the paths anymore, and therefore we cannot find a maximal path with 2 occurrences of $h$ without any occurrence of $g$.

**Lemma 3.** *The leaf of every path constructed by the algorithm is a deadlock, or is associated with a marking that is already present in the path.*

*Proof.* First we observe that every path constructed by the algorithm ends with a node equivalent to a leaf in the prefix tree. For each leaf, the path in the tree starting from the root and arriving to it is unique.

Let $r$ be the root of the tree, $\pi_0 \pi_1' ... \pi_n'$ be a path constructed by the algorithm, where $\pi_0$ is a maximal path in the prefix tree and $\pi_i'$ is an added segment isomorphic to a segment $\pi_i$ starting from $\text{rep}(l(\pi_{i-1}))$ (the repetition of the leaf $l(\pi_{i-1})$ of the segment $\pi_{i-1}$) and ending in $l(\pi_i)$, a leaf of the prefix tree. We have to prove that, if the leaf of the constructed path is not a deadlock, then the repetition $\text{rep}(l(\pi_n'))$ of the leaf $l(\pi_n')$ of the path belongs to the path itself, i.e., $\text{rep}(l(\pi_n'))$ is in $\pi_0 \pi_1' ... \pi_n'$.

We prove it by induction. Let $l(\pi_1')$ be the leaf of $\pi_0 \pi_1'$; if it is not a deadlock, then $\text{rep}(l(\pi_1'))$ is either in $\pi_1'$ or inside $[r, \text{rep}(l(\pi_0))]$, where $[r, \text{rep}(l(\pi_0))]$ is the path from the root $r$ to the repetition of the leaf of $\pi_0$ and then it is contained in $\pi_0$. Then $\text{rep}(l(\pi_1')) \in \pi_0 \pi_1'$.

We now assume the constructed path $\pi_0 \pi_1' ... \pi_i'$ ends either with a deadlock, or with a node whose repetition $\text{rep}(l(\pi_i'))$ is either in $\pi_i'$ or in the segment $[r, \text{rep}(l(\pi_{i-1}'))]$, which is contained in $\pi_0 \pi_1' ... \pi_{i-1}'$, and then $\text{rep}(l(\pi_i')) \in \pi_0 \pi_1' ... \pi_i'$.

We prove that the path $\pi_0 \pi_1' ... \pi_{i+1}'$ ends either with a deadlock, or with a node whose repetition $\text{rep}(l(\pi_{i+1}'))$ is either in $\pi_{i+1}'$ or in the segment $[r, \text{rep}(l(\pi_i'))]$, which is contained in $\pi_0 \pi_1' ... \pi_i'$, and therefore $\text{rep}(l(\pi_{i+1}')) \in \pi_0 \pi_1' ... \pi_{i+1}'$. In fact, $\pi_{i+1}'$ is isomorphic to a segment $\pi_{i+1}$ in the prefix tree starting from $\text{rep}(l(\pi_i))$, which is between $r$ and $l(\pi_i)$, and ending in a leaf $l(\pi_{i+1})$ of the prefix tree. This last leaf is either a deadlock, or has a repetition, which is either in $\pi_{i+1}$ or in $[r, \text{rep}(l(\pi_i))]$; since $\text{rep}(l(\pi_i'))$ is by inductive hypothesis in $\pi_0 \pi_1' ... \pi_i'$, we get the thesis. $\square$

**Lemma 4.** *Let $\pi$ be any maximal path in the $\text{RMG}_Y$-tree. If $\pi$ has in total at least $n$ occurrences of transitions belonging to $X$, then there is at least a path $\pi'$ analysed by the algorithm with in total at least $n$ occurrences of transitions of $X$, such that $\lambda(\pi') \subseteq \lambda(\pi)$.*

*Proof.* We show that we can peel $\pi$ and obtain a maximal path of the $RMG_Y$-tree such that its prefix is analysed. For Lemma 2, we can peel $\pi$ and obtain a path $\pi_1$ such that at least an occurrence of $X$ appears in its prefix in $fp(RMG_Y)$. Let $\pi_1'$ be such prefix. If $\pi_1'$ has $n$ occurrences of $X$, we don't need to proceed further; otherwise $\pi_1'$ must be followed in $\pi_1$ by a path isomorphic to a path starting from $rep(l(\pi_1'))$. Let $\pi_2'$ be this segment. If $\pi_2'$ has at least an occurrence of a transition of $X$, or $rep(l(\pi_2'))$ precedes $rep(l(\pi_1'))$, this elongation of the prefix has been considered by the algorithm. If $\pi_2'$ has no occurrences of $X$ and $rep(l(\pi_2')) \geq rep(l(\pi_1'))$, then we can peel $\pi_1$ of the part between $rep(l(\pi_2'))$ and $l(\pi_2')$, obtaining $\pi_1^2$. Since in $\pi_2'$ there are no elements of $X$, this cannot influence their number in $\pi_1^2$, and $\lambda(\pi_1^2) \subseteq \lambda(\pi_1)$. The path $\pi_1^2$ has also a prefix made by $\pi_1'$ concatenated with a segment starting from $rep(l(\pi_1'))$. Let $\pi_3'$ be this segment. If $rep(l(\pi_3')) \geq rep(l(\pi_1'))$, we repeat the peeling procedure. Since $\pi_1$ has $n$ occurrence of $X$ by hypothesis, after a finite number $i$ of steps, we will obtain a peeled maximal run $\pi_1^i$ such that $rep(l(\pi_i')) < rep(l(\pi_1'))$, with $\pi_i'$ segment starting from $rep(l(\pi_1'))$ elongating the segment $\pi_1'$, or $\pi_i'$ has at least an occurrence of $X$. We can repeat this reasoning until obtaining a prefix with at least $n$ occurrences of $X$. Since in our steps we never remove any of those, and $\pi$ includes them by hypothesis, this procedure ends after a finite number of steps. By construction, all the transitions in the constructed prefix are also in $\pi$, therefore we produced a prefix as required from the thesis. □

**Theorem 1.** *Algorithm 2 is correct.*

*Proof.* As first step we show that if the algorithm returns false, then $n.X \nrightarrow Y$. The algorithm returns false if the variable 'stop' is true. The value of 'stop' is selected into the function *extendPaths*, and it is set to true if a path is found with $n$ occurrences of $X$. Each prefix is constructed so that the final leaf is a deadlock for the path, or it is repeated previously; in the first case the path is already maximal, in the second case, the path can be extended to a maximal path without adding any new transition by repeating infinitely often the segment between the leaf of the prefix and its repetition. The existence of such a repetition is guaranteed by Lemma 3. In both cases there is a maximal run with at least $n$ occurrences of $X$ and none in $Y$ (by construction), therefore $n.X \nrightarrow Y$.

We now show that if the algorithm returns true, then either $n.X \rightarrow Y$, or the relation is undefined because there is no path with $n$ occurrences of $X$. This is a consequence of Lemma 4 and of the construction of $RMG_Y$: if there were a path with $n$ occurrences of $X$ and none in $Y$, by construction it would be a path of the $RMG_Y$-tree, and Lemma 4 guarantees that we would analyse a prefix with the same feature, but if this happens, the algorithm returns false. □

**Theorem 2.** *Algorithm 2 terminates.*

*Proof.* The algorithm ends when the variable 'Paths' becomes empty, or when a path with $n$ occurrences of $X$ was found. We show that 'Paths' becomes empty after a finite number of steps. The variable 'Paths' is a list of prefixes of paths in the $RMG_Y$-tree. Its content in each iteration of the while loop is entirely determined by the function *extendPaths*, that elongate some of its elements. In particular, the function elongates the paths with less of $n$ occurrences of $X$. Each path can be elongated in two ways: adding at least an additional occurrence of $X$, and this happens only finitely many times, since when the path has at least $n$ occurrences of $X$ it is not extended anymore, or with a segment whose repetition of the leaf is strictly closer to the root than the repetition of the previous leaf. Also in this second case the number of extension is finite, since the distance between each node and the root is finite.                    □

*Remark 8.* To compute the reveals relation, the algorithm needs to analyse only the maximal runs of the prefix tree, without further extensions. This is coherent with the result in [5], where the authors show that for 1-safe free-choice Petri nets, $\forall a, b \in T$, $a \rhd b$ iff for each maximal path $\pi$ in the prefix, if $a \in \pi$, then $b \in \pi$.

## 4.5  Variations of the Algorithm

In this section we discuss how the algorithm presented in Sect. 4.4 could be modified to extend its use for computing multiple reveals relations or for checking extended-reveals relations.

Algorithm 1 and Algorithm 2 can be used to compute a given collective reveals relation; it works on a tree structure derived from a reduction of MaxMg. This computation modifies the one presented in [3], where the tree is constructed for the entire MaxMg. In many cases, when we need to compute a single instance of a reveals relation, the reduced version is more efficient (see Sect. 5 for a performance comparison between the two). However, if we need to compute multiple relations on the same system, each one with a different set of revealed transitions, having the whole tree may save some computation, since the tree needs to be computed only once. As already discussed in Sect. 4.1, computing the MaxMg-tree is also useful when we need to know whether an instance of the relation is undefined.

Algorithm 2 can be adapted to compute the relation presented in Definition 4. Here we give a sketch of how this can be done. Let $X = \{t_1, ..., t_k\}$ and $Y$ be the input sets. Instead of having just a single threshold $n$ in input as for repeated reveals, the input must include all the thresholds $\{n_1, ..., n_k\}$ related to transitions of $X$, and the information about how they are associated to these transitions. Since the number of observations in which we are interested changes for every transition, when the algorithm needs to decide whether a path can stop or needs to be extended, it must consider all transitions of $X$ separately, each with its threshold. In addition, if a path has already reached the number of required occurrences of a certain transition, we should stop to consider this transition as useful when we evaluate the possible extensions. Analogously to collective reveals, we can use both the $RMG_Y$-tree or the MaxMg-tree to compute extended-repeated reveals, according to the number of relations that we need to compute on the same system.

Since extended reveals (Definition 2) can be expressed as a special case of extended-repeated reveals, modifying the algorithm as described would allow for its computation.

## 5  Implementation and Experiments

In order to get a better understanding of the usability of our algorithms in practice, we implemented and tested them on some examples. The code is available here: https://github.com/MC3-lab/mscTree. Since the contribution of this paper is mainly theoretical, we did not try to optimise the code and did not carry out a systematic set of experiments; this is left as future work. However, we think that the experiments and considerations presented in this section can be useful to get some insights on the algorithm efficiency and to suggest directions for future improvements.

Our tool takes as input a PT system specified in the PNML format [36], and has the following usage options.

1. The user can specify on the command line a collective reveals relation $n.X \rightarrow Y$. In this case, the tool proceeds as described in Sect. 4: first it computes $\mathrm{RMG}_Y$, then the $\mathrm{RMG}_Y$-tree, and finally decides whether $n.X \rightarrow Y$, using the tree.
2. The user may also not specify any relation on the command line, and require the computation of MaxMg and of the MaxMg-tree. In this case, after the computation of the MaxMg-tree, the user can specify any collective reveals relation in an interactive way. For the detailed algorithm, see [3].
3. Finally, the user may ask for the computation of all the (simple) reveals relations (Definition 1) on the tree. As in the previous case, this is done by computing MaxMg and the MaxMg-tree, and by looking at the leaves of the tree. To increase the efficiency, instead of checking the relations one by one, for each leaf we check all the reveals relations that cannot hold, since they are denied by that path, and if a relation is not excluded by any leaf, then it must hold in the system.

For our experiments we considered the following sets of PT systems. (1) We combined in different ways the nets shown in previous sections (rows pn1 through pn6 in the tables). (2) We developed a set of examples inspired by the Kanban PT systems in [1], used as benchmark for the tool [2] (rows k33, k34, and k4 in the tables). (3) Again from [1], we tested two PT systems describing industrial business process models [19] (rows IBM319 and IBM703); these are interesting models, since we expect business processes to be an application of the methods described in this paper.

For each PT system, we computed the number of reachable markings (column RMa); the number of markings in MaxMg (MM) and $\mathrm{RMG}_Y$ (MMY); the number of leaves in the MaxMg-tree (L) and $\mathrm{RMG}_Y$-tree for some set of transitions $Y$ (LY); the time needed for computing MaxMg (TMM); the time needed for computing the MaxMg-tree (Tt); the time for computing the $\mathrm{RMG}_Y$-tree

(TYt); the time for computing a collective reveals relation (Trev); the time to compute all the reveals relations (Tall). The results of our experiments are in Table 1 and Table 2. All times are given in seconds. The second column in Table 1 ($\#\Sigma$) denotes the sum of places and transitions in the PT system. Missing values denote cases in which we stopped the computation before termination, after at least an hour.

The PNML files for all these nets are available in the git repository of our tool.

**Table 1.** Results of the experiments using MaxMg.

| Name | $\#\Sigma$ | RMa | MM | L | TMM | Tt | Trev | Tall |
|------|------|-----|-----|-----|------|------|------|------|
| pn1 | 85 | 1289 | 172 | 44 | 0.244 | 0.018 | 0.001 | 0.384 |
| pn2 | 88 | 408630 | 1173 | 315 | 0.370 | 0.216 | 0.005 | 0.418 |
| pn3 | 91 | 2093213 | 3291 | 1494 | 0.953 | 1.150 | 0.012 | 0.511 |
| pn4 | 80 | 2252 | 408 | 182 | 0.267 | 0.101 | 0.002 | 0.397 |
| pn5 | 83 | 958197 | 3420 | 2656 | 0.970 | 4.529 | 0.021 | 0.613 |
| pn6 | 129 | $\sim 15 \cdot 10^6$ | 143341 | 132800 | 2622.647 | 374.301 | 5.997 | 424.937 |
| k33-f1 | 25 | 64 | 29 | 155 | 0.002 | 0.029 | 0.052 | 0.021 |
| k33-f2 | 25 | 64 | 29 | 155 | 0.002 | 0.029 | 0.001 | 0.021 |
| k34 | 25 | 160 | 129 | – | 0.012 | – | – | – |
| k4 | 32 | 160 | 49 | 3339 | 0.234 | 0.945 | 661.353 | 0.539 |
| IBM319 | 431 | 2482 | 325 | 1282 | 0.387 | 28.717 | 0.007 | 30.147 |
| IBM703 | 546 | 8370 | 732 | 1948 | 1.007 | 66.251 | 0.015 | 67.109 |

From the results we can observe that in some cases, such as the sets of examples (1) and (3), using maximal-step semantics significantly reduces the number of markings to analyse. In the sets of examples (2) and (3), the number of leaves in the tree is larger than the number of nodes in MaxMg and RMG; this suggests that some of the constructed subtrees may be isomorphic, and therefore it would be possible to prune them. However, deciding how to prune the tree is not trivial, since two nodes in the prefix associated to the same marking but with a different past, may be the starting point of non-isomorphic subtrees. Some criteria that we plan to test in future works consist in pruning the tree if it reaches a node whose marking has already been analysed and the set of markings preceding the repeated node includes all the marking in the past of the node already analysed, or in pruning the tree if we reach a node that has already been analysed, and that is not part of any cycle.

Set (2) is particularly interesting. These nets are critical for our algorithm and tool; the interplay between concurrency among components and local conflicts has two effects: first, there is no relevant difference between the number of reachable markings in the full marking graph and in the reduced marking graph;

**Table 2.** Results of the experiments using $RMG_Y$.

| Name | MMY | LY | TMMY | TYt | Trev |
|------|-----|-----|------|-----|------|
| pn1 | 146 | 32 | 0.243 | 0.013 | $1.27 \cdot 10^{-4}$ |
| pn2 | 895 | 207 | 0.350 | 0.150 | 0.001 |
| pn3 | 2086 | 684 | 0.675 | 0.491 | 0.003 |
| pn4 | 357 | 169 | 0.259 | 0.0900 | $4.15 \cdot 10^{-4}$ |
| pn5 | 1089 | 498 | 0.357 | 0.418 | 0.002 |
| pn6 | 29946 | 18592 | 148.412 | 52.011 | 0.109 |
| k33-f1 | 3 | 1 | $2.98 \cdot 10^{-4}$ | $3.89 \cdot 10^{-5}$ | $8.58 \cdot 10^{-6}$ |
| k34-f2 | 23 | 40 | 0.002 | 0.012 | $9.44 \cdot 10^{-5}$ |
| k34-f1 | 3 | 1 | 0.001 | $3.98 \cdot 10^{-5}$ | $8.34 \cdot 10^{-6}$ |
| k34-f2 | 41 | 690 | 0.006 | 0.158 | 0.001 |
| k4 | 16 | 38 | 0.232 | 0.005 | $7.25 \cdot 10^{-5}$ |
| IBM319 | 281 | 610 | 0.230 | 13.801 | 0.002 |
| IBM703 | 714 | 1860 | 0.971 | 61.861 | 0.006 |

second, the tree is very large, because many different combinations of maximal steps are possible, thus generating many branches, and long paths before returning to the same marking. Hence, for these nets, a small number of components can become unfeasible; the use of the reduction technique improves anyway the performance for these nets.

The reduction proposed in this paper seems to improve the performance in all the steps of the algorithm, and in case of a large numbers of markings in MaxMg or in the MaxMg-tree, it can become very convenient, even if we need to compute a few reveals relations. The efficiency of the reduction of the MaxMg-tree strongly depends on the set $Y$; in some cases, removing the arcs with $Y$ allows to cut a huge number of nodes in the tree, whereas in other cases, the number of nodes is similar in the $RMG_Y$-tree and in the MaxMg-tree.

## 6   Conclusion

In this paper, which extends [3], we have studied two variants of the "reveals" relation, namely extended-repeated reveals and collective reveals, which were introduced in [3]. The two relations, defined for transitions of general PT nets, express positive information flow. The existence of a reveals relation (or of its variants) between transitions means that the occurrence of one gives information about the other one. The security of a system can be compromised when a "low" transition reveals a "high" transition.

Building upon the results from [3,5], we have provided an algorithm to compute the parametric relations defined in [3], for distributed systems modelled with bounded equal-conflict PT systems. Unlike the algorithm presented in [3], the one presented in this paper does not need to construct the complete marking graph with maximal steps, but it constructs a reduction based on the specific relation that one needs to compute. In this way, the relation is computed on a smaller structure, allowing the algorithm to check it faster. As in [3], the methods provided in this paper cover the computation of all the reveals variants and can be used to perform information-flow analysis on bounded equal-conflict PT systems.

The algorithms presented in the paper have been implemented, and a first round of experiments has been carried out, as discussed in Sect. 5.

One of our next steps will be performing a complexity analysis of the proposed methods and working on improving their efficiency. This includes investigating a shorter prefix and more efficient algorithms. We plan to work on extending our results to more general classes of Petri nets such as unbounded equal-conflict PT systems. We will explore the practical use of our methods for both information-flow analysis and verification of other desired behavioural properties of complex distributed systems. We will also explore different approaches to information-flow analysis on Petri nets by considering games like in [4,9].

**Acknowledgements.** The authors thank the reviewers for their precious comments. This work is partially supported by the Italian MUR.

# References

1. Model Checking Contest 2023. https://mcc.lip6.fr/2023/models.php. Accessed 28 Nov 2022
2. SMART: Stochastic Model-checking Analyzer for Reliability and Timing. https://asminer.github.io/smart/. Accessed 28 Nov 2022
3. Adobbati, F., Bernardinello, L., Kilinç Soylu, G., Pomello, L.: Information flow among transitions of bounded equal-conflict Petri nets. In: Köhler-Bussmeier, M., Moldt, D., Rölke, H. (eds.) Petri Nets and Software Engineering 2022, Bergen, Norway. CEUR Workshop Proceedings, vol. 3170, pp. 60–79. CEUR-WS.org (2022). http://ceur-ws.org/Vol-3170/paper4.pdf
4. Adobbati, F., Bernardinello, L., Pomello, L.: A two-player asynchronous game on fully observable Petri nets. Trans. Petri Nets Other Model. Concurr. **15**, 126–149 (2021). https://doi.org/10.1007/978-3-662-63079-2_6
5. Adobbati, F., Kılınç Soylu, G., Puerto Aubel, A.: A finite prefix for analyzing information flow among transitions of a free-choice net. IEEE Access **10**, 38483–38501 (2022). https://doi.org/10.1109/ACCESS.2022.3165185
6. Balaguer, S., Chatain, T., Haar, S.: Building tight occurrence nets from reveals relations. In: Caillaud, B., Carmona, J., Hiraishi, K. (eds.) Proceedings of the 11th ACSD, Newcastle Upon Tyne, UK, pp. 44–53. IEEE (2011). https://doi.org/10.1109/ACSD.2011.16
7. Baldan, P., Carraro, A.: Non-interference by unfolding. In: Ciardo, G., Kindler, E. (eds.) PETRI NETS 2014. LNCS, vol. 8489, pp. 190–209. Springer, Cham (2014). https://doi.org/10.1007/978-3-319-07734-5_11
8. Basile, F., De Tommasi, G., Sterle, C.: Noninterference enforcement via supervisory control in bounded Petri nets. IEEE Trans. Automat. Contr. **66**(8), 3653–3666 (2021). https://doi.org/10.1109/TAC.2020.3024274

9. Bernardinello, L., Kılınç, G., Pomello, L.: Weak observable liveness and infinite games on finite graphs. In: van der Aalst, W., Best, E. (eds.) PETRI NETS 2017. LNCS, vol. 10258, pp. 181–199. Springer, Cham (2017). https://doi.org/10.1007/978-3-319-57861-3_12

10. Bernardinello, L., Kılınç, G., Pomello, L.: Non-interference notions based on reveals and excludes relations for Petri nets. Trans. Petri Nets Other Model. Concurr. **11**, 49–70 (2016). https://doi.org/10.1007/978-3-662-53401-4_3

11. Best, E., Darondeau, P., Gorrieri, R.: On the decidability of non interference over unbounded Petri nets. In: Chatzikokolakis, K., Cortier, V. (eds.) Proceedings of the 8th SecCo, Paris, France, EPTCS, vol. 51, pp. 16–33 (2010). https://doi.org/10.4204/EPTCS.51.2

12. Best, E., Devillers, R.: Sequential and concurrent behaviour in Petri net theory. Theor. Comput. Sci. **55**(1), 87–136 (1987). https://doi.org/10.1016/0304-3975(87)90090-9

13. Boudol, G., Castellani, I.: Noninterference for concurrent programs and thread systems. Theor. Comput. Sci. **281**(1–2), 109–130 (2002). https://doi.org/10.1016/S0304-3975(02)00010-5

14. Busi, N., Gorrieri, R.: A survey on non-interference with Petri nets. In: Desel, J., Reisig, W., Rozenberg, G. (eds.) ACPN 2003. LNCS, vol. 3098, pp. 328–344. Springer, Heidelberg (2004). https://doi.org/10.1007/978-3-540-27755-2_8

15. Busi, N., Gorrieri, R.: Structural non-interference in elementary and trace nets. Math. Struct. Comput. Sci. **19**(6), 1065–1090 (2009)

16. Desel, J., Esparza, J.: Free Choice Petri Nets. Cambridge Tracts in Theoretical Computer Science, Cambridge University Press (1995). https://doi.org/10.1017/CBO9780511526558

17. Engelfriet, J.: Branching processes of Petri nets. Acta Inf. **28**, 575–591 (1991). https://doi.org/10.1007/BF01463946

18. Esparza, J., Römer, S., Vogler, W.: An improvement of McMillan's unfolding algorithm. Formal Methods Syst. Des. **20**, 285–310 (2002). https://doi.org/10.1023/A:1014746130920

19. Fahland, D., et al.: Instantaneous soundness checking of industrial business process models. In: Dayal, U., Eder, J., Koehler, J., Reijers, H.A. (eds.) BPM 2009. LNCS, vol. 5701, pp. 278–293. Springer, Heidelberg (2009). https://doi.org/10.1007/978-3-642-03848-8_19

20. Focardi, R., Gorrieri, R.: A taxonomy of security properties for process algebras. J. Comput. Secur. **3**(1), 5–34 (1995)

21. Goguen, J.A., Meseguer, J.: Security policies and security models. In: Proceedings of the IEEE Symposium on Security and Privacy, pp. 11–20 (1982)

22. Goltz, U., Reisig, W.: The non-sequential behaviour of Petri nets. Inf. Control **57**(2), 125–147 (1983). https://doi.org/10.1016/S0019-9958(83)80040-0

23. Haar, S.: Unfold and cover: qualitative diagnosability for Petri nets. In: Proceedings of the 46th IEEE Conference on Decision Control (2007)

24. Haar, S., Rodríguez, C., Schwoon, S.: Reveal your faults: it's only fair! In: Proceedings of the 13th ACSD, Barcelona, Spain, pp. 120–129 (2013)

25. Janicki, R., Lauer, P.E., Koutny, M., Devillers, R.: Concurrent and maximally concurrent evolution of nonsequential systems. Theor. Comput. Sci. **43**, 213–238 (1986)

26. Kılınç, G.: Formal notions of non-interference and liveness for distributed systems. Ph.D. thesis, Univ. Milano-Bicocca, DISCo, Milano, Italy (2016)

27. Mantel, H.: A uniform framework for the formal specification and verification of information flow security. Ph.D. thesis, Saarland University, Saarbrücken, Germany (2003). http://scidok.sulb.uni-saarland.de/volltexte/2004/202/index.html

28. Mantel, H.: Information flow and noninterference. In: van Tilborg, H.C.A., Jajodia, S. (eds.) Encyclopedia of Cryptography and Security, 2nd edn, pp. 605–607. Springer, Heidelberg (2011). https://doi.org/10.1007/978-1-4419-5906-5_874

29. McCullough, D.: Specifications for multi-level security and a hook-up. In: Proceedings of the IEEE Symposium on Security and Privacy, p. 161 (1987). https://doi.org/10.1109/SP.1987.10009

30. McLean, J.: A general theory of composition for a class of "possibilistic" properties. IEEE Trans. Software Eng. **22**(1), 53–67 (1996). https://doi.org/10.1109/32.481534

31. Murata, T.: Petri nets: properties, analysis and applications. Proc. IEEE **77**(4), 541–580 (1989). https://doi.org/10.1109/5.24143

32. Smith, E.: On the border of causality: contact and confusion. Theor. Comput. Sci. **153**(1), 245–270 (1996). https://doi.org/10.1016/0304-3975(95)00123-9

33. Sutherland, D.: A model of information. In: Proceedings of the 9th National Computer Security Conference, vol. 247, pp. 175–183 (1986)

34. Teruel, E., Silva, M.: Liveness and home states in equal conflict systems. In: Ajmone Marsan, M. (ed.) Application and Theory of Petri Nets 1993. LNCS, vol. 691, pp. 415–432. Springer, Heidelberg (1993). https://doi.org/10.1007/3-540-56863-8_59

35. Thiagarajan, P.S.: Elementary net systems. In: Brauer, W., Reisig, W., Rozenberg, G. (eds.) Petri Nets: Central Models and Their Properties, Advances in Petri Nets 1986 Part I. LNCS, vol. 254, pp. 26–59. Springer, Heidelberg (1986). https://doi.org/10.1007/BFb0046835

36. Weber, M., Kindler, E.: The Petri net markup language. In: Ehrig, H., Reisig, W., Rozenberg, G., Weber, H. (eds.) Petri Net Technology for Communication-Based Systems. LNCS, vol. 2472, pp. 124–144. Springer, Heidelberg (2003). https://doi.org/10.1007/978-3-540-40022-6_7

# Analysing Adaption Processes of Hornets

Michael Köhler-Bußmeier[1]([✉]) and Heiko Rölke[2]

[1] University of Applied Science Hamburg, Berliner Tor 7, 20099 Hamburg, Germany
`michael.koehler-bussmeier@haw-hamburg.de`
[2] FH Graubünden, Pulvermühlestrasse 57, 7000 Chur, Switzerland
`heiko.roelke@fhgr.ch`

**Abstract.** In our research we study self-adapting multi-agent systems in the context of organisation-oriented design combined with the MAPE pattern (monitor, analyse, plan, and execute). We advocate a *models@run.time* approach for the planning phase to estimate the cost-benefit ratio of possible self-modifications.

In this paper we develop key values to describe the dynamics of self-adapting systems. Our main objective is to *compare* adaption dynamics of similar systems, i.e., systems that differ only slightly, e.g., w.r.t. their organisational networks.

We specify the MAPE-based adaption in the formalism of HORNETS – a formalism that uses nets as tokens, i.e., they follow the *nets-within-nets* approach. We identify abstractions of the reachability graph that focus on the adaption aspects of the processes. We develop key measures for adaption processes on these abstracted graphs. The key measures are used e.g., to compare two variations of the same adapting system.

The approach is illustrated by a case study: We analyse a HORNET-model of Axelrod's well-known tournament where the playing agents adapt their strategies during the game.

**Keywords:** Adaption · multi-agent systems · MAPE · Petri nets · Hornets · nets-within-nets · key measures

## 1 Introduction: The Dynamics of Adaption Processes

In general the evolution (i.e., adaption) of a system is determined by the inter-action aspect of adaptivity, i.e., how adaption is performed (e.g., via a cross-over of genes, when using the genetic system metaphor) and how the gene pool looks like (the "how") [1,2]. But, on the other hand, it is relevant which genes have the possibility to interact: Is there an opportunity for each pair of genes to meet and perform a cross-over in the system – or are they too separated? This aspect relates to the *network* aspect of adaptivity (the "who"). As genes are the acting entities in the system we will refer to them also as agents and the whole setting is usually formalised as a multi-agent system (MAS), which are typically based on game-theory and logic [3].[1]

---

[1] As a more practical example we may consider a company's workflow management system: The set of workflows is the gene pool, while the evolution of the workflows during the company's lifetime strongly relates to the organisational network.

© The Author(s), under exclusive license to Springer-Verlag GmbH, DE, part of Springer Nature 2024
M. Koutny et al. (Eds.): TPNOMCXVII, LNCS 14150, pp. 84–107, 2024.
https://doi.org/10.1007/978-3-662-68191-6_4

In our research, we study agent systems [4,5]. Our application domain are adaptive MAS. We use HORNETS to model the well-known MAPE-loop [6] for adaptive systems, which consists of the four phases: monitor, analyse, plan, and execute. The MAPE-loop is specified as a Petri net and this loop operates on interaction protocols of agents – a scenario, where nets-within-nets are a very reasonable formalism: The system net models the MAPE-loop and the net-tokens are the agent interaction protocols that are modified by the loop (cf. [7,8] for more details). For adaptive MAS the concept of *uncertainty* plays a major role [9]; the MAPE-loop never has perfect knowledge about the system's state; there is uncertainty about preferences of agents, duration of tasks, etc. Therefore, we do not assume that we have exactly one protocol net $N$ describing the agents' interaction, but we have a whole family of nets $N_\alpha$ where $\alpha$ is a parameter ranging over the domain of uncertainty. During our planning phase of our MAPE-loop we treat the different variants $N_\alpha$ as a *pool* of competing genes.

In this paper we study adaption processes, i.e., the trajectories of the gene pool, in the setting of discrete event system, namely in the formal framework of HORNETS [10], as this formalism has been developed to study adaptive systems [11]. In the context of HORNETS the two aspects – how and who – are naturally addressed: HORNETS are Petri nets where the tokens are Petri nets again. The surrounding net is called the system net and the net-tokens are instances of so-called object nets. The object nets model the adapting objects – as they define what can happen; and the system net models the network part together with the adaption logic itself – as the system net defines which object nets are involved and how adaption looks like. In the example of a multi-agent system the object nets describe the set of interaction protocols (multi-party workflows) and the net-tokens are the workflow instances while the system net models the whole adaption process of the MAS.

For HORNETS the concept of a gene pool is easily identified: It is the set of net-token types occurring in the given marking $\mu$. We are interested in the dynamics of this gene pool set. More specifically, our main objective is to *compare* adaption dynamics of similar systems. For the example of a workflow management system we like to compare two companies with the same initial set of workflows but with different organisational networks, i.e., we like to study the impact of the network on the adaption dynamics. We like to develop key values for these dynamics to answer questions like: *'Which multi-agent system adapts faster?'*, *'Which MAS develops a gene pool of greater diversity?'*, etc.

This paper is an extended version of [12]. The main extension is given in Sect. 2, which presents the application context of our theoretical studies, i.e., the adaption of multi-agent systems using the well-known MAPE-loop [6]. We will sketch how our analytical framework is used to study the *exploration vs. exploitation* balance – a well-known problem for adaptive systems, where one has to decide whether to explore unknown options or to optimise activities based on the observations made so far. Section 3 recalls the definition of HORNETS. The main purpose of this part is to explain the definition of the reachability graph of HORNETS. It can be skipped on first reading. The main contribution is given in Sect. 4, which describes how adaption processes can be studied in the formal framework of HORNETS. We will derive a structure describing the core adaption processes as an abstraction of the reachability graph of a given HORNET. The dynamics of the gene pool is somehow in between two other dynamics: on the one hand, it is much coarser than the dynamics of the whole HORNET as it abstracts from the internal actions of the net-tokens; on the other hand is much finer than the dynamics of the system net alone when considered as a normal P/T net. Different key values will be considered to capture essential aspects of the adaption dynamics. In Sect. 5 we exemplify the theoretical framework with a generalisation of Axelrod's well-known tournament. The tournament is a well-known example for adaption, especially in the context of genetic algorithms [1]. Here, we study the impact of differences in the agents' neighborhood for the adaption dynamics: We compare the dynamics on a *Erdős-Rényi graph* [13] to that on a *Watts-Strogatz graph* [14]. The work ends with a conclusion and an outlook.

## 2   Modelling Adaptive Systems Under Uncertainty

We investigate adaptivity of so-called *organisation-oriented MAS (Org-MAS)* [15], where one considers large-scale and agent-independent aspects of MAS, like roles, norms, positions, interaction protocols etc. Here, we discuss our insights in the context of our Org-MAS framework SONAR [16]. A SONAR model contains an organisation model together with models for the agent interaction protocols. In the following we concentrate on interaction protocols. In system models it is common that the general process structure is often well-understood, while quantitative aspects – like durations, delays etc. – are often less precisely known at design time. So, process models usually base on uncertainties $\alpha$. In many scenarios we have to make some design decisions (leading to a system's configuration $\beta$) w.r.t. these quantitative aspects $\alpha$. In our setting the system is specified by a Petri net over theses parameters: $N_\alpha(\beta)$.

We are aiming for a description of the system's changes that allows us to use the theory and methods described in this paper to analyse these adaptation processes as well. In general, we assume that our system is not exactly $N_\alpha$ – it can be any model $N_{\alpha'}$ where $\alpha'$ is a configuration that is (in some sense) similar to $\alpha$. Let $C(\alpha)$ denote the set of all configurations similar to $\alpha$. Usually, $C(\alpha)$ depends on the level of uncertainty, i.e. a higher degree of uncertainty leads to a larger set $C(\alpha)$. If one uses the analogy that the set $\{N_{\alpha'}(\beta) \mid \alpha' \in C(\alpha)\}$ is the gene-pool of the system we are able to study the impact of uncertainty within our theoretical framework presented here.

For example, the configuration $\beta$ may represent the selection logic for or-choices and $\beta$ has to be chosen in a way that minimises the total average delay. Due to the uncertainties in the quantitative parameters $\alpha$ it is highly likely that the chosen configuration $\beta$ is sub-optimal. Therefore, $\beta$ has to be adjusted at run-time whenever our knowledge about $\alpha$ improves via observations of the running system.

Consequently, we advocate to follow the models@run.time approach (cf. [11,17]) and use the system model as a part of our running system that describes the knowledge (K) about it [18]. This knowledge is used in the following way: We monitor (M) our system at run-time; observations are analysed (A) whether we have to correct our estimation of the quantitative parameters; whenever we adjust, this may lead to (re-)planning (P) of our configuration; the new config-uration is rolled out in the execution step (E). These four steps constitutes the phases of the well-known *MAPE-K execution loop* [6].

Adaptation of the configuration $\beta$ requires to evaluate different variations $N_\alpha$ of the model, where $\alpha$ is ranging over a region induced by the uncertainty about $\alpha$. Here, we evaluate by simulating variations $N_\alpha$ using a *digital twin* of the system. So, we need a formalism that allows for an easy simulation of models. We advocate a reflexive approach, i.e., we use a formalism that is able to execute itself as a sub-system. As we model our processes with Petri nets (more precisely: Petri nets including time and stochastic annotations), we argue in favour of the *nets-as-tokens* approach, also known as nets-within-nets [19]. Since our processes have an explicit algebraic structure (including usual operators like sequence, and-split, or-choice, etc.) we like to use a formalism that allows us to modify the structure of the net-tokens at run-time. These requirements is perfectly met by HORNETS [10].

While the general process structure is fixed (and described by the net $N$), the quantitative aspects $\alpha$ and $\beta$ will be changed during run-time. Let denote the process model as $N_\alpha(\beta)$. Here, $\alpha$ denotes all the quantitative aspects of the process net $N$, that are not under our control (i.e., we can only observe the system to improve our estimation of the current $\alpha$), while $\beta$ denotes all the quantitative aspects that we can adapt.

The EHORNET model is defined by the system net, which models the MAPE-loop, and the set of object nets $\mathcal{U} = \{N_\alpha(\beta) \mid \alpha, \beta\}$. The system net part (shown as an abstraction in Fig. 1) defines a MAPE-loop that operates in the following way: From observations (transition monitor), the MAPE-loop deduces (by the transition analyse) that our run-time model $N_\alpha(\beta)$ is not well described by $\alpha$ and that $\tilde{\alpha}$ is a better description. Whenever the change from $\alpha$ to $\tilde{\alpha}$ is considered as a significant one, the plan step of the loop is activated. As a result we calculate a new best response $\beta^\star$ and the execution phase replaces $N_{\tilde{\alpha}}(\beta)$ with $N_{\tilde{\alpha}}(\beta^\star)$.[2] From this point in time $N_{\tilde{\alpha}}(\beta^\star)$ is used as the process model and the loop restarts.

Instead of calculating the adjusted value $\beta^\star$ (which would restrict ourselves to exponential-distributions to obtain analytically feasible Markov-Models), we advocate for a simulative approach: Whenever we adjust our estimation for $\alpha$ we generate a family of similar parameters $\alpha_1, \ldots, \alpha_m \in C(\tilde{\alpha})$. For each $\alpha_i$ we generate several configuration candidates: $\beta_1, \ldots, \beta_n$. We evaluate all these candidate models $N_{\alpha_i}(\beta_j)$ by simulation.

---

[2] HORNETS allow also for a kind of second-order adaption in the plan step, as we are able to modify the net-token $N$ itself, e.g., we may adapt by replacing $N$ with some $N'$. This variant is studied in ongoing work.

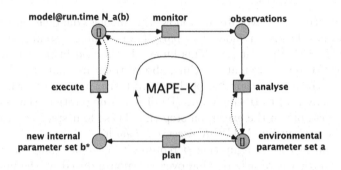

**Fig. 1.** The System Net describing the MAPE Loop.

However, the relationship of $m$ and $n$ depend on the uncertainty about the current configuration $\alpha$: Whenever our uncertainty about $\alpha$ is high we have to consider a larger number $m$ of similar parameter sets $\alpha_1, \ldots, \alpha_m$. Since we like to keep the simulation time constant, the product $m \cdot n$ is bounded/fixed. Therefore, a high uncertainty about $\alpha$ results in a large number of parameter sets $\alpha_i$, which restricts the number of configuration candidates $\beta_j$ under evaluation to a relatively small number. Conversely, a higher certainty in $\alpha$ allows for a broader exploration of configuration parameters $\beta$, i.e., a higher value of $n$. This balance is nothing else than the well known balance of *exploration vs exploitation*. Higher uncertainty demands for more exploration, while lower uncertainty allows for higher exploitation.

However, we could define the concrete impact of uncertainty for the balance of $m$ and $n$ in many different ways: Any monotonous function $f$ that maps uncertainty to a concrete value for $m$ is a possible candidate. In ongoing work we use our key values to compare how well these different candidates $f$ are able to handle uncertainty, especially in the execution of scientific calculations in computational clusters, e.g., at the *Center for Data Analytics, Visualization, and Simulation (DAViS)*, which is led by the second author.

## 3   Hornets and Object Nets

We use HORNETS to model the MAPE-loop of our multi-agent system (cf. [7,8] for more details on the MAPE-loop and [5,16] for SONAR, which is the underlying the organisation model). We have defined HORNETS in [10] as a generalisation of our object nets [20,21], which follow the *nets-within-nets* paradigm as proposed by Valk [19]. Nets-within-nets can be seen as the Petri net perspective on contextual change, in contrast to the process algebra view of the Ambient Calculus [22] or the $\pi$-calculus [23].

In this paper we will use the simplified model of Elementary Hornets (EHORNETS) from [24], where the nesting strcuture is restricted to two levels, while HORNETS [10] allow for an arbitrarily nested structure. This is done in analogy to the class of *elementary object net systems* (EOS) [20], which are the two-level specialisation of general object nets [20,21].

**Fig. 2.** An Elementary Object Net System (EOS).

*Example 1.* With HORNETS we study Petri nets where the tokens are nets again, i.e., we have a nested marking. Assume that we have the object net $N$ with places $P = \{q_1, q_2\}$ and transitions $T = \{t_1\}$. The marking of the HORNET of Fig. 2 is denoted by the nested multiset: $\widehat{p}_1[N, q_1]$. Events are also nested. We have three different kinds of events – as illustrated by the example given in Fig. 2:

1. System-autonomous: The system net transition $\widehat{t}$ fires autonomously, which moves the net-token from $\widehat{p}_1$ to $\widehat{p}_2$ without changing its marking.

$$\widehat{p}_1[N, q_1] \quad \rightarrow \quad \widehat{p}_2[N, q_1]$$

2. Object autonomous: The object net fires transition $t_1$ "moving" the black token from $q_1$ to $q_2$. The object net remains at its location $\widehat{p}_1$.

$$\widehat{p}_1[N, q_1] \quad \rightarrow \quad \widehat{p}_1[N, q_2]$$

3. Synchronisation: Whenever we add matching synchronisation inscriptions (using communication channels) at the system net transition $\widehat{t}$ and the object net transition $t_1$, then both must fire synchronously: The object net is moved to $\widehat{p}_2$ and the black token moves from $q_1$ to $q_2$ inside. Whenever synchronisation is specified, autonomous actions are forbidden.

For HORNETS we extend object nets with algebraic concepts that allow to modify the structure of the net-tokens as a result of a firing transition. This is a generalisation of the approach of algebraic nets [25], where algebraic data types replace the anonymous black tokens.

It is not hard to prove that the general HORNET formalism is Turing-complete. In [10] we have proven that there are several possibilities to simulate counter programs: One could use the nesting to encode counters. Another possibility is to encode counters in the algebraic structure of the net operators. We have also defined safeness for EOS and HORNETS to ensure finite state spaces (cf. [24, 26–30] for complexity results).

In the following we recall the definition of EHORNETS from [24]. First, we recall notations for p/t nets; then we will define the algebraic structure of the net-token and the logic used for guards. We introduce nested multisets as the marking structure. Finally, we define the firing rule, that, in general, involves a synchronisation of system net transitions with transitions of the net-tokens, i.e., we define nested events. The definition of the reachability graph will provide the ground for the analytical part in Sect. 4. The reader familiar with the firing rule of EHORNETS (Definition 2) can safely skip the remainder of this section.

*Multisets and P/T Nets.* A multiset $\mathbf{m}$ on the set $D$ is a mapping $\mathbf{m} : D \to \mathbb{N}$. Multisets can also be represented as a formal sum in the form $\mathbf{m} = \sum_{i=1}^{n} x_i$, where $x_i \in D$.

Multiset addition is defined component-wise: $(\mathbf{m}_1 + \mathbf{m}_2)(d) := \mathbf{m}_1(d) + \mathbf{m}_2(d)$. The empty multiset $\mathbf{0}$ is defined as $\mathbf{0}(d) = 0$ for all $d \in D$. Multiset-difference $\mathbf{m}_1 - \mathbf{m}_2$ is defined by $(\mathbf{m}_1 - \mathbf{m}_2)(d) := \max(\mathbf{m}_1(d) - \mathbf{m}_2(d), 0)$.

The cardinality of a multiset is $|\mathbf{m}| := \sum_{d \in D} \mathbf{m}(d)$. A multiset $\mathbf{m}$ is finite if $|\mathbf{m}| < \infty$. The set of all finite multisets over the set $D$ is denoted $MS(D)$. The *domain* of a multiset is $dom(\mathbf{m}) := \{d \in D \mid \mathbf{m}(d) > 0\}$.

Multiset notations are used for sets as well. The meaning will be apparent from its use.

Any mapping $f : D \to D'$ extends to a multiset-homomorphism $f^{\sharp} : MS(D) \to MS(D')$ by $f^{\sharp} \left( \sum_{i=1}^{n} x_i \right) = \sum_{i=1}^{n} f(x_i)$.

A *p/t net* $N$ is a tuple $N = (P, T, \mathbf{pre}, \mathbf{post})$, such that $P$ is a set of places, $T$ is a set of transitions, with $P \cap T = \emptyset$, and $\mathbf{pre}, \mathbf{post} : T \to MS(P)$ are the pre- and post-condition functions. A marking of $N$ is a multiset of places: $\mathbf{m} \in MS(P)$. We denote the enabling of $t$ in marking $\mathbf{m}$ by $\mathbf{m} \overset{t}{\to}$. Firing of $t$ is denoted by $\mathbf{m} \overset{t}{\to} \mathbf{m}'$.

*Net-Algebras.* We define the algebraic structure of object nets. For a general introduction of algebraic specifications cf. [31].

Let $K$ be a set of net-types (kinds). A (many-sorted) *specification* $(\Sigma, X, E)$ consists of a signature $\Sigma$, a family of variables $X = (X_k)_{k \in K}$, and a family of axioms $E = (E_k)_{k \in K}$.

A signature is a disjoint family $\Sigma = (\Sigma_{k_1 \cdots k_n, k})_{k_1, \cdots, k_n, k \in K}$ of operators. The set of terms of type $k$ over a signature $\Sigma$ and variables $X$ is denoted $\mathbb{T}_{\Sigma}^{k}(X)$.

We use (many-sorted) predicate logic, where the terms are generated by a signature $\Sigma$ and formulae are defined by a family of predicates $\Psi = (\Psi_n)_{n \in \mathbb{N}}$. The set of formulae is denoted $PL_{\Gamma}$, where $\Gamma = (\Sigma, X, E, \Psi)$ is the *logic structure*.

*Object Nets and Net-Algebras.* Let $\Sigma$ be a signature over $K$. A *net-algebra* assigns to each type $k \in K$ a set $\mathcal{U}_k$ of object nets – the net universe. Each object net $N \in \mathcal{U}_k, k \in K$ net is a p/t net $N = (P_N, T_N, \mathbf{pre}_N, \mathbf{post}_N)$. We identify $\mathcal{U}$ with $\bigcup_{k \in K} \mathcal{U}_k$ in the following. We assume the family $\mathcal{U} = (\mathcal{U}_k)_{k \in K}$ to be disjoint.

The nodes of the object nets in $\mathcal{U}_k$ are not disjoint, since the firing rule allows to transfer tokens between net tokens within the same set $\mathcal{U}_k$. Such a transfer is possible, if we assume that all nets $N \in \mathcal{U}_k$ have the same set of places $P_k$. $P_k$ is the place universe for all object nets of kind $k$.

In general, $P_k$ is not finite. Since we like each object net to be finite in some sense, we require that the transitions $T_N$ of each $N \in \mathcal{U}_k$ use only a finite subset of $P_k$, i.e., $\forall N \in \mathcal{U} : |{}^{\bullet}T_N \cup T_N{}^{\bullet}| < \infty$.

The family of object nets $\mathcal{U}$ is the universe of the algebra. A *net-algebra* $(\mathcal{U}, \mathcal{I})$ assigns to each constant $\sigma \in \Sigma_{\lambda, k}$ an object net $\sigma^{\mathcal{I}} \in \mathcal{U}_k$ and to each operator $\sigma \in \Sigma_{k_1 \cdots k_n, k}$ with $n > 0$ a mapping $\sigma^{\mathcal{I}} : (\mathcal{U}_{k_1} \times \cdots \times \mathcal{U}_{k_n}) \to \mathcal{U}_k$.

A net-algebra is called *finite* if $P_k$ is a finite set for each $k \in K$.

Since all nets $N \in \mathcal{U}_k$ have the same set of places $P_k$, which is required to be finite for EHORNETS, there is an upper bound for the cardinality of $\mathcal{U}_k$.

**Proposition 1 (Lemma 2.1 in [24]).** *For each $k \in K$ the cardinality of each net universe $\mathcal{U}_k$ is bound as follows: $|\mathcal{U}_k| \leq 2^{\left(2^{4|P_k|}\right)}$.*

A variable assignment $\alpha = (\alpha_k : X_k \to \mathcal{U}_k)_{k \in K}$ maps each variable onto an element of the algebra. For a variable assignment $\alpha$ the evaluation of a term $t \in \mathbb{T}_\Sigma^k(X)$ is uniquely defined and will be denoted as $\alpha(t)$.

A net-algebra, such that all axioms of $(\Sigma, X, E)$ are valid, is called *net-theory*.

*Nested Markings.* A marking of an EHORNET assigns to each system net place one or many net-tokens. The places of the system net are typed by the function $k : \widehat{P} \to K$, meaning that a place $\widehat{p}$ contains net-tokens of kind $k(\widehat{p})$. Since the net-tokens are instances of object nets, a *marking* is a *nested* multiset of the form:

$$\mu = \sum_{i=1}^{n} \widehat{p}_i[N_i, M_i] \quad \text{where} \quad \widehat{p}_i \in \widehat{P}, N_i \in \mathcal{U}_{k(\widehat{p}_i)}, M_i \in MS(P_{N_i}), n \in \mathbb{N}$$

Each addend $\widehat{p}_i[N_i, M_i]$ denotes a net-token on the place $\widehat{p}_i$ that has the structure of the object net $N_i$ and the marking $M_i \in MS(P_{N_i})$. The set of all nested multisets is denoted as $\mathcal{M}_H$. We define the partial order $\sqsubseteq$ on nested multisets by setting $\mu_1 \sqsubseteq \mu_2$ iff $\exists \mu : \mu_2 = \mu_1 + \mu$.

*Projections.* The projection $\Pi_N^1(\mu)$ is the multiset of all system-net places that contain the object net $N$:

$$\Pi_N^1 \left( \sum\nolimits_{i=1}^{n} \widehat{p}_i[N_i, M_i] \right) := \sum\nolimits_{i=1}^{n} \mathbf{1}_N(N_i) \cdot \widehat{p}_i \tag{1}$$

where the indicator function $\mathbf{1}_N$ is defined as: $\mathbf{1}_N(N_i) = 1$ iff $N_i = N$.

Analogously, the projection $\Pi_N^2(\mu)$ is the multiset of all net-tokens' markings (that belong to the object net $N$):

$$\Pi_N^2 \left( \sum\nolimits_{i=1}^{n} \widehat{p}_i[N_i, M_i] \right) := \sum\nolimits_{i=1}^{n} \mathbf{1}_k(N_i) \cdot M_i \tag{2}$$

The projection $\Pi_k^2(\mu)$ is the sum of all net-tokens' markings belonging to the same type $k \in K$:

$$\Pi_k^2 (\mu) := \sum\nolimits_{N \in \mathcal{U}_k} \Pi_N^2 (\mu) \tag{3}$$

*Synchronisation.* The transitions in an HORNET are labelled with synchronisation inscriptions. We assume a fixed set of channels $C = (C_k)_{k \in K}$.

- The function family $\widehat{l}_\alpha = (\widehat{l}_\alpha^k)_{k \in K}$ defines the synchronisation constraints. Each transition of the system net is labelled with a multiset $\widehat{l}^k(\widehat{t}) = (e_1, c_1) + \cdots + (e_n, c_n)$, where the expression $e_i \in \mathbb{T}_\Sigma^k(X)$ describes the called object net and $c_i \in C_k$ is a channel. The intention is that $\hat{t}$ fires synchronously with a multiset of object net transitions with the same multiset of labels. Each variable assignment $\alpha$ generates the function $\hat{l}^k_\alpha(\hat{t})$ defined as:

$$\hat{l}^k_\alpha(\hat{t})(N) := \sum_{\substack{1 \le i \le n \\ \alpha(e_i)=N}} c_i \quad \text{for} \quad \hat{l}^k(\hat{t}) = \sum_{1 \le i \le n} (e_i, c_i) \tag{4}$$

Each function $\hat{l}^k_\alpha(\hat{t})$ assigns to each object net $N$ a multiset of channels.
- For each $N \in \mathcal{U}_k$ the function $l_N$ assigns to each transition $t \in T_N$ either a channel $c \in C_k$ or $\perp_k$, whenever $t$ fires without synchronisation, i.e., autonomously.

*System Net.* Assume we have a fixed logic $\Gamma = (\Sigma, X, E, \Psi)$ and a net-theory $(\mathcal{U}, \mathcal{I})$. An *elementary higher-order object net* (EHORNET) is composed of a system net $\hat{N}$ and the set of object nets $\mathcal{U}$. W.l.o.g. we assume $\hat{N} \notin \mathcal{U}$. To guarantee finite algebras for EHORNETS, we require that the net-theory $(\mathcal{U}, \mathcal{I})$ is finite, i.e., each place universe $P_k$ is finite.

The system net is a net $\hat{N} = (\hat{P}, \hat{T}, \mathbf{pre}, \mathbf{post}, \hat{G})$, where each arc is labelled with a multiset of terms: $\mathbf{pre}, \mathbf{post} : \hat{T} \to (\hat{P} \to MS(\mathbb{T}_\Sigma(X)))$. Each transition is labelled by a guard predicate $\hat{G} : \hat{T} \to PL_\Gamma$. The places of the system net are typed by the function $k : \hat{P} \to K$. As a typing constraint we have that each arc inscription has to be a multiset of terms that are all of the kind that is assigned to the arc's place:

$$\mathbf{pre}(\hat{t})(\hat{p}), \quad \mathbf{post}(\hat{t})(\hat{p}) \quad \in \quad MS(\mathbb{T}^{k(\hat{p})}_\Sigma(X)) \tag{5}$$

For each variable binding $\alpha$ we obtain the evaluated functions $\mathbf{pre}_\alpha, \mathbf{post}_\alpha : \hat{T} \to (\hat{P} \to MS(\mathcal{U}))$ in the obvious way.

**Definition 1 (Elementary Hornet, eHornet).** *Assume a fixed many-sorted predicate logic* $\Gamma = (\Sigma, X, E, \Psi)$.

*An elementary* HORNET *is a tuple* $EH = (\hat{N}, \mathcal{U}, \mathcal{I}, k, l, \mu_0)$ *such that:*

1. $\hat{N}$ *is an algebraic net, called the* system net.
2. $(\mathcal{U}, \mathcal{I})$ *is a finite net-theory for the logic* $\Gamma$.
3. $k : \hat{P} \to K$ *is the typing of the system net places.*
4. $l = (\hat{l}, l_N)_{N \in \mathcal{U}}$ *is the labelling.*
5. $\mu_0 \in \mathcal{M}_H$ *is the initial marking.*

*Example 2.* We will illustrate Definition 1 with the example given in Fig. 3. We assume that we have one net type: $K = \{\text{WFN}\}$. We have only one operator $\|$ for parallel composition: $\| \in \Sigma_{\text{WFN}^2, \text{WFN}}$. The operator is interpreted by $\mathcal{I}$ as the usual AND operation on workflow nets. We have the universe with three object nets: $\mathcal{U}_{\text{WFN}} = \{N_1, N_2, N_3\}$. All places of the system net have the same type, i.e., $k(\hat{p}) = k(\hat{q}) = k(\hat{r}) = \text{WFN}$. The structure of the system net $\hat{N}$ and the object nets is given the usual way as shown in Fig. 3. This EHORNET uses no communication channels, i.e., all events occur autonomously: $\hat{l}^k_\alpha = \mathbf{0}$ and $l_N(t) = \perp_k$. In the initial marking we consider a EHORNET with two nets $N_1$ and $N_2$ as tokens (as shown on the left): $\mu_0 = \hat{p}[N_1, v] + \hat{q}[N_2, s]$.

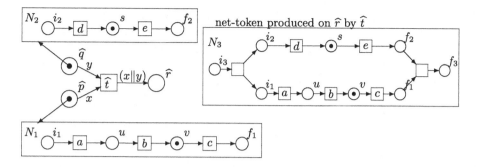

**Fig. 3.** Modification of the Net-Token's Structure.

*Events.* The synchronisation labelling generates the set of system events $\Theta$. We have three kinds of events:

1. Synchronised firing: There is at least one object net that has to be synchronised, i.e., there is a $N$ such that $\widehat{l}(\widehat{t})(N)$ is not empty.
   Such an event is a pair $\theta = \widehat{t}^\alpha[\vartheta]$, where $\widehat{t}$ is a system net transition, $\alpha$ is a variable binding, and $\vartheta$ is a function that maps each object net to a multiset of its transitions, i.e., $\vartheta(N) \in MS(T_N)$. It is required that $\widehat{t}$ and $\vartheta(N)$ have matching multisets of labels, i.e., $\widehat{l}(\widehat{t})(N) = l_N^\sharp(\vartheta(N))$ for all $N \in \mathcal{U}$. (Remember that $l_N^\sharp$ denotes the multiset extension of $l_N$.)
   The intended meaning is that $\widehat{t}$ fires synchronously with all the object net transitions $\vartheta(N), N \in \mathcal{U}$.
2. System-autonomous firing: The transition $\widehat{t}$ of the system net fires autonomously, whenever $\widehat{l}(\widehat{t})$ is the empty multiset $\mathbf{0}$.
   We consider system-autonomous firing as a special case of synchronised firing generated by the function $\vartheta_{id}$, defined as $\vartheta_{id}(N) = \mathbf{0}$ for all $N \in \mathcal{U}$.
3. Object autonomous firing: An object net transition $t$ in $N$ fires autonomously, whenever $l_N(t) = \perp_k$.
   Object autonomous events are denoted as $id_{\widehat{p},N}[\vartheta_t]$, where $\vartheta_t(N') = \{t\}$ if $N = N'$ and $\mathbf{0}$ otherwise. The meaning is that in object net $N$ fires $t$ autonomously within the place $\widehat{p}$.
   For the sake of uniformity we define for an arbitrary binding $\alpha$:

$$\mathbf{pre}_\alpha(id_{\widehat{p},N})(\widehat{p}')(N') = \mathbf{post}_\alpha(id_{\widehat{p},N})(\widehat{p}')(N') = \begin{cases} 1 & \text{if } \widehat{p}' = \widehat{p} \wedge N' = N \\ 0 & \text{otherwise.} \end{cases}$$

The set of all *events* generated by the labelling $l$ is $\Theta_l := \Theta_1 \cup \Theta_2$, where $\Theta_1$ contains synchronous events (including system-autonomous events as a special case) and $\Theta_2$ contains the object autonomous events:

$$\begin{aligned} \Theta_1 &:= \left\{ \widehat{t}^\alpha[\vartheta] \quad \mid \forall N \in \mathcal{U} : \widehat{l}_\alpha(\widehat{t})(N) = l_N^\sharp(\vartheta(N)) \right\} \\ \Theta_2 &:= \left\{ id_{\widehat{p},N}[\vartheta_t] \mid \widehat{p} \in \widehat{P}, N \in \mathcal{U}_{k(\widehat{p})}, t \in T_N \right\} \end{aligned} \tag{6}$$

*Firing Rule.* A system event $\theta = \widehat{\tau}^\alpha[\vartheta]$ removes net-tokens together with their individual internal markings. Firing the event replaces a nested multiset $\lambda \in \mathcal{M}_H$ that is part of the current marking $\mu$, i.e., $\lambda \sqsubseteq \mu$, by the nested multiset $\rho$. The enabling condition is expressed by the *enabling predicate* $\phi_{EH}$ (or just $\phi$ whenever $EH$ is clear from the context):

$$
\begin{aligned}
\phi_{EH}\left(\widehat{\tau}^\alpha[\vartheta], \lambda, \rho\right) &\iff \forall k \in K : \\
&\forall \widehat{p} \in k^{-1}(k) : \forall N \in \mathcal{U}_k : \Pi_N^1(\lambda)(\widehat{p}) = \mathbf{pre}_\alpha(\widehat{\tau})(\widehat{p})(N) \wedge \\
&\forall \widehat{p} \in k^{-1}(k) : \forall N \in \mathcal{U}_k : \Pi_N^1(\rho)(\widehat{p}) = \mathbf{post}_\alpha(\widehat{\tau})(\widehat{p})(N) \wedge \\
&\Pi_k^2(\lambda) \geq \sum_{N \in \mathcal{U}_k} \mathbf{pre}_N^\sharp(\vartheta(N)) \wedge \\
&\Pi_k^2(\rho) = \Pi_k^2(\lambda) + \sum_{N \in \mathcal{U}_k} \mathbf{post}_N^\sharp(\vartheta(N)) - \mathbf{pre}_N^\sharp(\vartheta(N))
\end{aligned}
\tag{7}
$$

The predicate $\phi_{EH}$ has the following meaning:

- Conjunct (1) states that the removed sub-marking $\lambda$ contains on $\widehat{p}$ the right number of net-tokens, that are removed by $\widehat{\tau}$.
- Conjunct (2) states that generated sub-marking $\rho$ contains on $\widehat{p}$ the right number of net-tokens, that are generated by $\widehat{\tau}$.
- Conjunct (3) states that the sub-marking $\lambda$ enables all synchronised transitions $\vartheta(N)$ in the object $N$.
- Conjunct (4) states that the marking of each object net $N$ is changed according to the firing of the synchronised transitions $\vartheta(N)$.

Note that conjuncts (1) and (2) assure that only net-tokens relevant for the firing are included in $\lambda$ and $\rho$. Conditions (3) and (4) allow for additional tokens in the net-tokens.

For system-autonomous events $\widehat{t}^\alpha[\vartheta_{id}]$ the enabling predicate $\phi_{EH}$ can be simplified further: Conjunct (3) is always true since $\mathbf{pre}_N(\vartheta_{id}(N)) = \mathbf{0}$. Conjunct (4) simplifies to $\Pi_k^2(\rho) = \Pi_k^2(\lambda)$, which means that no token of the object nets get lost when a system-autonomous events fires.

Analogously, for an object autonomous event $\widehat{\tau}[\vartheta_t]$ we have an idle-transition $\widehat{\tau} = id_{\widehat{p},N}$ and $\vartheta = \vartheta_t$ for some $t$. Conjunct (1) and (2) simplify to $\Pi_{N'}^1(\lambda) = \widehat{p} = \Pi_{N'}^1(\rho)$ for $N' = N$ and to $\Pi_{N'}^1(\lambda) = \mathbf{0} = \Pi_{N'}^1(\rho)$ otherwise. This means that $\lambda = \widehat{p}[M]$, $M$ enables $t$, and $\rho = \widehat{p}[M - \mathbf{pre}_N(\widehat{t}) + \mathbf{post}_N(\widehat{t})]$.

**Definition 2 (Firing Rule).** *Let $EH$ be an* EHORNET *and* $\mu, \mu' \in \mathcal{M}_H$ *markings.*

- *The event* $\widehat{\tau}^\alpha[\vartheta]$ *is enabled in* $\mu$ *for the mode* $(\lambda, \rho) \in \mathcal{M}_H^2$ *iff* $\lambda \sqsubseteq \mu \wedge$ $\phi_{EH}(\widehat{\tau}[\vartheta], \lambda, \rho)$ *holds and the guard* $\widehat{G}(\widehat{t})$ *holds, i.e.,* $E \models_{\mathcal{I}}^\alpha \widehat{G}(\widehat{\tau})$.
- *An event* $\widehat{\tau}^\alpha[\vartheta]$ *that is enabled in* $\mu$ *can fire – denoted* $\mu \xrightarrow[EH]{\widehat{\tau}^\alpha[\vartheta](\lambda, \rho)} \mu'$.
- *The resulting successor marking is defined as* $\mu' = \mu - \lambda + \rho$.

Note that the firing rule has no a-priori decision how to distribute the marking on the generated net-tokens. Therefore we need the mode $(\lambda, \rho)$ to formulate the firing of $\widehat{\tau}^\alpha[\vartheta]$ in a functional way.

*Example 3.* We will illustrate the firing rule considering the HORNET from Fig. 3 again. To model a run-time adaption, we combine $N_1$ and $N_2$ resulting in the net $N_3 = (N_1 \| N_2)$. This modification is modelled by system net transition $\hat{t}$ of the HORNET. In a binding $\alpha$ with $x \mapsto N_1$ and $y \mapsto N_2$ the transition $t$ is enabled. Let $(x \| y)$ evaluate to $N_3$ for $\alpha$. When $\hat{t}$ fires it removes the two net-tokens from $\hat{p}$ and $\hat{q}$ and generates one new net-token on place $\hat{r}$. This is the event $\theta_1 = \hat{t}^{\alpha}[\vartheta]$, where $\vartheta = \vartheta_{id}$. The net-token generated on $\hat{r}$ has the structure of $N_3$ and its marking is obtained as a transfer from the token on $v$ in $N_1$ and the token on $s$ in $N_2$ into $N_3$:

$$\hat{p}[N_1, v] + \hat{q}[N_2, s] \xrightarrow{\theta_1} \hat{r}\big[(N_1 \| N_2), s + v\big]$$

This transfer is possible since all the places of $N_1$ and $N_2$ are also places in $N_3$ and tokens can be transferred in the obvious way.

It is also possible that the net-tokens fire object autonomously. E.g., the net-token on place $\hat{q}$ enables the object net transition $e$ in $\mu_0$, i.e., the event $\theta_2 = id_{\hat{q}, N_2}[\vartheta_e]$:

$$\hat{p}[N_1, v] + \hat{q}[N_2, s] \xrightarrow{\theta_2} \hat{p}[N_1, v] + \hat{q}[N_2, f_2]$$

Analogously, the net-token on $\hat{p}$ enables the transition $c$.

*Reachability Graph.* Firing is extended to sequences $w \in \Theta_l^*$ in the usual way:

- The empty sequence $w = \epsilon$ is enabled iff $\mu' = \mu$.
- Whenever $\mu \xrightarrow[EH]{w} \mu'$ and $\mu' \xrightarrow[EH]{\theta} \mu''$ then $\mu \xrightarrow[EH]{(w \cdot \theta)} \mu'$.

We denote $\mu \xrightarrow[EH]{*} \mu'$ whenever there is some $w$ such that $\mu \xrightarrow[EH]{w} \mu'$ holds. We omit the subscript *EH* whenever it is clear from the context. The set of reachable markings is defined as:

$$RS(EH) := RS(\mu_0) := \left\{ \mu \mid \mu_0 \xrightarrow[EH]{*} \mu \right\} \tag{8}$$

The *reachability graph* $RG(EH) = (V, E, \mu_0)$ contains all nested markings $V = RS(EH)$ as vertices (or nodes), $E = \{(\mu, \mu') \mid \mu \xrightarrow{\theta} \mu'\}$ as edges and the initial marking $\mu_0$ as a distinguished node.

## 4   Adaption Processes

For EHORNETS it is quite obvious how to define the gene pool of a system state. Obviously, we are interested in the (multi-)set of object nets that are contained in the marking $\mu$. These are given by the projection $\Pi_{\mathcal{U}_k}(\mu)$:

$$\Pi_{\mathcal{U}_k} \left( \sum_{i=1}^n \hat{p}_i[N_i, M_i] \right) := \sum_{i=1}^n \mathbf{1}_{\mathcal{U}_k}(N_i) \cdot N_i \tag{9}$$

where the indicator function $\mathbf{1}_{\mathcal{U}_k}$ is defined as: $\mathbf{1}_{\mathcal{U}_k}(N_i) = 1$ iff $N_i \in \mathcal{U}_k$.

For the complete universe we define:

$$\Pi_{\mathcal{U}}(\mu) := \sum_{k \in K} \Pi_{\mathcal{U}_k}(\mu) = \sum_{i=1}^{n} N_i \qquad (10)$$

We define $\tilde{\Pi}_{\mathcal{U}} := dom \circ \Pi_{\mathcal{U}}$ to obtain the set of object nets. We use the metaphor that $\tilde{\Pi}_{\mathcal{U}}(\mu) = \{N_1, \ldots, N_n\}$ is the *gene pool* of the marking $\mu$.

Note that for safe HORNETS we have no more object nets than system net places and therefore $|\tilde{\Pi}_{\mathcal{U}}(\mu))| \leq |\Pi_{\mathcal{U}}(\mu)| \leq |\widehat{P}|$, i.e., the gene pool is bounded.

### 4.1   Adaption in the Reachability Graph

The set of reachable object nets of $EH$, defined as:

$$\mathcal{U}(EH) := \mathcal{U}(\mu_0) := \bigcup_{\mu \in RS(\mu_0)} \tilde{\Pi}_{\mathcal{U}}(\mu) \qquad (11)$$

describes the universe of reachable genes, but it does not contain any information about the adaption *dynamics* at all. So, we look at the reachability graph. But, the RG of a HORNET is usually too large to analyse, since the reachability problem requires exponential space for safe EHORNETS [24]. Fortunately, the RG contains much information that is not relevant when studying the adaption process. We like to define an abstracted version of the RG that describes the evolution of the gene pool (as specified by the HORNET).

As we are interested in the adaption dynamics of object nets we start with the reachability graph and abstract from "irrelevant" events. Roughly speaking, an event is considered as irrelevant whenever the set of object nets $\tilde{\Pi}_{\mathcal{U}}(\mu)$ doesn't change when firing the event (i.e., the HORNET is stuttering with respect to the set of object nets).

**Definition 3.** *The marking $\mu_{n+1}$ is $\mathcal{U}$-reachable in $(V, E)$ from $\mu_1$ whenever there is a sequence $\mu_1 \mu_2 \cdots \mu_{n+1}$ such that for all $i \in \{1, \ldots, n\}$ we have:*

$$\exists \theta_i : \mu_i \xrightarrow{\theta_i} \mu_{i+1} \wedge \tilde{\Pi}_{\mathcal{U}}(\mu_i) = \tilde{\Pi}_{\mathcal{U}}(\mu_{i+1})$$

*Given $RG(EH) = (V, E)$ we define the following relations on reachable markings:*

- $(\mu_1, \mu_2) \in R_1$ *iff $\mu_2$ is $\mathcal{U}$-reachable from $\mu_1$ in $(V, E)$ – and vice versa.*
- $(\mu_1, \mu_2) \in R_1'$ *iff $\mu_2$ is $\mathcal{U}$-reachable from $\mu_1$ in $(V, E)$.*
- $(\mu_1, \mu_2) \in R_2$ *iff $\mu_2$ is $\mathcal{U}$-reachable from $\mu_1$ in the undirected graph, i.e., in $(V, (E \cup E^{-1}))$.*
- $(\mu_1, \mu_2) \in R_3$ *iff $\tilde{\Pi}_{\mathcal{U}}(\mu_1) = \tilde{\Pi}_{\mathcal{U}}(\mu_2)$*

In other words, $R_1$ relates markings that are strongly connected in the reachability graph via irrelevant events; for $R_1'$ the connection may hold in only one direction; and $R_2$ relates markings that are weakly connected via irrelevant events. Unlike the other relations, $R_3$ does not assume any reachability relation between the markings.

Obviously, the relations have the following properties:

**Lemma 1.** – $R_1$ is reflexive, symmetric, and transitive.
- $R_1'$ is reflexive and transitive, but in general not symmetric.
- $R_1 = R_1' \cap (R_1')^{-1}$
- $R_2$ is reflexive, symmetric, and transitive.
- $R_3$ is reflexive, symmetric, and transitive.

Since $R_1$, $R_2$, and $R_3$ are equivalences we can use them to factor the RG, i.e., equivalence classes are condensed to a single node. All these graphs have $v_0 := [v_0]_{R_i}$ as a designated initial node.

**Definition 4.** Let $G = (V, E, v_0)$ be a graph with initial node and let $\approx \subseteq V^2$ be an equivalence on the vertices. The factorised graph is defined as $G_{/\approx} = (V', E', v_0')$ with

$$V' = [V]_\approx, \quad E' = \{([\mu]_\approx, [\mu']_\approx) \mid (\mu, \mu') \in E\}, \quad and \quad v_0' := [v_0]_\approx$$

Then, the abstracted graph $RG(EH)_{/R_i}$ where $i = 1, 2, 3$ describes the evolution of the gene pool that is specified by the HORNET.

The three relations leads to different kinds of abstraction due to the following inclusions:

**Lemma 2 (Abstraction Hierarchy).** $R_1 \subseteq R_1' \subseteq R_2 \subseteq R_3$

Here, a finer equivalence leads to a larger factorised graph. With Lemma 2 we obtain that $RG(EH)_{/R_1}$ is closer to the original RG, while $RG(EH)_{/R_3}$ leads to a more abstract factorisation. More specifically:

- The graph $AG_1(EH) := RG(EH)_{/R_1}$ collapses areas in the reachability graph where the set of used object nets (i.e., the gene pool) doesn't change, i.e., it abstracts away from stuttering.
- The graph $AG_2(EH) := RG(EH)_{/R_2}$ collapses greater areas in the RG since it is sufficient that there is a weak connectivity of the markings in the RG.
- The graph $AG_3(EH) := RG(EH)_{/R_3}$ collapses all markings into one single vertice whenever the projection $\tilde{\Pi}_\mathcal{U}(\mu)$ is the same.

## 4.2   Key Values of Abstract Graphs

In the following, we identify suitable graph theoretic measures to give key values of the abstract graph $(V, E, v_0)$. Assume that $n = |V|$ and $m = |E|$. For more aspects of graph measures cf. [32, Chapter 17].

**Number of Adaptivity Options.** On a macroscopic scale the *average degree* $\frac{1}{n} \cdot \sum_{v \in V} deg(v)$ tells us about how many evolution options the system has. A higher value indicates that the system has many options to adapt.

Similarly, the *density* $\frac{m}{n(n-1)}$ tells us something about the specificity of the adaption process on a macroscopic scale, where a higher value indicates that the system has no specific direction to evolve.

Graph *transitivity* looks at density on a more microscopic scale. It is the probability that $v$'s neighbours are connected, too:

$$C_T := \frac{|\{(u,v,w) \mid (u,v),(v,w),(u,w) \in E\}|}{|\{(u,v,w) \mid (u,v),(v,w) \in E\}|} \tag{12}$$

Transitivity tells us how dense the adaption process is on a small scale, i.e., when considering triplets of nodes. A higher value indicates that there are many ways of achieving the same adaption state, while a lower value indicates that some adaption states are reachable via a more specific process, only

**Measures for the Length of Adaption Processes.** We are interested in measurements of the length of the adaption process. The path length tells us something about the convergence speed. Let $d(v \to v')$ denote the shortest path length from node $v$ to $v'$. Then, the distances $d(v_0 \to v)$ describes how long the adaption dynamics is extended from initial node. A greater path length means a longer adaption dynamics.

The maximal distance from a given node is called its *eccentricity* $\epsilon(v)$:

$$\epsilon(v) := \max_{v' \in V} d(v \to v') \tag{13}$$

The eccentricity $\epsilon(v_0)$ tells us about the gene pool that is farthest away. We also consider the normalised variant $\epsilon(v_0)/n$.

**Identifying Central Gene Pools.** We also identify the most "central" states in the dynamics, which are in some sense the discrete, graph-theoretical analogue of an attractor. There are several concepts of centrality in graph theory. Here, we use *betweeness centrality* $c_B(v)$ that is the probability for the shortest path between two nodes to go through that node $v$.

$$c_B(v) := \frac{1}{(n-1)(n-2)} \sum_{u,w \in V : u \neq v, w \neq v, u \neq w} \frac{N_{sp}(u \xrightarrow{v} w)}{N_{sp}(u \to w)} \tag{14}$$

Here, $N_{sp}(u \to w)$ is the number of shortest paths from node $u$ to node $w$ and $N_{sp}(u \xrightarrow{v} w)$ is the number of the shortest paths that go through node $v$.

We use the stochastic distribution of betweenness centrality $c_b(v)$ to identify which of the nodes/genes are very central in the dynamics. The variance indicates whether the distribution is tight around its average value: a higher variance indicates that some nodes are more central than others.

## 4.3  Directedness of Adaption

Assumed that adaption always leads to an improvement, the abstract graph would contain no cycles. In general, a system will allow for some regression for exploration issues – a try-and-error strategy. But it is reasonable that on larger time scales adaption will lead to an improvement. So, longer cycles are typically less common than short ones. When 'ignoring' cycles, the abstract graph describes a partial order. Therefore, we have to find a maximal sub-graph that describes a partial order, i.e., a maximal DAG (directed acyclic graph). This sub-graph is interpreted as an underlying dynamics of *improvement* – when ignoring small phases of regression. We require that all the nodes remain reachable from the initial node $v_0$ in the DAG. So, we generate a maximal spanning DAG. The set of all such sub-graphs of $G = (V, E, v_0)$ being a DAG is:

$$DAGs(V, E, v_0) := \{D \mid D = (V, E_D, v_0) \text{ is a DAG } \wedge \\ E_D \subseteq E \wedge \forall v \in V : (v_0, v) \in E_D^*\} \tag{15}$$

We are interested in a sub-DAG of maximal size:

$$m_0(G) := \max\{|E_D| \mid (V, E_D, v_0) \in DAGs(G)\} \tag{16}$$

In other words, $|E| - m_0(G)$ is the minimal number of edges to be deleted to obtain an acyclic graph from the abstracted reachability graph $G$.

**Definition 5.** *The* degree of adaption directedness *is* $dad(G) := \frac{m_0(G)}{|E|}$.

The degree of adaption directedness indicates, how much the dynamics is going into a certain direction (which can be interpreted as an improvement). When $dad(G)$ is close to 1, then the RG is acyclic, and the adaption dynamics goes (almost) strictly into one direction; while a $dad(G)$ close to 0 indicates an adaption process heavily running in cycles. Of course, we hope for a dynamics with $dad(G) \approx 1$, since they are easier to interpret.

Any subgraph $D = (V, E_D, v_0)$ of $G = (V, E, v_0)$ being a DAG with maximally many edges, i.e., $|E_D| = m_0(G)$, is a candidate for the underlying *improvement dynamics*.

$$DAG_{m_0}(G) := \{(V, E_D, v_0) \in DAGs(G) \mid m_0(G) = |E_D|\} \tag{17}$$

We use depth and width of all the DAGs $D \in DAG_{m_0}(V, E, v_0)$ as our central key measures:

- The *DAG-depth* is the largest *line*, i.e., a maximal clique w.r.t. **li**, which is the *dependence* relation of a DAG $D = (V, E, v_0)$ defined as $\mathbf{li} := E^* \cup (E^*)^{-1} \cup id_V$:

$$depth_D(D) := \max\{|L| \mid L \text{ is maximal } \mathbf{li}\text{-clique }\} \tag{18}$$

A greater depth tell us that the system is very productive with respect to adaption, since it is going very straight into one direction.
- The *DAG-width* is the largest *cut*, i.e., a maximal independent set, or, alternatively, a maximal clique w.r.t. the *independence* relation $\mathbf{co} := \overline{\mathbf{li}} \cup id_V$:

$$width_D(D) := \max\{|C| \mid C \text{ is maximal } \mathbf{co}\text{-clique }\} \tag{19}$$

A greater width tells us that for a given gene pool there is a large amount of options to adapt – depending on structural aspects we have abstracted from in the adaption graph.

We average the depth and width over all the DAGs in $DAG_{m_0}(V, E, v_0)$:

$$depth(G) := \frac{1}{|DAG_{m_0}(G)|} \sum_{D \in DAG_{m_0}(G)} depth_D(D) \qquad (20)$$

Analogously for $width(G)$.

The depth-width ratio $depth(G)/width(G)$ tells us something about the number of adaption options given per productive evolution step.

## 4.4    Relationship Between Exploration and Exploitation

We can transform the DAG $D = (V, E, v_0)$ into a tree by using a different copy of a node for each path $p$ from the initial node to this node. (The definition is unproblematic, since our DAGs have finitely many nodes, and therefore also only finitely many paths.)

**Definition 6.** *Define the* tree unfolding $tree(D) = (V_{tr}, E_{tr}, v_0)$ *of a given DAG* $D = (V, E, v_0)$ *as:*

$$V_{tr} = \{p \mid p = v_0 \ldots v \text{ is a path in } D\}$$
$$E_{tr} = \{(p, p') \mid p' = p \cdot v'\}$$

The tree structure reveals information about the relationship between *exploration* of the adaption space, i.e., when the systems tests different options (and this accepts regression), and its *exploitation*, i.e., when the systems sticks to a pretty good option and tries to improve it with minor changes instead of evaluating some completely other option.

When the tree is growing the systems explores the adaption space. When the growth stagnates the system exploits the information gained. We try to capture this in the following measures: The adaption tree $T$ has a different branching structure, i.e., less successors here and more over there; additionally, exploration and exploitation does not necessarily come in two successive phases, but in many, intertwined ones. So, we compare our tree with a very "tidy" reference tree, namely a tree that starts with the exploration phase followed by the exploitation phase. When the root is drawn at the top the tree has a $\triangle\!\!\!\square$-like shape, where the triangle describes the exploration (with a high branching degree) and the rectangle describes the exploitation (with no branching). A dynamics that has a maximal exploration leads to a tree that consists of the triangle part only.

Assume that the original tree $T$ has height $h_0$ and $l_0$ leaves and $n_0$ nodes. Let $h$ be the height of the exploration-triangle and $h'$ the height of the exploitation-rectangle in the reference tree. Similarly, the triangle has $n$ nodes and $l$ leaves; the rectangle has $n'$ nodes and $l'$ leaves. As the rectangle has no branching, it has the same number of leaves as the triangle: $l = l'$. We want to have a $\triangle\!\!\!\square$-like tree that the same height and also the same number of nodes as the original tree: $h_0 = h + h'$ and $n_0 = n + n'$. We also require that the number of leaves does not change: $l_0 = l = l'$.

The new tree must have a (yet unknown) branching $b$ such that $b^h = l = l_0$ in the $\triangle$-part of the $\bigtriangleup$-like shape. Thus the complete triangle then has $n = \frac{b^{h+1}-1}{b-1}$ nodes and $l = b^h$ leaves. The rectangle has as many leaves as the triangle, as we have no branching here, and $n' = h' \cdot b^h$ nodes. So, we obtain:

$$n_0 = n + n'$$
$$= \frac{b^{h+1} - 1}{b - 1} + h' \cdot b^h$$
$$\approx b^h + h' \cdot b^h$$
$$= b^h(1 + h')$$
$$= l_0(1 + h')$$

Therefore, the exploitation rectangle $\square$ has the height $h' \approx \frac{n_0}{l_0} - 1$. From this we obtain the height $h$ of the exploration triangle $\triangle$ as $h = h_0 - h' \approx h_0 - \frac{n_0}{l_0} + 1$.

Let $D = (V, E, v_0)$ be a DAG and assume that its tree unfolding $T = tree(D)$ has $l_0$ leaves, $n_0$ nodes, and height $h_0$. Then, the *exploitation rate* of $T = tree(V, E, v_0)$ is the ratio of the rectangle height $h'$ to the total height $h_0$:

$$\chi(T) := \frac{h'}{h_0} \approx \frac{1}{h_0}\left(\frac{n_0}{l_0} - 1\right) \qquad (21)$$

Correspondingly, the *exploration rate* is given as $(1 - \chi(T))$.

We are interested in the corresponding exploration and exploitation rates in the adaption dynamics.

**Definition 7 (exploration and exploitation rates).** *For the DAG $D$ we define $\chi(D) := \chi(tree(D))$. For an abstract reachability graph $G$ we define:*

$$\chi(G) := \frac{1}{|DAG_{m_0}(G)|} \sum_{D \in DAG_{m_0}(G)} \chi(D) \qquad (22)$$

These rates are used to characterise adaption dynamics: Systems with a high exploration rate could be considered as adventurous, while systems with a high exploitation rate could be considered as more conservative.

## 5   Case Study: Axelrod's Tournament

As we have already mentioned multi-agent systems are usually studied using game-theory and logic [3]. The most prominent example to study evolution for a game is Axelrod's Tournament [33], where several agents are playing the well known prisoners' dilemma. The prisoners' dilemma is a two-player game. Both players are accused of a severe crime. If only one player confesses he can act as a principal witness and gets away with a minor punishment, while the other player is sent to prison for a long time; if both players confess, the witness strategy does not work and both are punished; but, if both players deny that they are involved in the crime, they get away almost without any punishment. Therefore, the optimal solution for both agents is to deny. But this is not a Nash-equilibrium since each agent can do better when confessing. Unfortunately, this leads to the worst situation, where both agents confess. This is also the Nash-equilibrium of the game. The problem that an *uncoordinated* choice of actions might result in a very bad equilibrium is sometimes called the price-of-anarchy.

The prisoners' game is formalised as follows: If both agents cooperate (C) they both obtain a payoff, e.g., $r = 3$; If only one agent cooperates the defecting agent (D) gets a higher payoff of e.g., $t = 5$, while the cooperating one obtains nothing $s = 0$. If both agents defect they both obtain a small payoff, e.g., $p = 1$.[3] In general, $t > r > p > s \geq 0$ is assumed. The payoff matrix is given as: Here,

|               | cooperate (C) | defect (D) |
|---------------|:-------------:|:----------:|
| cooperate (C) | 3,3           | 0,5        |
| defect (D)    | 5,0           | 1,1        |

the optimal solution $(C, C)$ has a payoff of $(3, 3)$. It is optimal in the sense that the social welfare, i.e., the sum of all individual payoffs, is maximised. As we have seen before each agent separately can do better by changing its strategy. Consequently, we arrive at the equilibrium $(D, D)$ with a payoff of $(1, 1)$, which is the minimal social welfare.

In the tournament version $n$ agents are playing this game pairwise over several rounds. The agents are allowed to adapt their strategy over time. We assume that each agent remembers a finite history of games already played with a given opponent. Assuming a history of size 3 a history is $h = g_3 g_2 g_1 = (a_3, b_3)(a_2, b_2)(a_1, b_1)$ where $a_i, b_i \in \{C, D\}$. A strategy is therefore a function $s : \{C, D\}^6 \to \{C, D\}$. When describing strategies by automata each history $h \in \{C, D\}^6$ is a state and the action chosen for the current game is given by state changes.

Even for this very restricted history size we have $2^{2^6} = 2^{64}$ different strategies, i.e., the strategy space is far too large to be explored directly. Axelrod invited researchers to submit their strategy to a tournament. Surprisingly, a very simple strategy performed best when played against all other strategies: tit-for-tat. This strategy starts cooperatively and then simply replays the opponents last choice.

---

[3] Here, cooperation means that the agent chooses a beneficial option, i.e., he denies the crime; the payoff is the amount of avoided punishment. It does not mean cooperation with law enforcement.

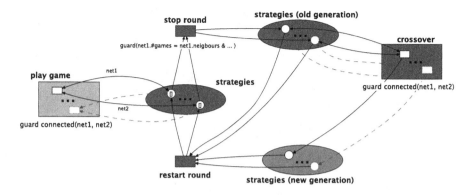

**Fig. 4.** The EHORNET's System Net for the Tournament.

The iterated prisoners dilemma is the most prominent case study for learning in games. The classical approach to adaption is genetic programming. The main idea is simple (cf. [1, pg 80ff]): Each strategy evaluates its payoff so far. The higher the payoff the higher the number of offsprings. An offspring is generated via a cross-over mechanism, i.e., the two parents' histories are split at some fixed point and recombined in a cross-over fashion.

We generalise the setting: We assume that there is a *network* that connects the agents and only *connected* agents can play the game. We assume that a network also determines which agents may be chosen as parents when generating a cross-over. For simplicity we assume both networks to be equal.

We have specified this scenario as an EHORNET. Here, the system net (shown in a simplified version in Fig. 4) specifies which agents are chosen for playing the game. It also specifies which agents are chosen in the adaption process for the cross-over. The system net is parameterised with the connection graph.

The object nets specify the agents, i.e., the strategy automata. One prominent strategy is known as *tit-for-tat*; it simply replays the opponent's action of the last round. The object net for this tit-for-tat strategy is shown in Fig. 5. In our case study we use a pool of several strategies, each modelled as an object net. The strategy nets are encoded as lists of transitions, so it is easy to create new strategies by a standard cross-over operation on sequences. The details of this case study can be found in [34].

We study the impact of the connection graph on the adaption process. Here we compare two different random graph topologies, namely a *Erdős-Rényi graph* [13] and a *Watts-Strogatz graph* [14] with a rewiring probability of $\beta = 0.01$ – both with the same number of nodes ($n = 27$) and the same number of edges ($m = 6n$), We have chosen these two kinds of graphs because they are both well known random graph structures. Moreover, the Erdős-Rényi graph is the special case of a Watts-Strogatz graph where $\beta = 1$. It is well known that for small values of $\beta$ each pair of nodes is connected in a Watts-Strogatz graph via a quite short path of length $\propto \log(n)$, a fact that is also known as the *small world* property [14].

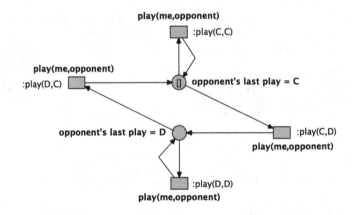

**Fig. 5.** The EHORNET's Object Net for the Tit-For-Tat Strategy.

**Table 1.** Summary of Key Measures of Adaption Processes for different Topologies.

| Adaption Dynamics | Erdős-Rényi | Watts-Strogatz |
|---|---|---|
| *average degree* $\frac{1}{n} \cdot \sum_{v \in V} deg(v)$ | 3.42 | 3.14 |
| *density* $\frac{m}{n(n-1)}$ | 0.13 | 0.26 |
| *transitivity* $C_T$ | 0.07 | 0.00 |
| *eccentricity* $\epsilon(v_0)$ | 4 | 3 |
| variance of *betweenness centrality* $c_B(v)$ | 0.05 | 0.10 |
| adaption directedness $dad(G)$ | 0.63 | 0.55 |
| $width(G)/depth(G)$ | 7/4 = 1.75 | 4/3 = 1.33 |
| rate of exploitation $\chi(G)$ | 0.20 | 0.25 |

Both topologies are modelled as instances of the system net shown in Fig. 4. The resulting EHORNETS are named $EH_1$ and $EH_2$. We generate the abstract adaption graphs $AG_3(EH_i), i = 1, 2$ for the two topologies. The key measures of the two abstracted reachability graphs are given in Table 1. One can observe, for example, that the Erdős-Rényi graph is more exploring than Watts-Strogatz graph as it has a higher average degree, a higher width/depth-ratio, and a lower exploitation rate $\chi(G)$. One may hypothesise that the reason for this lies in the *small world* property of the Watts-Strogatz, i.e., we have long-range connections and therefore every node is only some steps away from any other node, which is not the case for an Erdős-Rényi graph. Therefore, the Watts-Strogatz graph is faster in spreading good genes over the entire population.

## 6 Conclusion

In our research we study adaptive multi-agent systems. We use HORNETS to model the well-known MAPE-loop for adaptive systems. In this setting our analytical framework is used to explore the *exploration vs. exploitation* balance of a concrete MAS model that we use as a *model@run.time* to evaluate the cost-benefit ratio of possible adaption steps.

In this contribution, we developed key measures to compare adaption processes, usually adaption processes of variants of the same system. We used the nets-within-nets formalism of HORNETS as our formal model as they provide a natural description of what is adapted within the system: the set $\tilde{\Pi}_{\mathcal{U}}(\mu)$ of net-types occurring in the current marking $\mu$. Here, the system net describes the general system, while the marking's set of object net types describes the changing gene-pool. For the analysis we abstract from events in the HORNET that doesn't effect the gene pool and use network theoretical measures to describe a fingerprint of the adaption process.

In this paper, we abstracted from events that do not change the gene pool. Currently, we are relaxing this even further by ignoring events that change the gene pool only slightly, i.e., we use a distance $\epsilon$ between gene pools as an additional parameter.

In future work we plan to analyse the adaption dynamics via static properties of the Petri nets, like invariants etc. For most cases it may be sufficient to study an under- or an over-approximation of the state space.

# References

1. Holland, J.H.: Hidden Order: How Adaptation Builds Complexity. Helix Books, New York (1995)
2. Kennedy, J., Eberhart, R.C.: Swarm intelligence. Morgan Kaufmann Publishers Inc., San Francisco (2001)
3. Shoham, Y., Leyton-Brown, K.: Multiagent Systems: Algorithmic, Game-Theoretic, and Logical Foundations. Cambridge University Press, New York (2008)
4. Cabac, L., Moldt, D., Rölke, H.: A proposal for structuring petri net-based agent interaction protocols. In: van der Aalst, W.M.P., Best, E. (eds.) ICATPN 2003. LNCS, vol. 2679, pp. 102–120. Springer, Heidelberg (2003). https://doi.org/10.1007/3-540-44919-1_10
5. Köhler-Bußmeier, M., Wester-Ebbinghaus, M., Moldt, D.: A formal model for organisational structures behind process-aware information systems. In: Jensen, K., van der Aalst, W.M.P. (eds.) Transactions on Petri Nets and Other Models of Concurrency II. LNCS, vol. 5460, pp. 98–114. Springer, Heidelberg (2009). https://doi.org/10.1007/978-3-642-00899-3_6
6. Weyns, D.: Software engineering of self-adaptive systems: an organised tour and future challenges. In: ICAC/SASO (2017)
7. Sudeikat, J., Köhler-Bußmeier, M.: On combining domain modeling and organizational modeling for developing adaptive cyber-physical systems. In: ICAART'22 (2022)
8. Köhler-Bußmeier, M., Sudeikat, J.: On the micro-macro dynamics in MAPE-like adaption processes (2023) (submitted)
9. Hezavehi, S.M., Weyns, D., Avgeriou, P., Calinescu, R., Mirandola, R., Perez-Palacin, D.: Uncertainty in self-adaptive systems: a research community perspective. ACM Trans. Auton. Adapt. Syst. **15**, 1–36 (2021)

10. Köhler-Bußmeier, M.: Hornets: nets within nets combined with net algebra. In: Franceschinis, G., Wolf, K. (eds.) PETRI NETS 2009. LNCS, vol. 5606, pp. 243–262. Springer, Heidelberg (2009). https://doi.org/10.1007/978-3-642-02424-5_15
11. Weyns, D.: Software engineering of self-adaptive systems. In: Handbook of Software Engineering, pp. 399–443. Springer, Cham (2019). https://doi.org/10.1007/978-3-030-00262-6_11
12. Köhler-Bußmeier, M., Rölke, H.: Analysing adaption processes of Hornets. In: Köhler-Bußmeier, M., Moldt, D., Rölke, H., eds.: Petri Nets and Software Engineering 2022, PNSE 2022, vol. 3170, pp. 80–98. CEUR (2022)
13. Erdös, P., Rényi, A.: On random graphs. Publicationes Mathematicae **6**, 290–297 (1959)
14. Watts, D.J., Strogatz, S.H.: Collective dynamics of "small-world" networks. Nature **393**, 440–442 (1998)
15. Dignum, V., Padget, J.: Multiagent organizations. In Weiss, G., ed.: Multiagent Systems, 2nd ed. Intelligent Robotics; Autonomous Agents Series, pp. 51–98. MIT Press (2013)
16. Köhler-Bußmeier, M., Wester-Ebbinghaus, M.: SONAR$^*$: a multi-agent infrastructure for active application architectures and inter-organisational information systems. In: Braubach, L., van der Hoek, W., Petta, P., Pokahr, A. (eds.) MATES 2009. LNCS (LNAI), vol. 5774, pp. 248–257. Springer, Heidelberg (2009). https://doi.org/10.1007/978-3-642-04143-3_27
17. Bencomo, N., France, R., Cheng, B.H.C., Aßmann, U. (eds.): Models@run.time. LNCS, vol. 8378. Springer, Cham (2014). https://doi.org/10.1007/978-3-319-08915-7
18. Köhler-Bußmeier, M., Rölke, H.: Petri-nets@run.time: handling uncertainty during run-time adaptation using digital twins. In: Petri Nets and Software Engineering 2023, PNSE 2023 (2023)
19. Valk, R.: Object petri nets. In: Desel, J., Reisig, W., Rozenberg, G. (eds.) ACPN 2003. LNCS, vol. 3098, pp. 819–848. Springer, Heidelberg (2004). https://doi.org/10.1007/978-3-540-27755-2_23
20. Köhler, M., Rölke, H.: Properties of object petri nets. In: Cortadella, J., Reisig, W. (eds.) ICATPN 2004. LNCS, vol. 3099, pp. 278–297. Springer, Heidelberg (2004). https://doi.org/10.1007/978-3-540-27793-4_16
21. Köhler-Bußmeier, M., Heitmann, F.: On the expressiveness of communication channels for object nets. Fund. Inform. **93**, 205–219 (2009)
22. Cardelli, L., Ghelli, G., Gordon, A.D.: Mobility types for mobile ambients. In: Wiedermann, J., van Emde Boas, P., Nielsen, M. (eds.) ICALP 1999. LNCS, vol. 1644, pp. 230–239. Springer, Heidelberg (1999). https://doi.org/10.1007/3-540-48523-6_20
23. Milner, R., Parrow, J., Walker, D.: A calculus of mobile processes, parts 1–2. Inf. Comput. **100**, 1–77 (1992)
24. Köhler-Bußmeier, M.: On the complexity of the reachability problem for safe, elementary Hornets. Fundamenta Informaticae **129**, 101–116 (2014)
25. Reisig, W.: Petri nets and algebraic specifications. Theoret. Comput. Sci. **80**, 1–34 (1991)
26. Köhler-Bußmeier, M., Heitmann, F.: Safeness for object nets. Fund. Inform. **101**, 29–43 (2010)
27. Köhler-Bußmeier, M., Heitmann, F.: Liveness of safe object nets. Fund. Inform. **112**, 73–87 (2011)
28. Köhler-Bußmeier, M.: A survey on decidability results for elementary object systems. Fund. Inform. **130**, 99–123 (2014)

29. Köhler-Bußmeier, M., Heitmann, F.: An upper bound for the reachability problem of safe, elementary hornets. Fund. Inform. **143**, 89–100 (2016)
30. Köhler-Bußmeier, M.: Restricting HORNETS to support self-adaptive systems. In: van der Aalst, W., Best, E. (eds.) PETRI NETS 2017. LNCS, vol. 10258, pp. 288–306. Springer, Cham (2017). https://doi.org/10.1007/978-3-319-57861-3_17
31. Ehrig, H., Mahr, B.: Fundamentals of algebraic Specification. Springer-Verlag, EATCS Monographs on TCS (1985). https://doi.org/10.1007/978-3-642-69962-7
32. Sayama, H.: Introduction to the Modeling and Analysis of Complex Systems. Open SUNY Textbooks (2015)
33. Axelrod, R.: The Evolution of Cooperation. Basic Books (1984)
34. Jankowski, M., Dang, P.B., Krukenberg, J.: Analyse evolutionärer Strategien. Term paper, HAW Hamburg (2022)

# A Validated Learning Approach to Healthcare Process Analysis Through Contextual and Temporal Filtering

Bahareh Fatemi[1]($\boxtimes$), Fazle Rabbi[1], and Wendy MacCaull[2]

[1] Information Science and Media Studies, University of Bergen, Bergen, Norway
{Bahareh.Fatemi,Fazle.Rabbi}@uib.no
[2] Department of Computer Science, St Francis Xavier University, Antigonish, Canada
wmaccaul@stfx.ca

**Abstract.** The volume and diversity of healthcare data available using modern technology offers great potential for improving health services delivery. Giving clinicians and health system administrators the ability to easily investigate and analyze data from various perspectives can promote evidence-based decision-making. Current analysis approaches often result in process models where essential relations are difficult to depict and/or discern. Moreover, it is not easy to change the level of detail in order to accommodate user requirements by allowing them to analyze data from various perspectives or capture temporal aspects of the data. Further, inherent differences between patients and the vast variety of healthcare settings, even for one patient, make process mining extremely difficult. In this paper, we first discuss community detection methods which, together with filtering techniques based on dimensional modeling and ontologies, allow us to obtain "contextual" insights from event log data using what we call "contextual process mining". Then, to capture time-dependent relations in patient data, we propose a linear temporal logic-based language, $LTL_{EOT}$ ($LTL_{EOT}$: Event-Ontology-Time Linear Temporal Logic), which can be used to express both time and order-dependent conditions. The $LTL_{EOT}$ formulas are used to filter the event log data to find those patients who satisfy the conditions, thus capturing "temporal" insights in event log data. Both the investigations using community detection methods and those using the temporal logic methods are validated learning approaches: the first allows the user to experiment with the level of abstraction, while the second allows the user to experiment with the temporal logic formulas. This approach can give healthcare professionals insights into patterns of admission, diagnosis, and treatment among patients, which, in turn, lead to the overall goal of this research, which is improved resource management, scheduling, and other aspects of health services delivery. In a simple case study, we show this approach leads to an improved understanding of healthcare processes among comorbid patients.

**Keywords:** Healthcare data · Event logs · Process mining · Community detection · Abstraction · Linear temporal logic · Ontology · Context

© The Author(s), under exclusive license to Springer-Verlag GmbH, DE, part of Springer Nature 2024
M. Koutny et al. (Eds.): TPNOMCXVII, LNCS 14150, pp. 108–137, 2024.
https://doi.org/10.1007/978-3-662-68191-6_5

# 1    Introduction

Today's vast amount of healthcare information needs to be accessed easily, integrated intelligently and analyzed appropriately to support better health-care delivery. With intelligent integration and analysis, data can be used to gain deeper insights into patient health using historical healthcare information (including a patient's symptoms, appointments, exercise routines, lab results, vital signs, prescriptions, allergies, assessments, etc.) and also can be used to assess the effectiveness of treatment [62,64]. Context-relevant clinical information can enable improved decision-making as it provides a comprehensive under-standing of the patient's unique circumstances, optimizing treatment plans, and enhancing patient outcomes [15]. Healthcare data analysis across disciplines can facilitate the discovery of new knowledge, which can lead to streamlined work-flows, greater efficiency, and improved patient care. For instance, by analyzing large datasets from various sources, such as medical records, imaging studies, and clinical trials, Clinical Decision Support Systems (CDSS) can identify pat-terns and generate evidence-based recommendations for healthcare providers [58]. As another example, by analyzing data from electronic health records, pub-lic health databases, and socioeconomic information, healthcare organizations can develop targeted interventions, preventive strategies, and resource allocation plans [11,30]. Systematic analysis of healthcare data enables healthcare providers to identify patterns and trends, allowing them to allocate their resources more effectively [25]. By optimizing resource allocation and tailoring treatment plans based on data-driven insights, clinicians can improve health outcomes for indi-viduals, resulting in better overall patient care.

Healthcare systems consist of numerous health facilities that execute clini-cal and non-clinical (e.g., administrative) activities. Up-to-date information can influence decision-makers both at the level of the individual practitioner and at the system level. Both clinicians and administrators would benefit from more intuitive tools that would allow them to more fully utilize the data available to them without the need for sophisticated technical knowledge. They are partic-ularly interested in finding common pathways for patients, ascertaining how a process model can be improved, and determining to what extent existing systems are following clinical guidelines. However, it is not easy to meet these demands as healthcare processes are highly dynamic, complex, ad-hoc, and are increasingly multidisciplinary [54].

Data mining techniques present the opportunity to analyze and learn from healthcare information, from numerous viewpoints (i.e., contexts) such as with respect to patient populations with specific diseases, ages, gender, incidences of comorbidity, type of healthcare service setting (e.g., clinic, hospital, nursing home), home location (urban or rural), procedures used, etc. Community detec-tion [7,55] is a data mining technique that can provide useful information in order to understand relationships between a patient's symptoms and other infor-mation. Community detection algorithms have the potential to identify similar groups of patients but are limited as they do not include temporal information and therefore lack the capacity to determine patient pathways. On the other hand, process mining [1] techniques hold great potential to support health services by identifying common flows of patients, but they too are limited as they are not equipped with community detection methods. In order to adequately study the progression of diseases and the flow of patients from a group, we need an integrated approach combining community detection and process mining.

In [51], we introduced the idea of using a new approach, called model-based slicing, that utilizes ontologies and dimensional models to access the data required for improved data analysis. This approach exploits the use of structured information available in the healthcare industry such as standard ontologies (e.g., ICD (International Classification of Disease)-10 [44], designed to provide diagnostic codes for classifying diseases, and SNOMED-CT [8] which provides a comprehensive terminology for clinical health) as well as organizational frameworks within hospitals and other relevant hierarchies. In [50], we discussed community detection methods which, together with filtering techniques based on dimensional modeling and ontologies, built on the work of [51] to allow us to obtain "contextual insights" from event log data using what we called "contextual process mining". Our approach enhances existing process mining techniques by incorporating a flexible data mining technique for extracting healthcare information from a variety of perspectives and abstraction levels through the use of a data preprocessor.

Identifying the patterns of processes occurring frequently may contribute to streamlining healthcare processes. However, it is difficult to find such patterns due to the complexity of healthcare systems and the fact that they evolve due to a variety of reasons, such as the identification of new diseases and new medications and treatment procedures, etc. It is therefore important to support healthcare analysts with sophisticated, easy-to-use tools.

In this paper, we extend our previous work to support healthcare analysts to study frequently occurring process mining patterns. We focus on identifying comorbidity patterns from healthcare event logs, though the approach has wide applicability. The term "comorbidity" refers to the concurrent occurrence of two or more diseases [59]. Recent studies suggest that 50% of the patients visiting hospitals in the US are diagnosed with eleven or more co-occurring diseases [61]. The study of comorbid diseases can reveal not only the interaction between them but also, in some cases, their cause-effect relations [41]. The ultimate goals of such studies are primarily both understanding disease progression and prediction as well as identifying high-risk comorbidities, so that preventive measures can be taken. Moreover, in studying the cause-effect relations, the chronological order of the development of symptoms (or equivalently, the order of referral to different treatment departments or different diagnoses) is important. For example, the question that may be asked is whether depression led to drug use in a person or vice versa. Medical studies are often conducted to understand the nature of commodities but it is not straightforward to analyze a variety of comorbid conditions and the patient populations with comorbidities from a healthcare dataset. For instance, there have been several studies that prove that chronic kidney disease can both cause and be caused by hypertension [27]. Moreover, the endocrine system and genitourinary can interact in various syndromes [45].

This paper continues the analysis of event log data to determine and understand recurring patterns of patient admission, diagnosis, and treatment. Existing process mining tools such as Fluxicon Disco have a restricted capability to capture healthcare processes. In general, a process is a unique path or specific activity sequence from beginning to end; the inherent variations in patients and healthcare settings generally result in so much variation that healthcare processes are difficult to discern. Another way to capture the order and duration of events is needed. We propose a temporal logic-based language, $LTL_{EOT}$ (Event-Ontology-Time Linear Temporal Logic), which incorporates a variety of time-related concepts involving both order of and intervals between events, allowing us to capture temporal patterns. The user can formulate a query using $LTL_{EOT}$, then use it to filter event log data to find those patients which satisfy the query, thus capturing temporal insights in event log data. This is especially useful when a patient is being tested and/or treated at several sites by a variety of professionals dealing with different issues.

Healthcare professionals possess a high level of knowledge pertaining to their domains accumulated through their extensive experience. This knowledge lends itself to the use of validated learning, a concept introduced by Ries [53], to gain both contextual and temporal insights into healthcare data. Validated learning is the practice of systematically testing and verifying hypotheses or assumptions regarding software systems, algorithms, or data models using empirical evidence and data-driven experimentation. Our approach is meant to allow these professionals to query the system to better understand the processes the patient is undergoing.

The reader can refer to Fig. 1 which offers a high-level road map of our approach. Healthcare professionals can acquire insights from large amounts of data - by locating problem areas at a very high level and understanding temporal aspects of data. The overall goal of our work is to provide a means for health professionals to determine patterns in admission, diagnosis, and treatments. We promote the idea of using dimensional models which incorporate health care ontologies allowing the user to experiment with abstraction levels in the ontologies, then experiment with temporal queries to better understand the temporal aspects. This results in an approach to mine data to better distinguish patterns in patient treatment.

The main contributions of this paper are:

- We propose a novel approach to mining data that involves filtering and abstraction of event logs using ontological hierarchies (which we call "contextual insight") and filtering of event logs based on temporal queries (which we call "temporal insight").
- We propose a temporal logic-based language $LTL_{EOT}$ which incorporates the temporal aspects of order and interval. We define its semantics, so that the base case of the satisfaction relation incorporates ontological concepts, adapt the CTL model checking algorithm for checking the path satisfaction

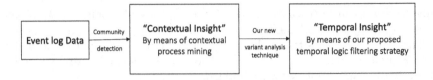

Fig. 1. A high-level road map of this study.

relationship for $LTL_{EOT}$ formulas, prove the correctness of the algorithm, and give its complexity.

- We promote a validated learning approach to be used by healthcare professionals in the investigation of event log data.
- We present some experiments illustrating aspects of contextual insights gained from event logs for contextual process mining and a case study involving temporal insights from event logs in the study of comorbidity patterns.

The rest of this paper is organized as follows. As this paper is a revised and extended version of [50] and forms the basis upon which the paper depends, we summarize the work done there in Sect. 2. In Sect. 3, we introduce the temporal logic-based language $LTL_{EOT}$, give its semantics, present the algorithm for checking a path for the satisfaction of an $LTL_{EOT}$ formula, and prove its correctness and complexity. We discuss the application of $LTL_{EOT}$ in the study of comorbidity. In Sect. 4, we outline related work. Section 5 concludes the paper and outlines some future work.

## 2    Towards Contextual Process Mining

In [50], we presented an approach for filtering and abstraction of event logs using ontologies, dimensional modeling, and community (cluster) analysis. In Sects. 2.1–2.3, we review some of the important concepts and proposed techniques from [50].

### 2.1    Process Mining

In many developed countries, most citizens use public healthcare services involving multiple service providers, providing diverse services supported by numerous software applications. Various types of data analysis are required due to the various roles played by healthcare professionals: e.g., while a clinician is interested to see the progression of diseases and to study the effects of different treatment procedures, healthcare managers wish to study the patient flow from one clinic to another and the number of patients waiting to get services.

In principle, process mining can be used to acquire and explore new knowledge about patient conditions, adherence to treatment programs, the effectiveness of treatment, etc. The main focus of process mining in healthcare is to provide evidence-based process analysis techniques for effective process management [47]. It combines community detection and process analysis techniques and is used to discover trends and patterns of process executions by analyzing the trace of activities performed in a system. These traces are referred to as 'event logs'. However, existing process mining techniques use event logs as input which typically consist of event information such as case-id, event time, event name, and attributes of events. Since healthcare information is much more complex than information from most other domains, current process mining techniques cannot adequately mine the information from the event logs required by the various health professionals and therefore are not exploited to their full potential.

In a healthcare setting, patients may need to visit various health facilities for various health-related issues and also may need to use certain online treatment programs. Hence, for effective process mining, event logs representing activities of various systems must be considered. Event logs from a variety of systems using various data definitions and formats must therefore be harmonized before they can be analyzed by any process mining algorithm. Another issue with applying process mining in healthcare data is related to the diversity of information. Identifying common pathways for patient flow in healthcare systems is complicated by the large variety of patient conditions and diagnoses. In healthcare, the data preparation task is very critical as healthcare data are very sensitive, and therefore semantics of the data must be preserved. Getting the right setup for data preparation is important to get the best understanding of the data as efficiently as possible [49]. The current situation in healthcare information systems makes this a complicated problem indeed.

Imagine a situation where we have event logs representing patient information with respect to patient visits to various clinics (or service points in the hospital) and patient diagnoses. Table 1 shows a portion of such an event log. The first column represents the *CaseId* information. In this case, it represents the patient's identification number. The second column, *EventId*, represents the identifier of the events. The third column, *Event-time*, represents the time when the event occurred; the fourth column, *Activity*, represents the name of the activity associated with the event, and the last column, *Resource*, represents the name of the corresponding resource. Due to the complexity in the process flow and diversity of diagnosis information, the process model discovered from such an event log is very large in size and it is difficult to extract meaningful information from it. Even after filtering, the event log to keep, e.g., only the patient cases which are admitted to the Radiology Department, the model is still very large. Figure 2 shows a fragment of radiology patients' flow (using a screenshot from Fluxicon Disco [23]) from a sample patient registry dataset. While the Fluxicon Disco process mining tool is equipped with several filtering mechanisms, for example, Fluxicon Disco can ignore low-frequency nodes to reduce the size of a diagram, this results in the loss of information that may be relevant. Fluxicon Disco and similar other process mining tools such as PROM [18] have some limitations, for example, they do not provide an overall view of a large process model from a higher level of abstraction.

Another issue with existing process mining tools is that they do not provide a flexible mechanism to perform context-aware process mining. While analyzing

**Table 1.** Portion of a healthcare event log (Sample data)

| CaseId | EventId | Event_time | Activity | Resource |
|---|---|---|---|---|
| 1 | 101 | 2017-03-20 13:30 | Surgical Clinic | Kristi Salazar |
| 1 | 102 | 2017-03-20 13:30 | (N39_9) Disorder of urinary system | Darla Ramirez |
| 2 | 103 | 2017-03-07 14:00 | Radiology Department | Ricky Alvarado |
| 2 | 104 | 2017-03-07 15:00 | (N63) Unspecified lump in breast | Deborah Tyler |
| 2 | 105 | 2017-03-07 15:15 | (N64_5) Other symptoms in breast | Johanna Buchanan |
| 3 | 106 | 2017-04-06 08:30 | Division of Mental Health Protection | Henrietta King |
| 3 | 107 | 2017-04-06 08:30 | (F321) Depressive episode | Beatrice French |

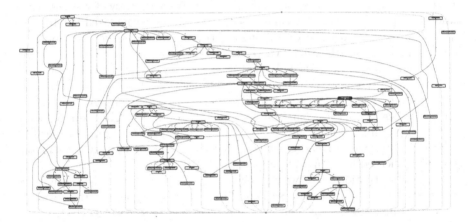

**Fig. 2.** A fragment of Radiology Patients flow visualized in Fluxicon Disco Process mining tool

common pathways for patients, different contexts are required to allow clinicians to focus on different groups of patients and visualize their care flows. Clinicians would be interested to study the comorbidity issues of patients and analyze the pathways of different patient groups. Existing process mining techniques may be used to visualize the flow of patients but the event logs need to be prepared in different ways in order to support a wider variety of queries. In the following, we provide an example to illustrate this need. Considering the event logs from Table 1, suppose we wish to investigate the flow of those patients to various departments in the hospital who have been diagnosed with some mental disorders, i.e., they have an ICD-10 code in the range F00-F99.9. We wish to focus on only those patients who are very similar or, in other words, belong to a community structure. The event logs in Table 1 consist of some information at a very low level, i.e., visits to clinics and specific diagnosis information. We need to relate clinics to their department hierarchy and specific diagnosis information to their diagnosis group from the ICD-10 ontology. Relating clinics to departments and diagnosis to diagnosis group allows us to choose the desired abstraction layer. Neither the choice of abstraction layer for defining the context nor integrating community detection algorithms are not supported by existing process mining tools. In [51], we argued that the current practice of process mining needs to be advanced by means of a rich information model which supports various perspectives needed to analyze event logs.

## 2.2  Contextualization Using Data Mining

Healthcare data are received from various healthcare service providers and personal health applications, such as patient monitoring applications and sensor devices. It is becoming a difficult task for health caregivers to analyze all these data from various sources and extract information in a meaningful way. Visualization of healthcare information can greatly help care providers gain insights from patients' data and make important decisions [52]. Data mining techniques such as community detection are used to identify useful information from healthcare data; the outcome of such data mining technologies can be useful to healthcare providers enabling them to understand the effectiveness of treatment processes and to streamline healthcare processes and treatment protocols [28]. Community structure in patient records based on patient condition and symptoms provide useful information for efficiently detecting unknown and valuable information. Data mining approaches can also be used to help medical researchers in making efficient healthcare policies, constructing drug recommendation systems, and developing health profiles of individuals [28]. Community detection algorithms are easy to apply for healthcare data as they are based on unsupervised learning techniques, i.e., the data does not need to be labeled.

One of the challenges for revolutionizing current healthcare systems is to adapt the treatment procedure according to the various needs of a diverse group of patients [56]. This requires a better understanding of each patient's condition including patient demographics, symptoms, preferences, interests, etc. In general, healthcare systems consist of various processes inside hospital organizations and several other processes outside the boundary of healthcare organizations to support online treatments. The central motivation of personalized medicine is the premise that an individual has a significant role in disease vulnerability and the selection of treatments [46]. Such personalization and adaptive treatment systems behave differently for different users. The decision on how these systems should behave for any particular user is based on a user model, which is a detailed representation of an individual user's information, such as *user preferences, interests, behavior, background, knowledge, individual traits,* and *others.* As these attributes are dynamic, it is essential to create, maintain, and update the user model.

There exist several algorithms to partition a dataset based on the association of its individuals. Patient demographic information along with other information can be effectively used to group patients using algorithms such as k-Means Clustering algorithm [28,39] and Community Detection algorithms [7,55]. Li et al. [35] constructs a lower-dimensional feature matrix of the weighted network using a deep sparse autoencoder and then performs a K-means algorithm for obtaining the community detection results. [33] proposes an embedding-based method that tackles the problem of overlapping communities. They design a Generative Adversarial Net (GAN) for optimization. [29] propose a Markov Random Field (MRF) method formalizing modularity as the energy function. However, such algorithms are not equipped with healthcare ontologies to provide perspectives from various abstraction levels. There are situations where domain experts would like to investigate patient problems in a specific area with greater detail but at the same time only get an overview of other areas at an abstract level. For example, a psychologist would be interested to see patients with specific mental problems and their comorbidity with ailments such as diabetes, cardiovascular disease, cancer, infectious diseases, etc.

In the next section, we discuss a solution that allows specifying contexts for mining patient information from a variety of abstraction levels, leading to improved process mining.

## 2.3    Contextual Process Mining

The main challenge in performing data analysis using existing process mining and clustering/community detection tools and techniques is the lack of support for the needed filtering and abstraction, which would give the individual practitioner or administrator the ability to extract and explore data from whatever perspective they deem appropriate. One may need to both filter information to select certain sub-populations of patients, or certain clinical contexts and also to group information to allow patterns to emerge from a more abstract view. In [51], Rabbi et al., presented a model-based slicing technique for process mining that utilizes dimensional modeling and ontological representations of healthcare information. The slicing techniques allow domain experts to analyze pathways for patients from various contexts, e.g., patients diagnosed with cancer, or patients admitted into the women's clinic, etc. The approach was based on a filtering mechanism where we allow filtering over the abstraction level on healthcare ontologies; however this approach was limited to selecting patient groups of similar kinds. For example, in [51] we show that it is possible to filter patients who have been diagnosed with any'mental disorder' but that may include patients who have a variety of other issues. Patient $P_1$ may be quite different than $P_2$ even though they have some commonalities. We now show how our approach promotes contextual process mining.

The graph in Fig. 3 consists of nodes with patient identifications (shown as integers). This figure is built with Gephi [4] tool, which is used here for visualization of the network of patients and their diagnoses. The network is constructed using NetworkX [24] Python library. We use the group code of the ICD-10 diagnostics code (i.e., diagnoses in the range F00_F09 are grouped, etc.). Different colors denote different communities and the size of the node representing the group code is determined by the degree of the node (i.e., the number of patients with that group code). This abstraction yields a good visualization: we can easily pick the patients who have been diagnosed with multiple mental issues. From

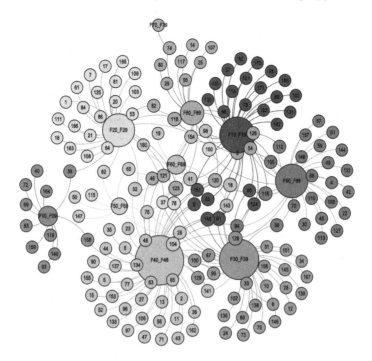

**Fig. 3.** Communities of patients based on their diagnosis (abstract view)

this figure we can see that many of the patients were diagnosed with F40_F48 (anxiety, dissociative, stress-related, somatoform, and other nonpsychotic mental disorders), F30_F39 (mood [affective] disorders), F20_F29 (schizophrenia, schizotypal and delusional disorders), F90_F98 (unspecified mental disorder), F10_F19 (mental and behavioral disorders due to psychoactive substance use) and the overlap is indicated by the patient nodes in the center of the graph with their association to multiple diagnoses nodes.

the above shows how ontologies can be incorporated into community detection; now we show how the selected group of patient event logs can be analyzed with process mining tools. An analyst may be interested in investigating the progression of diseases or the admission flow of patients in different departments. In our approach, appropriate events are prepared based on the selection of event types, e.g., diagnosis, admission, etc. We enrich the model-based slicing approach presented in [51] with an approach that contextualizes the dataset with patients from specific communities and then provides the contextual information to a process mining tool. Figure 4 illustrates the approach. The raw data includes patient diagnosis and admission-related information. We include a variety of hierarchical search dimensions (e.g., diseases, admissions) for the data analysis tasks. While applying community detection over patient records, we have the opportunity to specify which search dimension we would like to explore. In this example, we have specified a specific group of diagnosis code range (F00-F99).

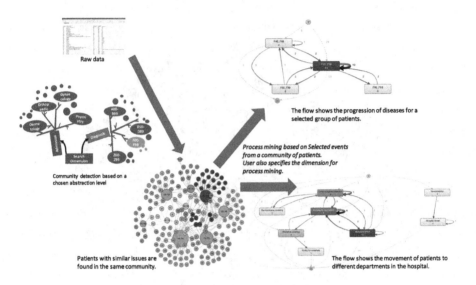

**Fig. 4.** Integration of community detection with model-based slicing for contextual process mining

The output of the community detection algorithm is shown on the bottom left side of the figure. The communities can be further analyzed by means of a process mining technique. While applying the process mining technique, we have the opportunity to specify which dimension we wish to explore. This selection is taken into account to prepare the event log for the process mining technique. The output of the process mining technique is shown on the right side of the figure. In this example, shows flows for two different dimensions: the progression of diseases of a particular group of patients (top right side of the figure) and patient admission flow in various departments (bottom right side of the figure). A prototype implementation supports the proposed approach.

## 3    Validated Learning for Healthcare Process Analysis

Although the approach proposed in Sect. 2 allows us to switch perspectives and analyze healthcare datasets from various abstraction levels, one of its limitations is that it cannot effectively find process variants. In healthcare, every patient is different, so it is challenging to identify process variations that represent patterns of patients using existing tools. For the remainder of the paper, we take the problem of comorbidity as a motivating example to illustrate our approaches.

We believe comorbidity can be inspected from both *contextual* and *temporal* aspects. By contextual we mean capturing the relations between diseases regardless of time, taking into account how they co-occur. Incorporating time to capture the order and time intervals results in temporal analysis. By performing community detection, as in Sect. 2, we can extract communities, each of which

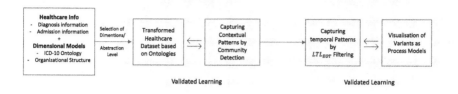

**Fig. 5.** Our proposed approach for healthcare data analysis

includes a set of patients and common diseases between them. We can apply this contextual approach to reduce the search space in huge volumes of event records to search for comorbidity patterns. However, we want to extract temporal information too. In administrative data, which is usually collected for the purpose of record keeping in medical centers [31], information such as the admission of the patients, their visits to different departments, various diagnoses made on them, and, most importantly, temporal information, including the time of occurrence of each event, is collected. Having a large volume of event logs and with the help of process mining, we can study comorbidity with a low processing load and time complexity. While existing process mining tools are equipped with some filtering facilities, they fail to filter the event log data based on more complex patterns. Here we introduce temporal logic $LTL_{EOT}$ and show how it can be used as a filtering strategy to include temporal information in our analysis. To the best of our knowledge, the temporal aspect of comorbidity has not been addressed in the literature, which means most of the existing methodologies do not take into account the time interval between the occurrence of two potentially comorbid diseases.

Healthcare professionals possess a certain level of knowledge pertaining to their domain, which has been accumulated through their extensive experience, but sometimes they need to support/verify their insights. We propose a validated learning-based mechanism to acquire insight from large amounts of healthcare data. Figure 5 summarizes our proposed approach. The grey ovals show two separate validated learning processes. In the first step, the user can zoom in and zoom out on the data by setting the desired level of abstraction provided with ontologies; in the second step, the user can query the healthcare dataset with a temporal logic formula and see the results in a process mining tool.

Capturing both contextual and temporal aspects of comorbidity in a validated learning approach enables end users to systematically test and validate their hypotheses.

## 3.1 $LTL_{EOT}$: Event-Ontology-Time Linear Temporal Logic

In this section we propose a temporal logic-based language, $LTL_{EOT}$, which incorporates a variety of time-related concepts involving both order of events and time intervals between events, allowing us to capture temporal patterns.

**Table 2.** Linear temporal logic time-related operations

| Operation | Description |
|-----------|-------------|
| $\Box\varphi$ | $\varphi$ will always hold. |
| $\Diamond\varphi$ | $\varphi$ will eventually hold. |
| $\bigcirc\varphi$ | $\varphi$ will hold next. |
| $\psi \cup \varphi$ | $\psi$ will eventually hold, and until then $\varphi$ will hold. |

Linear temporal logic (LTL) [21] is a modal temporal logic with modalities referring to (temporal) order of events. Temporal logic model checking using LTL [13], is a method for determining whether a given LTL formula holds in a finite state model of a system by searching for a counterexample (which is a sequence of states for which the formula does not hold). Some well-known applications of LTL include software and hardware verification, and automated verification of processes and programs [3]. Our approach is somewhat different: we use $LTL_{EOT}$ queries to search patient event logs for patients exhibiting the pattern articulated by the specified $LTL_{EOT}$ formula.

Contrary to first-order logic, LTL is empowered by a set of temporal operators, $\Box, \Diamond, \bigcirc, U, R, W$, which enables us to model and reason about systems as they evolve over time. Let $P$ be the set of the propositional symbols (or simply the alphabet) and $\psi, \varphi, \phi$ be propositional formulas over $P$. A well-formed $LTL$ formula, $\phi$, is recursively defined by the BNF formula as shown in Eq. (1) [32]. In this paper we restrict our discussion and examples to the more easily understood operators $\Box, \Diamond, \bigcirc, U$. Table 2 summarizes the common understandings of those temporal operators; the satisfaction relation $\models$ for $LTL$ is given in Definition 1.

$$\phi := \top \mid \bot \mid p \mid \neg\phi \mid \phi \wedge \phi \mid \phi \vee \phi \mid \bigcirc\phi \mid \Diamond\phi \mid \Box\phi \mid \phi\, U\phi \qquad (1)$$

**Definition 1.** *Let $S$ be a set of states and $\mathcal{P}(atom)$ be the power set of atoms. Let $\pi = s_1, s_2, s_3, \ldots$ be a path in $S$, and $L : S \to \mathcal{P}(atoms)$ be a labeling function. The satisfaction relation $\models$ for an LTL formula is defined as follows, where $\pi^i$ denotes the path $s_i, s_{i+1}, \ldots$:*

- $\pi \models \top$
- $\pi \not\models \bot$
- $\pi \models p$ *iff $p \in L(s_1)$*
- $\pi \models \neg\phi$ *iff $\pi \not\models \phi$*
- $\pi \models \phi_1 \wedge \phi_2$ *iff $\pi \models \phi_1$ and $\pi \models \phi_2$*
- $\pi \models \phi_1 \vee \phi_2$ *iff $\pi \models \phi_1$ or $\pi \models \phi_2$*
- $\pi \models \phi_1 \to \phi_2$ *iff $\pi \models \phi_2$ whenever $\pi \models \phi_1$*
- $\pi \models \bigcirc \phi$ *iff $\pi^2 \models \phi$*
- $\pi \models \Box \phi$ *iff, for all $i \geq 1, \pi^i \models \phi$*
- $\pi \models \Diamond \phi$ *iff, there is some $i \geq 1$ such that $\pi^i \models \phi$*
- $\pi \models \phi_1 \cup \phi_2$ *iff, there is some $i \geq 1$ such that $\pi^i \models \phi_2$ and for all $j = 1, 2, \ldots i - 1$ we have $\pi^j \models \phi_1$*

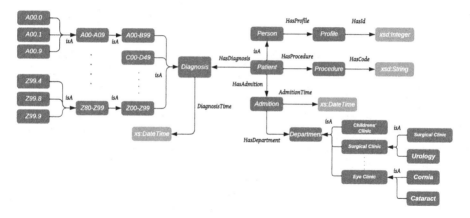

**Fig. 6.** Ontology model for patient profile and its relationship with ICD-10 and department ontologies

**Syntax and Semantics of $LTL_{EOT}$.** The original definition of $LTL$ describes the relative sequencing of states, or in our case, events, but does not include specific time-related information. We enrich the definition of $LTL$ for the purpose of specifying time intervals and propose $LTL_{EOT}$, Events-Ontology-Time linear temporal logic.

We use Web Ontology Language (OWL) [57] for modeling the concepts and relationships of patients with existing ontological hierarchies such as ICD-10 ontology, and department hierarchies. The patients have relationships with diagnosis, admission, and procedure concepts. Figure 6 shows the terminology (TBox $T$) of the ontology model. The figure includes the overall scheme of the ICD-10 hierarchy. Each node in this ICD-10 hierarchy (left top side of the figure) corresponds to a disease classification code.

Patient information from the healthcare dataset is used to assert individuals ($I$) for the concepts and roles from the TBox. The concept and role assertions represent the ABox of the ontology. An interpretation function $\cdot^{\mathcal{I}}$ maps every individual name $a \in I$ to the element $a^{\mathcal{I}} \in \Delta^{\mathcal{I}}$. where $\Delta^{\mathcal{I}}$ represents the domain of $\mathcal{I}$, and $\mathcal{I}$ satisfies

- a concept assertion $C(a)$ if $a^{\mathcal{I}} \in C^{\mathcal{I}}$, and
- a role assertion $r(a, b)$ if $\langle a^{\mathcal{I}}, b^{\mathcal{I}} \rangle \in r^{\mathcal{I}}$.

We use the OWL concepts in $LTL_{EOT}$ expressions and the interpretation function in the semantics of $LTL_{EOT}$.

A well-formed $LTL_{EOT}$ formula with time, $\phi$, is therefore recursively defined by the BNF formula below:

$$\phi := \top \mid \bot \mid C \mid \neg\phi \mid \phi \wedge \phi \mid \phi \vee \phi \mid \bigcirc_{(TimeInterval)}$$
$$\phi \mid \Diamond_{(TimeInterval)} \phi \mid \Box_{(TimeInterval)} \phi \mid \phi \cup_{(TimeInterval)} \phi \tag{2}$$

$$TimeInterval := \; < Time \mid \; \leq \; Time \mid \; > Time \mid \; \geq \; Time \mid \; = Time$$

$$Time := INT \; second \mid INT \; minute \mid INT \; hour \mid INT \; days$$
$$\mid INT \; week \mid INT \; month \mid INT \; year \mid Time \; and \; Time$$

In Definition 2, we define the semantics of $LTL_{EOT}$ formulas by means of a satisfaction relation over the notion of a path. A path consists of a sequence of events. The events are associated with instances that are classified by the terminologies from an ontology. For example, if an event $(e_j)$ is associated with (via an activity) a diagnosis instance $d_i$ which is classified by a disease concept N39_9 Disorder of the urinary system, the path satisfaction relation ensures that the instance is in the interpretation of the concept N39_9 Disorder of urinary system from the ontology, i.e., $\#_{Activity}(e_j) \in (N39\_9)^{\mathcal{I}}$.

The definition uses a function $diff_{Time}()$ to measure the time difference between two events.

$$diff_{Time}(e_i, e_{i+1}) = \#_{Event-time}(e_{i+1}) - \#_{Event-time}(e_i) \tag{3}$$

We will be using a $\#()$ function to refer to the values from the event log [60]. A subscript will be used for the function to indicate the name of the column. For example, with respect to Table 1 $\#_{Activity}(102)$ refers to the activity '(N39_9) Disorder of urinary system' of the event with id 102.

**Definition 2.** *Given an arbitrary path* $\pi = e_1, e_2, e_3, \ldots$ *where* $e_1, e_2, e_3$ *are events, the satisfaction relation* $\models$ *for an* $LTL_{EOT}$ *formula is defined as follows:*

- $\pi \models \top$
- $\pi \not\models \bot$
- $\pi \models C$ *iff* $\#_{Activity}(e_1) \in C^{\mathcal{I}}$
- $\pi \models \neg\phi$ *iff* $\pi \not\models \phi$
- $\pi \models \phi_1 \wedge \phi_2$ *iff* $\pi \models \phi_1$ *and* $\pi \models \phi_2$
- $\pi \models \phi_1 \vee \phi_2$ *iff* $\pi \models \phi_1$ *or* $\pi \models \phi_2$
- $\pi \models \phi_1 \rightarrow \phi_2$ *iff* $\pi \models \phi_2$ *whenever* $\pi \models \phi_1$
- $\pi \models \bigcirc_{(TimeInterval)} \phi$ *iff* $\pi^2 \models \phi$ *and* $diff_{Time}(e_1, e_2)$ *complies with* $TimeInterval$
- $\pi \models \square_{(TimeInterval)} \phi$ *iff, for all* $i \geq 1, \pi^i \models \phi$ *and* $diff_{Time}(e_1, e_i)$ *complies with* $TimeInterval$
- $\pi \models \lozenge_{(TimeInterval)} \phi$ *iff, there is some* $i \geq 1$ *such that* $\pi^i \models \phi$ *and* $diff_{Time}(e_1, e_i)$ *complies with* $TimeInterval$
- $\pi \models \phi_1 \; \cup_{(TimeInterval)} \phi_2$ *iff, there is some* $i \geq 1$ *such that* $\pi^i \models \phi_2$ *and for all* $j = 1, 2, \ldots i - 1$ *we have* $\pi^j \models \phi_1$ *and* $diff_{Time}(e_1, e_i)$ *complies with* $TimeInterval$

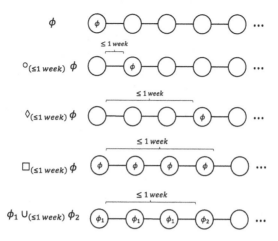

**Fig. 7.** Example of paths with events and time intervals.

**Table 3.** Examples $LTL_{EOT}$ temporal operations

| Operation | Description |
|---|---|
| $\Box_{(3\ hours)}\ \varphi$ | $\varphi$ will hold in all events within the next 3 $h$ |
| $\Diamond_{(\leq 2\ days)}\ \varphi$ | $\varphi$ will hold at some event within the next 2 $days$ |
| $\bigcirc_{(3\ years)}\ \varphi$ | $\varphi$ will hold at the next event occurring in 3 $years$ |
| $\psi\ \cup_{(>3\ days)}\ \varphi$ | $\psi$ will hold some time after 3 $days$, and at all events until then, $\varphi$ holds |

Figure 7 visualizes the semantics of some operations of our proposed temporal logic; and 3 illustrates some examples using these operators.

We adopt the CTL model checking algorithm from [32] for checking the path satisfaction relationship for $LTL_{EOT}$ formulas. The event log consists of data from multiple patients. Separating the event logs based on case ids give us the path representation of individual patients. We apply algorithm [32] for checking the satisfaction of each path. Algorithm 1 labels the events of a path with formulas. The algorithm iteratively labels the events with sub-formulas that satisfy fragments of the paths. It takes a parse tree of an $LTL_{EOT}$ formula and computes the satisfaction of sub-formulas against sub-paths. The computation stops when the root element of the parse tree is reached after processing of the satisfaction of the complete formula. The algorithm uses post-order traversal of the parse trees and checks for the satisfaction of the paths. To check the time interval constraints over paths, it needs to settle the starting events depending on part of the tree during the traversal. For example, a sub-formula $\Diamond_{(\leq 7months)}e_q)$ of a whole formula $\Box_{\geq 0seconds}(e_p \rightarrow \Diamond_{(\leq 7months)}e_q)$ needs to consider the fragment of the path where $e_p$ becomes true and needs to make sure that eventually $e_q$ happens within 7 months from the moment where $e_p$ happened. The algorithm takes that into account while processing a sub-formula in the form $\phi_l \rightarrow \phi_r$, by

**Algorithm 1.** Check for satisfaction

**Input**: A parse tree $\tau$ representing a $LTL_{EOT}$ formula $\phi$, a path $\pi$ in the form of sequence of events $e_1, e_2, e_3, ...e_n$

**Output**: True or False indicating whether the path $\pi$ satisfies $\phi$ or not.

**Step 1**: Starting from the bottom of the parse tree we check for path satisfaction of sub-formulas with the following steps and gradually move towards the root. The traversal is based on the Postorder traversal (Left-Right-Root) of a binary tree. The processing starts with $e_{start} = e_1$. We remark that in processing a sub-formula in the form $\phi_l \rightarrow \phi_r$, $e_{start}$ is set to the event where the left sub-formula is found true. This starting point is used for the computation of the right sub-formulas.

**Step 2**: For each node $\tau_i$ of the tree representing a sub-formula $\phi_i$ of $\phi$:

**Step 2.1**: If $\tau_i$ is a leaf node, THEN label any event $e_k$ with $\phi_i$ if $\#_{Activity}(e_k) \in \phi_i^{\mathcal{I}}$.

**Step 2.2**: If $\tau_i$ is an internal node and all its children have been processed, THEN the labeling of any event $e_k$ is determined by the following case analysis:

**Step 2.2.1**: if $\phi_i$ is in the form of $\psi_1 \wedge \psi_2$ and $e_k$ is labeled with both $\psi_1$ and $\psi_2$, THEN label $e_k$ with $\phi_i$.

**Step 2.2.2**: if $\phi_i$ is in the form of $\psi_1 \vee \psi_2$ and $e_k$ is labeled with either $\psi_1$ or $\psi_2$, THEN label $e_k$ with $\phi_i$.

**Step 2.2.3**: if $\phi_i$ is in the form of $\psi_1 \rightarrow \psi_2$ and $e_k$ is labeled with $\psi_2$ whenever $e_k$ is labeled with $\psi_1$, THEN label $e_k$ with $\phi_i$.

**Step 2.2.4**: if $\phi_i$ is in the form of $\bigcirc_{(TimeInterval)}\psi$ and $e_{k+1}$ is labeled with $\psi$ and $diff_{Time}(e_k, e_{k+1})$ complies with $TimeInterval$, THEN label $e_k$ with $\phi_i$.

**Step 2.2.5**: if $\phi_i$ is in the form of $\square(TimeInterval)\psi$ and $e_{start}, ..., e_{k-1}, e_k$ is labeled with $\psi$ and $diff_{Time}(e_{start}, e_k)$ complies with $TimeInterval$, THEN label $e_{start}$ with $\phi_i$.

**Step 2.2.6**: if $\phi_i$ is in the form of $\Diamond(TimeInterval)\psi$ and there exists an event $e_k$ with label $\psi$ and $diff_{Time}(e_{start}, e_k)$ complies with $TimeInterval$, THEN label $e_{start}, ...e_k$ with $\phi_i$.

**Step 2.2.7**: if $\phi_i$ is in the form of $\psi_1 U_{(TimeInterval)}\psi_2$ and there exists an event $e_k$ with label $\psi_2$ and for all $j = start, ...k - 1$, events $e_j$'s are labeled with $\psi_1$ and $diff_{Time}(e_{start}, e_k)$ complies with $TimeInterval$, THEN label $e_{start}, ...e_k$ with $\phi_i$.

**Step 3**: When all the computations of sub-formulas are finished, return True if $e_1$ is labeled with $\phi$; else return False

---

setting the $e_{start}$ from the left traversal of the tree. While traversing the right subtree the algorithm uses the $e_{start}$ as it was set from the context of the left sub-formulas. The processing of any other internal operator does not require such resetting of $e_{start}$.

**Proof of Correctness of Algorithm 1**: We demonstrate the correctness of Algorithm 1 by induction on the height of the parse tree.

**Base Case**: Parse tree $\tau$ consists of only one leaf node i.e., height 0. It is straightforward to show that the algorithm works for the base case. In this case, the root node is a leaf node and event $e_1$ must be labeled with formula $\phi$ if $\#_{Activity}(e_1) \in \phi^{\mathcal{I}}$.

**Induction Hypothesis**: For an arbitrary parse tree $\tau$ with height $k$ the algorithm provides correct results.

**Induction Step:** Let's assume we have a parse tree $\tau$ with height $k+1$; we need to show that the algorithm provides correct output. In this case, we have the following scenarios:

a) The root node has one subtree. The root node in this case must be one of the temporal operators $\bigcirc_{TimeInterval}$, $\square_{TimeInterval}$, $\lozenge_{TimeInterval}$. For all the temporal operators the algorithm will check for the satisfaction relation correctly because of the instructions provided in Step 2.2.4-Step 2.2.6.
b) The root node has two subtrees. Each of the subtrees is of at most height $k$ and we can assume from the induction hypothesis that the algorithm provides correct output for each subtree (representing sub-formulas $\psi_1$, $\psi_2$) individually.
   - If root node contains operator $\wedge$, the algorithm combines the results of the sub formulas and labels event $e_1$ with $\psi_1 \wedge \psi_2$ if $e_1$ is labeled with both $\psi_1$ and $\psi_2$.
   - If root node contains operator $\vee$, the algorithm combines the results of the sub formulas and labels event $e_1$ with $\psi_1 \vee \psi_2$ if $e_1$ is labeled with $\psi_1$ or $\psi_2$.
   - If the root node contains operator $\rightarrow$, the algorithm combines the results of the sub-formulas and labels event $e_1$ with $\psi_1 \rightarrow \psi_2$ under the following circumstances: $e_1$ is labeled with $\psi_2$ whenever it is labeled with $\psi_1$ then, label $e_1$ with $\psi_1 \rightarrow \psi_2$.
   - If root node contains operator $U_{TimeInterval}$, the algorithm combines the results of the sub formulas and label event $e_1$ with $\psi_1 U_{TimeInterval} \psi_2$ if there exists an event $e_k$ with label $\psi_2$ and all events $e_1, e_2, ... e_{k-1}$ are labeled with $\psi_1$ and $diff_{Time}(e_1, e_k)$ complies with the $TimeInterval$ (see Step 2.2.7).

Therefore we can conclude that the Algorithm 1 provides correct results in all situations.

**Complexity Analysis:** For a given parse tree with $n$ number of nodes and a sequence of events with length $m$, Algorithm 1 has the worst case time complexity $O((n/2) * m^2)$. It can be understood by considering situations where the algorithm needs to check the label of each pair of events in a sequence and compare the time differences in between. For an internal node with a binary temporal operator, the algorithm has time complexity $m^2$ because there are $m^2$ possible comparisons. Given the total number of nodes $n$, the algorithm's total complexity is therefore $O((n/2) * m^2)$.

## 3.2 The Motivating Comorbidity Example

Recall Table 1 shows a portion of a healthcare event log. The event log consists of the events associated with the admission-related information as well as diagnosis-related information. The diagnosis information is specified with a detailed ICD-10 code and name. In our approach, we manipulate the event log according to

**Table 4.** Portion of a healthcare event log (Sample data)

| CaseId | EventId | Event_time | Activity | Resource |
|--------|---------|------------|----------|----------|
| 1 | 102 | 2017-03-20 13:30 | (N39_9) Disorder of urinary system | Darla Ramirez |
| 2 | 104 | 2017-03-07 15:00 | (N63) Unspecified lump in breast | Deborah Tyler |
| 2 | 105 | 2017-03-07 15:15 | (N64_5) Other symptoms in breast | Johanna Buchanan |
| 3 | 107 | 2017-04-06 08:30 | (F321) Depressive episode | Beatrice French |

the selection of the dimensional model and the selection of abstraction based on ontological hierarchy. Table 4 shows a filtered and transformed event log where the activity has been selected based on the diagnosis information. A patient may be diagnosed with several diseases, within different time intervals during the treatment trajectory. In Table 4 the patient with $CaseId = 2$ has 2 records showing the event logs ($EventId = 104, 105$) corresponding to diagnoses. For this patient, the path, $\pi$ is then the sequence of events with $EventId$ 104 and 105; i.e., $\pi_2 = e_{104}, e_{105}$.

Having such paths for all patients, the patterns of comorbidity can be extracted by applying the query and filtering the transformed event log data. According to the definitions of comorbidity, a user might be interested to detect the following patterns in the event log data:

1. Diseases that appear right after one another.
2. Diseases that develop one after the other over short or extended periods of time.
3. Diseases that occur after a continuous period of a condition such as high blood pressure.
4. Diseases that appear continuously and at determinable time intervals.

Our proposed $LTL_{EOT}$ language has the expressive power to represent these patterns. A few examples are shown below:

- Find all events of patients who are diagnosed with iron deficiency anemia (D50), right after being diagnosed with chronic kidney disease (N18):

$$\Diamond_{(\geq\, 0\, s)}(N18) \wedge \Box_{(\geq\, 0\, s)}\left((N18) \rightarrow \bigcirc_{(\geq\, 0\, s)}(D50)\right) \qquad (4)$$

- Find all the events of patients who have been diagnosed with diabetes mellitus (E08-E13) and within 2 years have been diagnosed with chronic kidney disease (N18):

$$\Diamond_{(\geq\, 0\, s)}(E08 - E13) \wedge \Box_{(\geq\, 0\, s)}\left((E08 - E13) \rightarrow \Diamond_{(\leq\, 2\, years)}(N18)\right) \qquad (5)$$

- Find all events in which the patient has been diagnosed with hypertensive crisis (I16) for more than two months and then ended up being diagnosed with acute myocardial infarction (I21):

$$\Diamond_{(\geq\, 0\, s)}(I16\ \cup_{(\geq\, 2\, months)} I21) \qquad (6)$$

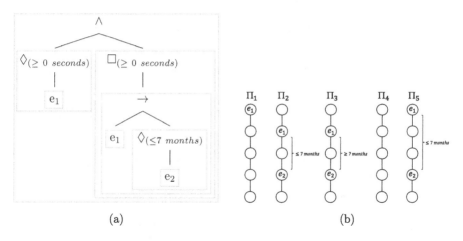

(a)                                                  (b)

**Fig. 8.** (8a) A sample parse tree $\tau$ representing the $LTL_{EOT}$ formula in query 8 and (8b) five sample paths. The dotted squares show the sub-formulas in $\tau$. Traversal starts in postorder manner (left-right-root) from the smaller squares towards the root. Once the formula in the most outer square returns true for a path, we say the path satisfies the formula. Following the Algorithm 1, only paths $\Pi_2$ and $\Pi_5$ satisfy formula (8).

– Find all the events of patients who have been repeatedly diagnosed with neoplasms (C00-D49) but there are at least 2 weeks between the diagnoses. Such events should be the conjunction of two properties:

$$\Diamond_{(\geq\ 0\ s)}(C00 - D49) \wedge \Box_{(\geq\ 0\ s)}\left((C00 - D49) \rightarrow \Diamond_{(\geq\ 0\ s)}(C00 - D49)\right)$$

$$\wedge \qquad\qquad (7)$$

$$\Box_{(\geq\ 0\ s)}\left((C00 - D49) \rightarrow \Diamond_{(\geq\ 2\ weeks)}(C00 - D49)\right)$$

Figure 8 illustrates a toy example of our proposed variant analysis approach on a sample event log of five patients $P1, \ldots, P5$. The parse tree corresponding to the sample query in (8) is shown in Fig. 8a, and in Fig. 8b we show five sample paths.

$$\Diamond_{(\geq\ 0\ s)}(e_1) \wedge \Box_{(\geq\ 0\ s)}\left((e_1) \rightarrow \Diamond_{(\leq\ 7\ months)}(e_2)\right) \qquad (8)$$

After filtering the event log based on the desired query, the sequence of events that finally pass the filter is provided as input to Fluxicon Disco for the purpose of visualization.

Query 9 shows the formula we used to identify the pattern of comorbidity diseases of the circulatory system (I00-I99) and diseases of the genitourinary system (N00-N99). The results of the execution of the query are presented in Fig. 9.

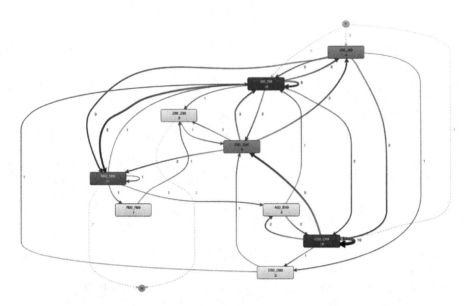

**Fig. 9.** Visualization of the pattern of comorbidity diseases of the circulatory system (I00-I99) and diseases of the genitourinary system (N00-N99)

$$\Diamond_{(\geq\ 0\,s)}(I00 - I99) \wedge \Box_{(\geq\ 0\,s)}\Bigg(\big(I00 - I99\big) \to \Diamond_{(\leq\ 2\ months)}(N00 - N99)\Bigg) \quad (9)$$

Figure 9 is a visualization of the comorbidity pattern of diseases of the circulatory system (I00-I99) and diseases of the genitourinary system (N00-N99) found by executing Algorithm 1 on query 9 over a sample filtered dataset from the local health authority. This figure shows the diagnosis map of all patients who have ever been diagnosed with a disease of the genitourinary system, one month after being diagnosed with diseases of the circulatory system.

This visualization also depicts the hypothetical association between other diseases such as endocrine, nutritional, and metabolic diseases (E00-E90) with I00-I99 and N00-N99, since they appear along paths between activities I00-I99 and N00-N99. However, obtaining such results in current process mining tools is not straightforward and requires more advanced data analysis techniques such as those discussed in this paper. The current tools available for clinicians and healthcare analysts are insufficient in their ability to support the study of healthcare process patterns for patients with multiple comorbidities in healthcare systems.

Using validated learning, clinicians and healthcare analysts can gain valuable insights from extensive event log datasets. Our hypothesis-driven approach allows them to formulate specific queries to test their assumptions. By navigating massive event log datasets strategically, clinicians and healthcare analysts can learn from data, empowering them to validate their hypotheses and uncover patterns that may have otherwise remained hidden. The following serve as examples of this approach:

1. *How many patients suffer from the comorbidity of diseases of the circulatory system (I00-I99) and diseases of the genitourinary system (N00-N99)?*
   - Contextual insight provides with an understanding of the frequency of co-occurrence of these diseases. Here we used the ICD group code (I00-I99) and (N00-N99) to include all diseases under the circulatory system and genitourinary system.
2. *Are patients who are diagnosed with diseases of the genitourinary system (N00-N99) likely to be diagnosed with diseases of the circulatory system (I00-I99) within 2 months (or 4 months or 6 months)?*
   - Temporal insight helps us to formulate appropriate queries and find evidence from the dataset.

## 4   Related Works

Van der Aalst presented four different analysis perspectives for process mining in [1] which include control-flow perspective, organizational perspective, case perspective, and time perspective. These perspectives are useful to understand the ordering of activities, the roles of resources, the attributes related to a particular case, and the frequency and timing of events. Although these perspectives can be used to derive useful insight by analyzing event logs from different points of view they lack an abstraction mechanism that will allow health professionals to both mine relevant information from highly discipline-specific data sources and also to process event data from often highly individualistic patient pathways in order to discover common pathways.

Bistarelli et al. presented a prototype tool called PrOnto in [6] which can discover business processes from an event log and classify them w.r.t. a business ontology. The tool takes an event log file as input and produces a UML-based activity diagram in XML format. The aim of the approach is to raise the level of abstraction in process mining by utilizing business ontologies. They proposed an ontology representing the hierarchy of resources. In their approach, resources are the actors of the activities. Since the resources are given an ontological hierarchy, it is possible to define which level of abstraction will be used for process mining. They proposed to use integer numbers to define the level of abstraction. Defining a high level of abstraction would merge several activities being performed by all the actors that belong to the high-level classification of resources. Our work is different from the approach presented in [6] in the sense that we proposed to use dimensional models and ontologies to classify event logs. Our approach is more flexible since it is possible to be more specific in one portion of the process model while being more generic in another portion of the process model. The idea of combining dimensional modeling with ontologies is novel in this paper. We have shown that the mining process includes some preprocessing steps. In these preprocessing steps, the user specifies the context (using dimensional modeling and ontologies) to define a patient group and also specifies the level of abstraction (using dimensional modeling and ontologies) that will be used to visualize the process mining output.

In [40], the authors discussed the application of process mining in healthcare and provided an overview of frequently asked questions by medical professionals in process mining projects. The questions reflect the medical professionals' interest in learning common pathways of different patient groups, determining their compliance with internal and external clinical guidelines, and also in gathering information about the throughput times for treating patients. The authors pointed out the need for accumulating data from different data sources and they claimed this to be a major challenge in healthcare. In the conclusion of the paper, the authors suggested that ontologies can be used for defining appropriate scope and for identifying the cases from different data sources. They urged the exploitation of ontology-based process mining approaches in the healthcare domain.

In [43], the authors discussed the necessity of relating elements in event logs with their semantic concepts. By linking event logs with the concepts from an ontology they presented a process mining approach that performs concept-based analysis. The idea of using semantics makes it possible to automatically reason or infer relationships between concepts that are related. They distinguished between the application of process mining in two different levels: instance level and conceptual level. They illustrated their ideas with an example process model to repair telephones in a company. That process model included three different ontologies: a Task ontology, a Role ontology, and a Performer ontology. The idea of using an ontology for process mining presented in [43] is very similar to our approach. The idea of filtering based on ontological concepts and the idea of grouping nodes by a high-level ontological concept are similar. However, in our approach, we emphasize the benefits of ontology-based process mining for the healthcare domain. While in [43] the authors implemented their technique in ProM, our approach is more general as it offers a pre-processing step where we filter events for patients from a tightly-knit group using the data mining technique and import the filtered events to Fluxicon Disco process mining tool.

A K-means clustering algorithm was presented in [36] where the authors enhanced the traditional K-means algorithm by means of a semantic model. The approach is similar to our community detection analysis where we utilize an abstract layer that gives semantics for our model. In our approach, we focused on the usability of incorporating a flexible abstraction layer for healthcare data analysis. Rosvall et al. in [55] provided a list of approaches for community detection and briefly presented the potential of utilizing network abstraction for understanding an air traffic system. Again, they did not present any example of abstraction which can be applied in healthcare data to enhance clustering and its visualization.

Machine learning techniques have been employed in a variety of healthcare studies such as diagnostic code assignment [42], patient representation [67], etc.

However, the potential for these machine learning algorithms and their integration with process mining techniques for analyzing healthcare information needs to be exploited. Healthcare data, due to its complex nature, can be modeled as a heterogeneous network. Representation learning methods [26] can be used to analyze the community structure of healthcare information represented as heterogeneous networks. According to [63] representation learning methods on heterogeneous networks could be divided into three categories: Path-based, Semantic unit-based, and Other methods. Similar to node2vec [22] for homogeneous node embedding methods that preserve the random-walk probabilities in the feature space, for heterogeneous networks, one might try to preserve metapath probabilities, which is a more sophisticated variation of the path. MetaPath2vec [17], MetaGraph2vec [66] fall into the Path based category which use path-based random-walks and a heterogeneous skip-gram model to learn node representation vectors. The basic principle of graph representation algorithms is to preserve the relationship and structural properties of the network in a low dimensional vector space which therefore can essentially be used for extracting information about the similarity of nodes from a network. Semantic unit based algorithms such as [20] define particular semantic units by means of capturing semantic information in the embedding space. Du et al. [19] presented an algorithm for network representation learning based on a graph partitioning strategy where a heterogeneous network is partitioned into homogeneous and bipartite subnetworks and the projective relations hidden in bipartite subnetworks are extracted by learning the projective embedding vectors. Although these machine learning-based approaches are relevant for studying healthcare information, they need to be adapted to support the analysis of healthcare information which includes large healthcare ontologies, and temporal aspects.

Scientists from various fields of research have investigated comorbidity and have exploited different methodologies. To identify the prevalence of comorbidities of mental and behavioral disorders, Cha et al. [12] propose an association rule-based analysis. Boytcheva et al. [10] propose a cascade data mining approach for frequent pattern mining. Several studies fall into the network analysis category. Jones et al. [34] define four network statistics to identify symptoms that connect two mental disorders. Social network analysis and graph theory have been also used to understand the comorbidity of two chronic diseases [31]. Crowson et al. [14] use unsupervised machine learning methods to cluster comorbidities in patients with rheumatoid arthritis. Maag et al. [38] propose a probabilistic model by developing a coupled hidden Markov model. Bottrighi et al. [9] proposed a knowledge-based approach to run-time comorbidity management to support physicians during the execution of the Clinical Practice Guidelines (CPGs) on a specific patient. Piovesan et al. [48] using Computer-Interpretable Guidelines, the history of the status of the patient, and the log of the clinical actions executed on them, propose an Answer Set programming-based method for the treatment of comorbid patients.

Batal et al. [5] proposed to use a method that uses Allen's temporal logic relations (before, meets, overlaps, is-finished-by, contains, starts, and equals) and relies on temporal abstractions and temporal pattern mining for learning classification models from healthcare data. Yousef Sanati et al. [65] developed a metric interval-based temporal logic, which is suitable for modeling Clinical Practice Guidelines in the healthcare domain. They used a tableau-based algorithm for checking the satisfiability of the formulas of the logic. Using that approach designers can model CPGs with the logic and check whether the CPGs are consistent.

Luca et al. [37] propose a trace retrieval and process mining approach introducing the notion of a log-tree.

Object-centric process mining [2] can deal with divergence (multiple instances of the same activity within a case) and convergence (one event may be related to different cases) related problems but they cannot provide contextual insight and temporal insight as we proposed in our paper. In [16] the authors focused on a problem which is about the efficient storage and exchange mechanism for making process mining possible. This could be potentially complementary to our approach for dealing with complex healthcare data.

Our approach differs from the above-mentioned approaches in the sense that we used an event-based formulation for paths where the events are linked with instances from ontologies and we use a variant of temporal logic. Our algorithm checks for the satisfaction of paths for temporal logic expressions with specific time intervals. Since our approach is based on multiple validated learning approaches combined with community analysis and process mining, and the output of our approach is visualized with Fluxicon Disco, the results are expected to provide an improved healthcare process analysis.

## 5   Conclusion and Future Work

In this paper, we proposed a validated learning approach to tackle healthcare process analysis. Our approach uses data mining (e.g., community detection and process mining algorithms) and formal methods techniques. The approach involves filtering and abstraction of event logs using ontologies, dimensional modeling, and community analysis to capture contextual insight, resulting in contextual process mining, and filtering the event logs using a temporal logic-based language $LTL_{EOT}$ to capture temporal insight. We demonstrate our approach in a case study involving comorbidity patterns in our administrative healthcare event log dataset. The syntax of traditional $LTL$ formulas was enhanced to permit the incorporation of the following:

- ontologies so that the base case of the satisfaction relation refers to an instance of ontology concept ($\pi \models C$ iff $\#_{Activity}(e_1) \in C^{\mathcal{I}}$); and,
- specific time intervals.

With this formulation, we specify comorbidity patterns, specifying the diagnoses and time intervals between events. This formulation greatly extended the expressive power of $LTL$ and allowed us to specify numerous comorbidity patterns.

One of the limitations of this language is that it cannot formulate expressions taking the state-based systems where we specify values of patient attributes (e.g., patient symptoms, demographic-related information such as age, race, gender, and clinical background). In the future, we will investigate the possible extension of the language, integrating state-based and event-based formulations. This will allow us to formulate queries such as "If the patient's blood pressure is higher than a specific threshold, and there is no drug interaction with medicines they take, then find the best medication for blood pressure reduction."

Development of a user interface suitable for use by domain experts (especially physicians), allowing them to filter and view the data with desired levels of abstraction and input queries to discover patterns among comorbid patients, is required as future work to make use of the approach discussed here. We are currently in discussion with some clinicians to evaluate our proposed approach.

**Acknowledgement.** We would like to express our sincere appreciation to the anonymous referees for their valuable comments, which greatly improved this paper. Their insights and feedback have been instrumental in enhancing the quality and clarity of our work.

# References

1. van der Aalst, W.M.P.: Process Mining: Discovery, 1st edn. Conformance and Enhancement of Business Processes. Springer Publishing Company, Incorporated (2011)
2. Aalst, W.M.P.: Object-centric process mining: dealing with divergence and convergence in event data. In: Ölveczky, P.C., Salaün, G. (eds.) SEFM 2019. LNCS, vol. 11724, pp. 3–25. Springer, Cham (2019). https://doi.org/10.1007/978-3-030-30446-1_1
3. Baader, F., Calvanese, D., McGuinness, D., Patel-Schneider, P., Nardi, D., et al.: The description logic handbook: Theory, implementation and applications. Cambridge University Press (2003)
4. Bastian, M., Heymann, S., Jacomy, M.: Gephi: An open source software for exploring and manipulating networks. In: Adar, E., Hurst, M., Finin, T., Glance, N.S., Nicolov, N., Tseng, B.L. (eds.) Proceedings of the Third International Conference on Weblogs and Social Media, ICWSM 2009, San Jose, California, USA, May 17–20, 2009. The AAAI Press (2009). https://aaai.org/ocs/index.php/ICWSM/09/paper/view/154
5. Batal, I., Valizadegan, H., Cooper, G.F., Hauskrecht, M.: A temporal pattern mining approach for classifying electronic health record data. ACM Trans. Intell. Syst. Technol. (TIST) 4(4), 1–22 (2013)
6. Bistarelli, S., Noia, T.D., Mongiello, M., Nocera, F.: Pronto: an ontology driven business process mining tool. Procedia Comput. Sci. **112**, 306–315 (2017)
7. Blondel, V.D., Guillaume, J.L., Lambiotte, R., Lefebvre, E.: Fast unfolding of communities in large networks. J. Stat. Mech: Theory Exp. **2008**(10), P10008 (2008)
8. Bodenreider, O., Cornet, R., Vreeman, D.J.: Recent developments in clinical terminologies - snomed ct, loinc, and rxnorm. Yearb. Med. Inform. **27**, 129–139 (2018)

9. Bottrighi, A., Piovesan, L., Terenziani, P.: Run-time support to comorbidities in glare-sscpm (2019)

10. Boytcheva, S., Angelova, G., Angelov, Z., Tcharaktchiev, D.: Mining comorbidity patterns using retrospective analysis of big collection of outpatient records. Health Inform. Sci. Syst. **5**(1), 1–9 (2017)

11. Braakhuis, H.E., Berger, M.A., Bussmann, J.B.: Effectiveness of healthcare interventions using objective feedback on physical activity: a systematic review and meta-analysis. J. Rehabil. Med. **51**(3), 151–159 (2019)

12. Cha, S., Kim, S.S.: Discovery of association rules patterns and prevalence of comorbidities in adult patients hospitalized with mental and behavioral disorders. In: Healthcare, vol. 9, p. 636. Multidisciplinary Digital Publishing Institute (2021)

13. Clarke, E.M., Enders, R., Filkorn, T., Jha, S.: Exploiting symmetry in temporal logic model checking. Formal Methods Syst. Des. **9**(1), 77–104 (1996)

14. Crowson, C.S., et al.: Using unsupervised machine learning methods to cluster comorbidities in a population-based cohort of patients with rheumatoid arthritis. Arthritis Care & Research (2022)

15. Dagliati, A., et al.: Big data as a driver for clinical decision support systems: a learning health systems perspective. Frontiers Digit. Humanit. **5**, 8 (2018)

16. Dfahland: Data Storage vs Data Semantics for Object-Centric Event Data, December 2022. https://multiprocessmining.org/2022/10/26/data-storage-vs-data-semantics-for-object-centric-event-data/

17. Dong, Y., Chawla, N.V., Swami, A.: Metapath2vec: scalable representation learning for heterogeneous networks. In: Proceedings of the 23rd ACM SIGKDD International Conference on Knowledge Discovery and Data Mining, KDD 2017, pp. 135–144. Association for Computing Machinery, New York (2017)

18. van Dongen, B.F., de Medeiros, A.K.A., Verbeek, H.M.W., Weijters, A.J.M.M., van der Aalst, W.M.P.: The ProM framework: a new era in process mining tool support. In: Ciardo, G., Darondeau, P. (eds.) ICATPN 2005. LNCS, vol. 3536, pp. 444–454. Springer, Heidelberg (2005). https://doi.org/10.1007/11494744_25

19. Du, W., Yu, S., Yang, M., Qu, Q., Zhu, J.: GPSP: graph partition and space projection based approach for heterogeneous network embedding. In: Champin, P., Gandon, F., Lalmas, M., Ipeirotis, P.G. (eds.) Companion of the The Web Conference 2018 on The Web Conference 2018, WWW 2018, Lyon, France, April 23–27, 2018, pp. 59–60. ACM (2018). https://doi.org/10.1145/3184558.3186928

20. Fu, G., Yuan, B., Duan, Q., Yao, X.: Representation learning for heterogeneous information networks via embedding events. In: Gedeon, T., Wong, K.W., Lee, M. (eds.) ICONIP 2019. LNCS, vol. 11953, pp. 327–339. Springer, Cham (2019). https://doi.org/10.1007/978-3-030-36708-4_27

21. Gabbay, D.M., Hodkinson, I., Reynolds, M.A.: Temporal logic: mathematical foundations and computational aspects (1994)

22. Grover, A., Leskovec, J.: Node2vec: scalable feature learning for networks. In: Proceedings of the 22nd ACM SIGKDD International Conference on Knowledge Discovery and Data Mining, KDD 2016, pp. 855–864. ACM, New York (2016)

23. Günther, C., Rozinat, A.: Disco: discover your processes. In: Lohmann, N., Moser, S. (eds.) Proceedings of the Demonstration Track of the 10th International Conference on Business Process Management (BPM 2012), pp. 40–44. CEUR Workshop Proceedings, CEUR-WS.org, January 2012. demonstration Track of the 10th International Conference on Business Process Management, BPM Demos 2012, Conference date: 04–09-2012 Through 04–09-2012

24. Hagberg, A., Swart, P., S Chult, D.: Exploring network structure, dynamics, and function using networkx. Technival report, Los Alamos National Lab. (LANL), Los Alamos, NM (United States) (2008)
25. Hall, W.W., Smith, N., Mitton, C., Urquhart, B., Bryan, S.: Assessing and improving performance: a longitudinal evaluation of priority setting and resource allocation in a Canadian health region. Int. J. Health Policy Manage. **7**(4), 328–335 (2017). https://doi.org/10.15171/ijhpm.2017.98
26. Hamilton, W.L., Ying, R., Leskovec, J.: Representation learning on graphs: Methods and applications (2017). cite arxiv:1709.05584Comment: Published in the IEEE Data Engineering Bulletin, September 2017; version with minor corrections
27. Hamrahian, S.M., Falkner, B.: Hypertension in chronic kidney disease. Hypertension: from basic research to clinical practice, pp. 307–325 (2017)
28. Haraty, R.A., Dimishkieh, M., Masud, M.: An enhanced k-means clustering algorithm for pattern discovery in healthcare data. Int. J. Distributed Sens. Networks **11**, 615740:1–615740:11 (2015)
29. He, D., Song, W., Jin, D., Feng, Z., Huang, Y.: An end-to-end community detection model: Integrating LDA into Markov random field via factor graph. In: Proceedings of the Twenty-Eighth International Joint Conference on Artificial Intelligence, IJCAI-19, pp. 5730–5736. International Joint Conferences on Artificial Intelligence Organization, July 2019
30. Hodkinson, A., et al.: Self-management interventions to reduce healthcare use and improve quality of life among patients with asthma: systematic review and network meta-analysis. BMj 370 (2020)
31. Hossain, M.E., Khan, A., Uddin, S.: Understanding the comorbidity of multiple chronic diseases using a network approach. In: Proceedings of the Australasian Computer Science Week Multiconference, pp. 1–7 (2019)
32. Huth, M., Ryan, M.: Logic in Computer Science: Modelling and reasoning about systems. Cambridge University Press (2004)
33. Jia, Y., Zhang, Q., Zhang, W., Wang, X.: Communitygan: community detection with generative adversarial nets. In: The World Wide Web Conference, pp. 784–794 (2019)
34. Jones, P.J., Ma, R., McNally, R.J.: Bridge centrality: a network approach to understanding comorbidity. Multivar. Behav. Res. **56**(2), 353–367 (2021)
35. Li, S., Jiang, L., Wu, X., Han, W., Zhao, D., Wang, Z.: A weighted network community detection algorithm based on deep learning. Appl. Math. Comput. **401**, 126012 (2021)
36. Liu, Z., Bao, J., Ding, F.: An improved k-means clustering algorithm based on semantic model. In: Proceedings of the International Conference on Information Technology and Electrical Engineering 2018, ICITEE 2018. Association for Computing Machinery, New York (2018)
37. Luca, C., Giorgio, L., Stefania, M., Paolo, T.: Mining the log-tree of process traces: current approach and future perspectives. In: 2015 IEEE 27th International Conference on Tools with Artificial Intelligence (ICTAI), pp. 310–316. IEEE (2015)
38. Maag, B., Feuerriegel, S., Kraus, M., Saar-Tsechansky, M., Züger, T.: Modeling longitudinal dynamics of comorbidities. In: Proceedings of the Conference on Health, Inference, and Learning, pp. 222–235 (2021)
39. MacQueen, J.: Some methods for classification and analysis of multivariate observations. In: Proceedings of the Fifth Berkeley Symposium on Mathematical Statistics and Probability, Volume 1: Statistics, pp. 281–297. University of California Press, Berkeley, Calif. (1967)

40. Mans, R.S., van der Aalst, W.M.P., Vanwersch, R.J.B., Moleman, A.J.: Process mining in healthcare: data challenges when answering frequently posed questions. In: Lenz, R., Miksch, S., Peleg, M., Reichert, M., Riaño, D., ten Teije, A. (eds.) KR4HC/ProHealth -2012. LNCS (LNAI), vol. 7738, pp. 140–153. Springer, Heidelberg (2013). https://doi.org/10.1007/978-3-642-36438-9_10

41. Matamalas, J.T., Arenas, A., Martínez-Ballesté, A., Solanas, A., Alonso-Villaverde, C., Gómez, S.: Revealing cause-effect relations in comorbidities analysis using process mining and tensor network decomposition. In: 2018 9th International Conference on Information, Intelligence, Systems and Applications (IISA), pp. 1–5 (2018). https://doi.org/10.1109/IISA.2018.8633613

42. Mayya, V., S., S.K., Krishnan, G.S., Gangavarapu, T.: Multi-channel, convolutional attention based neural model for automated diagnostic coding of unstructured patient discharge summaries. Future Gener. Comput. Syst. 118, 374–391 (2021)

43. Alves de Medeiros, A.K., van der Aalst, W.M.P.: Process mining towards semantics. In: Dillon, T.S., Chang, E., Meersman, R., Sycara, K. (eds.) Advances in Web Semantics I. LNCS, vol. 4891, pp. 35–80. Springer, Heidelberg (2008). https://doi.org/10.1007/978-3-540-89784-2_3

44. Organization., W.H.: ICD-10 : international statistical classification of diseases and related health problems/World Health Organization. World Health Organization Geneva, 10th revision, 2nd edn. (2004)

45. Özlük, Y., KILIÇASLAN, I.: Syndromes that link the endocrine system and genitourinary tract. Turkish Journal of Pathology 31 (2015)

46. Ozomaro, U., Wahlestedt, C., Nemeroff, C.B.: Personalized medicine in psychiatry: problems and promises. BMC Med. 11(1), 132 (2013)

47. Partington, A., Wynn, M., Suriadi, S., Ouyang, C., Karnon, J.: Process mining for clinical processes: a comparative analysis of four Australian hospitals. ACM Trans. Manage. Inf. Syst. 5(4), 19:1–19:18 (2015)

48. Piovesan, L., Terenziani, P., Dupré, D.T.: Conformance analysis for comorbid patients in answer set programming. J. Biomed. Inform. 103, 103377 (2020)

49. Pyle, D.: Data Preparation for Data Mining, 1st edn. Morgan Kaufmann Publishers Inc., San Francisco (1999)

50. Rabbi, F., Fatemi, B., MacCaull, W.: Analysis of patient pathways with contextual process mining. In: Lamo, Y., Rutle, A. (eds.) Proceedings of The International Health Data Workshop co-located with 10th International Conference on Petrinets (Petri Nets 2022), Bergen, Norway, June 26th-27th, 2022. CEUR Workshop Proceedings, vol. 3264. CEUR-WS.org (2022). https://ceur-ws.org/Vol-3264/HEDA22_paper_1.pdf

51. Rabbi, F., Lamo, Y., MacCaull, W.: A model based slicing technique for process mining healthcare information. In: Babur, Ö., Denil, J., Vogel-Heuser, B. (eds.) ICSMM 2020. CCIS, vol. 1262, pp. 73–81. Springer, Cham (2020). https://doi.org/10.1007/978-3-030-58167-1_6

52. Rabbi, F., Wake, J.D., Nordgreen, T.: Reusable data visualization patterns for clinical practice. In: Babur, Ö., Denil, J., Vogel-Heuser, B. (eds.) Systems Modelling and Management - First International Conference, ICSMM 2020, Bergen, Norway, June 25–26, 2020, Proceedings. Communications in Computer and Information Science, vol. 1262, pp. 55–72. Springer (2020). https://doi.org/10.1007/978-3-030-58167-1_5

53. Ries, E.: The lean startup: How today's entrepreneurs use continuous innovation to create radically successful businesses. Currency (2011)

54. Rojas, E., Munoz-Gama, J., Sepúlveda, M., Capurro, D.: Process mining in healthcare: a literature review. J. Biomed. Inform. **61**, 224–236 (2016)
55. Rosvall, M., Delvenne, J., Schaub, M.T., Lambiotte, R.: Different approaches to community detection. CoRR abs/1712.06468 (2017)
56. Schroeder, K., et al.: Building from patient experiences to deliver patient-focused healthcare systems in collaboration with patients: a call to action. Therapeutic Innov. Regulatory Sci. **56**(5), 848–858 (2022)
57. Staab, S., Studer, R. (eds.): Handbook on Ontologies. In: International Handbooks on Information Systems. Springer (2009). https://doi.org/10.1007/978-3-540-92673-3
58. Sutton, R.T., Pincock, D., Baumgart, D.C., Sadowski, D.C., Fedorak, R.N., Kroeker, K.I.: An overview of clinical decision support systems: benefits, risks, and strategies for success. NPJ Digital Med. **3**(1), 17 (2020)
59. Valderas, J.M., Starfield, B., Sibbald, B., Salisbury, C., Roland, M.: Defining comorbidity: implications for understanding health and health services. Ann. Family Med. **7**(4), 357–363 (2009)
60. Van Der Aalst, W.: Process mining: data science in action, vol. 2. Springer (2016)
61. Van Weenen, E., Feuerriegel, S.: Estimating risk-adjusted hospital performance. In: 2020 IEEE International Conference on Big Data (Big Data), pp. 1709–1719. IEEE (2020)
62. Vougas, K., et al.: Machine learning and data mining frameworks for predicting drug response in cancer: an overview and a novel in silico screening process based on association rule mining. Pharmacol. Therapeutics **203**, 107395 (2019)
63. Xie, Y., Yu, B., Lv, S., Zhang, C., Wang, G., Gong, M.: A survey on heterogeneous network representation learning. Pattern Recogn. **116**, 107936 (2021)
64. Yang, J., et al.: Brief introduction of medical database and data mining technology in big data era. J. Evid. Based Med. **13**(1), 57–69 (2020)
65. Yousef Sanati, M., MacCaull, W., Maibaum, T.S.E.: Analyzing clinical practice guidelines using a decidable metric interval-based temporal logic. In: Jones, C., Pihlajasaari, P., Sun, J. (eds.) FM 2014. LNCS, vol. 8442, pp. 611–626. Springer, Cham (2014). https://doi.org/10.1007/978-3-319-06410-9_41
66. Zhang, D., Yin, J., Zhu, X., Zhang, C.: MetaGraph2Vec: complex semantic path augmented heterogeneous network embedding. In: Phung, D., Tseng, V.S., Webb, G.I., Ho, B., Ganji, M., Rashidi, L. (eds.) PAKDD 2018. LNCS (LNAI), vol. 10938, pp. 196–208. Springer, Cham (2018). https://doi.org/10.1007/978-3-319-93037-4_16
67. Zhang, X., et al.: Learning robust patient representations from multi-modal electronic health records: a supervised deep learning approach. In: Proceedings of the 2021 SIAM International Conference on Data Mining (SDM), pp. 585–593. SIAM (2021)

# A Case Study on Data Protection for a Cloud- and AI-Based Homecare Medical Device

Philipp Bende[1], Olga Vovk[2]($\boxtimes$), David Caraveo[1,3], Ludwig Pechmann[3], and Martin Leucker[1,3]

[1] Institute for Software Engineering and Programming Languages, University of Lübeck, Lübeck, Germany
[2] School of Information Technologies, Department of Health Technologies, Tallinn University of Technology, Tallinn, Estonia
olga.vovk@taltech.ee
[3] UniTransferKlinik Lübeck GmbH, Lübeck, Germany

**Abstract.** To improve the treatment of many diseases, continuous monitoring of the patient at home with the ability of doctors to interact with individual cases demands an increasing number of medical devices connected to the cloud. To support the doctor's duties, such devices may benefit from AI-based diagnosis routines. In order for such devices to be approved and placed on the market, they need to comply with various legal, regulatory, economic, and social requirements. An integral part of these requirements is the protection of the patients' data.

In this paper, based on a current use case, we describe a workflow on how to identify risks and address their mitigations. To this end, we recall the relevant legal, regulatory, economic, and social data protection requirements. We pursue our findings on a Homecare OCT device that is intended to be used by elderly patients on a daily basis, by taking images of their eyes and sending them for further analysis to a cloud- and AI-based system. The patient's ophthalmologist gets notified for further dedicated treatment depending on the result. We then compare the Homecare OCT device with a clinical OCT System in regard to various risks to patient data which arise when a medical system is used outside of a secure hospital environment.

To perform the risk management, we describe (i) the architecture of both systems, (ii) analyze their data flow, (iii) discuss several vectors of attack, (iv) propose ways to mitigate the risks, and (v) discuss the handling of potential data breaches.

**Keywords:** Data Protection · Risk Management · Homecare Medical Devices · Cloud- and AI-based System · Data Breach Handling · Data Security · Medical Devices · Medical AI · Cloud-based Medical Systems · Decision Support System

This work has been conducted in the project "ICT programme" which was supported by the European Union through the European Social Fund.

# 1   Introduction

The rapidly developing field of medical devices using Artificial Intelligence (AI) has great potential in the healthcare domain by revolutionizing diagnosis, treatment, and patient care delivery. AI-based data analytics can provide clinicians with decision support for the diagnosis of patients' health care problems and risk assessment. This allows for a more individual treatment of the patient by providing better, more affordable and convenient health care and provide a higher level of support for health care professionals [36,39]. Despite the benefits that can be achieved, using technologies also raises concerns and one of them is personal data protection. To achieve the proper level of protection comprehensive measures shall be taken. These include considering legal, technical and administrative measures.

This article gives an overview of the requirements associated with data protection applicable in the health care field and provides an example of translation of the requirements to practice. In this work we present a case study of a homecare medical system and discuss risks concerning patient data protection associated with such a system, as well as ways to mitigate these risks in practice.

We created an overview of publications that address the question of data security in medical devices and AI. We performed a search on a combination of keywords "data security" "medical devices" or "medical AI". For our overview, we included papers published in recent years, not later than 2018. We excluded papers that were published in other languages than English. Also, we excluded papers that do not match our research topic and do not answer our research questions. Based on our findings, we can divide publications into papers that focus on legal aspects of data protection and technical aspects. The first category includes papers that focus on analyzing the legal requirements and frameworks. For example, in the article "The European Legal Framework for Medical AI" [33], the authors look into relevant laws, focusing on data protection. The article discusses the current European framework regulating medical AI and analyzes its specific areas of law, including data protection, product approval procedures, and liability law, while also highlighting proposed amendments to product approval procedures and liability law that will shape the future of medical AI in Europe by endorsing a human-centric approach. Nevertheless, this and similar papers use a theoretical approach. In contrast, we bring to the reader's attention requirements and related regulations but mainly focus on the practical implementation of those rules. In the second category we put articles focused on technical aspects, specifically medical devices cybersecurity. For example, the article "Secure health data sharing for medical cyber-physical systems for the healthcare 4.0" [28] focuses mainly on cybersecurity and technical aspects, such as encryption methods. The article proposes a secure data storage and sharing method for medical cyber-physical systems using a selective encryption algorithm combined with fragmentation and dispersion, based on a user-centric design that protects data safety and privacy even when transmission media and keys are compromised, and evaluates its efficiency on a smartphone platform. Based on this literature analysis we found out that research on the practical implementation of the requirements in real-life devices and comprehensive description of risks related to data protection is missing. Also, we would like to point out that papers are often focused on medical devices and networks located in hospitals and are usually more protected. In contrast, our work is dedicated to the homecare device that is used outside of a secure hospital environment and this usage can bring additional risks to data protection.

The article is structured as follows. In Sect. 2 we discuss legal, regulatory, social and economic requirements that need to be taken into account while dealing with personal data and requirements for data protection in software as a medical device. Following, Sect. 3 gives an overview of the homecare cloud system, including architecture and data flow in the system. Next, in Sect. 4 we describe potential risks associated with personal data protection in the current system and methods to mitigate those risks. Following, in Sect. 5 we perform risk analysis and risk management on a clinical cloud- and AI-based OCT system and compare the findings with the results of the Homecare OCT risk management. In Sect. 6 we discuss the handling of potential data breaches in the system according to regulatory and legal requirements. Finally, in Sect. 7, we discuss the main findings.

The Article is based on a preliminary version published in Proceedings of The International Health Data Workshop (HEDA 2022) [2] and extends the premilary version by describing and analyzing the clinical OCT system and comparing the finding with the results of our analysis of the Homecare OCT system.

## 2   Requirements

Personal data has a great value nowadays and to ensure its protection various requirements are implemented. In this article, we describe legal requirements, common and general rules that are set by law; regulatory, requirements that are set by specific normative acts in the field; economic requirements, that have a business impact; and social requirements, that include additional protection measures from sensitive personal data, such as medical and health care related data.

### 2.1   Legal Requirements

In order to harmonize legal requirements across European countries, the European Commission introduces the General Data Protection Regulation (GDPR) - a new law in the privacy protection field that is mandatory for all EU countries. This regulation is universal for EU countries and does not require additional implementation in the national legislation system. Although, if needed, countries can issue laws on the national level that complements GDPR [11].

Personal data is the central term in data protection laws. One of the core obligations under GDPR is to provide an adequate security level for personal data. Those measures include but are not limited to the following: ensuring confidentiality, integrity, availability of data; implementing pseudonymization, anonymization and encryption; ability to protect from incidents and minimize risks; process of testing, assessing and evaluating the system. According to Art.4 (1) GDPR "personal data" is defined as any information which is related to an identified or identifiable natural person [11].

Data anonymization is one of the ways to keep value while preventing privacy. GDPR defines anonymization as the "process of creating anonymous information", which means anonymized information shall not include an identified or identifiable natural person or personal data. It is important to emphasize that European legislation in the data protection field applies to personal data, which means if data is anonymized, it is out of the scope of GDPR, but it still can be a subject of other laws. Nevertheless, anonymized data or, in other words de-identified data, shall be distinguished from pseudonymized. Personal data to which pseudonymization methods were applied, that still can be attributed to a natural person shall be considered as information that may allow identification of a natural person [11]. In addition, the controller, defined by GDPR as a natural or legal person, public authority, agency or other body that determines the purposes and means of the processing of personal data and requires them to maintain necessary technical and organizational measures to keep personal data protected, shall assess whether a person is identifiable [11]. To do that, according to the Recital 26 GDPR, "account should be taken of all the means reasonably likely to be used, such as singling out, either by the controller or by another person to identify the natural person directly or indirectly" [11].

The Article 29 Working Party (WP29) Opinion on Anonymization Techniques, based on Directive 95/46/EC, understands anonymization as "results from processing personal data in order to irreversibly prevent identification". Although, the current directive is no longer in force, the given definition is still accurate [9]. EU guidelines, such as the Working Party mentioned above, aim to provide directions toward data anonymization. However, the final decision towards using privacy methods is the responsibility of the data controller and shall be decided case by case since there is no one universal method that fits them all [38].

In addition to GDPR, some EU countries issued additional guidelines on handling data on a national level. One of the examples is Guidance on health data protection (ger. "Orientierungshilfe zum Gesundheitsdatenschutz") issued in Germany [3]. The document provides a practical overview of the essential data protection requirements for companies in the healthcare sector.

According to ENISA (European Union Agency for Cybersecurity), the choice of anonymization and pseudonymization methods depends on different parameters, primarily the data protection level and the utility of the dataset [8]. Also, the choice of a method may be concerned by the complexity associated with a certain scheme in terms of implementation, scalability and database size.

There are multiple forms to protect personal data, for example, anonymization, pseudonymization, non-disclosure, hashing, encryption or tokenization [5]. Data anonymization is one of the ways to keep value while preventing privacy. GDPR defines anonymization as the "process of creating anonymous information", which means anonymized information shall not include an identified or identifiable natural person or personal data [11].

## 2.2 Regulatory Requirements

The GDPR is a major driver for data protection which was issued by the European Commission. Prior to the GDPR, which went into effect on May 2018, manufacturers of medical devices where already challenged by data protection through the ISO 13485:2016 and the Medical Device Regulation (MDR) [37]. The MDR requires data protection in cases like clinical trials and the ISO 13485 requires that the manufacturer has to ensure the confidentiality of health information and implement the necessary methods to do so [21]. This is needed on the actual device on the one hand and also during each process, where the manufacturer would have possible access to patient data.

The ISO 13485 defines the Quality Management Systems (QMS) for Medical Devices and ensures that the product is safe, effective and efficient. Therefore, the QMS documents the whole lifecycle from the product concept, development and verification until the post market phase and to the decommissioning of a product. Each phase of the product life cycle needs to be covered by risk management activities. Manufacturers usually implement an ISO 14971 compliant risk management process to identify hazards that could result in property damage, personal injury or death of users and/or patients or even reputation loss for the manufacturer.

The ISO 14971:2012 only defines two types of risks, unacceptable and acceptable, and all have to be mitigated as far as the risk benefit ratio does not get negative. Therefore, the manufacturer has to define his risk acceptance criteria which leads to a risk acceptance matrix [7,20]. The risk acceptance matrix is a tool to assess and categorize the potential risks and harms that a medical device poses to the patients who use it. The basic steps to set up a risk acceptance matrix are as follows: (i) Identify the potential harms that the medical device could cause. For example, potential harms can include: debilitating side effects, short-term injury or impairment, reduction in quality of vision or loss of vision. (ii) Estimate the risk of each individual harm. The risk is the product of the probability of occurrence and the severity of the harm. (iii) Build your matrix. The matrix is a table that shows the risk of each harm in relation to its probability and severity. The matrix should also include criteria for accepting or not accepting risks, based on qualitative factors such as the benefit of the product and the expectations of stakeholders. (iv) Train your team. All people involved in the design, development and distribution of the medical device should be familiar with the risk acceptance matrix and know how to apply it.

A source of input for backgrounds and risks to this topic which have to be covered through this process can be found from the Medical Device Coordination Group (MDCG) in the document 2019-16 "Guidance on Cybersecurity for medical devices". The MDCG document 2019-16 is a guideline for meeting the essential safety and performance requirements of medical devices with respect to IT risks (GSPR) [4]. It addresses manufacturers of medical devices that incorporate electronic programmable systems or software and provides them with recommendations for the safe design, manufacture, and Post-Market Surveillance (PMS) of their products. It also describes expectations for other stakeholders, such as integrators, operators, and users, who have a shared responsibility to ensure a safe environment for patient safety. The guideline also includes an overview of other EU and international legislation and guidance relevant to the field of cybersecurity for medical devices [25]. Also the ISO 27001 is an international standard for information security management systems (ISMS). It specifies the requirements for establishing, implementing, maintaining and continually improving an ISMS that protects the information assets of an organization. ISO 27001 also provides guidance for assessing and treating information security risks according to the needs and context of the organization [18]. A third source, which is repeated in parts but nevertheless plays a role especially in the context of the development and release of AI-supported medical products, is the questionnaire "Artificial Intelligence (AI) in medical devices" from the interest group of notified bodies for medical devices in Germany (IG-NB) [17]. It contains a series of questions that manufacturers of medical devices with artificial intelligence (AI)-based software must answer in order to meet the requirements of the European Medical Device Regulation 2017/745 (MDR). The questionnaire is not legally binding, but it provides important guidance for creating MDR-compliant documentation.

The risk acceptance matrix in Table 1 shows the correlation between the probability of occurrence and the severity of a hazard on a default risk assessment matrix as found in literature [20]. The probability is defined by five classes from frequent e.g. each use, to unthinkable, which may occur only once in the lifetime of a device. For severity there are also five classes ranging from marginal e.g. there is no harm at all, to catastrophic, which could lead to a severe injury or death. Therefore, a high probability and a high severity lead to unacceptable risks while on the other side low probability and a low severity may lead to an acceptable risk [19].

**Table 1.** Risk Acceptance Matrix (Probability to Severity) for the Homecare System.

|  | 1- Marginal | 2-Minor | 3-Moderate | 4-Serious | 5-Catastrophic |
|---|---|---|---|---|---|
| 1-Frequent | acceptable | unacceptable | unacceptable | unacceptable | unacceptable |
| 2-Occasional | acceptable | acceptable | unacceptable | unacceptable | unacceptable |
| 3-Rare | acceptable | acceptable | acceptable | unacceptable | unacceptable |
| 4-Unlikely | acceptable | acceptable | acceptable | acceptable | unacceptable |
| 5-Unthinkable | acceptable | acceptable | acceptable | acceptable | acceptable |

## 2.3 Economic Requirements

We can take a look at economic requirements from two perspectives. First, from the need to spend resources to apply proper measures to protect data, and second, from the possible losses in case of incompetence and data breach.

GDPR requires controllers to apply necessary measures in order to protect personal data [11]. However, considering that there is no standard set of measures that will fit all cases, and specific requirements may vary from country to country or detailed guidelines may be missing at all, in most cases it is still at the data controller's discretion to select appropriate measures. Nevertheless, applied measures shall be appropriate and relevant to the case. One of the ways to evaluate that is to conduct a risk-based data protection impact assessment. This procedure will help analyze, identify and mitigate risks associated with data processing. We want to point out that no single solution will enable data protection and data utility. It can be presented as a range of possible measures that can be implemented in specific case to find a suitable balance in each situation. This solution will depend on many factors. E.g. type and scope of processed data, risks associated with data processing, to whom data is shared and also, available resources. In each case can be defined the minimum level of protection measures applied as well as the maximum level of security that can be achieved.

The minimum level can be achieved with fewer resources, but is associated with higher risks of data loss or unauthorized access. Although, the maximum level of security provides a higher level of data protection, it also has drawbacks, such as high cost of implementation and maintenance, requirement for involvement of specialists from different fields, lower data utility associated with possible data loss resulting from anonymization or less convenient data access from a user's perspective. Violation of GDPR requirements can bring serious financial consequences for data controllers. In case of infringement of GDPR provisions, data controller can get a fine of up to 20 000 000 EUR or 4% of the total worldwide annual turnover [11]. In addition to those fines serious financial and reputation loss can be followed due to data breach. Based on IBM Security's 2020 data breach report, the average cost of a health care organization's data breach is $7.13 million, which is 10% more than in 2019 [15].

## 2.4  Social Requirements

According to GDPR, healthcare related data belong to the special type of data that requires additional protection measures compared to the regular personal data. This data may reveal information about the past or current status of a person's health, including physical or mental health conditions. Special information may contain results of body or tissue samples examinations, medical history, treatment details as well as data from health care professionals and medical devices [11]. Data protection requirements may also be specified in documents on a national level. For instance, Guidance on health data protection describes organizational precautions that must be taken by the companies that process sensitive health data in order to ensure the protection of this data. Those precautions include an obligation on the employees to maintain data securely, including to create a register of all data processing operations [3].

Certainly, the secondary usage of health data, such as for research purposes, can have significant social benefits, including developing solutions that improve people's lives, providing better support in decision making, and more affordable care. GDPR specifies that personal data shall be collected for specified, explicit, and legitimate purposes and applies restrictions for the usage of personal data in a way that is incompatible with those purposes [11]. Nevertheless, processing for archiving purposes in the public interest, scientific or historical research purposes is considered compatible with the initial purposes of the collection which means data can be used for research but may require implementation of safeguard measures [11].

# 3    Overview of the Homecare Cloud System

Age-related macular degeneration (AMD) is an eye disease that damages the macula of the retina and leads to blurred or loss of vision in the center of the visual field. There is no cure, but treatment slows the progression of the disease and reduces vision loss [1]. Treatment is administered by injecting vascular endothelial growth factor inhibitors into the eye at fixed intervals or adaptively, if worsening of the disease is detected [27].

The homecare system aims to develop a solution for the frequent monitoring of AMD patients' eyes and the AI-based prediction of the course of the disease. The frequent monitoring of the disease from the patient's home allows for the detection of the onset of the worsening of the disease and therefore scheduling the treatment at the best possible time. Thus, a cloud-based system that allows various different users to interact reliably and securely with multiple cloud services is realized.

When a patient is diagnosed with AMD, they can get a prescription for a homecare device. An optician provides the homecare device to the patient, who uses the device once every day to take a series of optical coherence tomography (OCT) [10] images of their eyes. These OCT images get uploaded to the cloud, where an AI-based service evaluates the progression of the AMD and suggests whether further treatment is required. If treatment is required, the patient's doctor is notified and can make an appointment for the treatment. Additionally, the patient and their doctor can view all past images and classification results in the cloud.

## 3.1    Architecture of the Homecare Cloud System

Figure 1 shows an overview of the cloud system and homecare device architecture. The part inside the dotted box represents serviced hosted on the cloud infrastructure. The left part of the figure shows the typical roles of patient, doctor and homecare device in the system. These users interact with the cloud system via different interfaces and access the cloud services through the internet. A patient can interact with the system by using the homecare device to take a series of OCT images of their eyes. The homecare device then uploads the raw images data to the cloud system. Within the cloud a preprocessing routine reconstructs a 3-dimensional DICOM-image from the uploaded data. Additionally, an AI-based classification service is notified that new images require evaluation.

The classification service evaluates the image and results in a recommendation if the disease progressed and thus requires further treatment. Current and past images and results can be accessed and viewed by the patient, as well as their doctor, via a mobile application or a web front-end application.

To ensure the integrity of the patient's data in the cloud, access to the system is restricted to authenticated and authorized users. Multiple standards for authentication and authorization exist, of which the three most commonly used ones are Open Authentication (OAuth) [13], OpenID Connect [32] and Security Assertion Markup Language (SAML) [23, 26]

There is precedence of OpenID in conjunction with OAuth2.0 being used in the context high security environments such as eHealth, eGoverment and Banking [6, 24].

For our implementation we utilize a server implementing OAuth2.0 [13] and OpenID Connect [32]. OAuth2.0 provides role-based access control (RBAC) mechanisms therefore allowing only authorized users access to resources [13]. The OpenID Connect standard provides web-based single-sign-on authentication and cross-domain identity management [32].

An AI-training service is used for further training and improvement, and the deployment and quality assurance of the AI-model. The classification algorithm runs as a cloud service and provides an interface where other services can request an evaluation of OCT images.

## 3.2   Data Flow in the Homecare Cloud System

To identify points of attack, where an intruder could attempt to gain access to a patient's data in the system, data- and information flow analysis can be performed. Information flow analysis results in an overview of which entities have access to the information in the system [31]. In addition to entities having access to data, a data flow analysis shows which processes and storage units have access to the data in the system [35]. Therefore, data flow analysis is preferred over information flow analysis for the identification of possible points of attack. In our data flow analysis we follow the methodology described by Seifermann et al. [35].

Figure 2 shows the data flow in the homecare system and visualizes which user is able to access the data.

Data is divided into three categories by the criticality of the data. Non-Identifying Non-Biometric data does not contain sensitive information (purple). The OCT images of a patient's eye are biometric data and contain sensitive information in pseudonymized form (yellow). The patient's identifying data, like the patient's name, is shown in blue. Access to a blue service therefore allows for the identification of a patient, while access to yellow services gives access pseudonymized biometric data but does not allow for the identification of the patient.

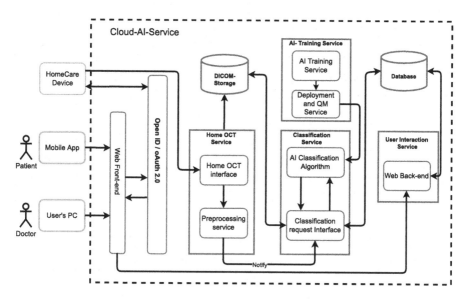

**Fig. 1.** Overview of the cloud architecture of system and homecare device. Users (left) interact via multiple interfaces (red boxes) with cloud services (blue boxes). The services consist of interfaces for user authentication, the upload, preprocessing and AI-based evaluation of data, a service for the training and quality assurance of the AI-service, and interfaces for users to access the results. (Color figure online)

The homecare device (top-left) takes the patient's OCT images and sends the images, as well as metadata describing the device to a preprocessing service running in the cloud (below). The images are related to the homecare device through the metadata and contain the patient's biometric data but no personal identifying information about the patient.

The preprocessing service generates a 3-dimensional image file from the raw OCT image data and the device's metadata and stores it as a DICOM file in the cloud. Similarly to the raw image data uploaded from the homecare device, the reconstructed DICOM file does not contain any patient identifying information.

The DICOM files can be retrieved from the storage by specifying the storage path of the requested file. Further, the image classification service (right of the preprocessing service) gets notified about a new upload. When notified, the classification service retrieves the DICOM file from the storage and evaluates the contained OCT image with an AI-based service also located in the cloud. The classification result, whether the patient's AMD worsened or not, is combined with the patient's ID to enable a correlation between a patient and their OCT image.

The correlation between a patient and an ID (above and right of the classification service), a patient and his doctor (middle right) and a patient ID and a device (top middle) is established by the patient's optician when the patient is initially entered into the system and provided with a homecare device.

The view result service (bottom middle) allows authenticated patients and their doctors to view an OCT image and the corresponding classification result. The user specifies the requested results (by patient.ID). The results contain the path to the corresponding image files, which are retrieved from the storage. A doctor further can view the results of all their patients (bottom right).

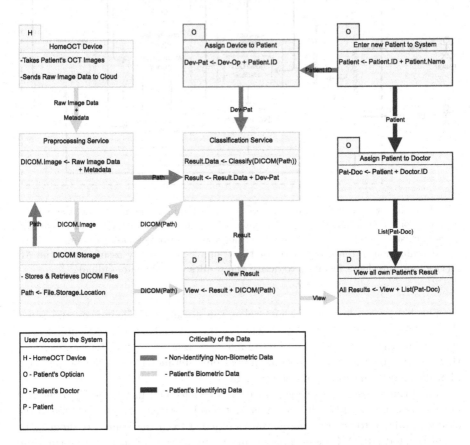

**Fig. 2.** The data flow in the homecare system. The boxes represent functions in the cloud system. The letters on top of the boxes show which user can access the function. A user has access to all information in the accessed function including information which is derived from other functions. The arrows represent information that is passed from one function to another one.

## 4    Analysis and Mitigation for Potential Risk to the Patients' Data

Following the regulatory requirements discussed in Sect. 2.2, risk management for the homecare medical system is implemented. This section describes the reasons for processing sensitive data, potential risks to the data, as well as the measures taken in order to minimize the risks.

### 4.1    Reasons to Process Sensitive Data in the System

GDPR Art. 9 protects personal and biometric data and prohibits the processing of such sensitive data. An exception is that processing can be permitted if a specific requirement for the processing, such as medical diagnosis, exists [11].

For the purpose of medical diagnosis, it is necessary to record and store the patient's full name in the system in order for their doctor to search and find a specific patient's data. When a new patient is stored in the database, it will be automatically generated an ID for this patient to guarantee the uniqueness of the database keys. Other personal information, such as age, sex or address are not processed in the system, since they are not required for the use case.

In addition to the personal identifying data, biometric data in the form of OCT-images of the patient's eyes are stored and processed in the system. It is necessary to store and process the biometric data because the purpose of the system is to detect AMD and evaluate the progress of the disease. The system creates a historical record of the patient's disease.

Since an AI detects the disease, multiple OCT-images are required to train of the neural network. The original training images are not retained in the system, but only the neural net's weights are based on these training images.

### 4.2    Potential Risks for Patients' Data

Based on the Risk Analysis in Table 1 we identify points of attack in the data flow of the system as depicted in Fig. 2, where a potential intruder or malicious user could attack the system in order to gain unauthorized access to a patient's sensitive data.

We differentiate between an intruder attempting to break into the system and a malicious user, for example, a rogue system administrator, attempting to access sensitive patient data.

An intruder could attempt to break into the cloud system or intercept data that is uploaded from the homecare device to the cloud (see Fig. 2 top left arrow). The intruder can also attempt to identify a patient and find out the patient's diagnosis.

In case AI models are not trained on identifiable personal data, they are not under the scope of GDPR [11]. However, an additional vector of attack on an AI-based system is the attempt to reconstruct training data from the learned weights of the model [30]. Therefore, an AI-model may be covered by GDPR if the training data itself is covered by GDPR. In this scenario, an intruder could perform a membership inference attack or reconstruction attack as defined in [29] to attempt to gain knowledge about the training data.

Different from an external intruder, a malicious user would already have access to the system itself and could attempt to access sensitive data or the AI-model without authorization. Such sensitive data could be accessed by gaining access to the database storing the patient's information and diagnosis (see Fig. 1 Database top right) or the patient's biometric data (see Fig. 1 DICOM-Storage top middle). A similar scenario is a doctor attempting to access patients' data for which he has no authorization, such as a different doctor's patient.

Additionally, a malicious user would have access to the AI-model and could attempt to gain information about the training data from the network's response, similar to an external intruder but with full access to the network.

### 4.3   Mitigation of Potential Risks

According to Table 1 the hazards discussed in Sect. 4.2 are unacceptable risks due the severity of the damage and frequency of occurrence and therefore need to be mitigated. Table 2 shows the mitigation strategy for each hazard in order to reduce the risks to an acceptable level.

In the following, we argue based on the assumption that the homecare device and the cloud system, including backend servers, databases and network, are trustworthy, act according to their specification and adhere to the security requirements of ISO 27001 [18].

The homecare device sends sensitive biometric data over an unsecure channel to the cloud. An intruder can intercept this communication. By encrypting all communication with HTTPS, the sensitive data cannot be recovered even if intercepted. The scenario, that an intruder gains hardware access to the homecare device and intercepts data pre-encryption is not further considered, since in that case the intruder would have to be in the patient's home and access the device while the patient is using it. If an intruder accessed the device after the patient was done using the device, the intruder would not be able to gain any identifying information from the device, since the device stores neither information about the patient, nor image data after the upload to the cloud.

In order to prevent an intruder or unauthorized user from gaining access to the databases, we do not allow direct access to the database but require access through a backend service. The backend only accepts requests from users who are authenticated and authorized by the authorization server. This ensures that as long as backend and database are not compromised, users need to be authorized to access the system itself and specific patient data.

Since a doctor must be able to access his patients' data, each patient is mapped to a doctor. The backend allows for requests from a doctor only for patients' data, for which this mapping exists. This ensures that the doctor can access their own patients' data but not to other doctors' patients' data.

To ensure the security and integrity of patient's sensitive data, all patients' information is encrypted in the database according to the requirements of ISO 27001 [18]. Furthermore, the biometric data is pseudonymized by not mapping it to the patients' name, but an ID. This makes it harder for an intruder to de-pseudonymize a patient, since he would need to get access to both, the biometric data and the database connecting IDs to patients.

The risk to the integrity of the AI model's training data is low since the model is not publicly available and the system allows only selected users a limited number of requests. These measures reduce the likelihood of an intruder gaining information about the AI-model's training data from observing the AI-model's answers to specific requests [29]. In case of the intruder gaining full access to the model, he could infer knowledge about the training data, but only access biometric data and no identifying information about the patient is exposed. To prevent a malicious user with full access to the AI-model from gaining knowledge about the training data set, privacy preserving machine learning techniques, such as differential privacy, as described in [22] can be utilized.

**Table 2.** A sample of the risk management for the homecare system. The risk acceptance is calculated from the probability and severity of the hazard according to Table 1

| Hazard | Risk acceptance before mitigation | Mitigation | Risk acceptance after mitigation |
|---|---|---|---|
| An intruder tries to fetch information sent by the Home OCT device | Frequent × Serious ⇒ Unacceptable | – Encrypt all communication with HTTPS | Frequent × Marginal ⇒ Acceptable |
| An intruder attempts to break into the cloud service and accesses data | Occasional × Serious ⇒ Unacceptable | – Limit system access to authorized users utilizing OpenID and oAuth2.0 protocols <br> – Restrict access to database only via backend service <br> – Backend checks user validation before forwarding data | Unlikely × Serious ⇒ Acceptable |
| Intruder or user gets access to the database in which the patient data is stored | Occasional × Serious ⇒ Unacceptable | – Restrict access to database only via backend service <br> – Backend checks user permission before forwarding data <br> – Encrypt database with secure standards according to ISO 27001 [18] | Unlikely × Serious ⇒ Acceptable |
| A doctor can see results of other doctors' patients | Occasional × Serious ⇒ Unacceptable | – Restrict access by mapping each patient with a doctor <br> – Allow access only to data from patients with correct mapping | Unlikely × Serious ⇒ Acceptable |
| A patient can see results of other patients | Rare × Serious ⇒ Unacceptable | – Restrict access by mapping each patient with a device <br> – Allow access only to data from device with correct mapping | Unlikely × Serious ⇒ Acceptable |
| An intruder attempts to gain information about a patient from the database | Unlikely × Catastrophic ⇒ Unacceptable | – Encrypt all patient's sensitive data in the database <br> – Encrypt patient's diagnosis | Unlikely × Moderate ⇒ Acceptable |
| An intruder tries to correlate biometric data with the patients | Rare × Serious ⇒ Unacceptable | – Pseudonymize biometric data by correlating patient's id with patient's sensitive data <br> – Not storing patient information on the homecare device | Rare × Moderate ⇒ Acceptable |
| An intruder attempts to gain information about the model's training data | Rare × Serious ⇒ Unacceptable | – Restrict number of classification requests to one per day <br> – Restrict access to the weights of the AI-model <br> – Biometric training data is pseudonymized | Unlikely × Serious ⇒ Acceptable |

### 4.4   Handling Errors and Inconsistencies in the Implementation

According to IEEE 610 a fault in software is defined as "an incorrect step, process, or data definition in a computer program" [16]. An error is "a difference between a computed result and the correct result" [12]. A failure "is the incorrect result of a fault" [12]. A mistake is "a human action that produces an incorrect result" [12]. In other words, a fault is a defect in the software code that may cause an error. An error is an incorrect internal state that may cause a failure. A failure is an external, incorrect behavior with respect to the expected behavior. A mistake is a human action that produces a fault.

In a previous version of the implementation of the HomeOCT cloud software, there was a fault that allowed for a patient to be entered into the system without being assigned to a doctor. This fault was the result of the implementation deviating from the specification. To prevent such mistakes from occurring conformance testing can be utilized. Conformance testing is a process that determines whether a system complies with its specification [14]. The fault described above resulted in a failure where it was possible for any doctor to view and to assign such unassigned patients to themselves.

## 5   Clinical OCT

A related use for a cloud- and AI-based medical system is a clinical OCT device depicted in Fig. 3. Similarly to the Homecare OCT, a clinical OCT can take multilayered images of the patient's retina and is used for the diagnosis of AMD and other diseases. Different from the Homecare OCT use case, the clinical OCT, as well as the data preprocessing and storage happens within the hospital's network (left dotted box in Fig. 3). The patient's data does not leave the hospital's network, except for the OCT images for the AI-based classification, which takes place in the cloud.

Before the patient's images are uploaded to the cloud, the images are pseudonymized by removing the patient identifying data, such as name, birthday, age, etc and instead assigning an ID to the images. The pseudonymized OCT images are sent to the cloud where a AI-model evaluates the images and returns the result to the clinic. After the classification is completed the pseudonymized images do not need to be retained in the cloud and are deleted from the cloud system. In the clinic the AI-model's classification result is combined with the original image and patient data by matching the IDs. The result is available as a recommendation for the doctor on how to proceed with the treatment.

### 5.1   Data Flow in the Clinical OCT Cloud System

Similar to the analysis performed in Sect. 3.2 we analyze the data flow in the clinical OCT cloud system in order to identify possible points of attack, where an intruder could attempt to gain access to data in the system. Figure 4 depicts the data flow of the clinical OCT use case. Part of the system is inside the hospital's network and therefore protected by the hospital's IT security. In this paper we do not go into details concerning the hospital's IT security but only address the pseudonymization, cloud-facing services and the cloud-based AI services. We assume, that any person with physical access to the OCT device or other PCs in the clinic is authorized to access these services.

As shown in Fig. 4, the Data is divided into non-identifying non-biometric, biometric and patient-identifying data. Patient identifying data does not leave the hospital's network. Pseudonymized biometric data leaves the hospital's network and is uploaded to the cloud for classification.

The data flow analysis shows that an intruder would have to break into the hospital's network, intercept data sent to cloud or break into the cloud service. The hospital's physical and IT security is not addressed in this paper.

Table 3 shows points of attack on the system, the resulting risks and how these risks are mitigated. The data sent to the cloud is encrypted with HTTPS, therefore an intruder listening can not decern useful information from data in transit. All data sent out of the hospital's network is pseudonymized and therefore an intruder breaking into the cloud service could not decern who the images belong to. Access to the AI-model is restricted, so only authorized users can request data classification. This prevents unauthorized parties to attempt to learn about the AI-model's and training data.

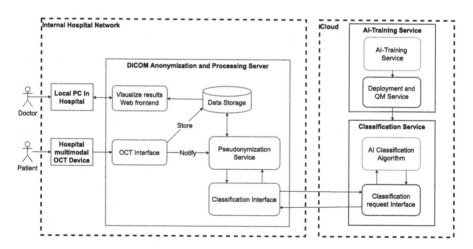

**Fig. 3.** Overview of the cloud architecture for the classification of clinical OCT images. The system consists of a server within the hospital's internal network (left) and a cloud service reachable over the internet (right). Within the hospital's network users can interface with the system to take OCT images and view results. The server accepts exports of DICOM files, pseudonymizes patient data, requests AI-based evaluation and allows the viewing of the results. The cloud consists of a classification service, which accepts classification requests and services for training deployment and quality assurance of the AI.

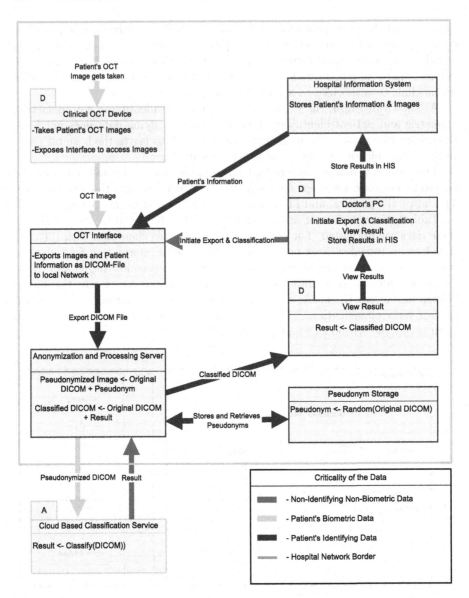

**Fig. 4.** The data flow in the clinical system. The boxes represent components and functions in the system. The letters on top of the boxes show which user can access the function. Only a doctor with access to the clinic infrastructure (D) is allowed to access the components within the clinic's network. The arrows represent information that is passed from one function to another one.

## 5.2   Comparison of the Risk Analysis for the Clinical and Homecare OCT Systems

From a security view, the main difference between the clinical OCT and Home-care OCT systems is that the clinical system is mostly located within a secure hospital environment, while the Homecare OCT system needs to allow access to many components directly via the internet. Additionally, the Homecare OCT system needs to provide access to the patient's images to the doctor remotely, therefore the images need to be stored in the cloud. In the Clinical OCT case, an OCT image is only temporary uploaded to the cloud in a pseudonymized form for classification, and is deleted after the classification result is returned to the hospital. Therefore, the Homecare OCT system faces additional risks with require further risk management as shown in Table 3, which are not required in the clinical OCT system as shown in Table 2.

**Table 3.** A sample of the risk management for the clinical OCT system. The risk acceptance is calculated from the probability and severity of the hazard according to Table 1

| Hazard | Risk acceptance before mitigation | Mitigation | Risk acceptance after mitigation |
|---|---|---|---|
| An intruder attempts to break into the hospital's network. | Frequent × Serious ⇒ Unacceptable | – High IT security in the hospital | Frequent × Marginal ⇒ Acceptable |
| An intruder tires to fecht information which is sent to the cloud. | Frequent × Serious ⇒ Unacceptable | – Encrypt all communication with HTTPS | Frequent × Marginal ⇒ Acceptable |
| An intruder attempts to break into the cloud service and accesses data | Occasional × Serious ⇒ Unacceptable | – Restrict access to Cloud service to only authorized users<br>– Store no data on the Cloud server | Unlikely × Serious ⇒ Acceptable |
| An intruder attempts to gain information about the AI-model's training data | Rare × Serious ⇒ Unacceptable | – Allow classification requests only for authorized users.<br>– Restrict access to the weights of the AI model. | Rare × Moderate ⇒ Acceptable |

# 6    Potential Data Breach Handling

The current paper describes potential risks related to the usage of homecare medical device and clinical OCT device and measures to be implemented to mitigate those risks. Based on our analysis we are able to mitigate risks from unacceptable to acceptable. It is unlikely, however not impossible for those things to happen. For this reason, it is important to analyze not only risks but also have an action plan that will help manage activities in case of a security breach.

## 6.1    Data Breach Handling According to GDPR

Article 4 of GDPR defines "personal data breach" as a "breach of security leading to the accidental or unlawful destruction, loss, alteration, unauthorized disclosure of, or access to, personal data transmitted, stored or otherwise processed" [11].

This regulation also provides certain obligations to the companies and organizations responsible for the data breach. In the event of data breach, GDPR requires organizations to notify the supervisory authority. This shall be done

**Table 4.** We specify for potentional data breach scenarios, which data is accessed by whom and the resulting risk for identifying a patient. Further, organizational and technical measures required by the GDPR [11] are described.

| Who got Access | What Data is Accessed | Risk of Identification | Organizational Measures | Technical Measures |
|---|---|---|---|---|
| Person inside organization (e.g. doctor) | Patient's data (names, diagnosis, images) | Can access personal data of people that are not their patients | – Inform the responsible person (procedure shall be in place)<br>– Responsibility for not informing about the event<br>– Evaluate and document if data breach is likely to result in a risk to the rights and freedoms of natural persons | Track which records can be accessed by which doctor |
| Outside intruder | Access to database with images | Can not de-pseudonymize patients because personal data stored separately | Evaluate and document if data breach is likely to result in a risk to the rights and freedoms of natural persons | Since there is a connection between the database with images and personal data, this connection shall be broken by modifying the pseudonyms such as the compromised pseudonyms are not linkable to personal data |
| Outside intruder | Access to database with personal data | High risk of identification. The database is encrypted but can be decrypted with a key. It is possible only if intruder got access to both database decryption key | Inform data protection organizations and people that may be affected by data breach | Subsequent measures for data breach handling |

without undue delay but not later than 72 h once the breach was discovered. This notification shall be done unless the personal data breach is unlikely to result in a risk to the rights and freedoms of natural persons [11]. Table 4 shows an overview of possible data breach scenarios and the resulting organizational and technical measures.

According to the article 34 of GDPR, individuals affected by the data breach shall be informed as well in case if data breach is likely to result in a high risk to their rights and freedoms.

Notification is not required in case of implementation appropriate technical and organisational protection measures (e.g. encryption), taken subsequent measures which ensure that the high risk to the rights and freedoms of data subjects is no longer likely to materialize or it would involve disproportionate effort - in this case public communication or similar [11].

Based on our analysis all described risks may be related to a potential personal data breach, which means if any of those risks happen personal data can be revealed.

## 6.2  Data Breach Handling According to MDR

The MDR recognizes the terms "incident" and "serious incident". A "serious incident" is also notifiable because, according to Article 2 No. 65 of Regulation (EU) 2017/745 [37], it could lead to "the death of a patient, user or another person", "the temporary or permanent serious deterioration of a patient's, user's or other person's state of health" or to "a serious public health threat". This means that the MDR threats data loss as a "malfunction or deterioration in the characteristics or performance of a device made available on the market, including use-error due to ergonomic features, as well as any inadequacy in the information supplied by the manufacturer and any undesirable side-effect" (Article 2 No. 64 of the MDR) [37]. According to Article 88, data loss would only be reported as a trend. However, the manufacturer must establish a Post-Market Surveillance (PMS) process to ensure that he discovers the malfunctions in the field, determines the severity of the error and implements appropriate corrective and preventive measures (CAPA) if an incident occurs [34].

# 7   Conclusion

Protection of personal data is a highly regulated field especially when they are used in medical devices and software. Various risks occur due to the high value of this data and its sensitive nature. Compliance becomes more challenging because of the diverse nature of those requirements and the lack of practical examples for implementation. To fill this gap, our paper demonstrates how legal, regulatory, and other requirements can be implemented on a real-life project. In detail, we describe risks, ways to mitigate them and strategies on how to handle potential data breaches in compliance with the GDPR [11]. We believe that other readers can benefit from our research by learning how theoretical requirements can be translated into practice.

We describe two main scenarios: a Homecare OCT system and a clinical OCT system and evaluate similarities and differences in the risk management.

In the case of the clinical OCT, the OCT device and the patients' data is located inside a secure environment and only pseudonymized images are sent to the cloud for classification and deleted afterwards. Therefore, no patient information is stored outside the secure environment. Contrary, in the case of the Homecare OCT, both the device and the patients' data is held outside of the secure hospital environment and therefore, additional risks exist, which require further mitigation.

In our data flow analysis, we identified two main types of attackers: intruder, a person outside the system, and malicious user, a person inside the system, e.g. administrator or doctor, who tries to get access to data without authorization.

Both types can have different vectors of attack and require mitigation measures to lower potential risks. The main mitigation strategy includes the following: encrypted communication between device and cloud, limited system access, restricted access to the databases and backend check of user's permissions, access mapping between doctor and user, encryption of sensitive personal data and pseudonymization when possible, storing patient's data in database encryption with secure standards, and avoid storage on homecare devices.

Even though achieving absolute security is not physically possible, our analysis shows that the implementation of the measures mentioned above significantly mitigates the risks of a successful attack and decreases possible damage in case of intrusion.

# References

1. Apte, R.S.: Age-related macular degeneration. N. Engl. J. Med. **385**(6), 539–547 (2021)
2. Bende, P., Vovk, O., Caraveo, D., Pechmann, L., Leucker, M.: A case study on data protection for a cloud- and AI-based homecare medical device. In: Lamo, Y., Rutle, A. (eds.) The International Health Data Workshop HEDA 2022. CEUR Workshop Proceedings (CEUR-WS.org) (2022)
3. BMWI: orientierungshilfe zum gesundheitsdatenschutz (2018). https://www.bmwi. de/Redaktion/DE/Downloads/M-O/orientierungshilfe-gesundheitsdatenschutz. pdf?__blob=publicationFile&v=16. Accessed 15 Feb 2022
4. Consulting, M.: GSPR: general safety and performance requirements for medical devices in the EU (2023). https://mdrc-consulting.com/gspr-en/. Accessed 09 May 2023
5. Datenschutz-Grundverordnung: verordnung (eu) 2016/679 des europäischen parlaments und des rates zum schutz natürlicher personen bei der verarbeitung personenbezogener daten, zum freien datenverkehr und zur aufhebung der richtlinie 95/46/eg (datenschutz-grundverordnung) (2016). https://eur-lex.europa.eu/eli/ reg/2016/679/oj?locale=de. Accessed 16 Feb 2022

6. Domenech, M.C., Comunello, E., Wangham, M.S.: Identity management in e-health: a case study of web of things application using OpenID connect. In: 2014 IEEE 16th International Conference on e-Health Networking, Applications and Services (Healthcom), pp. 219–224 (2014)

7. Eidel, O.: Template: risk management plan and risk acceptance matrix (2020). https://openregulatory.com/risk-management-plan-risk-acceptance-matrix-template-iso-14971/. Accessed 26 Apr 2023

8. ENISA: pseudonymisation techniques and best practices (2019). https://www.enisa.europa.eu/publications/pseudonymisation-techniques-and-best-practices. Accessed 11 Feb 2022

9. European Commission: article 29 working party opinion 05/2014 on anonymisation techniques (2014)

10. Fujimoto, J.G., Pitris, C., Boppart, S.A., Brezinski, M.E.: Optical coherence tomography: an emerging technology for biomedical imaging and optical biopsy. Neoplasia **2**(1–2), 9–25 (2000)

11. GDPR: regulation (eu) 2016/ 679 of the European parliament and of the council on the protection of natural persons with regard to the processing of personal data and on the free movement of such data, and repealing directive 95/46/ec (2016). https://eur-lex.europa.eu/eli/reg/2016/679/oj. Accessed 01 Feb 2022

12. Gurfinkel, A.: Fault, error, and failure (2019). https://ece.uwaterloo.ca/~agurfink/stqam.w19/assets/pdf/W01P2-FaultErrorFailure.pdf. Accessed 01 May 2023

13. Hardt, D.: The oauth 2.0 authorization framework. RFC 6749, RFC Editor (2012). https://www.rfc-editor.org/rfc/rfc6749.txt

14. Hwang, J., Aziz, A., Sung, N., Ahmad, A., Gall, F.L., Song, J.: AUTOCON-IoT: automated and scalable online conformance testing for IoT applications. IEEE Access **8**, 43111–43121 (2020)

15. IBM: IBM report: Compromised employee accounts led to most expensive data breaches over past year (2020). https://newsroom.ibm.com/2020-07-29-IBM-Report-Compromised-Employee-Accounts-Led-to-Most-Expensive-Data-Breaches-Over-Past-Year. Accessed 24 Mar 2022

16. IEEE: Standard glossary of software engineering terminology. IEEE Std 610.12-1990, pp. 1–84 (1990). https://doi.org/10.1109/IEEESTD.1990.101064

17. Interessengemeinschaft der Benannten Stellen für Medizinprodukte in Deutschland: questionnaire artificial intelligence in medical devices (2022). https://www.ig-nb.de/veroeffentlichungen/. Accessed 09 May 2023

18. ISO/IEC 27001: Information security management systems requirements. International Organization for Standardization, Vernier, Geneva, Switzerland (2022). https://www.iso.org/standard/27001

19. Johner, C.: ISO 14971 and risk management (2015). https://www.johner-institute.com/articles/risk-management-iso-14971/. Accessed 29 Mar 2022

20. Johner, C.: Risk assessment, risk acceptance matrix (2015). https://www.johner-institute.com/articles/risk-management-iso-14971/risk-acceptance/. Accessed 26 Apr 2023

21. Johner, C.: Datenschutz im gesundheitswesen bei medizinischen daten (2020). https://www.johner-institut.de/blog/regulatory-affairs/datenschutz-bei-medizinischen-daten/. Accessed 25 Mar 2022

22. Kumar, M., Rossbory, M., Moser, B.A., Freudenthaler, B.: Deriving an optimal noise adding mechanism for privacy-preserving machine learning. In: Anderst-Kotsis, G., et al. (eds.) DEXA 2019. CCIS, vol. 1062, pp. 108–118. Springer, Cham (2019). https://doi.org/10.1007/978-3-030-27684-3_15

23. Lewis, J.E.: Web single sign-on authentication using SAML. IJCSI Int. J. Comput. Sci. Issues **2** (2009)

24. Lodderstedt, T., Bradley, J., Labunets, A., Fett, D.: OAuth 2.0 security best current practice. Internet-Draft draft-ietf-oauth-security-topics-19, Internet Engineering Task Force (2021). https://datatracker.ietf.org/doc/html/draft-ietf-oauth-security-topics-19

25. Medical Device Coordination Group: Guidance on cybersecurity for medical devices (2020). https://health.ec.europa.eu/system/files/2022-01/md_cybersecurity_en.pdf. Accessed 09 May 2023

26. Naik, N., Jenkins, P.: Securing digital identities in the cloud by selecting an apposite federated identity management from SAML, OAuth and OpenID connect. In: 2017 11th International Conference on Research Challenges in Information Science (RCIS), pp. 163–174 (2017)

27. Okada, M., Kandasamy, R., Chong, E.W.T., McGuiness, M.B., Guymer, R.H.: The treat-and-extend injection regimen versus alternate dosing strategies in age-related macular degeneration: a systematic review and meta-analysis. Am. J. Ophthalmol. **192**, 184–197 (2018)

28. Qiu, H., Qiu, M., Liu, M., Memmi, G.: Secure health data sharing for medical cyber-physical systems for the healthcare 4.0. IEEE J. Biomed. Health Inf. **24**(9), 2499–2505 (2020)

29. Rigaki, M., Garcia, S.: A survey of privacy attacks in machine learning. CoRR abs/2007.07646 https://arxiv.org/abs/2007.07646 (2020)

30. Rigaki, M., Garcia, S.: A Survey of privacy attacks in machine learning. arXiv:2007.07646 (2021)

31. Sabaliauskaite, G., Adepu, S.: Integrating six-step model with information flow diagrams for comprehensive analysis of cyber-physical system safety and security. In: 2017 IEEE 18th International Symposium on High Assurance Systems Engineering (HASE), pp. 41–48 (2017)

32. Sakimura, N., Bradley, J., Jones, M., de Medeiros, B., Mortimore, C.: OpenID connect 1.0 specification (2014). https://openid.net/specs/openid-connect-core-1_0.html. Accessed 30 Mar 2022

33. Schneeberger, D., Stöger, K., Holzinger, A.: The European legal framework for medical AI. In: International Cross-Domain Conference for Machine Learning and Knowledge Extraction, pp. 209–226 (2020)

34. Seeck, A.: Post-market surveillance und Überwachung der produkte im markt (2022). https://www.johner-institut.de/blog/regulatory-affairs/post-market-surveillance/. Accessed 17 Nov 2022

35. Seifermann, S., Heinrich, R., Werle, D., Reussner, R.: Detecting violations of access control and information flow policies in data flow diagrams. J. Syst. Softw. **184**, 111138 (2022)

36. Sloane, E.B., J. Silva, R.: Chapter 83 - artificial intelligence in medical devices and clinical decision support systems. In: Iadanza, E. (ed.) Clinical Engineering Handbook (Second Edition), pp. 556–568. Academic Press, second edition edn. (2020)

37. Union, E.: Regulation (eu) 2017/745 of the European parliament and of the council of 5 April 2017 on medical devices, amending directive 2001/83/ec, regulation (ec) no 178/2002 and regulation (ec) no 1223/2009 and repealing council directives 90/385/eec and 93/42/eec (text with eea relevance. ) (2017). https://lexparency.org/eu/32017R0745/. Accessed 17 Nov 2022

38. Vovk, O., Piho, G., Ross, P.: Anonymization methods of structured health care data: a literature review. In: Attiogbé, C., Ben Yahia, S. (eds.) MEDI 2021. LNCS, vol. 12732, pp. 175–189. Springer, Cham (2021). https://doi.org/10.1007/978-3-030-78428-7_14

39. Zhou, S., et al.: A retrospective study on the effectiveness of artificial intelligence-based clinical decision support system (AI-CDSS) to improve the incidence of hospital-related venous thromboembolism (VTE). Ann. Transl. Med. 9(6), 491 (2021)

# Strategies for Minimising the Synthesised ENL-Systems

Aishah Ahmed and Marta Pietkiewicz-Koutny[✉]

School of Computing, Newcastle University, Newcastle upon Tyne NE4 5TG, UK
marta.koutny@ncl.ac.uk

**Abstract.** Elementary Net Systems with Localities (ENL-systems) is a class of Petri nets introduced to model GALS (globally asynchronous locally synchronous) systems, where some of the components might be considered as logically or physically close and acting synchronously, while others might be considered as loosely connected or residing at distant locations and communicating with the rest of the system in an asynchronous way. The specification of the behaviour of a GALS system comes very often in the form of a transition system. The automated synthesis, based on regions, is an approach that allows to construct Petri net models from their transition system specifications. In our previous papers we developed algorithms and tool support for the synthesis of ENL-systems from step transition systems, where arcs are labelled by steps (sets) of executed actions. In this paper we focus on the minimisation of the synthesised nets. In particular, we discuss the properties of minimal, companion, and complementary regions, and their role in the process of minimisation of ENL-systems. Furthermore, we propose strategies to eliminate redundant regions. Our theoretical results are backed by experiments (the algorithms for the minimisation are implemented within the WORKCRAFT framework).

**Keywords:** theory of concurrency · Petri nets · localities · analysis and synthesis · step sequence semantics · theory of regions · transition systems · WORKCRAFT framework

## 1 Introduction

A number of computational systems exhibit behaviour that follows the 'globally asynchronous locally (maximally) synchronous' paradigm. Examples can be found in hardware design, where a VLSI chip may contain multiple clocks responsible for synchronising different subsets of gates [13], and in biologically inspired membrane systems representing cells within which biochemical reactions happen in synchronised pulses [27]. To formalise such systems, [16] introduced *Place/Transition-nets with localities* (PTL-nets), where each locality defines a distinct set of events which must be executed synchronously, i.e., in a maximally concurrent manner (often called *local maximal concurrency*).

ⓒ The Author(s), under exclusive license to Springer-Verlag GmbH, DE, part of Springer Nature 2024
M. Koutny et al. (Eds.): TPNOMCXVII, LNCS 14150, pp. 162–188, 2024.
https://doi.org/10.1007/978-3-662-68191-6_7

An attractive way of constructing complex computing systems is their automated synthesis from behavioural specifications given in terms of suitable transition systems. In such a case, the synthesis procedure is often based on the regions of a transition system, a notion introduced in [15], and later used to solve the synthesis problem for different classes of Petri nets [5,8,9,22,23,25]. A comprehensive survey of the synthesis problem and region theory is presented in [4].

The vast majority of results in the area of synthesis of Petri nets use the standard transition systems, where the arcs are labelled with single events/actions, as initial specifications of systems' behaviour. In this paper, however, we follow the approach, used in [17–20,25], employing step transition systems instead, where arcs are labelled with sets of executed events/actions.

The nets with localities, as already mentioned, were first introduced in [16] using as a base a class of Place/Transition nets. The idea of actions' localities was later adapted to Elementary Net Systems (EN-systems) in [17], where a solution to the synthesis problem for ENL-systems was presented. Further advances in the area of synthesising nets with localities from step transition systems are the subjects of [18–20]. The last of them, [20], concentrated on finding the rules for reducing the number of regions that are essential to synthesise ENL-systems.

In our previous papers, [2,3], we developed algorithms and tool support for the synthesis of ENL-systems from step transition systems. In this paper we continue the work started in [20] and focus on the minimisation of ENL-systems. The nets obtained from the synthesis procedure, called saturated nets, contain many conditions that are redundant from their behaviour point of view. Removing such conditions is important to get more manageable and readable solutions to the synthesis problem. The approaches to remove redundant conditions from nets were investigated in the literature and implemented in several tools [1,7]. Many synthesis procedures concentrate on returning smaller solutions based on so-called minimal regions [6,10–12,21]. In our approach, minimal regions, as defined for our class of step transition systems, are also important for building smaller solutions to the synthesis problem. Furthermore, in this paper, following [8], we are interested in the role of minimal regions in defining state-machine components of the synthesised and minimised ENL-systems. When researching this second problem, the state-machine decomposability of minimised ENL-systems, we discovered that the definition of minimal regions introduced in [20] was not suitable to define subsets of minimal regions that would generate state-machine components of the synthesised and minimised ENL-systems. The cause of this problem was that the definition of minimal regions introduced in [20] was based on the composition operator for regions that was not associative. In this paper, we introduce a new definition of minimal regions based on a new definition of composition operator that we proved to be associative. This operator would allow the minimal regions to be grouped into families of regions that generate sequential subsystems of the synthesised and minimised ENL-systems. Furthermore, we prove in this paper that the reduction rules from [20] can still be used with the new definition of minimal regions. These results, presented in Sect. 5, constitute the main theoretical contribution of this paper. Having the necessary results regarding the properties of different kinds of regions, we propose and evaluate several strategies for eliminating redundant regions from the synthesised ENL-systems. Our theoretical results are backed by experiments (the algorithms for the minimisation are implemented within the WORKCRAFT framework [26,29]).

To explain the basic idea behind ENL-systems, let us consider the net in Fig. 1 modelling two co-located consumers and one producer residing in a remote location. In the initial state, the net can execute the singleton step $\{c_4\}$. Another enabled step is $\{p_2\}$ which removes the token from $b_1$ and puts a token, in both $b_0$ and $b_2$. In this new state, there are three enabled steps, viz. $\{p_1\}$, $\{c_1, c_4\}$ and $\{p_1, c_1, c_4\}$. The last one, $\{p_1, c_1, c_4\}$, corresponds to what is usually called *maximal concurrency* as no more activities can be added to it without violating the constrains imposed by the available resources (represented by tokens). However, the previously enabled step $\{c_4\}$ which is still *resource (or token) enabled* is disallowed by the control mechanism of ENL-systems. It rejects a resource enabled step like $\{c_4\}$ since we can add to it $c_1$ co-located with $c_4$ obtaining a step which is resource enabled. In other words, the control mechanism employed by ENL-systems (and PTL-nets) is that of *local maximal concurrency* as indeed postulated by the GALS systems execution rule.

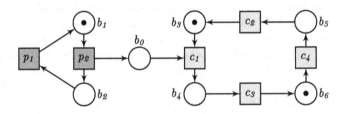

**Fig. 1.** An ENL-system modelling a system comprising one producer and two co-located consumers (the shading of boxes indicates the co-location of events they represent).

The paper is organised as follows. The next section recalls some basic notions concerning step transition systems as well as ENL-systems and their synthesis. Section 3 recalls, from [20], three reduction rules that can be used to safely eliminate redundant regions/conditions from the synthesised nets. Section 4 defines minimal regions for the class of ENLST-systems and Sect. 5 discusses the properties of different kinds of regions and their roles in the process of minimisation of the synthesised ENL-systems. Section 6 presents several strategies to eliminate redundant regions from the synthesised nets and Sect. 7 shows some selected results of the experiments. The paper ends with a conclusion that includes some directions for future work.

## 2   Preliminaries

In this section, we recall suitably adapted notions and results from [17,19,20].

The actions of net systems and transition systems discussed in this paper are called *events*. The sets of events used by both types of systems are assumed to be finite and nonempty. Let $E$ be a set of events. A *step* is a nonempty set of events from $E$, and a *co-location relation* $\asymp$ is any equivalence relation over $E$. For every event $e \in E$, $[e]_\asymp$ is the equivalence class of $\asymp$ to which $e$ belongs (i.e., the *locality* of $e$). For an event $e$ and a step $U$, we denote $e \asymp U$ whenever there is at least one event $f \in U$ satisfying $e \asymp f$.

**Definition 1.** *A* step transition system *(or* ST-*system) over a set of events $E$ is a triple* $\mathsf{ts} = (Q, A, q_0)$, *where $Q$ is a nonempty finite set of* states, $A \subseteq Q \times (\mathbb{P}(E) \setminus \{\varnothing\}) \times Q$ *is a set of* transitions (arcs), *and* $q_0 \in Q$ *is the* initial state.
*When we say that* $\mathsf{ts}$ *is an* ST-*system we implicitly assume the existence of its set of events $E$.* ◇

In diagrams, ST-systems are represented as labelled directed graphs, and singleton steps annotating transitions are denoted without brackets.

To ease the presentation, we assume that each event of $E$ occurs in at least one of the steps labelling the transitions of $\mathsf{ts}$.

The set of all steps labelling transitions outgoing from $q$ will be denoted by $allSteps_q$. For a transition $\mathsf{t} = (q, U, q') \in A$, we have therefore $U \in allSteps_q$, and respectively call $q$ and $q'$ the *source* and *target* of $\mathsf{t}$. Furthermore, $\mathsf{t}$ is *thick* if $|U| \geq 2$.

$\mathsf{ts}$ is called *thin* if, for every event $e \in E$, there is $(q, \{e\}, q') \in A$.

A sequence of transitions $(q_1, U_1, q_2)(q_2, U_2, q_3) \ldots (q_k, U_k, q_{k+1})$ is a *path* from $q_1$ to $q_{k+1}$. A state $q$ is *reachable* if there is a path from $q_0$ to $q$.

Two ST-systems, $\mathsf{ts} = (Q, A, q_0)$ and $\mathsf{ts}' = (Q', A', q_0')$, are *isomorphic* if there is a bijection $f : Q \to Q'$ such that $f(q_0) = q_0'$ and $A' = \{(f(q), U, f(q')) \mid (q, U, q') \in A\}$. We denote this by $\mathsf{ts} \cong \mathsf{ts}'$.

**Definition 2.** *An* elementary net system with localities *w.r.t. a co-location relation $\asymp$ (or* ENL$_\asymp$-*system) is a tuple* $\mathsf{enl} = (B, E, F, \asymp, c_0)$, *where $E$ is a set of* events *and $B$ is a finite nonempty set of* conditions *such that $B \cap E = \varnothing$, $F \subseteq (B \times E) \cup (E \times B)$ is the* flow relation, *and* $c_0 \subseteq B$ *is the* initial case *(in general, any $c \subseteq B$ is a* case*).*
*For every event $e$, its* pre-conditions *and* post-conditions *are given respectively by* $^\bullet e = \{b \mid (b, e) \in F\}$ *and* $e^\bullet = \{b \mid (e, b) \in F\}$, *and both sets are assumed to be nonempty and disjoint. Furthermore, we assume that there are no isolated conditions in* $\mathsf{enl}$.
*We will also say that* $\mathsf{enl}$ *is an elementary net system with localities (or* ENL-*system) if mentioning $\asymp$ is not important.* ◇

In diagrams, conditions (local states) are represented by circles, events (actions) by boxes, the flow relation by directed arcs, and each case (global state) by tokens (small black dots) placed inside those conditions which belong to this case. Moreover, boxes representing co-located events are shaded in the same way (see Fig. 1).

The dot-notation used in Definition 2 extends to sets of events in the usual way, e.g., $^\bullet U = \bigcup \{ ^\bullet e \mid e \in U \}$. Two distinct events, $e$ and $f$, are *in conflict* (or *conflicting*) if they share a pre-condition, or share a post-condition.

The semantics of $\mathrm{enl}$ is based on steps of simultaneously executed events, and can be understood as *local maximal concurrency*. We first define *potential steps* of $\mathrm{enl}$ as all nonempty sets of mutually non-conflicting events. A potential step $U$ is then *resource enabled* at a case $c$ if $^\bullet U \subseteq c$ and $U^\bullet \cap c = \varnothing$, and *control enabled* if, in addition, there is no event $e \notin U$ such that $e \risingdotseq U$ and the step $U \cup \{e\}$ is resource enabled at $c$. We denote these respectively by $U \in resenabled(c)$ and $U \in enabled(c)$. A control enabled step $U \in enabled(c)$ can be *executed* leading from $c$ to the case $c' = (c \setminus {}^\bullet U) \cup U^\bullet$. We denote this by $c[U\rangle c'$.

The set of *reachable* cases of $\mathrm{enl}$, denoted $reach_{\mathrm{enl}}$, is the smallest set of cases containing $c_0$ such that if $c \in reach_{\mathrm{enl}}$ and $c[U\rangle c'$, then $c' \in reach_{\mathrm{enl}}$.

The ST-system *generated* by $\mathrm{enl}$ is $\mathrm{ts}_{\mathrm{enl}} = (reach_{\mathrm{enl}}, A, c_0)$, where $A = \{(c, U, c') \mid c \in reach_{\mathrm{enl}} \wedge c[U\rangle c'\}$.

$\mathrm{enl}$ is a *net realisation* of an ST-system $\mathrm{ts}$ if $\mathrm{ts}_{\mathrm{enl}} \cong \mathrm{ts}$.

To ease the presentation, we assume that $\mathrm{enl}$ does not have *dead events*, i.e., for each event $e$, there are $c \in reach_{\mathrm{enl}}$ and $U \in enabled(c)$ such that $e \in U$.

**Definition 3.** *Let* $\mathrm{enl} = (B, E, F, \risingdotseq, c_0)$ *be an* $\mathrm{ENL}_{\risingdotseq}$*-system. We say that* $\mathrm{enl}$ *is a state machine* $\mathrm{ENL}_{\risingdotseq}$*-system iff:*

1. $\forall e \in E : |^\bullet e| = 1 = |e^\bullet|$;
2. $|c_0| = 1.$    ◇

**Definition 4.** *Let* $\mathrm{enl} = (B, E, F, \risingdotseq, c_0)$ *be an* $\mathrm{ENL}_{\risingdotseq}$*-system. A subsystem of* $\mathrm{enl}$ *is an* $\mathrm{ENL}_{\risingdotseq'}$*-system* $\mathrm{enl}' = (B', E', F', \risingdotseq', c_0')$ *such that the following conditions hold:*

1. $B' \subseteq B$ *and* $E' \subseteq E$;
2. $\forall b \in B' \; \forall e \in E : ((b, e) \in F \vee (e, b) \in F) \implies e \in E'$;
3. $F' = F \cap ((B' \times E') \cup (E' \times B'))$; $\risingdotseq' = \risingdotseq \cap E' \times E'$ *and* $c_0' = c_0 \cap B'.$

*A subsystem* $\mathrm{enl}'$ *is* connected *if the graph* $(B' \cup E', F')$ *is connected. Also, point 2 above says that the subsystem* $\mathrm{enl}'$ *is* generated *by the subset of conditions* $B'$ *of the* $\mathrm{ENL}_{\risingdotseq}$*-system* $\mathrm{enl}$.    ◇

**Definition 5.** *Let* $\mathrm{enl} = (B, E, F, \risingdotseq, c_0)$ *be an* $\mathrm{ENL}_{\risingdotseq}$*-system. We say that* $\mathrm{enl}$ *is a state machine decomposable* $\mathrm{ENL}_{\risingdotseq}$*-system iff there exists a set of connected subsystems of* $\mathrm{enl}$, $\mathrm{enl}_i = (B_i, E_i, F_i, \risingdotseq_i, c_0^i)$ $(i = 1, \ldots, m)$, *satisfying the following:*

1. $\forall i \in \{1, \ldots, m\} : \mathrm{enl}_i$ *is a state machine* $\mathrm{ENL}_{\risingdotseq_i}$*-system;*
2. $B = \bigcup_i B_i$, $E = \bigcup_i E_i$ *and* $F = \bigcup_i F_i.$

*The* $\mathrm{enl}_i$ *are called* state machine (or sequential) components *of* $\mathrm{enl}$.    ◇

The general synthesis problem we consider can be formulated thus:

*Problem 1.* Given an ST-system $\mathsf{ts}$ and a co-location relation $\frown$, find an effective way of checking whether there is an $\mathrm{ENL}_\frown$-system which is a net realisation of $\mathsf{ts}$. If the answer is positive construct such an $\mathrm{ENL}_\frown$-system.                $\Diamond$

The above problem can be approached by considering a link between the nodes (global states) of an ST-system with the conditions (local states) of a hypothetical ENL-system realising it, captured by the notion of regions with explicit input and output events.

**Definition 6.** *A* region (with explicit input and output events) *of an* ST-*system* $\mathsf{ts} = (Q, A, q_0)$ *is a triple* $\mathfrak{r} = (in, r, out) \in \mathbb{P}(E) \times \mathbb{P}(Q) \times \mathbb{P}(E)$, *such that* $in = out = \varnothing$ *implies* $r = Q$ *or* $r = \varnothing$ *and, for every transition* $(q, U, q')$ *of* $\mathsf{ts}$, *the following hold:*

R1  *If* $q \in r$ *and* $q' \notin r$ *then* $|U \cap out| = 1$.
R2  *If* $q \notin r$ *and* $q' \in r$ *then* $|U \cap in| = 1$.
R3  *If* $U \cap out \neq \varnothing$ *then* $q \in r$ *and* $q' \notin r$.
R4  *If* $U \cap in \neq \varnothing$ *then* $q \notin r$ *and* $q' \in r$.                $\Diamond$

In a region $\mathfrak{r} = (in, r, out)$, the set $in$ comprises events responsible for entering the set of states $r$, and $out$ comprises events responsible for leaving $r$. Note that $\bar{\mathfrak{r}} = (out, Q \setminus r, in)$ is also a region (the *complement* of region $\mathfrak{r}$).

In general, a region $\mathfrak{r}$ cannot be identified only by its set of states $r$. However, if $\mathsf{ts}$ is *thin*, then its different regions are based on different sets of states.

There are exactly two *trivial* regions satisfying $r = \varnothing$ or $r = Q$, viz. $(\varnothing, \varnothing, \varnothing)$ and $(\varnothing, Q, \varnothing)$.

The set of all non-trivial regions of $\mathsf{ts}$ will be denoted by $\mathfrak{R}_{\mathsf{ts}}$ and, for every state $q$, $\mathfrak{R}_q = \{\mathfrak{r} \in \mathfrak{R}_{\mathsf{ts}} \mid q \in r\}$ is the set of all non-trivial regions $(in, r, out)$ containing $q$.

The sets of *pre-regions* and *post-regions* of an event $e$, ${}^\circ e$ and $e^\circ$, comprise all the non-trivial regions $(in, r, out)$ respectively satisfying $e \in out$ and $e \in in$, viz. ${}^\circ e = \{\mathfrak{r} \in \mathfrak{R}_{\mathsf{ts}} \mid e \in out\}$ and $e^\circ = \{\mathfrak{r} \in \mathfrak{R}_{\mathsf{ts}} \mid e \in in\}$. This extends in the usual way to sets of events, for example, ${}^\circ U = \bigcup\{{}^\circ e \mid e \in U\}$. Also, we will write $e \in \mathfrak{r}^\circ \Longleftrightarrow \mathfrak{r} \in {}^\circ e$ and $e \in {}^\circ \mathfrak{r} \Longleftrightarrow \mathfrak{r} \in e^\circ$.

The set of *potential steps* of $\mathsf{ts}$ comprises all nonempty sets $U$ of events such that ${}^\circ e \cap {}^\circ f = e^\circ \cap f^\circ = \varnothing$, for each pair of distinct events $e, f \in U$. A potential step $U$ is then *region enabled* at $q \in Q$ if ${}^\circ U \subseteq \mathfrak{R}_q$ and $U^\circ \cap \mathfrak{R}_q = \varnothing$. We denote this by $U \in regenabled(q)$.

**Definition 7.** *An* ST-*system* $\mathsf{ts}$ *is an* ENL step transition system *w.r.t. a co-location relation* $\frown$ *(or* ENLST$_\frown$-*system) if the following hold:*

A1  *Each state is reachable.*
A2  *For every event* $e$, *both* ${}^\circ e$ *and* $e^\circ$ *are nonempty.*
A3  *For all distinct states* $q$ *and* $q'$, $\mathfrak{R}_q \neq \mathfrak{R}_{q'}$.
A4  *For every state* $q$ *and step* $U$, $U \in allSteps_q$ *iff* $U \in regenabled(q)$ *and there is no event* $e \notin U$ *such that* $e \frown U$ *and* $U \cup \{e\} \in regenabled(q)$.

*We also say that* ts *is an* ENLST-*system (if mentioning* $\backsimeq$ *is not important).* ◇

One can show that the ST-system generated by an ENL$_\backsimeq$-system is an ENLST$_\backsimeq$-system. The converse is also true, and a suitable translation is based on the regions of ST-systems.

**Definition 8.** *Let* ts *be an* ENLST$_\backsimeq$-*system. The tuple associated with* ts *is defined by* $enl_{ts}^{\backsimeq} = (\mathfrak{R}_{ts}, E, F_{ts}, \backsimeq, \mathfrak{R}_{q_0})$, *where* $q_0$ *is the initial state of* ts *and*

$$F_{ts} = \{(\mathfrak{r}, e) \in \mathfrak{R}_{ts} \times E \mid \mathfrak{r} \in {}^{\circ}e\} \cup \{(e, \mathfrak{r}) \in E \times \mathfrak{R}_{ts} \mid \mathfrak{r} \in e^{\circ}\}.$$

◇

The above construction always produces an ENL$_\backsimeq$-system which generates an ST-system isomorphic to ts (see [17]).

**Theorem 1.** *Let* ts *be an* ENLST$_\backsimeq$-*system. Then* $enl_{ts}^{\backsimeq}$ *is an* ENL$_\backsimeq$-*system such that* ts $\cong$ ts$_{enl_{ts}^{\backsimeq}}$. *Moreover, the unique isomorphism* $\psi$ *between* ts *and* ts$_{enl_{ts}^{\backsimeq}}$ *is given by* $\psi(q) = \mathfrak{R}_q$, *for every state* $q$ *of* ts.

# 3    Optimising Solutions to the Synthesis Problem

In this section we recall some notions and results from [20].

The ENL-system $enl_{ts}^{\backsimeq}$ obtained from the synthesis of the ENLST-system ts may contain many conditions which are *redundant* from the point of view of its behaviour, *i.e.*, deletion of such conditions (and their adjacent arcs) would lead to a net that generates the ST-system, which is still isomorphic to ts.

Suppose that we have reduced $enl_{ts}^{\backsimeq}$ in this way obtaining a sub-ENL-system enl. We would like to reduce enl further by deleting a condition/region $\mathfrak{r}$ (and its adjacent arcs) without, as before, violating the property of it being an ENL-system[1] and making sure that the resultant net still generates the ST-system isomorphic to ts. We denote the ENL-system after such one step reduction: $enl_{\mathfrak{r}}$.

In [20], it was proved that complement regions are very often redundant:

**Reduction Rule 1.** *If* $\mathfrak{r} = (in, r, out)$ *and* $\bar{\mathfrak{r}} = (out, Q \backslash r, in)$ *are two conditions in* enl *and deleting* $\bar{\mathfrak{r}}$ *leads to an* ENL-*system, then the* ST-*systems generated by* enl *and* $enl_{\bar{\mathfrak{r}}}$ *are isomorphic and* $\bar{\mathfrak{r}}$ *is redundant.* ◇

Another source of redundancy among conditions/regions in the synthesised net are "big" regions that are compositions of smaller regions. To define a composition operator, [20] introduces the concept of *compatible* regions.

**Definition 9.** *A region* $(in, r, out)$ *is compatible with another region* $(in', r', out')$ *iff the following three conditions hold:*

*1.* $r \cap r' = \varnothing$.

---

[1] Every ENL-system enl $= (B, E, F, \backsimeq, c_0)$ should satisfy: $\forall e \in E \ ({}^{\bullet}e \neq \varnothing \wedge e^{\bullet} \neq \varnothing \wedge {}^{\bullet}e \cap e^{\bullet} = \varnothing)$.

2. *For every $e \in out$ exactly one of the following holds:*
   - *For all the transitions $(q, U, q')$ such that $e \in U$ we have $q' \in r'$.*
   - *For all the transitions $(q, U, q')$ such that $e \in U$ we have $q' \notin r'$.*
3. *For every $e \in in$ exactly one of the following holds:*
   - *For all the transitions $(q, U, q')$ such that $e \in U$ we have $q \in r'$.*
   - *For all the transitions $(q, U, q')$ such that $e \in U$ we have $q \notin r'$.*

*If region $\mathfrak{r}$ is compatible with region $\mathfrak{r}'$ and region $\mathfrak{r}'$ is compatible with $\mathfrak{r}$ we say that the two regions are compatible.*                                                    ◇

In [20], it was proved that the *composition of two compatible regions* (defined below) is also a region. If $\mathfrak{r} = (in, r, out)$ and $\mathfrak{r}' = (in', r', out')$ are two non-trivial compatible regions of an ENLST-system $\mathfrak{ts}$, then the following is a (possibly trivial) region of $\mathfrak{ts}$:

$$\mathfrak{r} \oplus \mathfrak{r}' \stackrel{df}{=} (in \cup in' \setminus H, r \cup r', out \cup out' \setminus H),$$

where $H$ is a set of events that belong only to steps labelling transitions hidden/buried in $r \cup r'$ (with its source in $r$ and its target in $r'$ or the other way round). The region $\mathfrak{r} \oplus \mathfrak{r}'$ is called the composition of $\mathfrak{r}$ and $\mathfrak{r}'$. In [20], the following reduction rule was proved:

**Reduction Rule 2.** *If $\mathfrak{r} = (in, r, out)$, $\mathfrak{r}' = (in', r', out')$ and $\mathfrak{r} \oplus \mathfrak{r}'$ are three conditions/regions in $\mathfrak{enl}$, then the ST-systems generated by $\mathfrak{enl}$ and $\mathfrak{enl}_{\mathfrak{r} \oplus \mathfrak{r}'}$ are isomorphic and $\mathfrak{r} \oplus \mathfrak{r}'$ is redundant.*                                    ◇

The third reduction rule considers regions of $\mathfrak{ts} = (Q, A, q_0)$ based on the same set of states. We will call such regions *companion* regions. For a given set of states $r$, they will belong to the set denoted by $\mathfrak{R}^r_{\mathfrak{ts}}$.

In [20], it was proved that if the events contained in the set $in$ ($out$) of a region $\mathfrak{r} = (in, r, out)$ can be found in the $in$ ($out$) sets of other companion regions then $\mathfrak{r}$ is redundant and can be deleted. Formally:

**Reduction Rule 3.** *Let $\mathfrak{r} = (in, r, out)$ be a condition/region of $\mathfrak{enl}$ such that:*

$$in \subseteq \bigcup \{in' \mid (in', r, out') \text{ is condition in } \mathfrak{enl} \text{ different from } \mathfrak{r}\} \qquad (1)$$

$$out \subseteq \bigcup \{out' \mid (in', r, out') \text{ is condition in } \mathfrak{enl} \text{ different from } \mathfrak{r}\} \qquad (2)$$

*Then the ST-systems generated by $\mathfrak{enl}$ and $\mathfrak{enl}_{\mathfrak{r}}$ are isomorphic and $\mathfrak{r}$ is redundant.*
                                                                                          ◇

## 4    Minimal Regions

For many classes of Petri nets, for which the synthesis problem was investigated, a region was defined as a subset of states of a transition system. For such classes of nets and their transition systems a minimal region was defined *w.r.t.* the set inclusion $\subset$ [8,9,11,24]. Also, composition of regions (as sets) was defined by using the set union operator ($\cup$), which is both commutative and associative.

The regions of ENLST-systems are triples of the form: $\mathfrak{r} = (in, r, out)$. The minimal regions in this class of (step) transition systems are defined *w.r.t.* the strict pre-order $\prec$ on the set of regions, that utilises the idea of regions' composition by means of $\oplus$:

$$\mathfrak{r} \prec \mathfrak{r}' \text{ iff there is a non-trivial region } \mathfrak{r}'' \text{ such that } \mathfrak{r} \oplus \mathfrak{r}'' = \mathfrak{r}' \text{ [20]}.$$

Formally, we have the following definition of a *minimal region*:

**Definition 10.** *A region* $\mathfrak{r} \in \mathfrak{R}_{ts}$ *is* minimal *iff* $\forall \hat{\mathfrak{r}} \in \mathfrak{R}_{ts} : \hat{\mathfrak{r}} \not\prec \mathfrak{r}$. $\diamond$

The set of minimal regions of ts w.r.t. $\prec$ will be denoted by $\mathfrak{R}_{ts}^{min}$.

We observe that if a non-trivial region is *non-minimal* then it can be represented as a composition of two other non-trivial regions. This follows from the definition of the relation $\prec$ and the fact that the composition operator $\oplus$ is commutative, which, in turn, follows immediately from the definition of $\oplus$.

As an example, consider the ENLST-system in Fig. 2(a). Its non-trivial regions are:

$$\begin{aligned}
\mathfrak{r}_1 &= (\varnothing, \{q_0\}, \{e\}) & \mathfrak{r}_3 &= \bar{\mathfrak{r}}_1 = (\{e\}, \{q_1, q_2\}, \varnothing) \\
\mathfrak{r}_2 &= (\varnothing, \{q_0\}, \{e_1, e_2\}) & \mathfrak{r}_4 &= \bar{\mathfrak{r}}_2 = (\{e_1, e_2\}, \{q_1, q_2\}, \varnothing) \\
\mathfrak{r}_5 &= (\{e_1\}, \{q_1\}, \varnothing) & \mathfrak{r}_7 &= \bar{\mathfrak{r}}_5 = (\varnothing, \{q_0, q_2\}, \{e_1\}) \\
\mathfrak{r}_6 &= (\{e_2\}, \{q_2\}, \varnothing) & \mathfrak{r}_8 &= \bar{\mathfrak{r}}_6 = (\varnothing, \{q_0, q_1\}, \{e_2\})
\end{aligned}$$

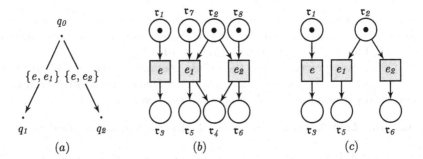

**Fig. 2.** An ENLST-system with three co-located events $e$, $e_1$ and $e_2$ (a); the ENL-system resulting from its synthesis (b); and the reduced ENL-system solution for (a) that uses only minimal regions (c).

The minimal regions of the ENLST-system in Fig. 2(a) are: $\mathfrak{r}_1$, $\mathfrak{r}_2$, $\mathfrak{r}_3$, $\mathfrak{r}_5$ and $\mathfrak{r}_6$. The remaining regions are non-minimal (their set is denoted by $\mathfrak{R}_{ts}^{\oplus}$): $\mathfrak{r}_4 = \mathfrak{r}_5 \oplus \mathfrak{r}_6$ ($H = \varnothing$); $\mathfrak{r}_7 = \mathfrak{r}_2 \oplus \mathfrak{r}_6$ ($H = \{e_2\}$); $\mathfrak{r}_8 = \mathfrak{r}_2 \oplus \mathfrak{r}_5$ ($H = \{e_1\}$).

The reduced ENL-system solution for the ENLST-system in Fig. 2(a) that uses only regions minimal *w.r.t.* $\prec$ is shown in Fig. 2(c).

Note that the operator $\oplus$ is not associative as can be shown by using, again, the example of the ENLST-system in Fig. 2(a). We can observe that: $(\mathfrak{r}_5 \oplus \mathfrak{r}_6) \oplus \mathfrak{r}_1 \neq$

$\mathfrak{r}_5 \oplus (\mathfrak{r}_6 \oplus \mathfrak{r}_1)$. While $\mathfrak{r}_5$ and $\mathfrak{r}_6$ are compatible and their composition produces $\mathfrak{r}_4$ $(\mathfrak{r}_4 = \mathfrak{r}_5 \oplus \mathfrak{r}_6)$, regions $\mathfrak{r}_6$ and $\mathfrak{r}_1$ are not compatible, because $\mathfrak{r}_1$ is not compatible with $\mathfrak{r}_6$, and they cannot be composed.

Also notice that there might be two companion regions (regions based on the same set of states) such that one of them is a minimal region and the second one is a non-minimal region. See, for example, regions $\mathfrak{r}_3 = (\{e\}, \{q_1, q_2\}, \varnothing)$ and $\mathfrak{r}_4 = (\{e_1, e_2\}, \{q_1, q_2\}, \varnothing)$ of the ENLST-system in Fig. 2(a), where $\mathfrak{r}_3$ is minimal and $\mathfrak{r}_4$ is non-minimal. So, the minimality of a region cannot be decided by looking at its set of states only.

The following result, about the representation of non-trivial regions, is similar to the results proved for other classes of nets (and their transition systems) that can be found in the literature: Elementary Net Systems [8], pure and bounded Place/Transition Nets [9], Safe Nets [11] or Elementary Net Systems with Inhibitor Arcs (ENI-systems) [24].

**Theorem 2.** *Every $\mathfrak{r} = (in, r, out) \in \mathfrak{R}_{ts}$ can be represented as a composition of minimal regions, where for each pair of different minimal regions in this representation, $\widehat{\mathfrak{r}} = (\widehat{in}, \widehat{r}, \widehat{out})$ and $\widetilde{\mathfrak{r}} = (\widetilde{in}, \widetilde{r}, \widetilde{out})$, $\widehat{r} \cap \widetilde{r} = \varnothing$.*

*Proof.* If $\mathfrak{r}$ is a minimal region then the result holds. If $\mathfrak{r}$ is non-minimal then there exists a minimal region $\mathfrak{r}' = (in', r', out') \prec \mathfrak{r}$. From the definition of the strict pre-order $\prec$ we have that there exists $\mathfrak{r}'' = (in'', r'', out'')$ such that $\mathfrak{r}' \oplus \mathfrak{r}'' = \mathfrak{r}$. If $\mathfrak{r}''$ is minimal we have $\mathfrak{r} = \mathfrak{r}' \oplus \mathfrak{r}''$. If $\mathfrak{r}''$ is non-minimal we continue in the same way with $\mathfrak{r}''$ as we have done before with $\mathfrak{r}$. In this way we will build a sequence of minimal regions, whose sets of states are mutually disjoint and their sum would define the set of states for $\mathfrak{r}$. As $Q$ is finite, the number of minimal regions in the representation of $\mathfrak{r}$ will be finite:

$$\mathfrak{r} = \mathfrak{r}_1 \oplus (\mathfrak{r}_2 \oplus \ldots (\mathfrak{r}_{n-2} \oplus (\mathfrak{r}_{n-1} \oplus \mathfrak{r}_n)) \ldots),$$

where $\mathfrak{r}_i = (in_i, r_i, out_i)$ (for $i = 1, \ldots, n$) are minimal regions.

Observe that by the definition of compatibility of regions and that of $\oplus$ operator, we have $r_{n-1} \cap r_n = \varnothing$ and $r_{n-2} \cap (r_{n-1} \cup r_n) = \varnothing$. We can proceed in this way from right to left of the above representation, ending with $r_1 \cap r'' = \varnothing$, where $r_1$ is the original $r'$ and $r'' = r_2 \cup r_3 \cup \ldots \cup r_{n-1} \cup r_n$. So, all the sets of states of the minimal regions in the representation are pairwise disjoint.     □

Theorem 2 and Reduction Rule 2 imply that one can construct a solution to the synthesis problem based on minimal regions *w.r.t.* the strict pre-order $\prec$. The consequence of the fact that the operator $\oplus$ is not associative is that we cannot drop the brackets, if there are any, when we represent a non-trivial region of an ENLST-system as a composition of minimal regions (see the proof of Theorem 2).

## 5   Properties of Regions

In this section we gather facts regarding relationships of complementary, compatible, companion and minimal regions of an ENLST-system $\mathsf{ts} = (Q, A, q_0)$.

**Fact 1.** *Any pair of complementary regions of $\mathsf{ts}$, $\mathfrak{r}$ and $\bar{\mathfrak{r}}$, form a pair of compatible regions and $\mathfrak{r} \oplus \bar{\mathfrak{r}} = (\varnothing, Q, \varnothing)$.* $\diamondsuit$

From Fact 1 it follows that if $\mathsf{ts}$ has only minimal regions among non-trivial regions, then only the pairs of complementary regions can be composed resulting in the trivial region $(\varnothing, Q, \varnothing)$.

**Fact 2.** *Let $\mathfrak{r}_1 = (in_1, r_1, out_1)$ and $\mathfrak{r}_2 = (in_2, r_2, out_2)$ be two non-trivial compatible regions of an ENLST-system $\mathsf{ts}$. Then $in_1 \cap in_2 = \varnothing$ and $out_1 \cap out_2 = \varnothing$.*

*Proof.* Since $\mathfrak{r}_1$ and $\mathfrak{r}_2$ are compatible regions, we have $r_1 \cap r_2 = \varnothing$. Suppose $in_1 \cap in_2 \neq \varnothing$. Then there exists $e \in in_1 \cap in_2$ and every transition labelled with a step containing $e$ enters both $r_1$ and $r_2$ (see Definition 6(R4)), but that is impossible as $r_1 \cap r_2 = \varnothing$ - a contradiction. So, $in_1 \cap in_2 = \varnothing$. Similarly, we can show that $out_1 \cap out_2 = \varnothing$. $\square$

Now, we introduce a notion of *strong compatibility* of regions.

**Definition 11.** *A region $(in, r, out)$ is strongly compatible with another region $(in', r', out')$ iff the following three conditions hold:*

1. *$r \cap r' = \varnothing$.*
2. *For every $e \in out$ exactly one of the following holds:*
   - *$e \in in'$.*
   - *For all the transitions $(q, U, q')$ such that $e \in U$ we have $q' \notin r'$.*
3. *For every $e \in in$ exactly one of the following holds:*
   - *$e \in out'$.*
   - *For all the transitions $(q, U, q')$ such that $e \in U$ we have $q \notin r'$.*

*If region $\mathfrak{r}$ is strongly compatible with region $\mathfrak{r}'$ and region $\mathfrak{r}'$ is strongly compatible with $\mathfrak{r}$ we say that the two regions are strongly compatible.* $\diamondsuit$

Notice that in Definition 11 (as before in Definition 9), in conditions 2 and 3, there are propositions expressed as 'exclusive or' ($\underline{\vee}$) of two sub-propositions, which can never be true together (see Definition 6(R3,R4)). We recall that for any two propositions $p$ and $q$ we have: $(p \underline{\vee} q) = (p \vee q) \wedge \neg(p \wedge q)$. Therefore, we can see that in the case of Definitions 9 and 11, the 'exclusive or' suggested by the phrase 'exactly one' used in conditions 2 and 3 of these definitions coincide with the 'regular or' ($\vee$). This observation will be important in the proof of Proposition 1.

**Fact 3.** *Two regions, which are strongly compatible are compatible.*

*Proof.* Follows from Definitions 9, 11 and 6. $\square$

The composition operator defined for the strongly compatible regions (rather than compatible regions) will be denoted by $\oplus_s$. The strict pre-order relation for the set of regions that utilises operator $\oplus_s$ instead of $\oplus$ will be denoted by $\prec_s$. The set of minimal regions of $\mathsf{ts}$ w.r.t. $\prec_s$ will be denoted by $\mathfrak{R}_{\mathsf{ts}}^{min,s}$.

The implication of Fact 3 is that Reduction Rule 2 works with strongly compatible regions (we can replace operator $\oplus$ by $\oplus_s$ in that rule). Furthermore, Definition 11 means that we can strengthen Fact 1 to:

**Fact 4.** *Any pair of complementary regions of* $\mathfrak{ts}$, $\mathfrak{r}$ *and* $\bar{\mathfrak{r}}$, *form a pair of strongly compatible regions and* $\mathfrak{r} \oplus_s \bar{\mathfrak{r}} = (\varnothing, Q, \varnothing)$. ◇

We will give examples of compatible and strongly compatible pairs of regions using the ENLST-system in Fig. 2(a). The pairs of regions $\{\mathfrak{r}_1, \mathfrak{r}_4\}$ and $\{\mathfrak{r}_2, \mathfrak{r}_3\}$ are compatible, but not strongly compatible. However, the pairs $\{\mathfrak{r}_1, \mathfrak{r}_3\}$, $\{\mathfrak{r}_2, \mathfrak{r}_4\}$, $\{\mathfrak{r}_2, \mathfrak{r}_5\}$, $\{\mathfrak{r}_2, \mathfrak{r}_6\}$, $\{\mathfrak{r}_5, \mathfrak{r}_6\}$, $\{\mathfrak{r}_5, \mathfrak{r}_7\}$ and $\{\mathfrak{r}_6, \mathfrak{r}_8\}$ are strongly compatible pairs of regions. Observe also that the pairs $\{\mathfrak{r}_1, \mathfrak{r}_5\}$ and $\{\mathfrak{r}_1, \mathfrak{r}_6\}$ are <u>not</u> compatible, because $\mathfrak{r}_1$ is not compatible with neither $\mathfrak{r}_5$ nor $\mathfrak{r}_6$.

The next proposition shows that unlike $\oplus$ operator, $\oplus_s$ is associative.

**Proposition 1.** *The operator* $\oplus_s$ *is associative.*

*Proof.* Let $\mathfrak{r}_1 = (in_1, r_1, out_1)$, $\mathfrak{r}_2 = (in_2, r_2, out_2)$ and $\mathfrak{r}_3 = (in_3, r_3, out_3)$ be non-trivial regions of $\mathfrak{ts} = (Q, A, q_0)$. Furthermore, we assume that $\mathfrak{r}_1$ and $\mathfrak{r}_2$ are strongly compatible and their composition $\mathfrak{r} = \mathfrak{r}_1 \oplus_s \mathfrak{r}_2$ is a non-trivial region such that $\mathfrak{r}$ and $\mathfrak{r}_3$ are strongly compatible.

We show that $\mathfrak{r}_2$ and $\mathfrak{r}_3$ are strongly compatible, their composition $\mathfrak{r}' = \mathfrak{r}_2 \oplus_s \mathfrak{r}_3$ is a non-trivial region such that $\mathfrak{r}'$ and $\mathfrak{r}_1$ are strongly compatible. Moreover, the following holds:

$$(\mathfrak{r}_1 \oplus_s \mathfrak{r}_2) \oplus_s \mathfrak{r}_3 = \mathfrak{r}_1 \oplus_s (\mathfrak{r}_2 \oplus_s \mathfrak{r}_3).$$

First we show that $\mathfrak{r}_2$ is strongly compatible with $\mathfrak{r}_3$. As $\mathfrak{r}_1$ and $\mathfrak{r}_2$ are strongly compatible regions and $\mathfrak{r} = \mathfrak{r}_1 \oplus_s \mathfrak{r}_2$, we have:

$$\mathfrak{r} = (in, r, out) = (in_1 \cup in_2 \setminus H, r_1 \cup r_2, out_1 \cup out_2 \setminus H),$$

where $H$ is a set of events that belong <u>only</u> to steps labelling transitions buried in $r_1 \cup r_2$. From assumptions we also have: $r_1 \cap r_2 = \varnothing$, $(r_1 \cup r_2) \cap r_3 = \varnothing$. So, $r_1 \cap r_3 = \varnothing$ and $r_2 \cap r_3 = \varnothing$.

Now, we show that:

$$\forall e \in out_2 : e \in in_3 \vee (\forall (q, U, q') \in A : e \in U \implies q' \notin r_3) \qquad (\dagger)$$

$$\forall e \in in_2 : e \in out_3 \vee (\forall (q, U, q') \in A : e \in U \implies q \notin r_3) \qquad (\dagger\dagger)$$

Suppose, to the contrary, that ($\dagger$) is not true. Then $\exists \hat{e} \in out_2 : \hat{e} \notin in_3 \wedge (\exists (\hat{q}, \hat{U}, \hat{q}') \in A : \hat{e} \in \hat{U} \wedge \hat{q}' \in r_3)$. So, there exists $(\hat{q}, \hat{U}, \hat{q}') \in A$ such that $\hat{e} \in \hat{U} \cap out_2$ and $\hat{q}' \in r_3$. This and $r_3 \cap r = \varnothing$ implies that $(\hat{q}, \hat{U}, \hat{q}')$ is a transition outgoing from $r = r_1 \cup r_2$, so we have $\hat{e} \notin H$ and, consequently, $\hat{e} \in out$. From assumptions we have that $\mathfrak{r}$ and $\mathfrak{r}_3$ are strongly compatible, so the existence of $(\hat{q}, \hat{U}, \hat{q}')$ with $\hat{q}' \in r_3$ means $\hat{e} \in in_3$, a contradiction with $\hat{e} \notin in_3$. So, ($\dagger$) holds.

($\dagger\dagger$) can be proved similarly as ($\dagger$). Consequently, $\mathfrak{r}_2$ is strongly compatible with $\mathfrak{r}_3$.

To prove that $\mathfrak{r}_3$ is strongly compatible with $\mathfrak{r}_2$ we still need to show:

$$\forall e \in out_3 : e \in in_2 \vee (\forall (q, U, q') \in A : e \in U \implies q' \notin r_2) \qquad (\ddagger)$$

$$\forall e \in in_3 : e \in out_2 \vee (\forall(q, U, q') \in A : e \in U \implies q \notin r_2) \qquad (\ddagger\ddagger)$$

Suppose, to the contrary, that ($\ddagger$) is not true. Then $\exists \widehat{e} \in out_3 : \widehat{e} \notin in_2 \wedge (\exists(\widehat{q}, \widehat{U}, \widehat{q}') \in A : \widehat{e} \in \widehat{U} \wedge \widehat{q}' \in r_2)$. From the assumption that $\mathfrak{r}$ and $\mathfrak{r}_3$ are strongly compatible and the existence of $(\widehat{q}, \widehat{U}, \widehat{q}')$ with $\widehat{q}' \in r_2 \subset r$ and $\widehat{e} \in out_3 \cap \widehat{U}$, we have $\widehat{e} \in in = in_1 \cup in_2 \setminus H$ and consequently $\widehat{e} \in in_2$ (see Facts 2 and 3), a contradiction with $\widehat{e} \notin in_2$. So, ($\ddagger$) holds.

($\ddagger\ddagger$) can be proved similarly as ($\ddagger$). Hence, $\mathfrak{r}_3$ is strongly compatible with $\mathfrak{r}_2$ and so $\mathfrak{r}_2$ and $\mathfrak{r}_3$ are strongly compatible regions. So, we can compose them obtaining:

$$\mathfrak{r}' = (in', r', out') = \mathfrak{r}_2 \oplus_s \mathfrak{r}_3 = (in_2 \cup in_3 \setminus H', r_2 \cup r_3, out_2 \cup out_3 \setminus H'),$$

where $H'$ is a set of events that belong <u>only</u> to steps labelling transitions buried in $r_2 \cup r_3$.

We need to show now that $\mathfrak{r}_1$ and $\mathfrak{r}'$ are strongly compatible. We already showed that $r_1 \cap r_2 = \varnothing$ and $r_1 \cap r_3 = \varnothing$. So, $r_1 \cap (r_2 \cup r_3) = \varnothing$.

Next we show that $\mathfrak{r}_1$ is strongly compatible with $\mathfrak{r}'$. To do so, we still need to show that:

$$\forall e \in out_1 : e \in in' \vee (\forall(q, U, q') \in A : e \in U \implies q' \notin r') \qquad (\triangle)$$

$$\forall e \in in_1 : e \in out' \vee (\forall(q, U, q') \in A : e \in U \implies q \notin r') \qquad (\triangle\triangle)$$

Suppose, to the contrary, that ($\triangle$) is not true. Then $\exists \widehat{e} \in out_1 : \widehat{e} \notin in' \wedge (\exists(\widehat{q}, \widehat{U}, \widehat{q}') \in A : \widehat{e} \in \widehat{U} \wedge \widehat{q}' \in r')$. We now consider two cases:

1. $\widehat{q}' \in r_2$.
   As $(\widehat{q}, \widehat{U}, \widehat{q}')$ is a transition incoming into $r_2$ and $\widehat{q} \in r_1$ ($\widehat{e} \in out_1$) and $r_1 \cap (r_2 \cup r_3) = \varnothing$ and $\mathfrak{r}_1$ and $\mathfrak{r}_2$ are strongly compatible, we have $\widehat{e} \notin H'$ and $\widehat{e} \in in_2$. So, $\widehat{e} \in in' = in_2 \cup in_3 \setminus H'$, a contradiction with $\widehat{e} \notin in'$.

2. $\widehat{q}' \in r_3$.
   From the assumption that $\mathfrak{r} = \mathfrak{r}_1 \oplus_s \mathfrak{r}_2$ and $\mathfrak{r}_3$ are strongly compatible we have $r \cap r_3 = \varnothing$. This and the existence of the transition $(\widehat{q}, \widehat{U}, \widehat{q}')$, where $\widehat{e} \in \widehat{U} \cap out_1$ and $\widehat{q}' \in r_3$, means that $\widehat{e} \notin H$ and consequently $\widehat{e} \in out = out_1 \cup out_2 \setminus H$. Furthermore, as $\mathfrak{r}$ and $\mathfrak{r}_3$ are strongly compatible, we have $\widehat{e} \in in_3$. Also, $\widehat{e} \notin H'$, because the transition $(\widehat{q}, \widehat{U}, \widehat{q}')$ has the source $\widehat{q} \in r_1$ $(r_1 \cap r' = \varnothing)$. So, $\widehat{e} \in in' = in_2 \cup in_3 \setminus H'$, a contradiction with $\widehat{e} \notin in'$.

We obtained a contradiction in both considered cases, so ($\triangle$) holds.

($\triangle\triangle$) can be proved similarly as ($\triangle$). Therefore, region $\mathfrak{r}_1$ is strongly compatible with region $\mathfrak{r}' = \mathfrak{r}_2 \oplus_s \mathfrak{r}_3$.

Now we prove that $\mathfrak{r}' = \mathfrak{r}_2 \oplus_s \mathfrak{r}_3$ is strongly compatible with $\mathfrak{r}_1$. To do so, we still need to show:

$$\forall e \in out' : e \in in_1 \vee (\forall (q, U, q') \in A : e \in U \implies q' \notin r_1) \qquad (\sharp)$$

$$\forall e \in in' : e \in out_1 \vee (\forall (q, U, q') \in A : e \in U \implies q \notin r_1) \qquad (\sharp\sharp)$$

Suppose, to the contrary, that $(\sharp)$ is not true. Then $\exists \widehat{e} \in out' : \widehat{e} \notin in_1 \wedge (\exists (\widehat{q}, \widehat{U}, \widehat{q}') \in A : \widehat{e} \in \widehat{U} \wedge \widehat{q}' \in r_1)$. We now consider two cases:

1. $\widehat{q} \in r_2$.
   As $(\widehat{q}, \widehat{U}, \widehat{q}')$ is a transition outgoing from $r_2$ and $\widehat{q}' \in r_1$, $r_1 \cap r' = \varnothing$ and $\widehat{e} \in out'$, we have $\widehat{e} \notin H'$ and $\widehat{e} \in out_2$ (as $out' = out_2 \cup out_3 \setminus H'$, and from Facts 2 and 3 we have $out_2 \cap out_3 = \varnothing$ as $\mathfrak{r}_2$ and $\mathfrak{r}_3$ are strongly compatible). Hence, from the fact that $\mathfrak{r}_1$ and $\mathfrak{r}_2$ are strongly compatible we have that $\widehat{e} \in in_1$, a contradiction with $\widehat{e} \notin in_1$.

2. $\widehat{q} \in r_3$.
   As $(\widehat{q}, \widehat{U}, \widehat{q}')$ is a transition outgoing from $r_3$ and $\widehat{q}' \in r_1$, $r_1 \cap r' = \varnothing$ and $\widehat{e} \in out'$, we have $\widehat{e} \notin H'$ and $\widehat{e} \in out_3$ (as $\widehat{e} \in out' = out_2 \cup out_3 \setminus H'$, and from Facts 2 and 3 we have $out_2 \cap out_3 = \varnothing$ as $\mathfrak{r}_2$ and $\mathfrak{r}_3$ are strongly compatible). From the fact that $\mathfrak{r} = \mathfrak{r}_1 \oplus_s \mathfrak{r}_2$ and $\mathfrak{r}_3$ are strongly compatible we have that $\widehat{e} \in in$ ($\widehat{q}' \in r_1 \subset r$). From the existence of the transition $(\widehat{q}, \widehat{U}, \widehat{q}')$, where $\widehat{e} \in \widehat{U}$, $\widehat{q} \in r_3$, $\widehat{q}' \in r_1 \subset r$ and $r \cap r_3 = \varnothing$, we have that $\widehat{e} \notin H$. As $\widehat{e} \in in = in_1 \cup in_2 \setminus H$ and $\widehat{q}' \in r_1$, we have $\widehat{e} \in in_1$ (from Facts 2 and 3 we have $in_1 \cap in_2 = \varnothing$ as $\mathfrak{r}_1$ and $\mathfrak{r}_2$ are strongly compatible). So, we obtained a contradiction with $\widehat{e} \notin in_1$.

We obtained a contradiction in both considered cases, so $(\sharp)$ holds.

$(\sharp\sharp)$ can be proved similarly as $(\sharp)$. Therefore, $\mathfrak{r}_2 \oplus_s \mathfrak{r}_3$ is strongly compatible with $\mathfrak{r}_1$, and consequently regions $\mathfrak{r}_2 \oplus_s \mathfrak{r}_3$ and $\mathfrak{r}_1$ are strongly compatible regions.

Finally, we need to show that:

$$(\mathfrak{r}_1 \oplus_s \mathfrak{r}_2) \oplus_s \mathfrak{r}_3 = \mathfrak{r}_1 \oplus_s (\mathfrak{r}_2 \oplus_s \mathfrak{r}_3),$$

where

$$\mathfrak{r} = \mathfrak{r}_1 \oplus_s \mathfrak{r}_2 = (in_1 \cup in_2 \setminus H, r_1 \cup r_2, out_1 \cup out_2 \setminus H) \text{ and}$$
$$\mathfrak{r}' = \mathfrak{r}_2 \oplus_s \mathfrak{r}_3 = (in_2 \cup in_3 \setminus H', r_2 \cup r_3, out_2 \cup out_3 \setminus H').$$

Let $H''$ be a set of events that belong only to steps labelling transitions buried in $r_1 \cup r_3$ and $\widehat{H} = H \cup H' \cup H''$.

We need to show: $L = R$, where

$$L = ((in_1 \cup in_2 \setminus H) \cup in_3 \setminus \widehat{H}, r_1 \cup r_2 \cup r_3, (out_1 \cup out_2 \setminus H) \cup out_3 \setminus \widehat{H}) \text{ and}$$
$$R = (in_1 \cup (in_2 \cup in_3 \setminus H') \setminus \widehat{H}, r_1 \cup r_2 \cup r_3, out_1 \cup (out_2 \cup out_3 \setminus H') \setminus \widehat{H}).$$

Observe first that $H \cap in_3 = \varnothing$ and $H \cap out_3 = \varnothing$, so in the equation for $L$ above we can use $\widehat{H}$ instead of $H' \cup H''$. Similarly, as $H' \cap in_1 = \varnothing$ and $H' \cap out_1 = \varnothing$, we can use $\widehat{H}$ instead of $H \cup H''$ in the equation for $R$.

Now we show that $L_{in} = (in_1 \cup in_2 \setminus H) \cup in_3 \setminus \widehat{H} = in_1 \cup (in_2 \cup in_3 \setminus H') \setminus \widehat{H} = R_{in}$. From the definitions of $H$, $H'$ and $H''$ we have $H \cap H' = \varnothing$, $H \cap H'' = \varnothing$ and $H' \cap H'' = \varnothing$. From Facts 2 and 3 and the fact that $\mathfrak{r}_1$ and $\mathfrak{r}_2$ and $\mathfrak{r}_2$ and $\mathfrak{r}_3$ are strongly compatible we have $in_1 \cap in_2 = \varnothing$ and $out_1 \cap out_2 = \varnothing$ as well as $in_2 \cap in_3 = \varnothing$ and $out_2 \cap out_3 = \varnothing$. Furthermore, $in_1 \cap in_3 = \varnothing$ as every transition labelled with a step containing $e \in in_1$ must enter $r_1$ and every transition labelled with a step containing $e \in in_3$ must enter $r_3$, but $r_1 \cap r_3 = \varnothing$, so $in_1 \cap in_3 \neq \varnothing$ is impossible. Hence, the difference between the sets of events of $L_{in}$ and $R_{in}$, before taking away events from $\widehat{H}$, results from the events that are contained in the intersections between the various sets of 'buried' events ($H$, $H'$, $H''$) and $in$ sets ($in_1$, $in_2$, $in_3$). However, since $H \subseteq \widehat{H}$, $H' \subseteq \widehat{H}$ and $H'' \subseteq \widehat{H}$, the events that cause the difference between the two sides of the equation will be removed when the set $\widehat{H}$ is subtracted from both sides of the equation, leaving $L_{in} = R_{in}$.

Similarly we can show that:

$$L_{out} = (out_1 \cup out_2 \setminus H) \cup out_3 \setminus \widehat{H} = out_1 \cup (out_2 \cup out_3 \setminus H') \setminus \widehat{H} = R_{out}.$$

$\square$

**Proposition 2.** *Let $\mathfrak{r}_1 = (in_1, r_1, out_1)$ and $\mathfrak{r}_2 = (in_2, r_2, out_2)$ be compatible regions of an* ST-*system* $\mathfrak{ts} = (Q, A, q_0)$, *which do not satisfy the conditions to be strongly compatible regions of* $\mathfrak{ts}$. *Then there exists a companion region of $\mathfrak{r}_1$, $\mathfrak{r}_1' \in \mathfrak{R}_{\mathfrak{ts}}^{r_1}$, and a companion region of $\mathfrak{r}_2$, $\mathfrak{r}_2' \in \mathfrak{R}_{\mathfrak{ts}}^{r_2}$, such that $\mathfrak{r}_1$ and $\mathfrak{r}_2'$ are strongly compatible and $\mathfrak{r}_1'$ and $\mathfrak{r}_2$ are strongly compatible. Furthermore, $\mathfrak{r}_1 \oplus_s \mathfrak{r}_2' = \mathfrak{r}_1' \oplus_s \mathfrak{r}_2 = \mathfrak{r}_1 \oplus \mathfrak{r}_2$.*

*Proof.* First, we show the existence of regions $\mathfrak{r}_1'$ and $\mathfrak{r}_2'$.

Since $\mathfrak{r}_1$ and $\mathfrak{r}_2$ are compatible we have $r_1 \cap r_2 = \varnothing$. Bearing in mind that $\mathfrak{r}_1$ and $\mathfrak{r}_2$ are compatible regions we now consider two cases:

1. There are no 'buried' transitions in $r_1 \cup r_2$.
   For this case the definitions of compatibility and strong compatibility (Definitions 9 and 11) coincide. Hence, $\mathfrak{r}_1$ and $\mathfrak{r}_2$ are strongly compatible and $\mathfrak{r}_1' = \mathfrak{r}_1$ and $\mathfrak{r}_2' = \mathfrak{r}_2$.

2. There are 'buried' transitions in $r_1 \cup r_2$.
   Then, without loss of generality, we can assume that there exists a transition $(q, U, q') \in A$ such that $q \in r_1$ and $q' \in r_2$. Hence, from Definition 6(R1) for $\mathfrak{r}_1$ and $(q, U, q')$, and $r_1 \cap r_2 = \varnothing$, we have $|U \cap out_1| = 1$. Let $e_1 \in U \cap out_1$. As $\mathfrak{r}_1$ and $\mathfrak{r}_2$ are <u>not</u> strongly compatible we can assume, again without loss of generality, that Definition 11 fails for $e_1 \in out_1$ resulting in $e_1 \notin in_2$. Furthermore, from Definition 6(R2) for $\mathfrak{r}_2$ and $(q, U, q')$, and $r_1 \cap r_2 = \varnothing$, we have $|U \cap in_2| = 1$. Since $e_1 \notin in_2$, there exists $e_2 \neq e_1$ such that $e_2 \in U \cap in_2$. Therefore, $|U| \geq 2$. From Definition 6(R1) for $\mathfrak{r}_1$ and $(q, U, q')$, we have that $e_2 \notin out_1$.

The manifestation of $e_1 \notin in_2$ (recall $e_1 \in out_1$) might be the existence of a transition $(q_1, U_1, q_1')$ such that $q_1 \in r_1$, $q_1' \notin r_1 \cup r_2$ and $e_1 \in U_1$. The manifestation of $e_2 \notin out_1$ (recall $e_2 \in in_2$) might be the existence of a transition $(q_2, U_2, q_2')$ such that $q_2 \notin r_1 \cup r_2$, $q_2' \in r_2$ and $e_2 \in U_2$. However, it is not possible for the two such transitions to exist considering the existence of the transition $(q, U, q')$. This is because $\mathfrak{r}_1$ and $\mathfrak{r}_2$ are compatible regions, and therefore they can be composed producing the region: $\mathfrak{r}_{sum} = \mathfrak{r}_1 \oplus \mathfrak{r}_2 = (in_{sum}, r_{sum}, out_{sum}) = (in_1 \cup in_2 \setminus H, r_1 \cup r_2, out_1 \cup out_2 \setminus H)$ and then $e_1 \notin H$ (because of $(q_1, U_1, q_1')$) and $e_2 \notin H$ (because of $(q_2, U_2, q_2')$). Hence, as $e_1 \in out_1$ and $e_2 \in in_2$, we have $e_1 \in out_{sum}$ and $e_2 \in in_{sum}$. Neither of these is possible, because of the existence of the transition $(q, U, q')$, as $e_1, e_2 \in U$ and this transition is 'buried' in $r_1 \cup r_2$. So, all transitions labelled by steps containing $e_1$ or $e_2$ are 'buried' in $r_1 \cup r_2$ and the transition $(q, U, q')$ has a label containing both of them.

For the thick transitions that are 'buried' in $r_1 \cup r_2$ (with source in $r_1$ and target in $r_2$) we can have a mismatch between the event that leads out from $r_1$ and the one that leads into $r_2$. We will now show how to alleviate such mismatches like the mismatch between $e_1 \in out_1$ and $e_2 \in in_2$ for the transition $(q, U, q')$. Let $U^{r_1, r_2} = \{U \mid \exists (q, U, q') \in A : q \in r_1, q' \in r_2 \text{ and } |U| \geq 2\}$. Also, let $pairs^{r_1, r_2} : U^{r_1, r_2} \to out_1 \times in_2$ be a function, which assigns, for labels of thick transitions going from $r_1$ to $r_2$, their pairs of events: leading out of $r_1$ and leading into $r_2$. Furthermore, let $N$ be a set of events from $E$, which are not contained in labels of transitions 'buried' in $r_1 \cup r_2$. We now define[2]:

$$out_1' = out_1 \cap N \cup second(pairs^{r_1, r_2}(U^{r_1, r_2})) \text{ and}$$
$$in_2' = in_2 \cap N \ \cup first(pairs^{r_1, r_2}(U^{r_1, r_2})).$$

We can then define tuples: $(in_1, r_1, out_1')$ and $(in_2', r_2, out_2)$. It is clear that the first tuple is a region as $\mathfrak{r}_1$ is a region and Definition 6(R1,R3) is satisfied for $out_1'$. Also, it is clear that the second tuple is a region as $\mathfrak{r}_2$ is a region and Definition 6(R2,R4) is satisfied for $in_2'$. Furthermore, assuming that we had only mismatches between events contained in the labels of transitions going from $r_1$ to $r_2$, it can be seen that $\mathfrak{r}_1' = (in_1, r_1, out_1')$ and $\mathfrak{r}_2$ are strongly compatible regions (as $out_1' \setminus out_1 \cap N \subseteq in_2$), and $\mathfrak{r}_1$ and $\mathfrak{r}_2' = (in_2', r_2, out_2)$ are strongly compatible regions (as $in_2' \setminus in_2 \cap N \subseteq out_1$). The mismatches between events contained in the labels of transitions going from $r_2$ to $r_1$ can be alleviated in a similar way.

Finally, we observe that $\mathfrak{r}_1 \oplus_s \mathfrak{r}_2' = \mathfrak{r}_1' \oplus_s \mathfrak{r}_2 = \mathfrak{r}_1 \oplus \mathfrak{r}_2$ is true as: (1) the sets of states for all three pairs of regions is $r_1 \cup r_2$; and (2) the only difference between the $in/out$ sets of regions involved in the three pairs are due to the events that belong only to steps labelling transitions 'buried' in $r_1 \cup r_2$, but they will be removed from the appropriate sums of the $in/out$ sets when the compositions of regions are formed. □

---

[2] For any sets $X$ and $Y$, $first : X \times Y \to X$ and $second : X \times Y \to Y$ are mappings defined as follows: $first(x, y) = x$ and $second(x, y) = y$, where $x \in X$ and $y \in Y$.

To illustrate the result of Proposition 2, we can use again the ENLST-system in Fig. 2(a). A pair of its regions, $\mathfrak{r}_4$ and $\mathfrak{r}_1$, are compatible, but not strongly compatible regions. However, there are regions $\mathfrak{r}_3 \in \mathfrak{R}_{ts}^{r_4}$ and $\mathfrak{r}_2 \in \mathfrak{R}_{ts}^{r_1}$, such that $\mathfrak{r}_4$ and $\mathfrak{r}_2$ are strongly compatible and $\mathfrak{r}_3$ and $\mathfrak{r}_1$ are strongly compatible. Also, we have $\mathfrak{r}_4 \oplus_s \mathfrak{r}_2 = \mathfrak{r}_3 \oplus_s \mathfrak{r}_1 = \mathfrak{r}_4 \oplus \mathfrak{r}_1 = (\varnothing, Q, \varnothing)$. Furthermore, using the same example, observe that when we express a composition of two <u>minimal</u> compatible regions by a composition of two strongly compatible regions, one of the two strongly compatible regions might be not a minimal region. For example, $\mathfrak{r}_2 \oplus \mathfrak{r}_3 = \mathfrak{r}_2 \oplus_s \mathfrak{r}_4$, where $\mathfrak{r}_2$ and $\mathfrak{r}_3$ are minimal regions, but $\mathfrak{r}_4$ is not. Proposition 2 does not take the minimality of regions into consideration.

**Corollary 1.** *Let* $ts = (Q, A, q_0)$ *be an* ENLST-*system. Then*

1. $\mathfrak{R}_{ts}^{min} = \mathfrak{R}_{ts}^{min,s}$.
2. *Every* $\mathfrak{r} \in \mathfrak{R}_{ts}$ *can be represented as a composition of minimal regions, where each pair of different minimal regions in this representation is a pair of strongly compatible regions.*
3. *Let* $\mathfrak{R} = \{\mathfrak{r}_1, \mathfrak{r}_2, \ldots, \mathfrak{r}_n\}$ *be a set of pairwise strongly compatible non-trivial regions of* $ts$, *where* $\mathfrak{r}_i = (in_i, r_i, out_i)$, $i \in \{1, \ldots, n\}$. *Then there exists a region* $\mathfrak{r} = (in, r, out) = \mathfrak{r}_1 \oplus_s \ldots \oplus_s \mathfrak{r}_n$, *where* $r = r_1 \cup \ldots \cup r_n$.

*Proof.* 1. The minimal regions of $ts$ can be obtained from $\mathfrak{R}_{ts}$ by elimination of non-minimal regions. From Proposition 2 it follows that any non-minimal region that can be represented as a composition of two compatible regions can also be represented as a composition of two strongly compatible regions. So, the same set of regions will be eliminated from $\mathfrak{R}_{ts}$ regardless of which strict pre-order is used ($\prec$ or $\prec_s$) when defining non-minimal (minimal) regions. Hence, $\mathfrak{R}_{ts}^{min} = \mathfrak{R}_{ts}^{min,s}$.

2. The proof is similar to the proof of Theorem 2. However, as $\oplus_s$ is an associative operator (see Proposition 1), we can drop the brackets, if there are any, in the final representation of $\mathfrak{r}$.

3. Assume first that $n = 3$. We show that each of the three regions ($\mathfrak{r}_1$, $\mathfrak{r}_2$ and $\mathfrak{r}_3$) and the region obtained by composing the two remaining regions by means of $\oplus_s$ form a pair of strongly compatible regions, which after being composed produce a region $\mathfrak{r}_1 \oplus_s \mathfrak{r}_2 \oplus_s \mathfrak{r}_3$. As an example, we can prove that $(\mathfrak{r}_1 \oplus_s \mathfrak{r}_2)$ and $\mathfrak{r}_3$ form a pair of strongly compatible regions. This part of the proof is omitted as it uses the same techniques as were employed in Proposition 1. Assuming now that $n > 3$, we can prove in a similar way that $(\mathfrak{r}_1 \oplus_s \mathfrak{r}_2)$ and $\mathfrak{r}_i$, $3 < i \leq n$, are pairs of strongly compatible regions. Since $\{\mathfrak{r}_3, \ldots, \mathfrak{r}_n\}$ is a set of pairwise strongly compatible regions by assumption, we have that the set $\{(\mathfrak{r}_1 \oplus_s \mathfrak{r}_2), \mathfrak{r}_3, \ldots, \mathfrak{r}_n\}$ is a set of $n - 1$ regions that are non-trivial and pairwise strongly compatible. We can continue this process, decrementing by 1 in each step the number of regions in this set of regions, till we have just one region in this set: $\mathfrak{r} = (in, r, out) = \mathfrak{r}_1 \oplus_s \mathfrak{r}_2 \oplus_s \ldots \oplus_s \mathfrak{r}_n$, where $r = r_1 \cup \ldots \cup r_n$. □

The next result, about special families of non-trivial regions of $\mathfrak{ts}$, is inspired by a result proved for the class of Elementary Net Systems in [8]. We have adapted this result here for the context of ENL-systems by changing one of the original conditions that a family of regions should satisfy, but the implied result is the same: a family of regions that satisfy the conditions of Theorem 3, treated as a set of conditions of the synthesised net, would generate a state machine component of this net. Points 2 and 3 of the consequent of Theorem 3 guarantee the satisfaction of Definition 3(1) and the point 1 of the consequent of Theorem 3 guarantees the satisfaction of Definition 3(2).

**Theorem 3.** *Let $\mathfrak{R} = \{\mathfrak{r}_1, \mathfrak{r}_2, \ldots, \mathfrak{r}_n\}$ be a family of non-trivial regions of $\mathfrak{ts} = (Q, A, q_0)$, where $\mathfrak{r}_i = (in_i, r_i, out_i)$, $i \in \{1, \ldots, n\}$, satisfy the following:*

1. *Every two different regions $\mathfrak{r}_i, \mathfrak{r}_j \in \mathfrak{R}$ are strongly compatible regions.*
2. $\forall \, \widehat{\mathfrak{r}} = (\widehat{in}, \widehat{r}, \widehat{out}) \in \mathfrak{R}_{\mathfrak{ts}} : \widehat{\mathfrak{r}} \notin \mathfrak{R} \implies (\exists \mathfrak{r}_i \in \mathfrak{R} : \widehat{r} \cap r_i \neq \varnothing).$

*Then:*

1. $\bigcup r_i = Q;$
2. $\forall e \in E : |{}^\circ e \cap \mathfrak{R}| \leq 1 \text{ and } |e^\circ \cap \mathfrak{R}| \leq 1;$
3. $\forall e \in E : e \in {}^\circ \mathfrak{r}_i \iff \exists j : e \in \mathfrak{r}_j{}^\circ.$

*Proof.* 1. Suppose $q \in Q \setminus \bigcup r_i$. As all regions of $\mathfrak{R}$ are pairwise strongly compatible then there exists a region $\mathfrak{r} = (in, r, out) = \mathfrak{r}_1 \oplus_s \ldots \oplus_s \mathfrak{r}_n$, where $r = r_1 \cup \ldots \cup r_n$ and $r_i \cap r_j = \varnothing$ for different $i, j \in \{1, \ldots, n\}$ (see Corollary 1(3)). Also, $\overline{\mathfrak{r}}$ is a region with $\overline{r} = Q \setminus \{r_1 \cup \ldots \cup r_n\}$ (disjoint from all $r_i$) and $\overline{\mathfrak{r}}$ is non-trivial ($q \in \overline{r}$), contradicting the second assumption that $\mathfrak{R}$ must satisfy.

2. Suppose to the contrary that there are $\mathfrak{r}_i$ and $\mathfrak{r}_j$ in $\mathfrak{R}$ such that $\mathfrak{r}_i, \mathfrak{r}_j \in {}^\circ e$. Hence, $e \in out_i \cap out_j$. So, for all transitions $(q, U, q') \in A$, where $e \in U$, we have $q \in r_i$ and $q \in r_j$ (see Definition 6(R3)), but $r_i \cap r_j = \varnothing$ - a contradiction. The second part of this point can be proved in a similar way.

3. Suppose $e \in {}^\circ \mathfrak{r}_i$. Then $\mathfrak{r}_i \in e^\circ$ and consequently $e \in in_i$. As, by definition, every event $e \in E$ occurs in at least one of the steps labelling the transitions of $\mathfrak{ts}$, we have a transition $(q, U, q') \in A$ such that $e \in U$. Therefore, from Definition 6(R4) we have $q \notin r_i$ and $q' \in r_i$. From Theorem 3(1), we have that $r_i = Q \setminus \bigcup_{k \in \{1, \ldots, n\} \setminus \{i\}} r_k$. So, there is $j \neq i$ such that $q \in r_j$ and $q' \notin r_j$ (the sets of states of $\mathfrak{r}_i$ and $\mathfrak{r}_j$ are disjoint as these regions are compatible). Hence, from Definition 6(R1), we have that $|U \cap out_j| = 1$, meaning that there is $\widehat{e} \in U$ such that $\widehat{e} \in out_j$. Since $\mathfrak{r}_i$ and $\mathfrak{r}_j$ are strongly compatible regions, we have $e = \widehat{e}$. So, $e \in out_j$, and therefore $\mathfrak{r}_j \in {}^\circ e$ and consequently $e \in \mathfrak{r}_j{}^\circ$. The converse implication can be proved in a similar way.

$\square$

The saturated ENL-system that is a solution to Problem 1 for a given ENLST-system $\mathfrak{ts}$, $\mathfrak{enl} = \mathfrak{enl}_{\mathfrak{ts}}^{\widehat{\approx}}$, and is based on all non-trivial regions, is state machine decomposable (see Definition 5), as due to Fact 4 every pair of complementary regions satisfies the conditions of Theorem 3 and would form a state machine component of $\mathfrak{enl}$. Furthermore, from Corollary 1 it follows that, similarly as for the class of Elementary Net Systems (see [8]), the ENL-system obtained from $\mathfrak{enl}$ by deleting all non-minimal regions following Reduction Rule 2 is also state machine decomposable as every region can be represented as a composition of minimal regions (w.r.t. $\prec_s$) and selected subsets of $\mathfrak{R}_{ts}^{min} = \mathfrak{R}_{ts}^{min,s}$ would satisfy the conditions of Theorem 3.

As an example we can take the saturated ENL-system synthesised from the ENLST-system in Fig. 2(a), shown in Fig. 2(b), and its minimised version shown in Fig. 2(c). The state machine components of the former ENL-system are generated by the following subsets of conditions/regions:

$$\mathfrak{r}_1 \oplus_s \mathfrak{r}_3 = \mathfrak{r}_2 \oplus_s \mathfrak{r}_5 \oplus_s \mathfrak{r}_6 = \mathfrak{r}_2 \oplus_s \mathfrak{r}_4 = \mathfrak{r}_7 \oplus_s \mathfrak{r}_5 = \mathfrak{r}_8 \oplus_s \mathfrak{r}_6 = (\varnothing, Q, \varnothing).$$

The minimised ENL-system in Fig. 2(c) has the first two state machine components from the components listed above.

# 6   Strategies to Eliminate Redundant Regions

The three reduction rules (see Sect. 3) give conditions for deleting one of the redundant regions at a time. Therefore, we need a *strategy* to delete as many redundant regions as possible to obtain a net, where all (or almost all) remaining regions are needed (essential). The regions are redundant or essential only in the context of other regions. Different strategies lead to different sets of essential (or nearly essential) regions. Such sets of regions were called in [14] *admissible*.

As an example we can take again the ENLST-system in Fig. 2(a). We observe that region $\mathfrak{r}_4 = \bar{\mathfrak{r}}_2$ can be deleted according to Reduction Rule 1 (as the complement of region $\mathfrak{r}_2$) or according to Reduction Rule 2 (as a non-minimal region: $\mathfrak{r}_4 = \mathfrak{r}_5 \oplus \mathfrak{r}_6$).

When looking for a strategy for deleting redundant regions, we will take into consideration the following criteria:

– Limiting as much as possible the non-determinism in the process of computing admissible regions.
– Effectiveness of the strategy gauged in terms of the number of the removed regions.
– Efficiency of the strategy gauged in terms of time needed to compute a set of admissible regions.

Our first attempt at formulating a strategy will be based on the first criterion listed above. Reduction Rule 2 showed that all non-minimal regions are redundant[3], so we can eliminate first the non-minimal regions. After this step, for a given ENLST-system $\mathfrak{ts}$, we obtain from the unique set of regions, $\mathfrak{R}_{ts}$, the unique set of minimal regions: $\mathfrak{R}_{ts}^{min}$. The application of Reduction Rule 1 and

---

[3] Reduction Rule 2 uses operator $\oplus$ and it was proved in [20] for this operator, but from Corollary 1(1) we have $\mathfrak{R}_{ts}^{min} = \mathfrak{R}_{ts}^{min,s}$, so it does not matter whether we use $\prec$ and $\oplus$, or $\prec_s$ and $\oplus_s$, to define the set of minimal regions.

Reduction Rule 3 might not lead to a unique resultant set of regions. We might decide to keep certain companion regions and delete other companion regions in case of Reduction Rule 3. Similarly, we can keep both or one (random one) out of two complementary regions. As, in general, the Reduction Rule 3, leads to fewer possible choices of regions to delete, and might be even irrelevant in the case of thin step transition systems, where there are no companion regions, we might decide that this rule should be applied before the Reduction Rule 1, which can lead to many possible combinations of regions to keep/delete. This strategy, called *Strategy (2,3,1)*, can be defined as follows:

1. Use Reduction Rule 2 to delete all non-minimal regions.
2. Use Reduction Rule 3 to delete any redundant companion regions that might be present among the minimal regions.
3. Use Reduction Rule 1 to delete any redundant complementary regions that might be present after the first two steps of the strategy.

To check how good this strategy is from the second criterion point of view we consider a set of ENLST-systems generated by nets composed of several sequential subsystems, where all the events are co-located. Such systems have a lot of companion regions. We will call them $\mathsf{ts}_{i,j}^{co-loc}$, where the index $i$ denotes the number of sequential subsystems, and the index $j$ denotes the number of events in each of the line-like sequential subsystems. As an example of such a step transition system we can see an ENLST-system $\mathsf{ts}_{2,2}^{co-loc}$ in Fig. 3(a).

Using the set of step transition systems $\mathsf{ts}_{i,j}^{co-loc}$ ($i = 2, \ldots, 4$; $j = 2, \ldots, 5$), we compare the effectiveness of region removal of Strategy (2,3,1) and Strategy (3,2,1) (Strategy (2,3,1) with the first two steps reversed). The result of this comparison is presented in Table 1.

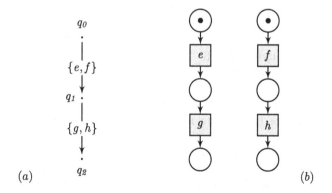

(a)

(b)

**Fig. 3.** An ENLST-system $\mathsf{ts}_{2,2}^{co-loc}$ with co-located events $e$, $f$, $g$ and $h$ (a), and one of the possible ENL-systems generating it (b).

**Table 1.** Comparison between the effectiveness of Strategy (3,2,1) and Strategy (2,3,1), where x - y - z in the last two columns reports the number of remaining regions after the first (x), the second (y) and the third (z) stage of the strategies.

| ts | $|Q|$ | $|E|$ | $|\mathfrak{R}_{ts}|$ | Strategy (3,2,1) | Strategy (2,3,1) |
|---|---|---|---|---|---|
| $ts_{2,2}^{co-loc}$ | 3 | 4 | 16 | 12 - 6 - 6 | 8 - 6 - 6 |
| $ts_{2,3}^{co-loc}$ | 4 | 6 | 52 | 28 - 10 - 10 | 12 - 8 - 8 |
| $ts_{2,4}^{co-loc}$ | 5 | 8 | 160 | 60 - 12 - 12 | 16 - 10 - 10 |
| $ts_{2,5}^{co-loc}$ | 6 | 10 | 484 | 124 - 26 - 26 | 20 - 12 - 12 |
| $ts_{3,2}^{co-loc}$ | 3 | 6 | 30 | 22 - 11 - 11 | 15 - 11 - 11 |
| $ts_{3,3}^{co-loc}$ | 4 | 9 | 126 | 66 - 20 - 20 | 24 - 16 - 16 |
| $ts_{3,4}^{co-loc}$ | 5 | 12 | 510 | 190 - 52 - 51 | 33 - 21 - 21 |
| $ts_{3,5}^{co-loc}$ | 6 | 15 | 2046 | 546 - 147 - 143 | 42 - 26 - 26 |
| $ts_{4,2}^{co-loc}$ | 3 | 8 | 48 | 36 - 18 - 18 | 24 - 18 - 18 |
| $ts_{4,3}^{co-loc}$ | 4 | 12 | 248 | 140 - 48 - 47 | 40 - 28 - 28 |
| $ts_{4,4}^{co-loc}$ | 5 | 16 | 1248 | 540 - 165 - 159 | 56 - 38 - 38 |
| $ts_{4,5}^{co-loc}$ | 6 | 20 | 6248 | 2108 - 532 - 508 | 72 - 48 - 48 |

The results in Table 1 are not so surprising. The removal of non-minimal regions makes only sense in the context of all non-trivial regions (as the first step of the strategy). When removing companion regions, the algorithm processes groups of companion regions (each based on a shared set of states) separately from each other. From each group some subset of regions may be removed, at random, according to Reduction Rule 3. Once some of the minimal companion regions are removed (if we remove companion regions first), some of the regions that were previously non-minimal would become minimal as it won't be possible to represent them as compositions of minimal regions using the remaining minimal regions. Therefore, they won't be deleted by the Reduction Rule 2, if it is applied after Reduction Rule 3. The results in Table 1 show how great would be the loss of effectiveness if we used Strategy (3,2,1) for ENLST-systems with a big number of companion regions.

While the Reduction Rule 2, applied first in our strategy, can be considered as a method for eliminating non-minimal regions, non-minimal from the 'state information' point of view, the Reduction Rule 3 can be understood as a method for eliminating regions that are redundant from the 'event information' point of view. However, some subsets of companion regions will remain after the application of Reduction Rule 3, because they are essential as shown below:

**Fact 5.** Let $\mathfrak{r} = (in, r, out)$ be a non-trivial region of $ts = (Q, A, q_0)$ and let $\mathfrak{R}^r \subseteq \mathfrak{R}_{ts}^r$ be a set of its companion regions (including $\mathfrak{r}$) that remained after the application of the Reduction Rule 3 and let $|\mathfrak{R}^r| \geq 2$. Then all the regions of $\mathfrak{R}^r$ do not satisfy the same conditions of the Reduction Rule 3 (all do not satisfy condition (1) or all do not satisfy condition (2) or all do not satisfy both conditions: (1) and (2)).

*Proof.* Suppose, $\widehat{\mathfrak{r}} \in \mathfrak{R}^r$ and $\widehat{\mathfrak{r}} \neq \mathfrak{r}$. Furthermore, suppose that $\mathfrak{r}$ does not satisfy condition (1) of the Reduction Rule 3, and therefore we have:

$$\exists\, e \in in \; \forall\, \mathfrak{r}' = (in', r, out') \in \mathfrak{R}^r : \mathfrak{r}' \neq \mathfrak{r} \implies e \notin in' \tag{3}$$

Since $e \in in$ we have that there is a transition $(q, U, q') \in A$ such that $e \in U$ and $q \notin r$ and $q' \in r$. As $\widehat{\mathfrak{r}} = (\widehat{in}, r, \widehat{out}) \in \mathfrak{R}^r$ and $\widehat{\mathfrak{r}} \neq \mathfrak{r}$, we have from (3) that $e \notin \widehat{in}$, and therefore there must be $\widehat{e} \neq e$ such that $\widehat{e} \in U \cap \widehat{in}$. From Definition 6(R2) for $\mathfrak{r}$ we have that $\widehat{e} \notin in$. As $\mathfrak{r} \in \mathfrak{R}^r$ is an example of a companion region of $\widehat{\mathfrak{r}}$ (different than $\widehat{\mathfrak{r}}$), we can see that $\widehat{\mathfrak{r}}$ satisfies (3) with $\widehat{\mathfrak{r}}$ taking the role of $\mathfrak{r}$ and $\mathfrak{r}$ taking the role of $\mathfrak{r}'$ in (3). Hence, $\widehat{\mathfrak{r}}$ does not satisfy condition (1) of the Reduction Rule 3. Similar arguments can be used if $\mathfrak{r}$ does not satisfy condition (2) of the Reduction Rule 3. $\qquad\square$

**Corollary 2.** *Let $\mathfrak{R}^r = \{\mathfrak{r}_1, \mathfrak{r}_2, \ldots, \mathfrak{r}_n\} \subseteq \mathfrak{R}^r_{\mathsf{ts}}$ be a set of companion regions based on $r$ that remained after the application of the Reduction Rule 3. Then, for every region $\mathfrak{r}_i = (in_i, r, out_i)$ of $\mathfrak{R}^r$ that does not satisfy condition (1) (respectively (2)) of Reduction Rule 3 there exists a unique $E_i \subseteq in_i$ (respectively $E'_i \subseteq out_i$) with events that are not present in the in (respectively out) sets of other regions from $\mathfrak{R}^r$. So, companion regions of $\mathfrak{R}^r$ are 'indexed' by the unique subsets of events of their in (respectively out) sets. We will call these subsets of events in-indices (respectively out-indices) of $r$ for the regions of $\mathfrak{R}^r$.* $\diamond$

Notice that sets $\mathfrak{R}^r$ in Corollary 2 (and in Fact 5) might be equal to $\mathfrak{R}^r_{\mathsf{ts}}$. For example, for $\mathsf{ts}$ in Fig. 2(a), we have $\mathfrak{R}^{\{q_0\}} = \mathfrak{R}^{\{q_0\}}_{\mathsf{ts}} = \{\mathfrak{r}_1, \mathfrak{r}_2\}$. Also, the indexing sets of events do not need to be singleton sets (as, for example, set $\{e_1, e_2\}$ for $\{q_0\}$ of $\mathfrak{r}_2$ of $\mathsf{ts}$ in Fig. 2(a)).

We will further illustrate the above results using the ENLST-system in Fig. 3(a). Its non-trivial regions are listed below:

$$
\begin{aligned}
\mathfrak{r}_1 &= (\varnothing, \{q_0\}, \{e\}) & \bar{\mathfrak{r}}_1 &= (\{e\}, \{q_1, q_2\}, \varnothing) \\
\mathfrak{r}_2 &= (\{e\}, \{q_1\}, \{g\}) & \bar{\mathfrak{r}}_2 &= (\{g\}, \{q_0, q_2\}, \{e\}) \\
\mathfrak{r}_3 &= (\{g\}, \{q_2\}, \varnothing) & \bar{\mathfrak{r}}_3 &= (\varnothing, \{q_0, q_1\}, \{g\}) \\
\mathfrak{r}_4 &= (\{e\}, \{q_1\}, \{h\}) & \bar{\mathfrak{r}}_4 &= (\{h\}, \{q_0, q_2\}, \{e\}) \\
\mathfrak{r}_5 &= (\{h\}, \{q_2\}, \varnothing) & \bar{\mathfrak{r}}_5 &= (\varnothing, \{q_0, q_1\}, \{h\}) \\
\mathfrak{r}_6 &= (\varnothing, \{q_0\}, \{f\}) & \bar{\mathfrak{r}}_6 &= (\{f\}, \{q_1, q_2\}, \varnothing) \\
\mathfrak{r}_7 &= (\{f\}, \{q_1\}, \{g\}) & \bar{\mathfrak{r}}_7 &= (\{g\}, \{q_0, q_2\}, \{f\}) \\
\mathfrak{r}_8 &= (\{f\}, \{q_1\}, \{h\}) & \bar{\mathfrak{r}}_8 &= (\{h\}, \{q_0, q_2\}, \{f\})
\end{aligned}
$$

The implemented tool, after applying Reduction Rule 2, will delete 8 out of 16 regions, leaving the minimal regions ($\mathfrak{r}_1$ - $\mathfrak{r}_8$). The set of minimal regions will be the same whether they are defined w.r.t. $\prec$ or $\prec_s$ strict pre-order (see Corollary 1(1)) as every non-minimal region that can be expressed as a composition of compatible regions can be also expressed as a composition of strongly compatible regions (see Proposition 2). For example, $\bar{\mathfrak{r}}_3 = \mathfrak{r}_1 \oplus_s \mathfrak{r}_2 = \mathfrak{r}_1 \oplus \mathfrak{r}_7$, where the first two regions are strongly compatible, but the second two regions are only compatible, but not strongly compatible. The algorithm that implements Reduction Rule 3, when applied to this example, would delete two out of four regions based on the set of states $\{q_1\}$ leaving either $r_2$ and $r_8$ or $r_4$ and $r_7$. The remaining pairs of companion regions, based on sets of states $\{q_0\},\{q_1\}$ and $\{q_2\}$, will remain as they are essential (having different in-indices or/and out-indices for the shared sets of states; see Corollary 2). The Reduction Rule 1, the last to be used in Strategy $(2, 3, 1)$, is not applicable to this example as all the complementary regions of $r_1$ - $r_8$ were already deleted as non-minimal regions (see the results for $ts_{2,2}^{co-loc}$ in Table 1).

## 7   Selected Results of the Experiments

The algorithms for the minimisation of the synthesised ENL-systems are implemented within the WORKCRAFT framework [26, 29]. They are a part of the tool support for the synthesis of ENL-systems, SYNTHCRAFT [28], which introduced two plugins into WORKCRAFT: one to represent ENL-systems, and another one to represent ST-systems.

In this section, we illustrate the process of net minimisation and its implementation in SYNTHCRAFT on an example of a system modelling interactions between one 'producer' and one 'consumer' system that reside in different localities (notice that in Fig. 1 we have an ENL-system modelling interactions of one producer and <u>two</u> co-located consumers). Starting the synthesis procedure with the specification of this system in the form of an ST-system, we obtain the saturated net depicted in Fig. 4, which shows the screenshot from WORKCRAFT.

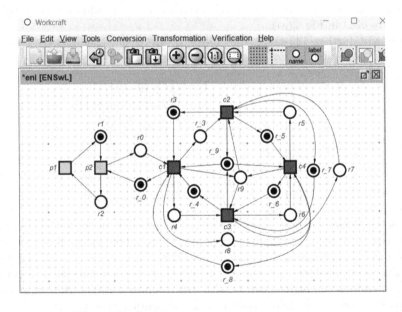

**Fig. 4.** Synthesising ENL-systems in WORKCRAFT.

The obtained ENL-system has redundant conditions. The SYNTHCRAFT tool allows the user to run each of the reduction rules (see Sect. 3) separately or combine them together to form a particular strategy. If we only apply Reduction Rule 2 to the saturated net obtained for this example (to eliminate non-minimal regions), we obtain the ENL-system that will be much smaller (having 8 conditions rather than 18 conditions) as shown in Fig. 5.

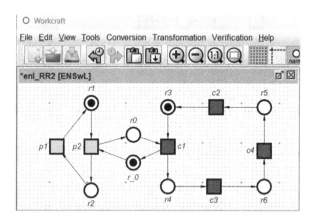

**Fig. 5.** Applying Reduction Rule 2 to the ENL-system of Fig. 4.

The resultant ENL-system uses now only minimal regions as its conditions, but it is still state-machine decomposable as the saturated net from which it was obtained. The three state-machine components of this reduced ENL-system are generated by the following subsets of conditions: $\{r1, r2\}$, $\{r0, r\_0\}$ and $\{r3, r4, r5, r6\}$.

In the ENL-system of Fig. 5 there is still one redundant condition, $r0$ or its complement $r\_0$, which can be eliminated by applying Reduction Rule 1. Note also that the initial ST-system, from which the ENL-system of Fig. 4 was obtained, is a thin step transition system (see page 4 for definition) and therefore Reduction Rule 3 does not apply to this example. The results of running Strategy $(2,3,1)$ for this example is shown in Fig. 6. The ENL-system there is <u>not</u> state-machine decomposable.

We can observe that, depending on the particular requirements of the minimisation, we might choose different minimisation strategies or only some of their constituent reduction rules. If the property of being state-machine decomposable is the most important feature of the synthesised net that the designer requires, then only Reduction Rule 2 can be applied, but if the aim is to have the smallest number of conditions in the synthesised net, then our experiments with various examples of ENL-systems/ENLST-systems show that the best strategy would be Strategy $(2, 3, 1)$ as discussed in Sect. 6.

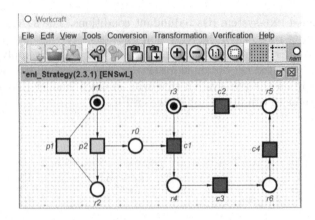

**Fig. 6.** Applying minimisation Strategy (2, 3, 1) to the ENL-system of Fig. 4.

# 8   Conclusions

In this paper we discussed the minimisation of the synthesised ENL-systems and the strategies to eliminate redundant regions that involve three reduction rules. Also, we investigated the properties of minimal regions that play a crucial role in the minimisation process. We showed that synthesised and minimised nets that are based on all minimal regions (after the application of the Reduction Rule 2) do not lose the property of the saturated ENL-systems of being state machine decomposable. We believe[4] that after the application of the Reduction Rule 3 this property still holds for the resultant net. However, after applying Reduction Rule 1, some synthesised ENL-systems are no longer decomposable. As an example, we can take the ENLST-system generated by the ENL-system in Fig. 1. The synthesis procedure for this example will produce a saturated net that has only minimal regions (12 regions). Some of them are redundant and can be deleted according to Reduction Rule 1. Figure 1 shows one of the possible minimised versions of this net that is not state-machine decomposable.

In the future work, we plan to investigate the relationship between the split of ENL-systems into state machine components (based on conditions) and the split into localities (based on events). Also, we want to develop an improved algorithm implementing Reduction Rule 1, which would allow to target certain regions for deletion from the pairs of complementary regions.

**Acknowledgement.** We are grateful to the anonymous reviewers for their constructive comments, which have helped us to improve the presentation of the paper and to clarify our ideas.

The first author is grateful to the National Transitional Council of Libya for funding her PhD studentship and research.

---

[4] This still needs to be formally proved.

# References

1. van der Aalst, W.M.P., van Dongen, B.F., Günther, C.W., Rozinat, A., Verbeek, E., Weijters, T.: Prom: the process mining toolkit. In: de Medeiros, A.K.A., Weber, B. (eds.) Proceedings of the Business Process Management Demonstration Track (BPMDemos 2009), Ulm, Germany, September 8, 2009. CEUR Workshop Proceedings, vol. 489. CEUR-WS.org (2009)

2. Ahmed, A., Koutny, M., Pietkiewicz-Koutny, M.: Synthesising elementary net systems with localities. Theoret. Comput. Sci. **908**, 123–140 (2022)

3. Ahmed, A., Pietkiewicz-Koutny, M.: Algorithms for the synthesis of elementary net systems with localities. In: Köhler-Bußmeier, M., Kindler, E., Rölke, H. (eds.) Proceedings of the International Workshop on Petri Nets and Software Engineering, PNSE 2020, Paris, France, June 24, 2020 (due to COVID-19: virtual workshop). CEUR Workshop Proceedings, vol. 2651, pp. 86–107. CEUR-WS.org (2020)

4. Badouel, É., Bernardinello, L., Darondeau, P.: Petri Net Synthesis. Texts in Theoretical Computer Science. An EATCS Series. Springer (2015)

5. Badouel, E., Darondeau, P.: Theory of regions. In: Reisig, W., Rozenberg, G. (eds.) ACPN 1996. LNCS, vol. 1491, pp. 529–586. Springer, Heidelberg (1998). https://doi.org/10.1007/3-540-65306-6_22

6. Bergenthum, R.: Prime miner - process discovery using prime event structures. In: International Conference on Process Mining, ICPM 2019, Aachen, Germany, June 24–26, 2019, pp. 41–48. IEEE (2019)

7. Bergenthum, R., Desel, J., Lorenz, R., Mauser, S.: Synthesis of Petri nets from scenarios with viptool. In: van Hee, K.M., Valk, R. (eds.) Applications and Theory of Petri Nets, 29th International Conference, PETRI NETS 2008, Xi'an, China, June 23–27, 2008. Proceedings. Lecture Notes in Computer Science, vol. 5062, pp. 388–398. Springer, Cham (2008)

8. Bernardinello, L.: Synthesis of net systems. In: Ajmone Marsan, M. (ed.) ICATPN 1993. LNCS, vol. 691, pp. 89–105. Springer, Heidelberg (1993). https://doi.org/10.1007/3-540-56863-8_42

9. Bernardinello, L., Michelis, G.D., Petruni, K., Vigna, S.: On the synchronic structure of transition systems. In: Desel, J. (ed.) Proceedings of the International Workshop on Structures in Concurrency Theory, STRICT 1995, Berlin, Germany, May 11–13, 1995, pp. 69–84. Workshops in Computing. Springer, Cham (1995). https://doi.org/10.1007/978-1-4471-3078-9_5

10. Carmona, J., Cortadella, J., Kishinevsky, M.: Genet: a tool for the synthesis and mining of Petri nets. In: Application of Concurrency to System Design 2009, 9th International Conference, ACSD 2009, Augsburg, Germany, 1–3 July 2009, pp. 181–185. IEEE Computer Society (2009)

11. Cortadella, J., Kishinevsky, M., Kondratyev, A., Lavagno, L., Yakovlev, A.: Logic Synthesis of Asynchronous Controllers and Interfaces. Springer, Heidelberg (2002)

12. Cortadella, J., Kishinevsky, M., Kondratyev, A., Lavagno, L., Yakovlev, A.: Petrify: a tool for manipulating concurrent specifications and synthesis of asynchronous controllers. IEICE Trans. Inf. Syst. **E80-D**, 315–325 (1997)

13. Dasgupta, S., Potop-Butucaru, D., Caillaud, B., Yakovlev, A.: Moving from weakly endochronous systems to delay-insensitive circuits. Electron. Notes Theor. Comput. Sci. **146**(2), 81–103 (2006)

14. Desel, J., Reisig, W.: The synthesis problem of Petri nets. Acta Inform. **33**(4), 297–315 (1996)

15. Ehrenfeucht, A., Rozenberg, G.: Partial (set) 2-structures. Part I: basic notions and the representation problem. Part II: state spaces of concurrent systems. Acta Inform. **27**(4), 315–368 (1990)

16. Kleijn, J.H.C.M., Koutny, M., Rozenberg, G.: Towards a Petri net semantics for membrane systems. In: Freund, R., Păun, G., Rozenberg, G., Salomaa, A. (eds.) WMC 2005. LNCS, vol. 3850, pp. 292–309. Springer, Heidelberg (2006). https://doi.org/10.1007/11603047_20

17. Koutny, M., Pietkiewicz-Koutny, M.: Transition systems of elementary net systems with localities. In: Baier, C., Hermanns, H. (eds.) CONCUR 2006. LNCS, vol. 4137, pp. 173–187. Springer, Heidelberg (2006). https://doi.org/10.1007/11817949_12

18. Koutny, M., Pietkiewicz-Koutny, M.: Synthesis of elementary net systems with context arcs and localities. Fund. Inform. **88**(3), 307–328 (2008)

19. Koutny, M., Pietkiewicz-Koutny, M.: Synthesis of Petri nets with localities. Sci. Ann. Comput. Sci. **19**, 1–23 (2009)

20. Koutny, M., Pietkiewicz-Koutny, M.: Minimal regions of ENL-transition systems. Fund. Inform. **101**(1–2), 45–58 (2010)

21. Mannel, L.L., Bergenthum, R., van der Aalst, W.M.P.: Removing implicit places using regions for process discovery. In: van der Aalst, W.M.P., Bergenthum, R., Carmona, J. (eds.) Proceedings of the International Workshop on Algorithms & Theories for the Analysis of Event Data 2020, ATAED 2020, Paris, France, June 24, 2020 (due to COVID-19: virtual workshop). CEUR Workshop Proceedings, vol. 2625, pp. 20–32. CEUR-WS.org (2020)

22. Mukund, M.: Petri nets and step transition systems. Int. J. Found. Comput. Sci. **3**(4), 443–478 (1992)

23. Nielsen, M., Rozenberg, G., Thiagarajan, P.S.: Elementary transition systems. Theoret. Comput. Sci. **96**(1), 3–33 (1992)

24. Pietkiewicz-Koutny, M.: Synthesis of ENI-systems using minimal regions. In: Sangiorgi, D., de Simone, R. (eds.) CONCUR 1998. LNCS, vol. 1466, pp. 565–580. Springer, Heidelberg (1998). https://doi.org/10.1007/BFb0055648

25. Pietkiewicz-Koutny, M.: The synthesis problem for elementary net systems with inhibitor arcs. Fund. Inform. **40**(2–3), 251–283 (1999)

26. Poliakov, I., Khomenko, V., Yakovlev, A.: WORKCRAFT – a framework for interpreted graph models. In: Franceschinis, G., Wolf, K. (eds.) PETRI NETS 2009. LNCS, vol. 5606, pp. 333–342. Springer, Heidelberg (2009). https://doi.org/10.1007/978-3-642-02424-5_21

27. Păun, G.: Membrane Computing: An Introduction. Springer, Natural Computing Series (2002)

28. https://github.com/SYNTHCRAFTTool/workcraft/tree/SYNTHCRAFT/workcraft (2023)

29. (2018). https://workcraft.org/

# Implementable Strategies for a Two-Player Asynchronous Game on Petri Nets

Federica Adobbati[1,2] , Luca Bernardinello[1(✉)] , Lucia Pomello[1] ,
and Riccardo Stramare[1]

[1] Università degli studi di Milano–Bicocca, DISCo, viale Sarca 336 U14, Milano,
Italy
luca.bernardinello@unimib.it
[2] National Institute of Oceanography and Applied Geophysics - OGS, Trieste, Italy

**Abstract.** We consider a two-player game on Petri nets, in which each player controls a subset of transitions. The players are called 'user' and 'environment'; we assume that the environment must guarantee progress on its transitions. A play of this game is a run in the unfolding of the net, satisfying the progress assumption. In general, we define a strategy for the user as a map from the set of 'observations' to subsets of transitions owned by the user. Different restrictions on strategies can be used to encode observability assumptions. We say that a given strategy is implementable if the net can be endowed with new places so that the runs of the new net coincide with the plays of the original net, complying with the strategy. We propose an algorithm based on the search of regions to decide whether a strategy is implementable.

**Keywords:** Asynchronous games · Petri nets · system control · region theory

## 1 Introduction

We consider the problem of controlling the behaviour of a system by guaranteeing that some undesirable behaviours are not executed or that some desirable properties are satisfied.

Such kind of problem has been studied for a long time, in different formal frameworks. Section 5 of this paper gives a concise review of a number of contributions close in spirit to our approach.

Here, we assume the system is modelled by a Petri net where some transitions are controlled by a 'user' who may choose which enabled transitions, among the ones under its control, fire and this on the basis of its 'partial' knowledge of the current state of the net system and of the behavioural properties it wants to achieve.

We model such a situation by a two-player game on the Petri net, where the players are called 'user' and 'environment', the transitions are partitioned in

M. Koutny et al. (Eds.): TPNOMCXVII, LNCS 14150, pp. 189–211, 2024.
https://doi.org/10.1007/978-3-662-68191-6_8

such a way that each one is under the control of exactly one player; we assume that the environment must guarantee progress on its transitions, whereas the user may wait to fire, or even not fire, a transition under its control.

A play of this game is a run in the unfolding of the net, satisfying the progress assumption. We say that a user has a winning strategy if it is able to win any play, i.e.: to force the behaviour of the system to satisfy the desired properties. In general, we define a strategy for the user as a map from the set of 'observations' to subsets of transitions owned by the user.

We have studied such a game and the problem of finding a winning strategy for the user, on the basis of different properties one wants to achieve, in different papers, see for example [1,2].

In this paper, which is an extension of [3], we assume the user has a strategy and, given this strategy, we want to decide whether it is *implementable*, i.e.: whether it is possible to add some places limiting the behaviours of the system so that, in the corrected system, each execution corresponds to one of the behaviours prescribed by the strategy.

Such a problem is solved, on the basis of the theory of regions, by considering the reduced marking graph, in which the not chosen transitions are deleted, and by searching a set of regions solving the 'state-transition separation problems' originated by removing those transitions. If such a set of regions exists, then we say the strategy is implementable and the identified regions correspond to the places to be added to constrain the system behaviour to the desired one.

The paper is organised as follows. Section 2 provides the necessary background on Petri nets, as well as the basic notions on the theory of regions of transition systems and on the synthesis problem. Section 3 presents the two-player game on bounded Petri nets. Section 4 defines when a given strategy is implementable and presents an algorithm that checks whether a strategy is implementable and, in the positive case, adds the places that restrict the behaviour as desired. Section 5 discusses some related work. Finally, Sect. 6 concludes the paper and discusses some possible future work.

## 2    Preliminary Definitions

In this section we recall basic notions on Petri nets and on regions of transition systems, which will be used in the rest of the paper. For a detailed overview on Petri nets refer to [15].

### 2.1    Petri Nets

A Petri net is a graph with two kinds of nodes: *places* (or *conditions*) represented with circles, and *transitions* (or *events*), represented with squares. Let $P$ be the set of places, and $T$ be the set of transitions, with $P$ and $T$ disjoint; the relation between the elements of the net is expressed through a function $W :$ $(P \times T) \cup (T \times P) \to \mathbb{N}$. In the graphical representation, given a pair of elements $(x, y) \in (P \times T) \cup (T \times P)$, if $W(x, y) > 0$ we draw a directed arc from $x$ to $y$.

If $W(x, y) > 1$ we label the arc with the value of $W(x, y)$. Formally, a Petri net can be denoted as a triple $N = (P, T, W)$.

A net $N' = (P', T', W')$ is a *subnet* of $N = (P, T, W)$ if $P' \subseteq P$, $T', \subseteq T$, and $W'$ is $W$ restricted to the elements in $N'$.

For each element of the net $x \in P \cup T$, the *pre-set* of $x$ is the set $^\bullet x = \{y \in P \cup T \mid W(y, x) > 0\}$, the *post-set* of $x$ is the set $x^\bullet = \{y \in P \cup T \mid W(x, y) > 0\}$. If $x \in T$, its pre-set (resp. post-set) is also called set of *preconditions* (resp. *postconditions*). Analogously, if $x \in P$, its pre-set and post-set are also called set of *pre-transitions* and *post-transitions* respectively. The previous notation can be extended to subsets of elements $A \subseteq P \cup T$: $^\bullet A = \bigcup_{x \in A} {}^\bullet x$ and $A^\bullet = \bigcup_{x \in A} x^\bullet$. If there are arcs in both directions between a place $p$ and a transition $t$, i.e.: $W(p, t) > 0$ and $W(t, p) > 0$, then this situation is called *loop* or *self-loop*.

We assume that the net is *T-restricted*, i.e.: each transition has non-empty pre-set and post-set, and it has no self-loops.

A *marking* is a function $m : P \to \mathbb{N}$ describing the global state of the net. A P/T *system* is a net with an initial marking $m_{in}$, and it is denoted with $\Sigma = (P, T, W, m_{in})$. A marking $m$ is graphically represented with *tokens* (small black circles) inside places, i.e.: each place $p$ has as many tokens as $m(p)$.

A transition $t \in T$ is *enabled* in a marking $m$, denoted with $m[t\rangle$, if, for each place $p \in {}^\bullet t$, $m(p) \geq W(p, t)$. An enabled transition can occur, or *fire*, producing a new marking $m'$ (denoted $m[t\rangle m'$), such that for each $p \in P$, $m'(p) = m(p) - W(p, t) + W(t, p)$.

Let $m$ be a marking of $\Sigma$, the set $[m\rangle$ is the smallest set of markings such that: $m \in [m\rangle$, and if $m' \in [m\rangle$ and $m'[t\rangle m''$, then $m'' \in [m\rangle$. The set $M = [m_{in}\rangle$ is the set of *reachable markings* of $\Sigma$.

Two transitions $t_1$ and $t_2$ are in *structural conflict* iff they share at least a place in their pre-sets: $^\bullet t_1 \cap {}^\bullet t_2 \neq \emptyset$; they are in *behavioural conflict* iff there exists a reachable marking $m$ such that it enables both of them, whereas the occurrence of one on them disables the other one, i.e.: $m[t_1\rangle m'$, $m[t_2\rangle m''$, $\neg(m''[t_1\rangle)$ and $\neg(m'[t_2\rangle)$.

A P/T system is *1-live* if for any transition $t \in T$ there exists a reachable marking $m$ such that: $m[t\rangle$.

The sequential behaviour of a P/T system $\Sigma = (P, T, W, m_{in})$ can be described by its *sequential marking graph* $\mathsf{MG}(\Sigma) = (M, T, A, m_{in})$, that is a labelled transition system where the states are the reachable markings $M = [m_{in}\rangle$, with $m_{in}$ the initial one, and each arc in $A$ is labelled by the transition leading from the source marking to the target one, $A = \{(m, t, m') \mid m, m' \in M, t \in T, and\ m[t\rangle m'\}$.

A P/T system is *bounded* (*k-bounded*) if there is $k \in \mathbb{N}$ such that: for any reachable marking $m$ and for any place $p$, $m(p) \leq k$. If $k = 1$ then the P/T system is said to be *safe*.

If a P/T system is bounded then the set of its reachable markings, and then also its sequential marking graph, is finite.

In the rest of the paper we consider 1-live bounded P/T systems, whose nets are finite, i.e.: $P$ and $T$ are finite sets, T-restricted and without self loops. In the special case of safe systems, we will interpret markings as sets of places: for each marking $m$, for each place $p$, $p \in m$ iff $m(p) = 1$.

The non-sequential behaviour of a P/T system can be modelled by the class of *occurrence nets*, see [8]. An occurrence net is a triple $N = (B, E, F)$, where $B$ and $E$ are disjoint, possibly infinite, sets called *conditions* and *events*, respectively, $F \subseteq (B \times E) \cup (E \times B)$ is the *flow* relation, and such that the graph of $N$ satisfies further restrictions. In order to formalize these restrictions we need to introduce some other relations on the elements of the net: the relation $\prec$ denotes the transitive closure of $F$, and $\preceq$ the transitive and reflexive closure of $F$. Let the pre-set and the post-set of an element of the net be defined analogously as above, let $x, y \in B \cup E$, then $x \# y$ iff there exists $e_1, e_2 \in E : e_1 \neq e_2, e_1 \preceq x, e_2 \preceq y$ and there exists $b \in {}^\bullet e_1 \cap {}^\bullet e_2$.

The net $N = (B, E, F)$ is an occurrence net if the following restrictions hold:

1. $\forall x \in B \cup E : \neg(x \prec x)$
2. $\forall x \in B \cup E : \neg(x \# x)$
3. $\forall e \in E : \{x \in B \cup E \mid x \preceq e\}$ is finite
4. $\forall b \in B : |{}^\bullet b| \leq 1$

In an occurrence net the transitive and reflexive closure of $F$, $\preceq$, forms a *partial order*. The set of minimal elements of an occurrence net $N$ with respect to $\preceq$ will be denoted by $min(N)$. Since we only consider T-restricted nets, the elements of $min(N)$ are conditions.

On the elements of an occurrence net the relation of concurrency, **co**, is defined as follows: let $x, y \in B \cup E$, $x$ **co** $y$, if neither $(x \prec y)$ nor $(y \prec x)$ nor $(x \# y)$.

A *B-cut* of $N$ is a maximal set of pairwise concurrent elements of $B$, and can be intuitively seen as a global state of the net in a certain moment.

A *branching process* of a bounded 1-live PT system $\Sigma = (P, T, W, m_{in})$, whose underlying net is finite, T-restricted and without loops, is a pair $(N, \lambda)$, where $N = (B, E, F)$ is an occurrence net, and $\lambda$ is a map from $B \cup E$ to $P \cup T$ such that:

1. $\lambda(B) \subseteq P$; $\lambda(E) \subseteq T$
2. $\forall e \in E$, $\forall p \in P$, $W(p, \lambda(e)) = |\lambda^{-1}(p) \cap {}^\bullet e|$ and $W(\lambda(e), p) = |\lambda^{-1}(p) \cap e^\bullet|$
3. $\forall p \in P$ $m_{in}(p) = |\lambda^{-1}(p) \cap min(N)|$
4. $\forall x, y \in E$, if ${}^\bullet x = {}^\bullet y$ and $\lambda(x) = \lambda(y)$, then $x = y$.

A branching process $(N_1, \lambda_1)$ is a *prefix* of a branching process $(N_2, \lambda_2)$ if $N_1$ is a subnet of $N_2$ and $\lambda_1$ is the restriction of $\lambda_2$ to $B_1 \cup E_1$.

Any finite P/T system $\Sigma = (P, T, W, m_{in})$ has a unique branching process which is maximal with respect to the prefix relation. This maximal branching process, called the *unfolding* of $\Sigma$, will be denoted by $\text{Unf}(\Sigma) = ((B, E, F), \lambda)$, where $\lambda$ is the map from $B \cup E$ to $P \cup T$.

Any B-cut $\gamma$ of the unfolding corresponds to a reachable marking: $\lambda(\gamma) \in [m\rangle$. By analogy with net systems, we say that an event $e$ of an unfolding is *enabled* at a B-cut $\gamma$, denoted $\gamma[e\rangle$, if ${}^\bullet e \subseteq \gamma$.

A *run* $\rho = (B_\rho, E_\rho, F_\rho)$ records a possible non sequential behaviour of the system, it is a prefix of $\mathsf{Unf}(\Sigma) = (B, E, F)$, whose occurrence net is free of conflicts, i.e., for any $e_1, e_2 \in E_\rho$, $\neg(e_1 \# e_2)$. A run $\rho$ is *maximal* if there is no event $e \in E \setminus E_\rho$ such that $\rho \cup \{e\} \cup \{e^\bullet\}$ is a run.

A *configuration* is a subset of events $C \subseteq E$ of the unfolding which is causally closed and free of conflicts; the set of events $E_\rho$ of any run $\rho$ is therefore a configuration. A configuration $C$ is *local* if there is an event $e \in C$ such that $C = \{e' \in E \mid e' \leq e\}$, with $E$ set of events of the unfolding, such a local configuration is denoted $\lfloor e \rfloor$. Any local configuration is a finite set, and this is due to condition 3. of the definition of occurrence nets. $\mathsf{Cut}(\lfloor e \rfloor)$ denotes the B-cut of the run $\rho$ with events $E_\rho = \lfloor e \rfloor$ which enables $e$, i.e.: $\mathsf{Cut}(\lfloor e \rfloor) = ((E_\rho^\bullet \setminus {}^\bullet E_\rho) \setminus \{e^\bullet\}) \cup \{{}^\bullet e\}$.

Two B-cuts of a run $\rho$, $\gamma$ and $\gamma'$, are ordered, denoted $\gamma < \gamma'$, iff $\gamma \neq \gamma'$ and $\forall b \in \gamma, \exists b' \in \gamma'$ such that: $b \leq b'$. A sequence $\gamma_1 \gamma_2 ... \gamma_n ...$ of B-cuts is *increasing* if $\gamma_i < \gamma_j$ for each $i, j \in \mathbf{N}$ with $i < j$.

## 2.2 Regions and the Synthesis Problem

In this section we recall some basic notions on the theory of regions of transition systems. Regions, introduced by Ehrenfeucht and Rozenberg (see [7]) have been used as a tool to solve synthesis problems for Petri nets: given a labelled transition system, decide if there is a Petri net, of a given class, such that its marking graph is isomorphic to the given transition system. Intuitively, a region corresponds to a potential place of the net, and the synthesis problem is solvable if the given transition system has enough regions to solve all the so-called separation problems (defined below). Here, we will focus on regions for P/T systems. For a thorough treatment of region theory, see [4].

A *labelled transition system* is given by a set $Q$ of states, a set $L$ of labels, and a set $A$ of arcs (or transitions), with $A \subseteq Q \times L \times Q$; each arc $(q, z, q')$ represents a change of state from $q$ to $q'$ produced by an occurrence of the action labelled with $z$. We will consider finite transition systems ($Q$ and $L$ are finite) with a distinguished initial state $q_0$. Formally, we will write $\mathsf{TS} = (Q, L, A, q_0)$ to denote such a transition system.

The word *transition*, already used to denote one of the two types of nodes in a Petri net (Sect. 2.1), assumes a different meaning when we consider transition systems. In this section, when we refer to transitions we mean arcs in a transition system.

We assume that in all transition systems under consideration all the states are reachable from the initial state, that every label appears in at least one arc, and that there are no *loops*, namely transitions of the form $(q, z, q)$. Formally, we define a path in $\mathsf{TS}$ as a sequence of transitions

$$\pi = (q_1, z_1, q_2)(q_2, z_2, q_3) \cdots (q_{k-1}, z_{k-1}, q_k);$$

we will say that this path goes from $q_1$ to $q_k$, and that $q_k$ is reachable from $q_1$.

Our assumptions on $\mathsf{TS}$ can then be formalized like in the definition below.

**Definition 1.** *A labelled initialized transition system is a structure*

$$\mathsf{TS} = (Q, L, A, q_0)$$

*where $Q$ and $L$ are finite sets of states and labels, respectively, $A \subseteq Q \times L \times Q$ is a set of transitions, $q_0 \in Q$ is the initial state, satisfying the following:*

1. *For all $q$ in $Q$, there is a path from $q_0$ to $q$; for all $z$ in $L$, there is an arc $(q, z, q')$ in $A$*
2. *For each arc $(q, z, q')$, $q \neq q'$*

The marking graph of a 1-live P/T system without self-loops is a labelled transition system fulfilling these properties.

In the rest of this section, let $\mathsf{TS} = (Q, L, A, q_0)$ be a fixed labelled transition system satisfying 1 and 2.

**Definition 2.** *A region of $\mathsf{TS}$ is a map $r : Q \to \mathbb{N}$ such that, for all $t$ in $L$, and for all pairs of transitions $(q, t, q')$ and $(q_1, t, q_1')$ in $A$, the following holds:*

$$r(q') - r(q) = r(q_1') - r(q_1)$$

If we think of $r$ as a map giving the number of tokens in a potential place in each state, then the condition of Definition 2 says that every firing of $t$ has the same effect on $r$.

Given a region $r$, we can define a map $w_r : L \to \mathbb{Z}$ as follows: for all $t$ in $L$, $w_r(t) = r(q') - r(q)$, for a transition $(q, t, q')$ in $A$. From the definition of region, it follows that the definition of $w_r$ does not depend on the choice of the transition. The value of $w_r(t)$ expresses the change in the value of $r$ produced by any transition labelled by $t$.

*Example 1.* Consider the labelled transition system in Fig. 1. Then the two maps, $r_1$ and $r_2$ tabulated on the right of the picture are regions, and, for instance, $w_{r_1}(a) = 1$, $w_{r_1}(c) = -1$.

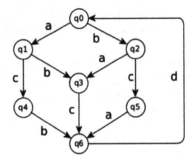

| | $q_0$ | $q_1$ | $q_2$ | $q_3$ | $q_4$ | $q_5$ | $q_6$ |
|---|---|---|---|---|---|---|---|
| $r_1$ | 0 | 1 | 1 | 2 | 0 | 0 | 1 |
| $r_2$ | 1 | 0 | 1 | 0 | 0 | 1 | 0 |

**Fig. 1.** A labelled transition system and two of its regions.

Let now $q_1$ and $q_2$ be two distinct states of TS; we say that a region $r$ *separates* $q_1$ and $q_2$ if $r(q_1) \neq r(q_2)$. We also say in this case that $r$ solves the *state separation problem* $(q_1, q_2)$.

Let $t$ be a label in $L$, and $q$ a state such that $t$ is not enabled in $q$; a region $r$ separates $t$ from $q$ if $w_r(t) < 0$ and $r(q) < -w_r(t)$. Intuitively, think of $r$ as a place of a P/T system, with $r(q)$ the number of tokens in $r$ in state $q$; the inequality $w_r(t) < 0$ means that a firing of $t$ has the effect of taking $|w_r(t)|$ tokens from $r$, hence $r$ is an input place of $t$; then $r(q) < -w_r(t)$ means that in state $q$, $r$ does not contain enough tokens to allow for the firing of $t$. We will then say that $r$ solves the state-event separation problem $(q, t)$.

A labelled transition system TS is *separated* if, for each pair of distinct states, there is a region solving the corresponding separation problem, and, for each state $q$ and for each label $t$ not enabled in $q$, there is a region solving the corresponding separation problem.

If the transition system is not separated, we cannot synthesize a Petri net such that its marking graph is isomorphic to the transition system.

We will say that a set $D$ of regions *separates* TS if it contains enough regions to solve all separation problems. If this is the case, then we can define a P/T system $\Sigma = (D, L, W, m_{in})$ in this way: for each $r$ in $D$, and for each $t$ in $L$, $W(r, t) = -w_r(t)$ if $w_r(t) < 0$, $W(t, r) = w_r(t)$ if $w_r(t) > 0$, and $W(r, t) = W(t, r) = 0$ in all other cases; for all $r$ in $D$, $m_{in}(r) = r(q_0)$.

If $D$ separates TS, then the marking graph of $\Sigma$ is isomorphic to TS (see [4] for a proof).

For each separation problem, there is an algorithm, polynomial in the size of TS, which decides if there is a region solving it, and, if so, effectively finds a separating region. For details on the algorithm, again see [4].

|    | $q_0$ | $q_1$ | $q_2$ | $q_3$ | $q_4$ | $q_5$ | $q_6$ |
|----|----|----|----|----|----|----|----|
| $r_1$ | 0 | 1 | 1 | 2 | 0 | 0 | 1 |
| $r_2$ | 1 | 0 | 1 | 0 | 0 | 1 | 0 |
| $r_3$ | 1 | 1 | 0 | 0 | 1 | 0 | 0 |
| $r_4$ | 0 | 1 | 0 | 1 | 1 | 0 | 1 |
| $r_5$ | 1 | 1 | 1 | 1 | 0 | 0 | 0 |
| $r_6$ | 0 | 0 | 0 | 0 | 1 | 1 | 1 |
| $r_7$ | 0 | 0 | 1 | 1 | 0 | 1 | 1 |

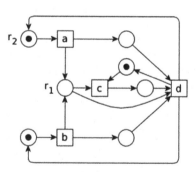

**Fig. 2.** A P/T system realization of the TS given in Fig. 1

*Example 2.* Consider again the transition system TS shown in Fig. 1. The rows of the table on the left of Fig. 2 correspond to a separating set of regions for TS. The P/T net system on the right is the corresponding net system.

Let now $r$ be a region of TS. If we remove a transition from TS, we obtain a new transition system, $TS'$; from the definition of region it is clear that $r$ is a region also of $TS'$. After removing a subset $U$ of transitions, some states and some labels might become unreachable from the initial state; define $TS'$ by taking only the reachable states and labels after removing $U$; then, the restriction of $r$ to the set of reachable states is a region of $TS'$. This removal operation will be used in Sect. 4.1.

In order to clarify the correspondence between regions of a transition system and places of a net system, consider a bounded P/T system $\Sigma = (P, T, W, m_{in})$ and its marking graph $MG(\Sigma) = (M, T, A, m_{in})$, where $M$ is the set of reachable markings. Choose a place $p$ and define a map $f_p : M \to \mathbb{N}$ as follows:

$$\forall m \in M : f_p(m) = m(p).$$

As a consequence of the firing rule of P/T nets, such a map satisfies a uniformity property: for each transition $t$, and for each edge $(m, t, m')$ in $A$, the difference $f_p(m) - f_p(m')$ is the same, and is equal to $W(p, t) - W(t, p)$. The marking graph $MG(\Sigma)$ is separated by the set of regions corresponding to the places of $\Sigma$.

Suppose now that $g : M \to \mathbb{N}$ satisfies the same uniformity property for each transition. We can add to $\Sigma$ a new place $g$; for a given transition $t$, we add an arc from $t$ to $g$ if there is an arc $(m, t, m')$ in $MG(\Sigma)$ with $g(m') > g(m)$, and we put $W(t, g) = g(m') - g(m)$; symmetrically, if $g(m) > g(m')$, we add an arc from $g$ to $t$, with $W(g, t) = g(m) - g(m')$. The resulting net system has a marking graph isomorphic to $MG(\Sigma)$.

## 3    Asynchronous Games

Let us introduce a two-player, asynchronous game on bounded Petri nets through an example. Consider the P/T system in Fig. 3. Two players interact on it, the *user*, by controlling the light grey transitions, and the *environment*, by controlling the white ones. The game is asynchronous: the players can concurrently fire their transitions. The game is asymmetric: the user has the right to keep its transitions blocked when they are enabled, whereas the environment must guarantee progress of its transitions. In this example, we suppose that the user has full knowledge of the current marking, and that it has the goal of marking place $q$ infinitely often. In order to win, the user must wait for the environment to choose between firing $t_1$ or $t_2$. It can do this, since the environment cannot delay this choice forever. In the former case, the user chooses $u_1$, otherwise $u_2$. The environment is then forced to fire either $v_1$ or $v_2$, with the effect of marking $q$, and then to fire $z$, reproducing the initial marking.

Formally, we define a game on a bounded P/T system $\Sigma = (P, T, W, m_{in})$, where the transitions are partitioned into two sets: $T_u$, the *controllable* transitions, i.e.: the ones controlled by the user, and $T_{env}$, the *uncontrollable* transitions, i.e. the ones controlled by the environment; $T = T_u \cup T_{env}$, $T_u \cap T_{env} = \emptyset$.

Since in the case of a conflict between a controllable transition and an uncontrollable one, which are both enabled, we assume that the user is not always able

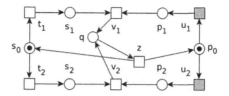

**Fig. 3.** A game net

to fire its transition before the environment, we impose that the net is such that there is no structural conflict between a controllable transition and an uncontrollable one: $\forall t_1, t_2: t_1 \in T_u, t_2 \in T_{env}, \ {}^\bullet t_1 \cap {}^\bullet t_2 = \emptyset$.

We consider the unfolding of the P/T system $\Sigma$ where events are partitioned into *controllable* $(E_u)$ and *uncontrollable* $(E_{env})$ events, depending on their correspondence to occurrences of controllable or uncontrollable transitions, respectively.

**Definition 3.** *A* play *in the game is formally defined as a run* $\rho = (B_\rho, E_\rho, F)$ *in the unfolding of $\Sigma$, which must be maximal with respect to uncontrollable events, because of the progress constraint for the environment, namely there cannot be any event $e \in E_{env}$ such that ${}^\bullet e \in \rho$, and $({}^\bullet e)^\bullet \cap E_\rho = \emptyset$.*

The *winning condition* for the user is a set of plays, satisfying a certain property. The user wins a play if the play belongs to the winning condition. The goal of the user is to win all the plays.

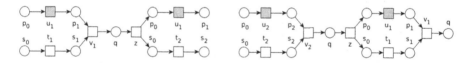

**Fig. 4.** A terminating play (left) and a partial play (right)

In the example discussed above, the winning condition is formed by all the maximal runs with an infinite number of occurrences of the place $q$. Figure 4 shows, on the left, a play ending in a deadlock (the environment wins) and, on the right, the initial segment of an infinite play (the user wins).

In order to reach its goal, the user can apply a *strategy*. We assume that the user has in general only a partial knowledge of the current state of the net system. This is formalized by a notion of *observation*. An observation is given by an equivalence relation on the set of B-cuts of the unfolding, denoted by $\equiv$, where two B-cuts are equivalent if they are indistinguishable for the user. Examples of observations are discussed in Subsect. 3.1. A strategy $\alpha$ is defined as a map from the set of observations, denoted by Obs, to sets of controllable enabled transitions: $\alpha : \mathsf{Obs} \to 2^{T_u}$.

**Definition 4.** *A play* $\rho = (B_\rho, E_\rho, F)$ *is* consistent *with a strategy* $\alpha$ *if the following conditions hold.*

1. *For each controllable event* $e \in E_\rho \cap E_u$ *there is an increasing sequence* $\mu = \gamma_1 \gamma_2 ... \gamma_n ...$ *of B-cuts in* $\rho$, *and a B-cut* $\gamma_j \in \mu$ *such that* $\lambda(e) \in \alpha([\gamma_j])$ *and* $\lambda(\gamma_j)[\lambda(e)\rangle$, *where* $[\gamma_j]$ *denotes the equivalence class w.r.t.* $\equiv$ *containing* $\gamma_j$.
2. *There is no event* $e \in E_u$, $e \notin E_\rho$ *such that there is a B-cut* $\gamma_j : \lambda(e) \in \alpha([\gamma])$, *for each B-cut* $\gamma \geq \gamma_j$.

Loosely speaking, a play is consistent with a strategy if each choice of the user in the play is justified by the strategy, and there is no event constantly enabled and constantly selected by the strategy which never fires.

### 3.1   Examples of Observations

In this section we propose some possible equivalence relations to define the observations of the user.

*Subset of Places of the Net.* At the beginning of this section, we discussed the example in Fig. 3 assuming that the user observes all the places on the system, and can distinguish between different markings. In this context, given two B-cuts $\gamma_1$ and $\gamma_2$, $\gamma_1 \equiv \gamma_2$ iff $\lambda(\gamma_1) = \lambda(\gamma_2)$.

We could also consider the case in which some value of some place is never observable by the user. Consider the case in which the user cannot see whether $s_1$ and $s_2$ are marked. In this case all the cuts $\gamma_i$ such that $\lambda(\gamma_i) = \{s_1, p_0\}$ are in the same equivalence class of the cuts $\gamma_j$ such that $\lambda(\gamma_j) = \{s_2, p_0\}$, therefore the strategy cannot distinguish between the case in which $t_1$ occurred and the case in which $t_2$ occurred, and therefore cannot choose between $u_1$ and $u_2$ so to be sure that $q$ will be eventually reached.

*Stable Parts of Markings.* As in the previous case, we assume that each pair of cuts associated to the same marking is in the same equivalence class (but the following reasoning may be applied without this assumption). In the net in Fig. 5, the user controls the transitions $v_0$ and $v_1$. Assume that the goal of the user is to fire $v_0$ if the marking is $\{p_0, c_0, n_0\}$, and $v_1$ if the marking is $\{p_1, c_0, n_0\}$. It is reasonable to state that the user has no winning strategy for this goal, even if the value of $p_0$ and $p_1$ is not hidden in the system: since their value may be modified by the environment alone, the user can never be sure that while executing $v_0$ or $v_1$, the environment did not execute $t_0$ or $t_1$, changing the state of the system. In other words, in an asynchronous system the user may not be sure of the current state of the system, if this can be modified by the environment. This leads us to a notion of observation that, in each marking, distinguishes only between the places that cannot be modified by uncontrollable transitions. Considering this notion, all the cuts associated to the marking $\{p_0, c_0, n_0\}$ are equivalent to all those associated to $\{p_1, c_0, n_0\}$, since both $p_0$ and $p_1$ can be modified by the environment in these markings.

*Remark 1.* By considering this notion of observation, the same place may be observable or not depending on the marking: in $\{p_0, c_0, n_0\}$ the place $n_0$ is observable, since no uncontrollable transition can modify its value. After the occurrence of $v_0$, the uncontrollable transition $h_0$ is enabled, therefore the information that $n_0$ is marked may be modified and is no longer available for the user.

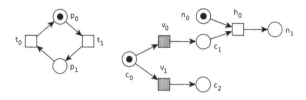

**Fig. 5.** A net with no winning strategy.

*Subset of Conditions on the Unfolding.* As a last example, consider the net in Fig. 6. We assume that the user cannot observe any occurrence of the places $p_3, p_4$ and $p_7$. In the figure, observable places are represented with bold lines. Let $O = \{b \in B : \lambda(b) \in P \setminus \{p_3, p_4, p_7\}\}$ be the set of conditions observable on the unfolding. Given two B-cuts $\gamma_1$ and $\gamma_2$, we define an observation so that $\gamma_1 \equiv \gamma_2$ iff $\gamma_1 \cap O = \gamma_2 \cap O$. In Fig. 6, assume that the goal is to never reach a deadlock. The user does not have a winning strategy defined on markings, since, in order to win, it must choose $t_1$ in $\{p_0, p_4\}$, and $t_2$ in $\{p_0, p_3\}$, but these two makings are not distinguishable due to the observability constraint. However, the user has a winning strategy, if we consider an observation as previously defined. Consider the prefix of the unfolding of Fig. 6 represented in Fig. 7. In the B-cut $\gamma_1 = \{b5, b7\}$, the user can observe only $b7$; in the B-cut $\gamma_2 = \{b2, b8\}$ the user can observe only $b8$. Although $\lambda(b7) = \lambda(b8)$, $b7 \neq b8$, and therefore, based on the notion of observation given above $\gamma_1 \not\equiv \gamma_2$. This notion of observation, where the user can distinguish different B-cuts associated to the same marking, implies that the user has full memory of what happened on the system: by observing a condition on the unfolding, the user knows its entire past. In general, this information cannot be recovered by observing a place on the system.

## 4    Implementable Strategies

In the game described in Sect. 3, the goal of the user is to limit the possible behaviours of the system so that all the executions satisfy a certain property. The strategy for the user describes how the behaviours should be limited. In this section, we discuss how the system could be corrected by adding the limitations given by the strategy in form of places, so that, in the corrected system, each

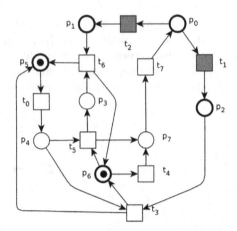

**Fig. 6.** A net where a winning strategy can be defined on B-cuts.

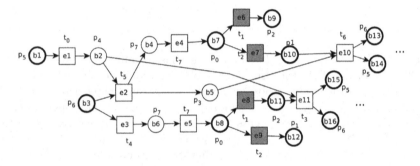

**Fig. 7.** Prefix of the unfolding of the net in Fig. 6

execution follows one of the behaviours prescribed by the strategy. If such a corrected system exists, we say that the strategy is *implementable*.

In this section, we are neither interested in the specific goal a user pursues, nor in the fact that a strategy is winning, but only in determining whether a given strategy is implementable. Before giving a formal definition of implementable strategy, we need some auxiliary definitions.

**Definition 5.** *Let* $\Sigma = (P, T, W, m_{in})$ *be a bounded P/T system. A restriction of* $\Sigma$ *is a P/T system* $\Sigma' = (P \cup H, T, W', m'_{in})$ *such that* $W = W'|_{(P \times T) \cup (T \times P)}$ *and* $m_{in} = m'_{in}|_P$, $P \cap H = \emptyset$.

Let $\Sigma$ be a bounded P/T system, and $\Sigma'$ be a restriction of $\Sigma$. A sequence of transition firings in $\Sigma'$ from $m'_{in}$ can always be reproduced in $\Sigma$ from $m_{in}$.

**Definition 6.** *Let* $\rho' = (B'_{\rho'}, E'_{\rho'}, F'_{\rho'})$ *be a run in the unfolding of* $\Sigma'$, *and* $\gamma'$ *be a B-cut of* $\rho'$. *A projection of* $\rho'$ *on* $\mathrm{Unf}(\Sigma)$ *is a run* $\rho = (B_\rho, E_\rho, F_\rho)$ *such that* $\rho$ *is isomorphic to* $\rho' \setminus J$, *with* $J = \{j \in B' : \lambda(j) \in H\}$. *Analogously, a projection of* $\gamma'$ *on* $\rho$ *is a B-cut* $\gamma \subseteq B_\rho$ *such that* $\gamma = \gamma' \setminus J$.

By construction, for each $\rho'$ run of $\mathrm{Unf}(\Sigma')$, and for each B-cut $\gamma'$, there is always at least a projection on $\mathrm{Unf}(\Sigma)$.

While following a strategy, the user has complete control over controllable transitions, for example it can decide to fire controllable transitions only after the occurrence of some uncontrollable transitions, to completely block their occurrence, or to order the occurrence of concurrently enabled controllable transitions in a specific way. However, it cannot force uncontrollable transitions to fire in any order and it cannot be sure to fire a controllable transition before an enabled uncontrollable transition has occurred. An implementation of a strategy must reflect these properties, therefore, we cannot allow for places that limit the behaviour of the environment. A naive solution for this would be to allow to add only places that are preconditions of controllable transitions. However, Example 3 shows a system in which the new places are preconditions of uncontrollable transitions, without limiting the behaviour of the environment.

**Definition 7.** *Let $\Sigma = (P, T, W, m_{in})$ be a P/T system, and $\Sigma' = (P \cup H, T, W', m'_{in})$ a restriction of $\Sigma$. A place $p \in H \setminus P$ is environment-fair if $p^\bullet \cap T_{env} = \emptyset$, or if the following conditions hold.*

1. *There is a transition $t \in T$ such that $p \in t^\bullet$.*
2. *For each $t_n \in T_{env}$ such that $t_n \in p^\bullet$, for each run $\rho \in \mathrm{Unf}(\Sigma')$ including the elements $b, e_1, e_2$ such that $\lambda(b) = p$, $\lambda(e_1) = t$, $\lambda(e_2) = t_n$, $e_1 \in {}^\bullet b, b \in {}^\bullet e_2$, then $e_1 \prec e_2$ in the projection of $\rho$ on $\mathrm{Unf}(\Sigma)$.*
3. *For each transition $t_n \in T_{env}$ such that $t_n \in p^\bullet$, for each transition $t_i \in p^\bullet$, and for each marking $m' \in [m'_{in}\rangle$, if $t_i$ and $t_n$ are in behavioural conflict in $m'$, then they are also in behavioural conflict also in $m = m' \cap P$.*

In Definition 7, the second condition expresses that if an uncontrollable transition is forced by a new place to occur after another one, then this same order constraint must hold also in the initial net. The third condition expresses that all the conflicts derived from a new place involving at least an uncontrollable transition must be structural and not behavioural.

**Definition 8.** *Let $\Sigma = (P, T, W, m_{in})$ be a bounded P/T system. A strategy $\alpha$ is weakly implementable iff there is a bounded restriction $\Sigma' = (P \cup H, T, W', m'_{in})$ of $\Sigma$ such that the following conditions hold.*

1. *Each place in $H \setminus P$ is environment fair.*
2. *For each maximal run $\rho'$ in $\mathrm{Unf}(\Sigma')$, its projection on $\mathrm{Unf}(\Sigma)$ is a play consistent with $\alpha$.*
3. *For each maximal run $\rho'$ in $\mathrm{Unf}(\Sigma')$, for each controllable event $e'$ in $\rho'$, let $\gamma' = \mathsf{Cut}(\lfloor e' \rfloor)$ be the cut preceding the local configuration of $e'$ in $\rho'$, and $\gamma$ its projection on $\mathrm{Unf}(\Sigma)$. Then $\lambda(e') \in \alpha([\gamma])$.*

*If such a $\Sigma'$ exists, we say that it is a weak implementation of $\alpha$ on $\Sigma$.*

**Definition 9.** *Let $\Sigma = (P, T, W, m_{in})$ be a bounded P/T system. A strategy $\alpha$ is strongly implementable iff there is a bounded restriction $\Sigma' = (P \cup$*

$H, T, W', m'_{in})$ of $\Sigma$ such that $\Sigma'$ is a weak implementation of $\alpha$, and each play consistent with $\alpha$ is a projection of a maximal run in $\mathrm{Unf}(\Sigma')$.

If such a $\Sigma'$ exists, we say it is a strong implementation of $\alpha$ on $\Sigma$.

Loosely speaking, $\Sigma'$ is a weak implementation of $\alpha$ on $\Sigma$ if all its maximal runs follow the behaviour prescribed by $\alpha$ on $\Sigma$, possibly restricting it. It is a strong implementation if all the behaviours allowed by $\alpha$ on $\Sigma$ are reproducible on $\Sigma'$.

*Remark 2.* By definition, a weak implementation $\Sigma'$ of a strategy $\alpha$ on a P/T system $\Sigma$ has at least a maximal run in $\mathrm{Unf}(\Sigma')$, since its initial marking cannot be empty. Hence, in the unfolding of a weak implementation there must always be at least a maximal run projecting on a play consistent with $\alpha$ in $\mathrm{Unf}(\Sigma)$.

To illustrate the definitions and the different cases that can occur, we discuss three examples of nets and strategies.

*Example 3.* Consider the safe (1-bounded) P/T system on Fig. 8 where, in order to simplify the drawing, the output arcs of the five transitions labelled by $R$ have been omitted. These transitions reproduce the initial marking, hence they all have as post-set the places $\{p_1, p_2, p_{10}\}$. In this system, the user has the goal to infinitely often reach a marking containing place $p_{12}$, and it can observe the value of the places $\{p_1, p_2, p_3, p_4, p_5, p_6, p_{10}, p_{12}\}$, which are represented with bold lines.

In the initial marking, there are two independent conflicts controlled by the environment (between A and B, and between C and D), and a conflict controlled by the user, between H and I. In order to fulfil its goal, the user has to wait for the environment to make its choices.

The system is safe, so we can take the powerset of the set of observed places as **Obs**. A winning strategy is: $\alpha(\{p_1, p_2, p_{10}\}) = \emptyset$, $\alpha(\{p_4, p_6, p_{10}\}) = \{H\}$, $\alpha(\{p_3, p_5, p_{10}\}) = \alpha(\{p_3, p_6, p_{10}\}) = \alpha(\{p_4, p_5, p_{10}\}) = \{I\}$. A strong implementation of this strategy is given by the P/T system on Fig. 9. Since the choice of H depends on the occurrence of both B and D, this is represented by adding place $p_{14}$ from B to H, and place $p_{15}$ from D to H. Instead, the choice of I depends on the occurrence of either A or C, hence it may be represented adding place $p_{13}$ from both A and C to I. In this way, if it is the case that both A and C occur, the added place $p_{13}$ may get two tokens and then the net system with this added place becomes 2-bounded and no more safe (1-bounded). In order to correctly reproduce the initial marking, the added places may be emptied by the uncontrollable transitions R, and this without limiting the behaviour of the environment, indeed it is possible to show that the added places, $p_{13}$, $p_{14}$ and $p_{15}$ are environment-fair, since they satisfy conditions 1., 2. and 3. of Definition 7.

*Example 4.* A strategy can be weakly implementable, but not strongly implementable. Consider the net system $\Sigma$ on the left of Fig. 10, and the following strategy, defined on markings, under the hypothesis that the user can see all places, but cannot distinguish distinct occurrences of them (braces are omitted in the arguments of the map): $\alpha(p_0, p_3) = \{t_0, t_1\}$, $\alpha(p_1, p_3) = \{t_2\}$,

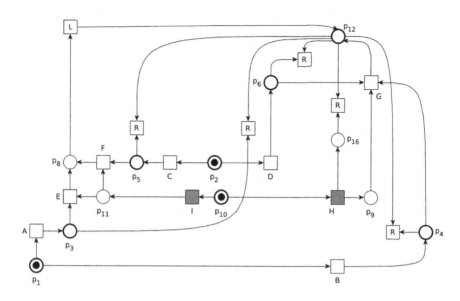

**Fig. 8.** A P/T system where the user observes the thick places and has the goal to reach place $p_{12}$ infinitely often.

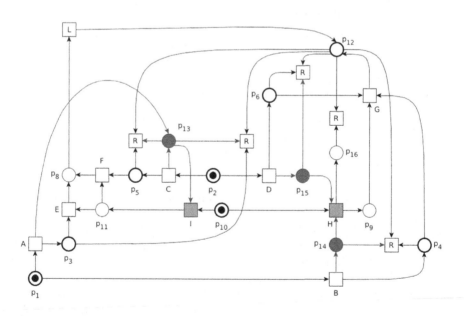

**Fig. 9.** An implementation of a strategy for system of Fig. 8, adding preconditions also to uncontrollable transitions.

$\alpha(p_7, p_3) = \{t_2\}$, $\alpha(p_2, p_3) = \{t_3\}$, and $\alpha(m) = \emptyset$ for all other markings. The marking graph shown on the right of Fig. 10 is obtained from $\mathsf{MG}(\Sigma)$ by removing arcs corresponding to controllable transitions which are not chosen by the strategy, and states which are no more reachable from the initial state. This transition system is not separated for bounded P/T systems without self-loops. As we will see in the next section, this means that the strategy is not strongly implementable. However, we can notice that the unsolvable separation problem is given by the absence of label $t_2$ in state $\{p_2, p_3\}$, and by the absence of label $t_3$ in the state $\{p_1, p_3\}$, which are reached if the user fires $t_0$ in the initial state. The strategy $\alpha$ gives the user the freedom to choose either $t_0$ or $t_1$ in that state, therefore a weak implementation of $\alpha$ can be realized by blocking $t_0$, so that the critical states are not reached, adding a place from $t_6$ to $t_2$, and blocking $t_3$.

An alternative weak implementation consists in adding a place from $t_6$ to $t_2$, and blocking the occurrence of $t_3$. In this way, if $t_0$ fires in the implementation, neither $t_2$ nor $t_3$ can fire. This execution on the implementation projects on a consistent play, since neither $t_2$ nor $t_3$ are constantly selected by $\alpha$ after the choice of $t_0$. In the run selecting $t_1$ we are in the same case discussed above, therefore the requirements for the weak implementation are satisfied.

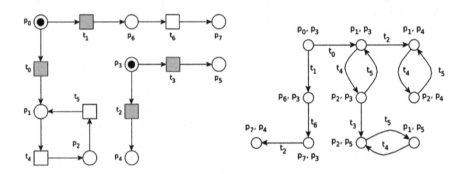

**Fig. 10.** A weakly implementable strategy.

*Example 5.* In some cases, neither a weak implementation nor a strong implementation exist. Consider the net $\Sigma$ in Fig. 11, and assume that the user can distinguish each B-cut in $\mathsf{Unf}(\Sigma)$. Consider the strategy $\alpha$ such that $\alpha(\gamma_0) = \alpha(\gamma_1) = \emptyset$, $\alpha(\gamma_2) = \alpha(\gamma) = \{t_0\}$, for each $\gamma > \gamma_2$ enabling $t_0$. An implementation cannot block $t_0$, since in all the plays consistent with $\alpha$, $t_0$ must fire, since it is constantly enabled and selected from $\gamma_2$ on. Hence, $t_0$ needs to be blocked until the first occurrence of $t_2$, and we need to add a place from $t_2$ to $t_0$. Such a place is not bounded, therefore the resulting net is not a weak implementation of $\Sigma$.

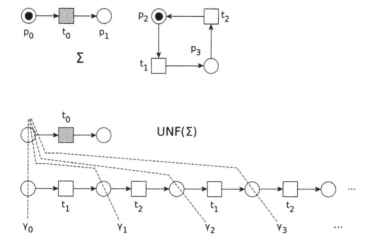

**Fig. 11.** A 1-bounded net and its unfolding

## 4.1 An Algorithm to Check Whether a Strategy Is (Strongly) Implementable

We are interested in characterizing cases in which a given strategy is implementable. In this section we focus on P/T systems where the user cannot discriminate between two B-cuts associated to the same marking, namely, for each pair of B-cuts $\gamma_1, \gamma_2$ such that $\lambda(\gamma_1) = \lambda(\gamma_2)$, $\gamma_1 \equiv \gamma_2$. Any class of observations satisfying this condition is allowed. Hence, from now on, we consider strategies consistent with this assumption.

For this case, we propose an algorithm which, given a strategy, defined as a map from equivalence classes of markings to sets of controllable transitions, decides if the strategy is strongly implementable, and constructs an actual implementation, in the positive case. Its pseudo-code is presented in Algorithm 1.

The algorithm builds on region theory, and is conceptually simple: we first construct a reduced marking graph of $\Sigma$, where we remove all arcs corresponding to controllable transitions which are not compatible with the strategy, and remove states which are no longer reachable from the initial marking. In practice, we can think of directly building the reduced marking graph, starting from the initial marking. Given a strategy $\alpha$, the reduced marking graph will be denoted $MG_\alpha(\Sigma)$.

We then try to synthesize the reduced marking graph by the calculus of regions. To this end, we first observe that, for each region $r$ of the full marking graph $MG(\Sigma)$, the restriction of $r$ to the set of states of the reduced marking graph $MG_\alpha(\Sigma)$ is a region of the latter. This implies that all the state separation problems in $MG_\alpha(\Sigma)$ are solved by restrictions of the "old" regions. Such restrictions also solve the state-transition separation problems which were already in $MG(\Sigma)$.

---

**Algorithm 1.** Implementable strategy

---

**procedure** IMPL($\Sigma$, $\alpha$)
$\qquad\qquad\qquad\qquad\qquad\qquad$ ▷ $\Sigma$ is a bounded P/T system, $\alpha$ a strategy.
$\quad \Sigma' \leftarrow \Sigma$
$\quad$ build $\mathsf{MG}_\alpha(\Sigma) = (M', T, A)$
$\quad$ compute $\mathsf{SP} = \{(m, t) \mid m \in M', m[t\rangle$ in $\Sigma, t \notin \alpha(m)\}$
$\quad$ **for all** $(m, t)$ in $\mathsf{SP}$ **do**
$\qquad$ **if** there is a region $r$ solving $(m, t)$ **then**
$\qquad\qquad$ add to $\Sigma'$ a place corresponding to $r$
$\qquad$ **else**
$\qquad\qquad$ **return** failure $\qquad\qquad\qquad$ ▷ $\alpha$ is not strongly implementable
$\qquad$ **end if**
$\quad$ **end for**
$\quad$ add a new place $\omega$ to $\Sigma'$, with $m'_{in}(\omega) = 0$, and make it an input place of
$\quad$ each $t$ unreachable in $\mathsf{MG}_\alpha$.
$\quad$ **return** $\Sigma'$ $\qquad\qquad\qquad\qquad\qquad$ ▷ $\Sigma'$ is a strong implementation of $\alpha$.
**end procedure**

---

On the other hand, removing some transitions from $\mathsf{MG}(\Sigma)$ creates new state-transition separation problems. The algorithm we propose looks for a set of regions solving these new problems. If no such set of regions exist, then the strategy is not strongly implementable, as will be proved below. If $U = \{r_1, \ldots, r_K\}$ is a set of separating regions for the new separation problems, then we can add to $\Sigma$ the set $H$ of corresponding places, and the arcs with the corresponding weights.

**Proposition 1.** *Let $\Sigma = (P, T, W, m_{in})$ be a bounded P/T system with $T = T_u \cup T_{env}$, $T_u \cap T_{env} = \emptyset$. Let RMG be a transition system obtained from $\mathsf{MG}(\Sigma)$ by removing a subset of transitions labelled with elements in $T_{env}$, and the states unreachable from the initial marking. Let $U$ be a set of regions solving the new state-event separation problems, and $H$ the set of places derived from them. The restriction $\Sigma' = (P \cup H, T, W', m'_{in})$ of $\Sigma$ is a bounded P/T system, and all the places in $H$ are environment-fair.*

*Proof.* Boundedness follows from the fact that $\Sigma'$ is separated, and its marking graph is finite. To show that the new places are environment-fair, we proceed in two steps. First, we note that by removing arcs labelled by controllable transitions, we cannot introduce new behavioural conflicts between uncontrollable transitions. Second, suppose that in a run of $\Sigma'$, there is a B-cut $\gamma$ enabling an occurrence $e_1$ of an uncontrollable transition $t_1$; suppose moreover that in the same run there is an occurrence $e_2$ of another uncontrollable transition, $t_2$, and that $e_1$ precedes $e_2$ in this run, while $e_1$ and $e_2$ are not ordered in the projection of the run. Then, in $\Sigma$, the reachable marking $\lambda(\gamma)$ must enable $t_1$ and $t_2$, and these two transitions must be concurrent in $m$. Hence, there must be reachable markings $m_1$, $m_2$, and $m_3$, with $m[t_1\rangle m_1$, $m[t_2\rangle m_2$, $m_1[t_2\rangle m_3$, and $m_2[t_1\rangle m_3$. None of these arcs in $\mathsf{MG}(\Sigma)$ can be removed by the reduction operation, hence $e_1$ and $e_2$ should be concurrent in $\gamma$. $\qquad\qquad\qquad\qquad\qquad\qquad\qquad$ □

**Proposition 2.** *Let $\Sigma = (P, T, W, m_{in})$ be a bounded P/T system whose transitions are partitioned into controllable $(T_u)$ and uncontrollable $(T_{env})$. A strategy $\alpha : \mathsf{Obs} \rightarrow 2^{T_u}$ is strongly implementable if, and only if, the reduced marking graph $\mathsf{MG}_\alpha(\Sigma)$ is separated. Furthermore, if $\mathsf{MG}_\alpha(\Sigma)$ is separated, $\Sigma'$ returned by Algorithm 1 is a strong implementation of $\alpha$ on $\Sigma$.*

*Proof.* First, we prove that if a strategy $\alpha$ is strongly implementable on $\Sigma$, then $\mathsf{MG}_\alpha(\Sigma)$ is separated. Let $\Sigma'$ be a strong implementation of $\alpha$ on $\Sigma$. By contradiction, assume that $\mathsf{MG}_\alpha(\Sigma)$ is not separated. Then, $\mathsf{MG}(\Sigma')$ cannot be isomorphic to $\mathsf{MG}_\alpha(\Sigma)$ and either there is a path $\sigma'$ in $\mathsf{MG}(\Sigma')$ that cannot be reproduced in $\mathsf{MG}_\alpha(\Sigma)$, or there is a path $\sigma$ in $\mathsf{MG}_\alpha(\Sigma)$ that cannot be reproduced in $\mathsf{MG}(\Sigma')$. In the first case, there must be a run in $\mathsf{Unf}(\Sigma')$ that cannot be associated to any part of a play in $\mathsf{Unf}(\Sigma)$; in the latter case, there must be a play on $\mathsf{Unf}(\Sigma)$ that is not associated to any run in $\mathsf{Unf}(\Sigma')$. Hence, in both cases $\Sigma'$ is not a strong implementation of $\alpha$ on $\Sigma$, contradicting the hypothesis.

Next, we show that if the marking graph is separated, $\alpha$ is strongly implementable, and $\Sigma'$ returned by Algorithm 1 is a strong implementation. Proposition 1 shows that the places added to $\Sigma'$ are environment fair. We need to show that also the other conditions in Definition 8 and Definition 9 are satisfied. The second point of Definition 8 and the condition in Definition 9 follow from the observation that, by construction, $\mathsf{MG}(\Sigma')$ and $\mathsf{MG}_\alpha(\Sigma)$ are isomorphic. For point 3 in Definition 8, we observe that for each maximal run $\rho'$ in $\mathsf{Unf}(\Sigma')$, and for each controllable event $e'$ in $\rho'$, the state in $\mathsf{MG}(\Sigma')$ associated to $m' = \lambda(\mathsf{Cut}(\lfloor e' \rfloor))$ must have an outgoing transition labelled with $\lambda(e')$, otherwise $e'$ could not be allowed to occur in $\mathsf{Cut}(\lfloor e' \rfloor)$. Let $\gamma$ be the projection of $\mathsf{Cut}(\lfloor e' \rfloor)$, then $\lambda(e')$ must be in $\alpha([\lambda(\gamma)])$, since $\mathsf{MG}_\alpha(\Sigma) = \mathsf{MG}(\Sigma')$ by hypothesis, and the state $m'$ in $\mathsf{MG}(\Sigma')$ is associated to $\lambda(\gamma)$ in $\mathsf{MG}_\alpha(\Sigma)$.  $\square$

The computational cost of solving one state-event separation problem is polynomial in the size of the transition system, so the overall cost of our algorithm depends mainly on the construction of the reduced marking graph. If $\Sigma$ is $k$-bounded and has $h$ places, then the marking graph has at most $(k+1)^h$ reachable markings. Hence the complexity in the worst case is exponential in the number of places. For a given strategy, the number of reachable markings in the reduced graph can be much smaller, but this depends strongly on the specific strategy.

*Example 6.* Consider the P/T system $\Sigma$ in Fig. 3 (recalled also in Fig. 12), and the associated discussion. A winning strategy is given by the following map: $\alpha(\{p_0, s_1\}) = \{u_1\}$, $\alpha(\{p_0, s_2\}) = \{u_2\}$, and $\alpha(\{m\}) = \emptyset$ for all other markings.

The marking graph of $\Sigma$ is shown on the left of Fig. 13. The reduced marking graph, obtained by removing controllable transitions not chosen by the strategy, is on the right. This reduced transition system turns out to be separated. Beyond the regions corresponding to places of $\Sigma$, we need to find regions solving four new state-transition separation problems: $(1, u_1)$, $(1, u_2)$, $(3, u_1)$, $(2, u_2)$. The map $f(2) = 1$, $f(x) = 0$ for any $x$ other than 2 is a region separating $u_1$ from

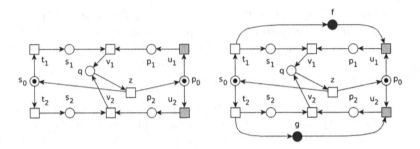

**Fig. 12.** An implemented strategy

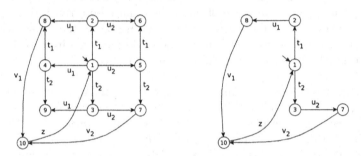

**Fig. 13.** A marking graph and its reduction.

states 1 and 3; the map $g(3) = 1$, $g(x) = 0$ for any state $x$ other than 3 is a region, and separates $u_2$ from states 1 and 2.

## 5    State of the Art

This section provides a non-exhaustive overview of techniques for the implementation of controllers on Petri nets, selected between those closer to our approach.

Most of the first relevant works on this topic developed from the line started by Ramadge and Wonham in the late 80 s [17,18], on supervisory control of discrete event systems (DES). In Chap. 3 and Chap. 4 of their book [5], Cassandras and Lafortune collect some results about the control of a DES with a supervisor. Supervising a DES means to limit its behaviours, so to avoid that it can generate unwanted strings of its language. In the DES only some events are controllable, and only some are observable. A supervisor is a function that, for each given observation, chooses some controllable events to disable. A realization of a supervisor is an automaton representation of the supervisor; composing the supervisor with the uncontrolled DES results in an automaton whose language is a subset of the one generated by the uncontrolled DES.

In Chap. 4 the authors discuss how these results can be adapted when DES are modelled as Petri nets. This line was first developed in [10,11]. In 2019, Lacerda and Lima proposed an application of these formalisms to robotics [13].

Differently from this paper, the approach presented in Chap. 4 allows for labelled Petri nets, Petri nets having the same label on multiple transitions. Every finite automaton can be transformed into a labelled Petri net, and it is always possible to use techniques on automata to construct a supervised net. A supervised net resulting from an automaton may have a greater number of transitions than the initial one. This is not allowed in our context, where we require that the structure of the net cannot change, except for some additional places, and without repeated labels on transitions, some automata are not synthesizable into Petri nets, as discussed in Sect. 2.2.

More related to the approach of this paper, [19] introduced the use of region theory for synthesising a supervisor on a Petri net. In [19], the supervisor needs to avoid a set of bad states. In a later work [9], the authors extended their work by requiring that the supervised system needs to be able to always restore the initial marking, in addition to the avoidance of bad states. In [14, 16, 20], the authors improve the efficiency of the search for regions and consider applications of this approach in the control of flexible manufacturing systems.

Our work is also based on region theory, but it considers a set of more general specifications: in some cases, implementing the strategy may not cause the avoidance of any state, but just put some constraints on the order in which they need to be visited.

Finally, some works propose the supervision of a Petri net through monitor places (see [12] for a survey). As for the methods based on region theory, the supervised net is the initial net with a set of additional places. The places are found by solving linear inequalities, and can be found as linear combinations of the places in the net, without constructing the marking graph. Although this can produce more efficient solutions, in some cases this approach fails, whereas a solution can be found with nonlinear techniques [4, 6].

# 6   Conclusion and Perspectives

In this work, we considered a two-player game on a P/T system where one of the two player follows a strategy, and we defined when such a strategy is weakly implementable, namely there is P/T system in which all the maximal runs are justified by the strategy, and strongly implementable, if all and only the behaviours allowed by the strategy can be associated to maximal runs on the implementation. We also provide an algorithm that computes a strong implementation, if one exists, for a special class of observations.

There are several directions to consider for future works. One of them consists in characterizing which strategies are strongly implementable. We conjecture that, if the strategy is based on observations of stable parts of markings, it is always strongly implementable, since we avoid to try to force an occurrence of a controllable transition before the occurrence of an uncontrollable one. Also related to equivalence classes of observations, we plan to study techniques to determine implementations of strategies with memory, when they exist (as for example in the case discussed in this paper of observations of conditions on the unfolding).

We also plan to study weak implementable strategies, by characterizing when a strategy is implementable, finding algorithms to implement it, and finding how to determine the most permissive weak implementation, if a strong implementation does not exist.

In this work we focussed on a two player game and bounded P/T systems, but in future works we plan to consider multi-agent systems and allow for unbounded implementations.

Finally, we plan to implement our algorithm and check its performance on practical cases.

**Acknowledgement.** The authors thank the anonymous reviewers for their valuable comments and suggestions. This work is supported by the Italian MUR.

# References

1. Adobbati, F., Bernardinello, L., Pomello, L.: A two-player asynchronous game on fully observable Petri nets. Trans. Petri Nets Other Model. Concurr. **15**, 126–149 (2021)
2. Adobbati, F., Bernardinello, L., Pomello, L.: Looking for winning strategies in two-player games on Petri nets with partial observability (2022). https://doi.org/10.48550/ARXIV.2204.01603
3. Adobbati, F., Bernardinello, L., Pomello, L., Stramare, R.: Implementable strategies for a two-player asynchronous game on Petri nets. In: Algorithms and Theories for the Analysis of Event Data, Bergen, Norway, pp. 69–75. CEUR-WS.org (2022). https://ceur-ws.org/Vol-3167/paper5.pdf
4. Badouel, E., Bernardinello, L., Darondeau, P.: Petri Net Synthesis. Texts in Theoretical Computer Science. An EATCS Series. Springer (2015). https://doi.org/10.1007/978-3-662-47967-4
5. Cassandras, C.G., Lafortune, S.: Introduction to discrete event systems. Springer (2021). https://doi.org/10.1007/978-3-030-72274-6
6. Chen, Y., Pan, L., Li, Z.: Design of optimal supervisors for the enforcement of nonlinear constraints on petri nets. IEEE Trans. Autom. Sci. Eng. (2022)
7. Ehrenfeucht, A., Rozenberg, G.: Partial (set) 2-structures. part II: state spaces of concurrent systems. Acta Inf. **27**(4), 343–368 (1990). https://doi.org/10.1007/BF00264612
8. Engelfriet, J.: Branching processes of Petri nets. Acta Inf. **28**(6), 575–591 (1991). https://doi.org/10.1007/BF01463946
9. Ghaffari, A., Rezg, N., Xie, X.: Design of a live and maximally permissive Petri net controller using the theory of regions. IEEE Trans. Robot. Autom. **19**(1), 137–141 (2003). https://doi.org/10.1109/TRA.2002.807555
10. Giua, A., DiCesare, F.: Petri net structural analysis for supervisory control. IEEE Trans. Robot. Autom. **10**(2), 185–195 (1994)
11. Holloway, L.E., Krogh, B.H., Giua, A.: A survey of petri net methods for controlled discrete event systems. Discrete Event Dyn. Syst. **7**(2), 151–190 (1997)
12. Iordache, M.V., Antsaklis, P.J.: Supervision based on place invariants: a survey. Discrete Event Dyn. Syst. **16**(4), 451–492 (2006)
13. Lacerda, B., Lima, P.U.: Petri net based multi-robot task coordination from temporal logic specifications. Robot. Auton. Syst. **122**, 103289 (2019)

14. Li, Z., Zhou, M., Jeng, M.: A maximally permissive deadlock prevention policy for FMS based on petri net siphon control and the theory of regions. IEEE Trans. Autom. Sci. Eng. **5**(1), 182–188 (2008)

15. Murata, T.: Petri nets: properties, analysis and applications. Proc. IEEE **77**(4), 541–580 (1989)

16. Pan, Y.L., Huang, Y.S., Jeng, M., Chung, S.L.: Enhancement of an efficient control policy for FMSs using the theory of regions and selective siphon method. Int. J. Adv. Manuf. Technol. **66**(9), 1805–1815 (2013)

17. Ramadge, P.J., Wonham, W.M.: Supervisory control of a class of discrete event processes. SIAM J. Control. Optim. **25**(1), 206–230 (1987)

18. Ramadge, P.J., Wonham, W.M.: The control of discrete event systems. Proc. IEEE **77**(1), 81–98 (1989)

19. Rezg, N., Xie, X., Ghaffari, A.: Supervisory control in discrete event systems using the theory of regions. In: Discrete Event Systems, pp. 391–398. Springer (2000)

20. Rezig, S., Ghorbel, C., Achour, Z., Rezg, N.: PLC-based implementation of supervisory control for flexible manufacturing systems using theory of regions. Int. J. Autom. Control **13**(5), 619–640 (2019)

# Confusion-Tolerant Computation
# of Probability in Acyclic Nets

Anirban Bhattacharyya$^{(\boxtimes)}$ and Maciej Koutny

School of Computing, Newcastle University, Newcastle upon Tyne NE4 5TG, UK
{Anirban.Bhattacharyya, Maciej.Koutny}@ncl.ac.uk

**Abstract.** This paper presents a solution to the issue of how to compute probabilities in nets with confusion, where confusion is interference between concurrent choices of which enabled transition to perform. A formal framework is developed – using a novel formula based on event weights – for computing the probabilities of execution traces of an acyclic net, which in turn are used to compute the probabilities of the markings, steps, and nodes of the net. We prove the framework satisfies generic probability requirements. We also prove the formula simplifies to the standard formula for computing the probability of independent concurrent events in confusion-free concurrent simple acyclic nets with choice, in the maximally concurrent and interleaving models of concurrency.

## 1 Introduction

Computation of probability in nets has been the subject of considerable research effort over many years [7,11,14]. Nevertheless, the issue of how to compute probabilities in nets with *confusion* has remained open [3]. Informally, confusion is interference between concurrent choices of which enabled transition to perform at a reachable marking of a net. A formal definition of confusion for interleaving concurrency is given in Definition 9, based on [3]. To motivate our approach, we illustrate the standard approach to calculating probability using simple examples of free-choice and extended free-choice nets (which do not have confusion) [5], then show where this approach fails using classic examples of the two types of confusion: symmetric and asymmetric.

In the free-choice net FCN1 in Fig. 1, $s1$ and $s2$ are the initial concurrent places (individual states) of the net at which transitions (individual events) can be chosen for firing (execution). At $s1$ either $e1$ or $e2$ can execute, at $s2$ either $e3$ or $e4$ can execute, and the set of alternative events at either state remains unchanged by the execution of an event at the other state. Hence, the choices of event at $s1$ and $s2$ are independent. Therefore, the Bayesian probabilities [16] of alternative events at $s1$ and $s2$ can be determined purely from the net structure at $s1$ and $s2$. In the absence of additional information about events $e1$, $e2$, $e3$, and $e4$, their respective Bayesian probabilities are $p(e1|s1) = p(e2|s1) = 0.5$ and $p(e3|s2) = p(e4|s2) = 0.5$.

M. Koutny et al. (Eds.): TPNOMCXVII, LNCS 14150, pp. 212–245, 2024.
https://doi.org/10.1007/978-3-662-68191-6_9

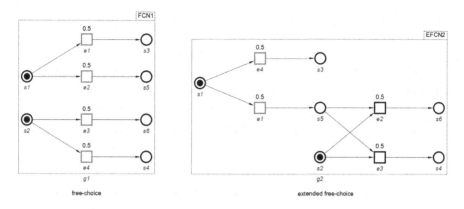

**Fig. 1.** Bayesian probabilities in free-choice and extended free-choice nets.

In the extended free-choice net EFCN2, the alternative events at $s1$ are $e4$ and $e1$, the alternative events at $\{s5, s2\}$ are $e2$ and $e3$, and execution of either $e4$ or $e1$ at $s1$ has no effect on the set of alternative events at $\{s5, s2\}$. Hence, the Bayesian probabilities of events $e4$, $e1$, $e2$, and $e3$ can be determined structurally: $p(e4|s1) = p(e1|s1) = 0.5$ and $p(e2|\{s5, s2\}) = p(e3|\{s5, s2\}) = 0.5$.

In contrast to FCN1, net N1 in Fig. 2 has symmetric confusion, where event $e2$ is shared between concurrent states $s1$ and $s2$. Hence, the choices of event at $s1$ and $s2$ are *not* independent. If $e1$ is executed first then $e3$ must be executed second, because $e2$ becomes disabled (the probability of execution of $e3$ becomes 1, and the probability of execution of $e2$ becomes 0). $e2$ is a choice of execution synchronized between $s1$ and $s2$ with a non-zero probability of execution.

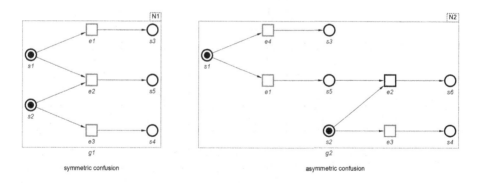

**Fig. 2.** Nets with symmetric and asymmetric confusion.

In net N2 (which has asymmetric confusion), at $s2$ only $e3$ can be executed initially (the Bayesian probability of $e3$ is 1); but if $e1$ is executed first then either $e2$ or $e3$ can be executed at $s2$ (the Bayesian probability of $e3$ becomes less than 1). Thus, the Bayesian probability of $e3$ depends on the execution order of the net. Therefore, our approach to computing probabilities in nets is based on net behaviour (execution traces), rather than on net structure.

## Related Work

Existing research on computation of probability in nets with confusion is limited. Much of the research on probabilistic nets is focused on confusion-free nets [1,4,12,15]. Other research is engineering orientated: imposing restrictions or additional structure on a net to manage or handle confusion. For example in [9], the nodes of a net are grouped into (possibly overlapping) regions termed *agents* that do not contain confusion and choose which of their events to fire according to their (local) state. Agents are selected for execution nondeterministically by a global scheduler that allows their concurrent execution unless their pairwise union contains confusion, in which case the scheduler orders the execution of the agents involved prioritized by the degree of choice of event available to the agent. Thus, confusion is managed by removing the concurrency that causes confusion. In [3], additional states are added to an occurrence net in order to represent 'negative' information, that is, states that will not be reached after an event is fired. These 'negative' states are causally linked to events in order to remove confusion, resulting in a confusion-free net with the same event traces as the original net. Thus, confusion is handled by removing confusion.

## Contribution

In contrast to existing research, we use a novel *general* formula (in Definition 11) to calculate the Bayesian probability of concurrent events. Our approach imposes no restriction or additional structure on a net, and thereby tolerates confusion. Therefore, our probability framework is descriptive, rather than prescriptive. That is, we assume a net is given to model and analyse, rather than to engineer. The framework is expressed in terms of acyclic nets, although we expect the framework can be extended to cyclic nets with satisfying conditions similar to well-formedness (see Definition 7). Acyclic nets support efficient algorithms because they are acyclic [2], they are scalable through the use of abstraction relations [10], and they are supported by modeling and analysis tools such as SONCraft [13], screen captures of which have been used in the diagrams of this paper.

The rest of the paper is organized as follows: Section 2 provides the basic definitions of acyclic net used in the paper and defines confusion for interleaving concurrency. Section 3 defines our probability framework and formula for computing the probabilities of execution traces and concurrent events, and defines generic requirements that a probability framework must satisfy. We prove the framework satisfies the requirements (Theorems 4 and 5). Section 4 explores the framework and demonstrates that in the *presence* of confusion, the probabilities of traces with identical initial markings and identical final markings, and also their sum, depend on the concurrency model of the traces. We prove that in the *absence* of confusion, our formula simplifies to the standard formula for computing the probability of independent concurrent events in the maximally concurrent and interleaving models of concurrency for concurrent simple acyclic nets with choice (Theorems 6 and 7).

## 2   Acyclic Nets

An acyclic net can be regarded as a Petri net. Hence, our terminology borrows extensively from Petri net theory and set theory.

**Definition 1 (sets and relations).** *Let* $\mathbb{N}$ *be the set of natural numbers including* 0 *and* $\mathbb{N}^+ \triangleq \mathbb{N} - \{0\}$. *All other sets are defined to be finite. Given a set* $X$ *and a binary relation* $R \subseteq X \times X$, $id_X \triangleq \{(x,x) \mid x \in X\}$ *is the* identity *relation on* $X$, $R^+ \triangleq \bigcup_{i \in \mathbb{N}^+} R^i$ *is the irreflexive transitive closure of* $R$, *and* $R$ *is acyclic iff* $R^+ \cap id_X = \emptyset$. ◇

Each acyclic net *acnet* represents the actual or hypothesized behaviours of a system or system component. That is, the possible executions of a system, where each execution trace is expressed as a sequence of sets of events (*steps*) that represent sets of actions performed by the system in parallel according to a concurrency model, alternating with sets of states (*markings*) that represent global states of the system. The start state of the system at the beginning of its execution is expressed by the *initial marking* of *acnet* ($P_{acnet}^{init}$), and an end state of the execution that does not 'deadlock' is expressed by a *final marking* of *acnet* (a subset of $P_{acnet}^{fin}$). This motivates the following definitions.

**Definition 2 (acyclic net).** *An* acyclic net *is a triple* $acnet = (P, T, F)$, *where* $P$ *and* $T$ *are disjoint sets of* places *and* transitions *respectively, and* $F \subseteq (P \times T) \cup (T \times P)$ *is a* flow relation *such that:*

1. $P$ *is nonempty and* $F$ *is acyclic.*
2. *For every* $t \in T$, *there are* $p, q \in P$ *such that* $pFt$ *and* $tFq$.

*The set of all acyclic nets is denoted by* AN. ◇

The terms *place* and *state* are synonymous, also *transition* and *event*. The states and events of *acnet* are collectively termed the *nodes* of *acnet*. The *flow relation* expresses the direct *causality* (causal relationship) between the nodes. The direct causes and consequences of a node $x \in P \cup T$ and $X \subseteq P \cup T$ are defined as follows:

$$
\begin{array}{ll}
{}^\bullet x \triangleq \mathrm{pre}_{acnet}(x) \triangleq \{z \mid zFx\} & {}^\bullet X \triangleq \mathrm{pre}_{acnet}(X) \triangleq \bigcup\{{}^\bullet z \mid z \in X\} \\
x^\bullet \triangleq \mathrm{post}_{acnet}(x) \triangleq \{z \mid xFz\} & X^\bullet \triangleq \mathrm{post}_{acnet}(X) \triangleq \bigcup\{z^\bullet \mid z \in X\}.
\end{array}
$$

The *initial* and *final* states of *acnet* are respectively defined by:

$$
P_{acnet}^{init} \triangleq \{p \mid p \in P \wedge {}^\bullet p = \emptyset\} \quad \text{and} \quad P_{acnet}^{fin} \triangleq \{p \mid p \in P \wedge p^\bullet = \emptyset\}.
$$

For example in Fig. 3, *acnet1* is an acyclic net (our running example) with ${}^\bullet s5 = \mathrm{pre}_{acnet1}(s5) = \{e3, e4\}$ and $e1^\bullet = \mathrm{post}_{acnet1}(e1) = \{s2, s3\}$.

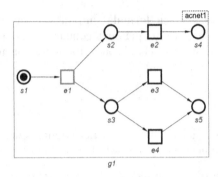

**Fig. 3.** Acyclic net *acnet*1 with initial marking {s1} and enabled step {e1}.

**Definition 3 (step and marking).** *Let acnet = $(P, T, F)$ be an acyclic net.*

1. steps($acnet$) $\triangleq \{U \mid U \in \mathbb{P}(T) \setminus \{\emptyset\} \wedge \forall t, u \in U \ (t \neq u \implies {}^\bullet t \cap {}^\bullet u = \emptyset)\}$ *are the* steps *of acnet*[1].
2. markings($acnet$) $\triangleq \mathbb{P}(P)$ *are the* markings *of acnet.*
3. $M_{acnet}^{init} \triangleq P_{acnet}^{init}$ *is the* initial marking *of acnet.*    ◇

A marking is indicated graphically by black tokens in states. For example in Fig. 3, the token indicates that the marking of *acnet*1 is the initial marking $M_{acnet1}^{init}$, which is {s1}, and steps($acnet$1) = $\{U \mid U \in \mathbb{P}(\{e1, e2, e3, e4\}) \setminus \{\emptyset\} \wedge$ ($e3 \notin U \vee e4 \notin U$)}.

The following two definitions are necessary in order to define the Bayesian probability of a step and the probability of an execution trace.

**Definition 4 (enabled and executed step).** *Let M be a marking of an acyclic net acnet.*

1. enabled$_{acnet}(M) \triangleq \{U \mid U \in$ steps($acnet$) $\wedge {}^\bullet U \subseteq M\}$ *are the* steps *enabled at M.*
2. *A step $U \in$ enabled$_{acnet}(M)$ can be* executed *and yields $M' \triangleq (M \cup U^\bullet) \setminus {}^\bullet U$, denoted by $M[U\rangle_{acnet} M'$.*    ◇

Enabling a step means that all its input states are marked in a global state. The execution of such a step first adds tokens to all its output states and then removes tokens from all its input states. This is different from the 'standard' way of executing a step, where one first removes tokens from all the input states and after that adds tokens to all the output states. For the class of well-formed acyclic nets defined later in this paper, these two execution modes are equivalent. However, only the former execution mode is suitable to define the semantics of an extended framework supporting structured acyclic nets with communicating subnets and subnets at different levels of abstraction.

In Fig. 3, the execution of step $U = \{e1\}$ enabled by marking $M = \{s1\}$ of *acnet*1 yields marking $M' = (\{s1\} \cup \{e1\}^\bullet) \setminus {}^\bullet\{e1\} = (\{s1\} \cup \{s2, s3\}) \setminus \{s1\} = \{s2, s3\}$, as shown in Fig. 4.

---

[1] $\mathbb{P}(T)$ denotes the power set of $T$, that is, the set of all subsets of $T$.

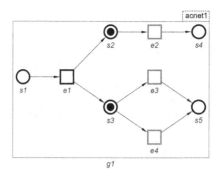

**Fig. 4.** Acyclic net $acnet1$ following the execution of step $\{e1\}$ resulting in new marking $\{s2, s3\}$ and new enabled steps $\{e2\}$, $\{e3\}$, $\{e4\}$, $\{e2, e3\}$, and $\{e2, e4\}$.

**Definition 5 (mixed step sequence and step sequence).**
*For $k \in \mathbb{N}$, let $M_0, \ldots, M_k$ be markings and for $1 \le i \le k$, let $U_1, \ldots, U_k$ be steps of an acyclic net acnet such that $M_{i-1}[U_i\rangle_{acnet} M_i$.*

1. *$\mu = M_0 U_1 M_1 \ldots U_k M_k$ is a mixed step sequence from $M_0$ to $M_k$, denoted by $M_0[\mu\rangle\rangle_{acnet} M_k$.*
2. *$\sigma = U_1 \ldots U_k$ is a step sequence from $M_0$ to $M_k$, denoted by $M_0[\sigma\rangle_{acnet} M_k$.*
3. *$\mu' = M_0 U_1 M_1 \ldots U_j M_j$ such that $0 \le j < k$ is a prefix of $\mu$, denoted by $\mu' < \mu$ or equivalently $(M_0[\mu'\rangle\rangle_{acnet} M_j) < (M_0[\mu\rangle\rangle_{acnet} M_k)$.*
4. *The length of $\mu$ is denoted by $|\mu| \triangleq k$.*

*Furthermore, $M_0[\sigma\rangle_{acnet}$ denotes that $\sigma$ is a step sequence enabled at $M_0$, and $M_0[\rangle_{acnet} M_k$ denotes that $M_k$ is reachable from $M_0$.* ◇

If $k = 0$ then $\mu = M_0$, $|\mu| = 0$, and the corresponding step sequence $\sigma$ is the *empty* sequence denoted by $\lambda$. An example of a mixed step sequence of $acnet1$ is $\mu = \{s1\}\{e1\}\{s2, s3\}\{e2, e3\}\{s4, s5\}$ with step sequence $\sigma = \{e1\}\{e2, e3\}$; $\mu$ has prefixes $\{s1\}\{e1\}\{s2, s3\}$ and $\{s1\}$, and $|\mu| = 2$, see Fig. 4. Notice that $\{s1\}$ is the prefix of every mixed step sequence of $acnet1$ originating at $\{s1\}$. The notions of *prefix* and *length* of a mixed step sequence are used to prove results by induction.

The following two definitions take $M_0$ in Definition 5 to be the initial marking and complete our framework for acyclic nets.

**Definition 6 (behavioural notions).** *The following sets capture various behavioural notions related to step sequences and reachable markings of an acyclic net acnet.*

1. $\mathrm{sseq}(acnet) \triangleq \{\sigma \mid M_{acnet}^{init}[\sigma\rangle_{acnet} M\}$        step sequences.
2. $\mathrm{mixsseq}(acnet) \triangleq \{\mu \mid M_{acnet}^{init}[\mu\rangle\rangle_{acnet} M\}$
                     mixed step sequences (or execution traces).

3. $\mathrm{maxsseq}(acnet) \triangleq \{\sigma \mid \sigma \in \mathrm{sseq}(acnet) \wedge \neg\exists U(\sigma U \in \mathrm{sseq}(acnet))\}$

maximal step sequences.

4. $\mathrm{maxmixsseq}(acnet) \triangleq$
   $\{\mu \mid \mu \in \mathrm{mixsseq}(acnet) \wedge \neg\exists U, M(\mu U M \in \mathrm{mixsseq}(acnet))\}$

maximal mixed step sequences (or maximal execution traces).

5. $\mathrm{reachable}(acnet) \triangleq \{M \mid M_{acnet}^{init}[\rangle_{acnet} M\}$          reachable markings.

6. $\mathrm{finreachable}(acnet) \triangleq \{M \mid \exists\sigma \in \mathrm{maxsseq}(acnet)(M_{acnet}^{init}[\sigma\rangle_{acnet} M)\}$

final reachable markings.

*We can treat individual transitions as singleton steps; for instance, a step sequence $\{t\}\{u\}\{w,v\}\{z\}$ can be denoted by $tu\{w,v\}z$.*          ◇

For example in *acnet1*:

1. $\mathrm{sseq}(acnet1) = \{\lambda, e1, e1e2, e1e3, e1e4, e1\{e2e3\}, e1\{e2e4\}, e1e2e3, e1e3e2,$
   $e1e2e4, e1e4e2\}$.
2. $\mathrm{mixsseq}(acnet1) = \{\{s1\}, \{s1\}\{e1\}\{s2, s3\}, \{s1\}\{e1\}\{s2, s3\}\{e2\}\{s3, s4\},$
   $\{s1\}\{e1\}\{s2, s3\}\{e3\}\{s2, s5\}, \{s1\}\{e1\}\{s2, s3\}\{e4\}\{s2, s5\},$
   $\{s1\}\{e1\}\{s2, s3\}\{e2, e3\}\{s4, s5\}, \{s1\}\{e1\}\{s2, s3\}\{e2, e4\}\{s4, s5\},$
   $\{s1\}\{e1\}\{s2, s3\}\{e2\}\{s3, s4\}\{e3\}\{s4, s5\},$
   $\{s1\}\{e1\}\{s2, s3\}\{e3\}\{s2, s5\}\{e2\}\{s4, s5\},$
   $\{s1\}\{e1\}\{s2, s3\}\{e2\}\{s3, s4\}\{e4\}\{s4, s5\},$
   $\{s1\}\{e1\}\{s2, s3\}\{e4\}\{s2, s5\}\{e2\}\{s4, s5\}\}$.
3. $\mathrm{maxsseq}(acnet1) = \{e1\{e2e3\}, e1\{e2e4\}, e1e2e3, e1e3e2, e1e2e4, e1e4e2\}$.
4. $\mathrm{maxmixsseq}(acnet1) = \{\{s1\}\{e1\}\{s2, s3\}\{e2, e3\}\{s4, s5\},$
   $\{s1\}\{e1\}\{s2, s3\}\{e2, e4\}\{s4, s5\},$
   $\{s1\}\{e1\}\{s2, s3\}\{e2\}\{s3, s4\}\{e3\}\{s4, s5\},$
   $\{s1\}\{e1\}\{s2, s3\}\{e3\}\{s2, s5\}\{e2\}\{s4, s5\},$
   $\{s1\}\{e1\}\{s2, s3\}\{e2\}\{s3, s4\}\{e4\}\{s4, s5\},$
   $\{s1\}\{e1\}\{s2, s3\}\{e4\}\{s2, s5\}\{e2\}\{s4, s5\}\}$.
5. $\mathrm{reachable}(acnet1) = \{\{s1\}, \{s2, s3\}, \{s3, s4\}, \{s2, s5\}, \{s4, s5\}\}$.
6. $\mathrm{finreachable}(acnet1) = \{\{s4, s5\}\}$.

A basic property we require of acyclic nets is *well-formedness*. The purpose of this requirement is to ensure an unambiguous representation of causality in the behaviours the acyclic nets represent, which supports causal analysis. Such nets also avoid the occurrence of multiset steps, which is important because our probability framework is currently based on ordinary sets. The definition of a well-formed acyclic net is derived from the notion of a well-formed step sequence, in which no place receives a token more than once. Specifically, in a well-formed step sequence, no place is a pre-place of an executed step more than once, the order of execution of transitions does not influence the resulting marking, and each step sequence can be sequentialised to a firing sequence. To develop a sound treatment of causality in an acyclic net, it is required that all step sequences are well-formed. Furthermore, there should be no redundant transition that can never be executed from the initial marking.

**Definition 7 (well-formedness).**

1. *A step sequence $U_1 \ldots U_k$ with $k \in \mathbb{N}^+$ of an acyclic net acnet is well-formed iff the following conditions are satisfied:*
   *(a) $\forall i \in [1..k]\, \forall e, e' \in U_i\, (e \neq e' \implies e^\bullet \cap e'^\bullet = \emptyset)$*
   *(b) $\forall i, j \in [1..k]\, (i \neq j \implies U_i^\bullet \cap U_j^\bullet = \emptyset)$*
2. *An acyclic net acnet is well-formed iff each transition occurs in at least one step sequence and all step sequences in* sseq(*acnet*) *are well-formed.*    ◇

For example, *acnet*1 in Fig. 5 is a well-formed acyclic net. In contrast, *acnet*2 is not well-formed because condition 2 of Definition 7 is not satisfied (∵ the maximally concurrent step sequence $\{e1, e2\}\{e3\}$ fails to satisfy condition 1(a), and the interleaving concurrent step sequences $\{e1\}\{e2\}\{e3\}$ and $\{e2\}\{e1\}\{e3\}$ fail to satisfy condition 1(b))[2]. Thus, it is impossible to determine which event $e1$ or $e2$ causes $e3$. Well-formed nets can have confusion. For example in Fig. 2, N1 and N2 are well-formed nets (by Definition 7) with symmetric and asymmetric confusion respectively.

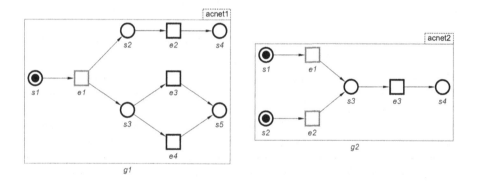

**Fig. 5.** Comparison of well-formed *acnet*1 and not well-formed *acnet*2 acyclic nets.

An execution trace (or simply trace) represents an execution sequence of possible global states of a system alternating with possible parallel actions performed by the system in the context of a concurrency model. Therefore, a trace is a mixed step sequence of an acyclic net. A concurrency model of a system represents alternative execution sequences of the system. Therefore, a concurrency model is a set of execution traces (i.e. mixed step sequences) of an acyclic net. Formally:

**Definition 8 (execution trace elements and concurrency models).**
*Let acnet be a well-formed acyclic net, and let each element $\mu$ of* mixsseq(*acnet*) *be such that $\mu = M_0^\mu U_1^\mu M_1^\mu \ldots U_{k_\mu}^\mu M_{k_\mu}^\mu$ with $k_\mu \in \mathbb{N}$ and $M_0^\mu = M_{acnet}^{init}$.*

---

[2] The symbol ∵ denotes 'because'.

1. $\forall \mu \in \text{mixsseq}(acnet)\,(\text{mixsseqsteps}(\mu) \triangleq \{U_i^{\mu} \mid i \in [1..|\mu|]\})$        trace steps.
2. $\forall \mu \in \text{mixsseq}(acnet)\,(\text{mixsseqmarkings}(\mu) \triangleq \{M_j^{\mu} \mid j \in [0..|\mu|]\})$

                                         trace markings.
3. $\forall S \subseteq \text{mixsseq}(acnet)\,(maxlen(S) \triangleq max\{|\mu| \mid \mu \in S\})$

                  length of longest trace in a set of traces.
4. $\forall S \in \mathbb{P}(\text{mixsseq}(acnet)) \setminus \{\emptyset\}$                      trace prefix sets.

   (a) $\forall \mu \in S\,(prfx(\mu) \triangleq \{\mu' \mid \mu' < \mu\})$

   (b) $prfx(S) \triangleq \bigcup\{prfx(\mu) \mid \mu \in S\}$

5. $cmodel \in \mathbb{P}(\text{mixsseq}(acnet)) \setminus \{\emptyset\}$ *is a* concurrency model *of acnet iff it satisfies the following conditions:*

   (a) $\forall \mu \in cmodel\,(prfx(\mu) \subset cmodel)$            prefix closure.

   (b) $cmodel \setminus \text{maxmixsseq}(acnet) \subseteq prfx(cmodel)$     trace extension.

   (c) $\forall \mu U M, \mu U' M' \in cmodel\,(U \not\subset U')$         subset exclusion.

6. $S_{max}^{cmodel} \triangleq cmodel \cap \text{maxmixsseq}(acnet)$

            maximal execution traces of a concurrency model.

7. $cmodel_{ic}(acnet) \triangleq$

   $\{\mu \mid \mu \in \text{mixsseq}(acnet) \wedge \forall U \in \text{mixsseqsteps}(\mu)\,(|U| = 1)\}$

            interleaving concurrency model of *acnet*.

8. $cmodel_{mc}(acnet) \triangleq$

   $\{\mu \mid \mu \in \text{mixsseq}(acnet) \wedge \forall i \in [1..|\mu|]\,\forall U \in \text{enabled}_{acnet}(M_{i-1}^{\mu})\,(U_i^{\mu} \not\subset U)\}$

          maximal concurrency model of *acnet*.         ◇

If $k = 0$ then $\mu = M_{acnet}^{init}$ and $\text{mixsseqsteps}(\mu) = \emptyset$, which is used in proofs. Concurrency models are key to our approach in two ways: (i) the computation of net probabilities is based on the mixed step sequences in a concurrency model; (ii) a concurrency model identifies the alternative steps enabled at a reachable marking that are necessary to compute the Bayesian probability of a step in a mixed step sequence. Therefore, restrictions are imposed on concurrency models to ensure that trace probabilities are well-defined. Specifically: a concurrency model must contain the prefix traces (if any) of every trace in the model and also the maximal traces. Furthermore, alternative steps enabled at a reachable marking can overlap but no step can be a subset of another step, which helps to achieve exclusive outcomes. The maximal traces of a concurrency model are used to define the probabilities of the markings and steps of the model and (therefore) are collected into the set $S_{max}^{cmodel}$.

A concurrency model of an acyclic net can be defined *implicitly* using a restriction on the steps enabled at a marking. For example, the interleaving concurrency model of *acnet1* restricts the steps of traces to singleton steps[3]. $\therefore cmodel_{ic}(acnet1) = \{\{s1\}, \{s1\}\{e1\}\{s2, s3\}, \{s1\}\{e1\}\{s2, s3\}\{e2\}\{s3, s4\},$
$\{s1\}\{e1\}\{s2, s3\}\{e3\}\{s2, s5\}, \{s1\}\{e1\}\{s2, s3\}\{e4\}\{s2, s5\},$
$\{s1\}\{e1\}\{s2, s3\}\{e2\}\{s3, s4\}\{e3\}\{s4, s5\},$
$\{s1\}\{e1\}\{s2, s3\}\{e3\}\{s2, s5\}\{e2\}\{s4, s5\},$
$\{s1\}\{e1\}\{s2, s3\}\{e2\}\{s3, s4\}\{e4\}\{s4, s5\},$
$\{s1\}\{e1\}\{s2, s3\}\{e4\}\{s2, s5\}\{e2\}\{s4, s5\}\}.$

---

[3] The symbol $\therefore$ denotes 'therefore'.

The maximal concurrency model of *acnet1* restricts the steps of traces to maximally concurrent enabled events.

$\therefore cmodel_{mc}(acnet1) = \{\{s1\}, \{s1\}\{e1\}\{s2, s3\},$
$\{s1\}\{e1\}\{s2, s3\}\{e2, e3\}\{s4, s5\}, \{s1\}\{e1\}\{s2, s3\}\{e2, e4\}\{s4, s5\}\}.$

Concurrency models other than maximal concurrency (i.e. non-maximal concurrency models) consist of traces where each step of events enabled at a marking is a subset of a step of maximally concurrent events enabled at the marking, if the marking is reachable in the maximal concurrency model.

Alternatively, a concurrency model can be defined *explicitly* by a user. Thus, traces can be used to represent different concurrency models uniformly.

Different traces represent alternative execution paths through a system and can have different probabilities. Calculating such probabilities is complicated by *confusion*, which is defined below for interleaving concurrency, based on [3]:

**Definition 9 (confusion in interleaving concurrency of a well-formed acyclic net).** *A well-formed acyclic net has confusion iff there exists a reachable marking $M$ and distinct events $e_1$, $e_2$, $e_3$ such that one of the following holds:*

1. *symmetric confusion:*
   *(a) $e_1$, $e_2$, $e_3$ are enabled at $M$ and*
   *(b) ${}^\bullet e_1 \cap {}^\bullet e_2 \neq \emptyset$ and*
   *(c) ${}^\bullet e_2 \cap {}^\bullet e_3 \neq \emptyset$ and*
   *(d) ${}^\bullet e_1 \cap {}^\bullet e_3 = \emptyset$*
2. *asymmetric confusion:*
   *(a) $e_1$, $e_3$ are enabled at $M$ and*
   *(b) $e_2$ is not enabled at $M$ but becomes enabled after the execution of $e_1$ and*
   *(c) ${}^\bullet e_2 \cap {}^\bullet e_3 \neq \emptyset$ and*
   *(d) ${}^\bullet e_1 \cap {}^\bullet e_3 = \emptyset$*

Notice that confusion does *not* occur in the maximal concurrency model of an acyclic net. This is because confusion is defined as interference between concurrent *ordered* choices of event enabled at a reachable marking. Such ordering is absent in maximal concurrency because the event choices are synchronised.

## 3    Probabilistic Acyclic Nets

A probabilistic acyclic net *pacnet* is defined in terms of an acyclic net, a concurrency model, and a weight function, as follows:

**Definition 10 (probabilistic acyclic net).** *A probabilistic acyclic net is a triple pacnet = (acnet, cmodel, $w : T \longrightarrow \mathbb{N}^+$), where acnet = $(P, T, F)$ is a well-formed acyclic net, cmodel $\in \mathbb{P}(\text{mixsseq}(acnet)) \setminus \{\emptyset\}$ is a concurrency model of acnet, and $w$ is a weight function that allocates a strictly positive integer-valued weight to each event of acnet.*
*The set of all probabilistic acyclic nets is denoted by PAN.*    ◇

Event weight is used for three reasons. First, weight is more fundamental than probability, because probability can be computed from weight but not the reverse. Second, weight provides indirection in computing probability, which allows experimentation with different ways of calculating probability. Third, weight is easier to understand for naive users than probability. The probability of a trace is defined as follows:

**Definition 11 (execution trace probability).** *Given a probabilistic acyclic net pacnet* $= (acnet, cmodel, w)$ *with execution trace* $\mu \in cmodel$ *defined by* $\mu = M_{acnet}^{init} U_1 M_1 \ldots U_n M_n$ *with step sequence* $\sigma = U_1 \ldots U_n$ *and* $n \in \mathbb{N}$, *the probability of* $\mu$ *is defined by*

$$p(\mu) \triangleq p(\sigma) \quad where \quad p(\sigma) \triangleq \prod_{i=1}^{n} p(U_i|\sigma_{i-1}) \quad and \quad p(U_i|\sigma_{i-1}) \triangleq \frac{\prod\limits_{e \in U_i} w(e)}{\sum\limits_{d=1}^{m_i} \prod\limits_{e \in U_{i,d}} w(e)},$$

*and* $\sigma_{i-1} \triangleq U_1 \ldots U_{i-1}$ *where* $\sigma_0 \triangleq \lambda$,
*and* $\{U_{i,1}, \ldots, U_{i,m_i}\} = \{U \mid M_{acnet}^{init} U_1 M_1 \ldots U_{i-1} M_{i-1} U M \in cmodel\}$.
*If* $n = 0$ *then* $p(\mu) \triangleq p(M_{acnet}^{init}) \triangleq 1$.    ◇

$U_{i,1}, \ldots, U_{i,m_i}$ are the alternative steps of $U_i$ (one of which is $U_i$) in traces with prefix $M_{acnet}^{init} U_1 M_1 \ldots U_{i-1} M_{i-1}$ in the concurrency model *cmodel* of the well-formed acyclic net *acnet*. This restriction allows the choice of alternative steps to be trace dependent, that is, dependent on the execution history up to the marking $M_{i-1}$, which is useful for concurrency models explicitly defined by a user. The restriction also allows the choice of alternative steps to be marking dependent, that is, dependent on $M_{i-1}$ only, which is useful for implicitly defined concurrency models such as the interleaving and maximal models of concurrency. Use of the product of weights of events in a step preserves the conventional correspondence between the conjunction of events and the multiplication of probabilities. Similarly, use of the summation preserves the conventional correspondence between the disjunction of events and the addition of probabilities. This correspondence helps to simplify our general formula for $p(U_i|\sigma_{i-1})$ to the standard formula for the probability of independent concurrent events (given in Definition 16).

Applying Definition 11 to *acnet*1 with event weights shown in Fig. 6, the probabilities of the traces in the maximal concurrency model of *acnet*1 are:
$p(\{s1\}) = 1$,
$p(\{s1\}\{e1\}\{s2, s3\}) = p(\{e1\}) = \frac{10}{10} = 1$,
$p(\{s1\}\{e1\}\{s2, s3\}\{e2, e3\}\{s4, s5\})$
$= p(\{e1\}) \times p(\{e2, e3\}|\{e1\}) = p(\{e2, e3\}|\{e1\}) = \frac{10 \times 8}{10 \times 8 \, + \, 10 \times 2} = 0.8$,
$p(\{s1\}\{e1\}\{s2, s3\}\{e2, e4\}\{s4, s5\})$
$= p(\{e1\}) \times p(\{e2, e4\}|\{e1\}) = p(\{e2, e4\}|\{e1\}) = \frac{10 \times 2}{10 \times 8 \, + \, 10 \times 2} = 0.2$.

Clearly, the sum of the probabilities of the traces exceeds 1, and (therefore) is not a valid probability value. The reason is that the traces of the maximal concurrency model are not exclusive, since some traces are prefixes. Therefore, partitioning the concurrency model into sets of traces that do not contain a prefix ensures the required trace exclusivity. For example, $\{\{s1\}\}$, $\{\{s1\}\{e1\}\{s2, s3\}\}$,

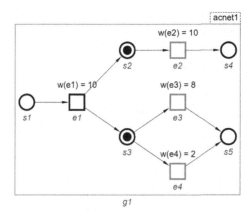

**Fig. 6.** Acyclic net *acnet*1 with weighted events.

and $\{\{s1\}\{e1\}\{s2, s3\}\{e2, e3\}\{s4, s5\}, \{s1\}\{e1\}\{s2, s3\}\{e2, e4\}\{s4, s5\}\}$ is such a partition, and each cell of the partition is termed an *exclusive set of execution traces* of a concurrency model. The sum of the probabilities of the traces in each cell is 1, which motivates the following definition.

**Definition 12 (exclusive sets of execution traces).**
*Let pacnet* $= (acnet, cmodel, w)$ *be a probabilistic acyclic net.*

1. exclusivetracesset($cmodel$) $\triangleq \{S \mid S \in \mathbb{P}(cmodel) \setminus \{\emptyset\} \wedge \forall \mu, \mu' \in S(\mu \not\prec \mu')\}$
   exclusive sets of execution traces of a concurrency model.
2. maxexclusivetracesset($cmodel$) $\triangleq$
   $\{S \mid S \in$ exclusivetracesset($cmodel$) $\wedge$
   $\quad \forall \mu \in cmodel \setminus S (S \cup \{\mu\} \notin$ exclusivetracesset($cmodel$))$\}$
   maximum exclusive sets of execution traces of a concurrency model.

$\Diamond$

Thus, in an exclusive set of execution traces $(S)$ of a concurrency model ($cmodel$) of a well-formed acyclic net ($acnet$), no trace is a prefix of another trace. Such a set is maximum if and only if the addition of a new trace from the concurrency model creates a prefix trace in the set.

The maximum property of each $S \in$ maxexclusivetracesset($cmodel$) ensures that $S$ is both *exclusive* and *exhaustive*, so that $\sum_{\mu \in S} p(\mu) = 1$, which is a basic requirement on a set of outcomes in probability theory [6]. This result is proved in Theorem 4.

For example, applying Definitions 11 and 12 to the interleaving concurrency model of *acnet*1, the maximum exclusive sets of execution traces of $cmodel_{ic}(acnet1)$ grouped using trace length are:
$S_0 = \{\{s1\}\}$,
$S_1 = \{\{s1\}\{e1\}\{s2, s3\}\}$,

$S_2 = \{\{s1\}\{e1\}\{s2, s3\}\{e2\}\{s3, s4\}, \{s1\}\{e1\}\{s2, s3\}\{e3\}\{s2, s5\},$
$\{s1\}\{e1\}\{s2, s3\}\{e4\}\{s2, s5\}\},$
$S_3 = \{\{s1\}\{e1\}\{s2, s3\}\{e2\}\{s3, s4\}\{e3\}\{s4, s5\},$
$\{s1\}\{e1\}\{s2, s3\}\{e3\}\{s2, s5\}\{e2\}\{s4, s5\},$
$\{s1\}\{e1\}\{s2, s3\}\{e2\}\{s3, s4\}\{e4\}\{s4, s5\},$
$\{s1\}\{e1\}\{s2, s3\}\{e4\}\{s2, s5\}\{e2\}\{s4, s5\}\}.$

For $S_0$, $p(\{s1\}) = 1$ (by Definition 11).

Probability of the trace in $S_1$ is: $p(\{e1\}) = \frac{10}{10} = 1$ (as required).

The sum of the probabilities of the traces in $S_2$ is:

$p(\{e1\})p(\{e2\}|\{e1\}) + p(\{e1\})p(\{e3\}|\{e1\}) + p(\{e1\})p(\{e4\}|\{e1\})$
$= p(\{e2\}|\{e1\}) + p(\{e3\}|\{e1\}) + p(\{e4\}|\{e1\})$
$= \frac{10}{10+8+2} + \frac{8}{10+8+2} + \frac{2}{10+8+2} = 1$ (as required).

The sum of the probabilities of the traces in $S_3$ is:

$p(\{e1\})p(\{e2\}|\{e1\})p(\{e3\}|\{e1\}\{e2\}) + p(\{e1\})p(\{e3\}|\{e1\})p(\{e2\}|\{e1\}\{e3\}) +$
$p(\{e1\})p(\{e2\}|\{e1\})p(\{e4\}|\{e1\}\{e2\}) + p(\{e1\})p(\{e4\}|\{e1\})p(\{e2\}|\{e1\}\{e4\})$
$= p(\{e2\}|\{e1\})p(\{e3\}|\{e1\}\{e2\}) + p(\{e3\}|\{e1\})p(\{e2\}|\{e1\}\{e3\}) +$
$\quad p(\{e2\}|\{e1\})p(\{e4\}|\{e1\}\{e2\}) + p(\{e4\}|\{e1\})p(\{e2\}|\{e1\}\{e4\})$
$= \frac{10}{10+8+2}\frac{8}{8+2} + \frac{8}{10+8+2}\frac{10}{10} + \frac{10}{10+8+2}\frac{2}{8+2} + \frac{2}{10+8+2}\frac{10}{10}$
$= \frac{10}{20}\frac{8}{10} + \frac{8}{20} + \frac{10}{20}\frac{2}{10} + \frac{2}{20} = \frac{4}{10} + \frac{4}{10} + \frac{1}{10} + \frac{1}{10} = 1$ (as required).

Thus, $S_0$, $S_1$, $S_2$, and $S_3$ are all exclusive and exhaustive subsets of $cmodel_{ic}(acnet1)$ and the sum of the probabilities of their respective traces is 1. In addition, $S_3$ consists of the maximal traces in $cmodel_{ic}(acnet1)$. Consequently, the traces in $S_3$ contain all reachable markings and all performable steps of the traces in $cmodel_{ic}(acnet1)$, unlike $S_0$, $S_1$, and $S_2$. These properties of $S_3$ motivate the following lemma, three theorems, and definition.

In the context of the concurrency model $cmodel$ of a probabilistic acyclic net $pacnet = (acnet, cmodel, w)$, Lemma 1 states that every non-maximal trace is a prefix of a maximal trace. Theorem 1 states that the set of maximal traces $S_{max}^{cmodel}$ and its set of prefix traces $prfx(S_{max}^{cmodel})$ cover the concurrency model exactly. Theorem 2 states that the markings and steps of the non-maximal traces are markings and steps of the maximal traces.

**Lemma 1.** *For any probabilistic acyclic net* $pacnet = (acnet, cmodel, w)$,
$\forall \mu' \in cmodel \setminus S_{max}^{cmodel} \exists \mu \in S_{max}^{cmodel} (\mu' < \mu).$

*Proof.* $\mu' \in cmodel \setminus S_{max}^{cmodel}$
$\implies \exists \mu'' \in cmodel (\mu' < \mu'')$
(by definitions of $S_{max}^{cmodel}$, trace extension, and $prfx(cmodel)$)
$\implies \exists \mu \in S_{max}^{cmodel} (\mu' < \mu)$
(by definition of $S_{max}^{cmodel}$, iteration, and transitivity of $<$
($\because$ $acnet$ is acyclic and finite))
$\implies \forall \mu' \in cmodel \setminus S_{max}^{cmodel} \exists \mu \in S_{max}^{cmodel} (\mu' < \mu)$ ($\because \mu'$ is arbitrary). ◇

**Theorem 1.** *For any probabilistic acyclic net* $pacnet = (acnet, cmodel, w)$, $\{S_{max}^{cmodel}, prfx(S_{max}^{cmodel})\}$ *is an exact cover of* $cmodel$.

*Proof.* $\{S_{max}^{cmodel}, prfx(S_{max}^{cmodel})\}$ is an exact cover of *cmodel* iff the following conditions hold (by definition of exact cover[4]):

1. $S_{max}^{cmodel} \cup prfx(S_{max}^{cmodel}) = cmodel$
2. $S_{max}^{cmodel} \cap prfx(S_{max}^{cmodel}) = \emptyset$

*Proof of Item 1.*
$S_{max}^{cmodel} \subseteq cmodel$ (by definition of $S_{max}^{cmodel}$) $\wedge$
$prfx(S_{max}^{cmodel}) \subseteq cmodel$
(by definitions of $S_{max}^{cmodel}$, $prfx(S_{max}^{cmodel})$, and prefix closure)
$\Longrightarrow S_{max}^{cmodel} \cup prfx(S_{max}^{cmodel}) \subseteq cmodel$ (by set theory).
Now $\mu' \in cmodel \Longrightarrow \mu' \in S_{max}^{cmodel} \vee \mu' \in cmodel \setminus S_{max}^{cmodel}$
(by definition of $S_{max}^{cmodel}$ and set theory).
If $\mu' \in cmodel \setminus S_{max}^{cmodel}$ then $\exists \mu \in S_{max}^{cmodel} (\mu' < \mu)$ (by Lemma 1)
$\Longrightarrow \mu' \in prfx(S_{max}^{cmodel})$ (by definition of $prfx(S_{max}^{cmodel})$)
$\Longrightarrow \mu' \in S_{max}^{cmodel} \cup prfx(S_{max}^{cmodel})$ (by first-order logic and set theory)
$\Longrightarrow cmodel \subseteq S_{max}^{cmodel} \cup prfx(S_{max}^{cmodel})$ ($\because \mu'$ is arbitrary)
$\Longrightarrow S_{max}^{cmodel} \cup prfx(S_{max}^{cmodel}) = cmodel$ ($\because S_{max}^{cmodel} \cup prfx(S_{max}^{cmodel}) \subseteq cmodel$).

*Proof of Item 2.*
$\mu' \in S_{max}^{cmodel} \cap prfx(S_{max}^{cmodel})$
$\Longrightarrow \exists \mu \in S_{max}^{cmodel} (\mu' < \mu)$ (by definition of $prfx(S_{max}^{cmodel})$)
$\Longrightarrow \mu' \notin maxmixsseq(acnet)$ (by definition of $maxmixsseq(acnet)$)
$\Longrightarrow \mu' \notin S_{max}^{cmodel}$ (by definition of $S_{max}^{cmodel}$; which is a contradiction).
$\therefore S_{max}^{cmodel} \cap prfx(S_{max}^{cmodel}) = \emptyset$.    $\diamond$

**Theorem 2.** *For any probabilistic acyclic net* $pacnet = (acnet, cmodel, w)$ *the following hold:*

1.  $\bigcup\{mixsseqmarkings(\mu') \mid \mu' \in cmodel \setminus S_{max}^{cmodel}\}$
     $\subset \bigcup\{mixsseqmarkings(\mu) \mid \mu \in S_{max}^{cmodel}\}$
2.  $\bigcup\{mixsseqsteps(\mu') \mid \mu' \in cmodel \setminus S_{max}^{cmodel}\}$
     $\subseteq \bigcup\{mixsseqsteps(\mu) \mid \mu \in S_{max}^{cmodel}\}$

The proof uses Theorem 1 to establish weak set inclusion in Items 1 and 2, and proves the terminal marking of a maximal trace does not occur in any nonmaximal trace to establish strong set inclusion in Item 1, see Appendix. The set inclusion in Item 2 is weak because the final step of a maximal trace can be performed in a prefix of another maximal trace. For example, $S_{max}^{cmodel_{ic}(acnet1)} = S_3$ and $\bigcup\{mixsseqsteps(\mu) \mid \mu \in S_{max}^{cmodel_{ic}(acnet1)}\} = \{\{e1\}, \{e2\}, \{e3\}, \{e4\}\}$. These steps are performed collectively by the following non-maximal traces of $cmodel_{ic}(acnet1)$: $\{s1\}\{e1\}\{s2, s3\}\{e2\}\{s3, s4\}$, $\{s1\}\{e1\}\{s2, s3\}\{e3\}\{s2, s5\}$, and $\{s1\}\{e1\}\{s2, s3\}\{e4\}\{s2, s5\}$.

---

[4] See [8] for a definition of *exact cover*.

The following theorem states that the set of maximal execution traces of a probabilistic acyclic net is a maximum exclusive set. This theorem is necessary to ensure marking and step probabilities defined in Definition 13 satisfy their respective generic probability requirements.

**Theorem 3.** *For any probabilistic acyclic net pacnet* $=(acnet, cmodel, w)$, $S_{max}^{cmodel} \in \text{maxexclusivetracesset}(cmodel)$.

The hypothesis $S_{max}^{cmodel}$ is not an exclusive set of *cmodel* leads to a contradiction using Theorem 1, and Lemma 1 is used to prove $S_{max}^{cmodel}$ is a maximum set, which proves the theorem, see Appendix.

**Definition 13 (marking, step, and node probabilities).** *Given a probabilistic acyclic net pacnet* $=(acnet, cmodel, w)$, *the probabilities of each marking* $M$, *step* $U$, *state* $s$, *and event* $e$ *are denoted by* $p(M)$, $p(U)$, $p(s)$, *and* $p(e)$ *respectively, defined as follows:*

1. $p(M) \triangleq \sum\limits_{\mu \in S_M} p(\mu)$                                                        marking probability.

   *where* $S_M \triangleq \{\mu \mid \mu \in S_{max}^{cmodel} \wedge M \in \text{mixsseqmarkings}(\mu)\}$

2. $p(U) \triangleq \sum\limits_{\mu \in S_U} p(\mu)$                                                        step probability.

   *where* $S_U \triangleq \{\mu \mid \mu \in S_{max}^{cmodel} \wedge U \in \text{mixsseqsteps}(\mu)\}$

3. $p(s) \triangleq \sum\limits_{\mu \in S_s} p(\mu)$                                                        state probability.

   *where* $S_s \triangleq \{\mu \mid \mu \in S_{max}^{cmodel} \wedge s \in \bigcup \text{mixsseqmarkings}(\mu)\}$

4. $p(e) \triangleq \sum\limits_{\mu \in S_e} p(\mu)$                                                        event probability.

   *where* $S_e \triangleq \{\mu \mid \mu \in S_{max}^{cmodel} \wedge e \in \bigcup \text{mixsseqsteps}(\mu)\}$                    ◇

Thus, the probability $p(M)$ of a marking $M$ of a probabilistic acyclic net *pacnet* is the sum of the probabilities of the maximal traces of the concurrency model *cmodel* of *pacnet* of which $M$ is an element. Similarly, the probability $p(U)$ of a step $U$ of *pacnet* is the sum of the probabilities of the maximal traces of *cmodel* of which $U$ is an element. The probability $p(s)$ of a state $s$ and the probability $p(e)$ of an event $e$ are defined similarly, using their containing marking and step respectively.

To be well-defined, the probability framework should satisfy the following generic requirements [6].

## Generic Requirements on a Probability Framework

1. Any probability value must be in the closed real interval [0..1].
2. The sum of probabilities of exclusive and exhaustive outcomes must be equal to 1.

Requirement 1 is conventional in probability theory. In the context of the probability framework, the outcomes in Requirement 2 can be execution traces, markings, and steps.

To confirm the probability framework satisfies the generic requirements, and thereby correctly computes probabilities in nets with confusion, the framework is used to compute the probabilities of weighted versions of the classic examples of nets with symmetric and asymmetric confusion, see Fig. 7.

In the interleaving concurrency model of N1, $S_{max}^{cmodel_{ic}(N1)} = \{\mu_a, \mu_b, \mu_c\}$ where $\mu_a \triangleq \{s1, s2\}\{e1\}\{s3, s2\}\{e3\}\{s3, s4\}$,

$$\mu_b \triangleq \{s1, s2\}\{e3\}\{s1, s4\}\{e1\}\{s3, s4\}, \quad \mu_c \triangleq \{s1, s2\}\{e2\}\{s5\}.$$

$$p(\mu_a) = \frac{w(e1)}{w(e1)+w(e2)+w(e3)}\frac{w(e3)}{w(e3)} = \frac{5}{15} = \frac{1}{3} \wedge$$

$$p(\mu_b) = \frac{w(e3)}{w(e1)+w(e2)+w(e3)}\frac{w(e1)}{w(e1)} = \frac{5}{15} = \frac{1}{3} \wedge$$

$$p(\mu_c) = \frac{w(e2)}{w(e1)+w(e2)+w(e3)} = \frac{5}{15} = \frac{1}{3}$$

(by Definition 11, and definitions of $\mu_a$, $\mu_b$, $\mu_c$, and definitions of $w(e1)$, $w(e2)$, $w(e3)$), which clearly satisfies Requirements 1 and 2.

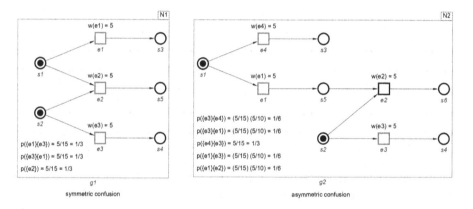

**Fig. 7.** Weight-based probabilities in the interleaving concurrency model of acyclic nets with symmetric and asymmetric confusion.

In the interleaving concurrency model of N2, $S_{max}^{cmodel_{ic}(N2)} = \{\mu_d, \mu_e, \mu_f, \mu_g, \mu_h\}$ where $\mu_d \triangleq \{s1, s2\}\{e3\}\{s1, s4\}\{e4\}\{s3, s4\}$,

$$\mu_e \triangleq \{s1, s2\}\{e3\}\{s1, s4\}\{e1\}\{s5, s4\}, \quad \mu_f \triangleq \{s1, s2\}\{e4\}\{s3, s2\}\{e3\}\{s3, s4\},$$
$$\mu_g \triangleq \{s1, s2\}\{e1\}\{s5, s2\}\{e3\}\{s5, s4\}, \quad \mu_h \triangleq \{s1, s2\}\{e1\}\{s5, s2\}\{e2\}\{s6\}.$$

$$p(\mu_d) = \frac{w(e3)}{w(e3)+w(e4)+w(e1)}\frac{w(e4)}{w(e4)+w(e1)} = \frac{5}{15}\frac{5}{10} = \frac{1}{6} \wedge$$

$$p(\mu_e) = \frac{w(e3)}{w(e3)+w(e4)+w(e1)}\frac{w(e1)}{w(e4)+w(e1)} = \frac{5}{15}\frac{5}{10} = \frac{1}{6} \wedge$$

$$p(\mu_f) = \frac{w(e4)}{w(e3)+w(e4)+w(e1)}\frac{w(e3)}{w(e3)} = \frac{5}{15} = \frac{1}{3} \wedge$$

$$p(\mu_g) = \frac{w(e1)}{w(e3)+w(e4)+w(e1)}\frac{w(e3)}{w(e3)+w(e2)} = \frac{5}{15}\frac{5}{10} = \frac{1}{6} \wedge$$

$$p(\mu_h) = \frac{w(e1)}{w(e3)+w(e4)+w(e1)}\frac{w(e2)}{w(e3)+w(e2)} = \frac{5}{15}\frac{5}{10} = \frac{1}{6}$$

(by Definition 11, and definitions of $\mu_d$, ..., $\mu_h$, and definitions of $w(e1)$, ..., $w(4)$), which satisfies Requirements 1 and 2 (by inspection).

In the maximal concurrency model of N1 (which does not have confusion), $S_{max}^{cmodel_{mc}(N1)} = \{\mu_A, \mu_B\}$ where
$\mu_A \triangleq \{s1, s2\}\{e1, e3\}\{s3, s4\}$  and  $\mu_B \triangleq \{s1, s2\}\{e2\}\{s5\}$.
$p(\mu_A) = \frac{w(e1)w(e3)}{w(e1)w(e3)+w(e2)} = \frac{25}{30} = \frac{5}{6} \wedge p(\mu_B) = \frac{w(e2)}{w(e1)w(e3)+w(e2)} = \frac{5}{30} = \frac{1}{6}$
(by Definition 11, and definitions of $\mu_A$, $\mu_B$, and definitions of $w(e1)$, $w(e2)$, $w(e3)$), which satisfies Requirements 1 and 2 (by inspection).

In the maximal concurrency model of N2 (which does not have confusion), $S_{max}^{cmodel_{mc}(N2)} = \{\mu_C, \mu_D\}$ where
$\mu_C \triangleq \{s1, s2\}\{e4, e3\}\{s3, s4\}$  and  $\mu_D \triangleq \{s1, s2\}\{e1, e3\}\{s5, s4\}$.
$p(\mu_C) = \frac{w(e4)w(e3)}{w(e4)w(e3)+w(e1)w(e3)} = \frac{25}{50} = \frac{1}{2} \wedge$
$p(\mu_D) = \frac{w(e1)w(e3)}{w(e4)w(e3)+w(e1)w(e3)} = \frac{25}{50} = \frac{1}{2}$
(by Definition 11, and definitions of $\mu_C$, $\mu_D$, and definitions of $w(e1)$, $w(e3)$, $w(e4)$), which clearly satisfies Requirements 1 and 2.

Thus, for application of the interleaving concurrency model to two simple examples of symmetric and asymmetric confusion, and application of the maximal concurrency model to these examples, our probability framework satisfies the two generic probability requirements. Theorem 4 generalises this result for trace probabilities. To prove Theorem 4, we need the following notions of truncation function and truncation set of traces, as well as Lemmas 2 and 3.

Truncation sets are used to layer a collection of traces in a concurrency model by trace length using the truncation function. The layers are used in backward inductive proofs in Lemma 2 and Theorem 4. Lemma 2 states that each truncation set of a maximum exclusive set of traces of a concurrency model is also maximum exclusive. This property is used to prove Lemma 3, which states that any extension of a trace in a truncation set into a larger truncation set must include *all* the alternative extension steps of the trace allowed by the concurrency model. This property is key to proving Item 2 of Theorem 4, see Appendix.

**Definition 14 (truncation function and truncation set of traces).**
*Let pacnet* $= (acnet, cmodel, w)$ *be a probabilistic acyclic net,*
*and let* $S \in \mathbb{P}(cmodel) \setminus \{\emptyset\}$.

1. *trunc* : *cmodel* $\times \mathbb{N} \longrightarrow$ *cmodel  such that*
$$trunc(\mu, n) \triangleq \begin{cases} \mu & \text{if } |\mu| \leq n \\ M_{acnet}^{init} U_1^\mu M_1^\mu \ldots U_n^\mu M_n^\mu & \text{if } |\mu| > n \end{cases} \quad \text{truncation function.}$$

2. $\forall n \in [0..maxlen(S)] \, (Trunc(S, n) \triangleq \{trunc(\mu, n) \mid \mu \in S\})$
truncation set of traces.   $\diamond$

**Lemma 2.** *For any probabilistic acyclic net pacnet* $= (acnet, cmodel, w)$,
$\forall S \in \text{maxexclusivetracesset}(cmodel) \, \forall n \in [0..maxlen(S)]$
$(Trunc(S, n) \in \text{maxexclusivetracesset}(cmodel))$.

The proof uses backward induction and contradiction. The hypothesis $Trunc(S, n-1) \notin \text{maxexclusivetracesset}(cmodel)$ for
an $S \in \text{maxexclusivetracesset}(cmodel)$ and an $n \in [1..maxlen(S)]$ leads to contradictions, which proves the lemma, see Appendix.

**Lemma 3.** *For any probabilistic acyclic net* $pacnet = (acnet, cmodel, w)$,
$\forall S \in \text{maxexclusivetracesset}(cmodel) \setminus \{\{M^{init}_{acnet}\}\} \forall n \in [1..maxlen(S)]$
$(\mu'' \in Trunc(S, n-1) \wedge \mu''UM \in Trunc(S, n)$
$\implies (\mu''U'M' \in cmodel \implies \mu''U'M' \in Trunc(S, n)))$.

The proof is by contradiction. The negation of the lemma predicate in combination with Lemma 2 applied to $Trunc(S, n)$ leads to a contradiction with Lemma 2 for $Trunc(S, n)$, which proves the lemma, see Appendix.

**Theorem 4.** *For any probabilistic acyclic net* $pacnet = (acnet, cmodel, w)$ *the following hold:*

1. $\forall \mu \in cmodel (p(\mu) \in [0..1])$
2. $\forall S \in \text{maxexclusivetracesset}(cmodel) (\sum_{\mu \in S} p(\mu) = 1)$

The proof of Item 1 follows directly from Definition 11 and arithmetic. Proof of Item 2 uses backward induction on trace length, based on the proposition that the sum of the probabilities of the traces in a truncation set $Trunc(S, n)$ is $\sum_{\mu \in S} p(\mu)$. The induction step proves using Lemma 3 that the sum of the probabilities of the traces in a truncation set $Trunc(S, n)$ is the same as that of $Trunc(S, n-1)$. This is because the steps differentiating the two maximum exclusive truncation sets of traces are exactly those allowed by the underlying concurrency model, which ensures that the factor consisting of the sum of the probabilities of alternative steps is 1, see Appendix.
Therefore, $\sum_{\mu \in S} p(\mu) = p(M^{init}_{acnet}) = 1$ (by Definition 11).

The following definition and theorem extend the notion of exclusive and exhaustive outcomes in the Generic Requirements to the reachable markings $cmmarkings(cmodel)$ and the execution steps $cmsteps(cmodel)$ of the concurrency model $cmodel$ of a probabilistic acyclic net $pacnet$, based on the set of maximal execution traces $S^{cmodel}_{max}$ of the concurrency model. A set of markings $\mathcal{M}$ is exclusive if and only if the sets of maximal traces that contain the individual markings of $\mathcal{M}$ are disjoint. $\mathcal{M}$ is also exhaustive if and only if the union of these sets of maximal traces is $S^{cmodel}_{max}$. Similarly, a set of steps $\mathcal{U}$ is exclusive and exhaustive if and only if the sets of maximal traces that contain the individual steps of $\mathcal{U}$ are disjoint and the union of these sets is $S^{cmodel}_{max}$.

**Definition 15 (exclusive and exhaustive sets of reachable markings and execution steps).** *Let* $pacnet = (acnet, cmodel, w)$ *be a probabilistic acyclic net.*

1. $cmmarkings(cmodel) \triangleq \bigcup \{\text{mixsseqmarkings}(\mu) \mid \mu \in cmodel\}$
   markings of a concurrency model.
2. $\forall M \in cmmarkings(cmodel) \forall S \in \mathbb{P}(cmodel) \setminus \{\emptyset\}$
   $(markingtraces(M, S) \triangleq \{\mu \mid \mu \in S \wedge M \in \text{mixsseqmarkings}(\mu)\})$
   traces containing a marking.

3. $exclusivemarkingsset(cmodel) \triangleq$
   $\{\mathcal{M} \mid \mathcal{M} \subseteq cmmarkings(cmodel) \wedge$
   $\qquad \forall M, M' \in \mathcal{M}$
   $\qquad (M \neq M'$
   $\qquad \qquad \Longrightarrow markingtraces(M, S_{max}^{cmodel}) \cap markingtraces(M', S_{max}^{cmodel}) = \emptyset)\}$
   $\qquad \qquad \qquad \qquad$ exclusive sets of markings of a concurrency model.

4. $maxexclusivemarkingsset(cmodel) \triangleq$
   $\{\mathcal{M} \mid \mathcal{M} \in exclusivemarkingsset(cmodel) \wedge$
   $\qquad \bigcup\{markingtraces(M, S_{max}^{cmodel}) \mid M \in \mathcal{M}\} = S_{max}^{cmodel}\}$
   $\qquad \qquad$ maximum exclusive sets of markings of a concurrency model.

5. $cmsteps(cmodel) \triangleq \bigcup\{\text{mixsseqsteps}(\mu) \mid \mu \in cmodel\}$
   $\qquad \qquad \qquad \qquad \qquad$ execution steps of a concurrency model.

6. $\forall U \in cmsteps(cmodel) \, \forall S \in \mathbb{P}(cmodel) \setminus \{\emptyset\}$
   $(steptraces(U, S) \triangleq \{\mu \mid \mu \in S \wedge U \in \text{mixsseqsteps}(\mu)\})$
   $\qquad \qquad \qquad \qquad$ traces containing an execution step.

7. $exclusivestepsset(cmodel) \triangleq$
   $\{\mathcal{U} \mid \mathcal{U} \subseteq cmsteps(cmodel) \wedge$
   $\qquad \forall U, U' \in \mathcal{U}$
   $\qquad (U \neq U' \Longrightarrow steptraces(U, S_{max}^{cmodel}) \cap steptraces(U', S_{max}^{cmodel}) = \emptyset)\}$
   $\qquad \qquad$ exclusive sets of execution steps of a concurrency model.

8. $maxexclusivestepsset(cmodel) \triangleq$
   $\{\mathcal{U} \mid \mathcal{U} \in exclusivestepsset(cmodel) \wedge$
   $\qquad \bigcup\{steptraces(U, S_{max}^{cmodel}) \mid U \in \mathcal{U}\} = S_{max}^{cmodel}\}$
   $\qquad \qquad$ maximum exclusive sets of execution steps of a concurrency model.

$\qquad \qquad \qquad \qquad \qquad \qquad \qquad \qquad \qquad \qquad \qquad \qquad \qquad \Diamond$

**Theorem 5.** *For any probabilistic acyclic net* $pacnet = (acnet, cmodel, w)$ *the following hold:*

1. $\forall M \in cmmarkings(cmodel) \, (p(M) \in [0..1])$
2. $\forall \mathcal{M} \in maxexclusivemarkingsset(cmodel) \, (\sum_{M \in \mathcal{M}} p(M) = 1)$
3. $\forall U \in cmsteps(cmodel) \, (p(U) \in [0..1])$
4. $\forall \mathcal{U} \in maxexclusivestepsset(cmodel) \, (\sum_{U \in \mathcal{U}} p(U) = 1)$

The proof relies on the previous definition and on two properties of $S_{max}^{cmodel}$, namely: (i) $S_{max}^{cmodel}$ is a maximum exclusive set of traces of $cmodel$ (Theorem 3), and (ii) $S_{max}^{cmodel}$ satisfies the generic requirements (Theorem 4).

## 4  Investigation of Probabilistic Acyclic Nets

We examine the effect of different concurrency models on the trace probabilities of acyclic nets with and without confusion. First, the trace probabilities of the maximal and interleaving concurrency models are compared for the acyclic nets with symmetric and asymmetric confusion shown in Fig. 7. Then, the trace probabilities of the concurrency models are compared for the confusion-free acyclic nets shown in Figs. 8 and 9.

For the probabilistic acyclic net $(\text{N}1, cmodel_{mc}(\text{N}1), w)$, the maximal traces are $\mu_A$ and $\mu_B$; and for the net $(\text{N}1, cmodel_{ic}(\text{N}1), w)$, the maximal traces are $\mu_a$, $\mu_b$, and $\mu_c$. The traces $\mu_A$, $\mu_a$, and $\mu_b$ correspond, that is, the traces have the same initial markings and the same final markings; and $\mu_B$ and $\mu_c$ correspond.
$$p(\mu_A) = \tfrac{5}{6} \wedge p(\mu_a) = \tfrac{1}{3} \wedge p(\mu_b) = \tfrac{1}{3} \quad \text{and} \quad p(\mu_B) = \tfrac{1}{6} \wedge p(\mu_c) = \tfrac{1}{3}.$$
Therefore, $p(\mu_A)$ is not equal to $p(\mu_a)$, or $p(\mu_b)$, or $p(\mu_a) + p(\mu_b)$; and $p(\mu_B)$ is not equal to $p(\mu_c)$.

Similarly, $\mu_C$ and $\mu_D$ are the maximal traces of $(\text{N}2, cmodel_{mc}(\text{N}2), w)$, and $\mu_d$, $\mu_e$, $\mu_f$, $\mu_g$, and $\mu_h$ are the maximal traces of $(\text{N}2, cmodel_{ic}(\text{N}2), w)$. Traces $\mu_C$, $\mu_d$, and $\mu_f$ correspond, and $\mu_D$, $\mu_e$, and $\mu_g$ correspond. No maximally concurrent trace corresponds to the interleaving concurrent trace $\mu_h$.
$$p(\mu_C) = \tfrac{1}{2} \wedge p(\mu_d) = \tfrac{1}{6} \wedge p(\mu_f) = \tfrac{1}{3} \quad \text{and} \quad p(\mu_D) = \tfrac{1}{2} \wedge p(\mu_e) = \tfrac{1}{6} \wedge$$
$$p(\mu_g) = \tfrac{1}{6}.$$
Therefore, $p(\mu_D)$ is not equal to $p(\mu_e)$, or $p(\mu_g)$, or $p(\mu_e) + p(\mu_g)$; but $p(\mu_C) = p(\mu_d) + p(\mu_f)$.

Therefore, in general, if an acyclic net has confusion, then the probabilities of corresponding traces (i.e. traces with identical initial markings and identical final markings), and also their sum, depend on the concurrency model of the traces.

Now the trace probabilities of the maximal and interleaving concurrency models of the *confusion-free* acyclic net with binary choice shown in Fig. 8 are compared.

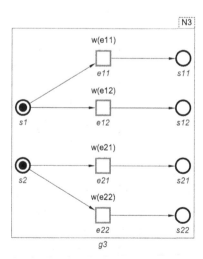

**Fig. 8.** Confusion-free acyclic net consisting of two disjoint simple sequential acyclic nets with binary choice.

The probabilistic acyclic net $(\text{N3}, cmodel_{mc}(\text{N3}), w)$ has the following four traces:

$\mu_E \triangleq \{s1, s2\}\{e11, e21\}\{s11, s21\}$, $\mu_F \triangleq \{s1, s2\}\{e11, e22\}\{s11, s22\}$,
$\mu_G \triangleq \{s1, s2\}\{e12, e21\}\{s12, s21\}$, $\mu_H \triangleq \{s1, s2\}\{e12, e22\}\{s12, s22\}$

with respective probabilities:

$p(\mu_E) = \frac{w(e11)w(21)}{w(e11)w(e21)+w(e11)w(e22)+w(e12)w(e21)+w(e12)w(e22)}$ $\wedge$

$p(\mu_F) = \frac{w(e11)w(22)}{w(e11)w(e21)+w(e11)w(e22)+w(e12)w(e21)+w(e12)w(e22)}$ $\wedge$

$p(\mu_G) = \frac{w(e12)w(21)}{w(e11)w(e21)+w(e11)w(e22)+w(e12)w(e21)+w(e12)w(e22)}$ $\wedge$

$p(\mu_H) = \frac{w(e12)w(22)}{w(e11)w(e21)+w(e11)w(e22)+w(e12)w(e21)+w(e12)w(e22)}$

(by Definition 11 and definitions of $\mu_E$, $\mu_F$, $\mu_G$, $\mu_H$).

The probabilistic acyclic net $(\text{N3}, cmodel_{ic}(\text{N3}), w)$ has the following eight traces:

$\mu_i \triangleq \{s1, s2\}\{e11\}\{s11, s2\}\{e21\}\{s11, s21\}$,
$\mu_j \triangleq \{s1, s2\}\{e21\}\{s1, s21\}\{e11\}\{s11, s21\}$,
$\mu_k \triangleq \{s1, s2\}\{e11\}\{s11, s2\}\{e22\}\{s11, s22\}$,
$\mu_l \triangleq \{s1, s2\}\{e22\}\{s1, s22\}\{e11\}\{s11, s22\}$,
$\mu_m \triangleq \{s1, s2\}\{e12\}\{s12, s2\}\{e21\}\{s12, s21\}$,
$\mu_n \triangleq \{s1, s2\}\{e21\}\{s1, s21\}\{e12\}\{s12, s21\}$,
$\mu_o \triangleq \{s1, s2\}\{e12\}\{s12, s2\}\{e22\}\{s12, s22\}$,
$\mu_p \triangleq \{s1, s2\}\{e22\}\{s1, s22\}\{e12\}\{s12, s22\}$

with respective probabilities:

$p(\mu_i) = \frac{w(e11)}{w(e11)+w(e12)+w(e21)+w(e22)}\frac{w(e21)}{w(e21)+w(e22)}$ $\wedge$

$p(\mu_j) = \frac{w(e21)}{w(e11)+w(e12)+w(e21)+w(e22)}\frac{w(e11)}{w(e11)+w(e12)}$ $\wedge$

$p(\mu_k) = \frac{w(e11)}{w(e11)+w(e12)+w(e21)+w(e22)}\frac{w(e22)}{w(e21)+w(e22)}$ $\wedge$

$p(\mu_l) = \frac{w(e22)}{w(e11)+w(e12)+w(e21)+w(e22)}\frac{w(e11)}{w(e11)+w(e12)}$ $\wedge$

$p(\mu_m) = \frac{w(e12)}{w(e11)+w(e12)+w(e21)+w(e22)}\frac{w(e21)}{w(e21)+w(e22)}$ $\wedge$

$p(\mu_n) = \frac{w(e21)}{w(e11)+w(e12)+w(e21)+w(e22)}\frac{w(e12)}{w(e11)+w(e12)}$ $\wedge$

$p(\mu_o) = \frac{w(e12)}{w(e11)+w(e12)+w(e21)+w(e22)}\frac{w(e22)}{w(e21)+w(e22)}$ $\wedge$

$p(\mu_p) = \frac{w(e22)}{w(e11)+w(e12)+w(e21)+w(e22)}\frac{w(e12)}{w(e11)+w(e12)}$

(by Definition 11 and definitions of $\mu_i$, ..., $\mu_p$).

Relating the probabilities of corresponding traces $\mu_E$, $\mu_i$, and $\mu_j$ of the two probabilistic acyclic nets:

$p(\mu_E) = \frac{w(e11)w(21)}{w(e11)w(e21)+w(e11)w(e22)+w(e12)w(e21)+w(e12)w(e22)}$

$= \frac{w(e11)}{w(e11)+w(e12)}\frac{w(21)}{w(e21)+w(e22)}$ $\wedge$

$p(\mu_i) + p(\mu_j) = \frac{w(e11)}{w(e11)+w(e12)+w(e21)+w(e22)}\frac{w(e21)}{w(e21)+w(e22)} +$

$\frac{w(e21)}{w(e11)+w(e12)+w(e21)+w(e22)}\frac{w(e11)}{w(e11)+w(e12)}$

$= \frac{w(e11)}{w(e11)+w(e12)}\frac{w(21)}{w(e21)+w(e22)}$

(by Definition 11, and definitions of $\mu_E$, $\mu_i$, and $\mu_j$, and arithmetic)
$\implies p(\mu_E) = p(\mu_i) + p(\mu_j)$ (by arithmetic), and the formulae for $p(\mu_E)$ and $p(\mu_i) + p(\mu_j)$ are equal to the standard formula for computing the probability of occurrence of the independent concurrent events $e11$ and $e21$, see Definition 16.

Similarly, $\mu_F$, $\mu_k$, $\mu_l$ correspond, $\mu_G$, $\mu_m$, $\mu_n$ correspond, $\mu_H$, $\mu_o$, $\mu_p$ correspond, with $p(\mu_F) = p(\mu_k) + p(\mu_l)$, $p(\mu_G) = p(\mu_m) + p(\mu_n)$, $p(\mu_H) = p(\mu_o) + p(\mu_p)$, and the formulae are equal to their respective standard formulae for computing the probability of independent concurrent events.

Thus, for a confusion-free well-formed acyclic net consisting of two disjoint sequential acyclic nets with binary choice, in the maximal and interleaving concurrency models, the sum of the probabilities of corresponding traces in a concurrency model is independent of the concurrency model. Figure 9 shows the general case and Theorems 6 and 7 generalise the result, for which we need to define the notion of standard probability of independent concurrent events.

**Definition 16 (standard probability of independent concurrent events).** *Let pacnet $= (acnet, cmodel, w)$ be a probabilistic acyclic net, where $acnet = (P, T, F)$ is a well-formed acyclic net. Let $E \subseteq T$ be a set of events of acnet partitioned by $E_1, \ldots, E_z$, where $z \in \mathbb{N}^+$ and*

$$\forall j \in [1..z] \left( (^\bullet E_j)^\bullet = E_j \ \wedge \ \bigcap_{e \in E_j} {}^\bullet e \neq \emptyset \right). \text{ Let } \widetilde{E} \triangleq \prod_{j=1}^{z} E_j.$$

*Events $e_1 \in E_1, \ldots, e_z \in E_z$ are defined to be independent concurrent events iff $\exists M \in \mathrm{reachable}(acnet) \, \forall (t_1, \ldots, t_z) \in \widetilde{E} \, (\{t_1, \ldots, t_z\} \in \mathrm{enabled}_{acnet}(M))$.*
*The standard probability of $e_1, \ldots, e_z$ in the context $M$ is defined by*

$$p_{\mathrm{STD}}(M, \{e_1, \ldots, e_z\}) \triangleq \prod_{j=1}^{z} \frac{w(e_j)}{\sum\limits_{e \in E_j} w(e)} \qquad \qquad \Diamond$$

The standard probability equation is valid for $z = 1$, although there is no concurrency with only one event $e_1 \in E_1$. The conditions on the $E_j$s help to ensure that the concurrent events in $E$ are located in different $E_j$s so that no two concurrent events are co-located within the same $E_j$, event choice is within an $E_j$, and the $E_j$s are disjoint. For example, see Fig. 9.

**Theorem 6.** *Let pacnet $= (\mathrm{N4}, cmodel_{mc}(\mathrm{N4}), w)$ be the probabilistic acyclic net with maximal concurrency model $cmodel_{mc}(\mathrm{N4})$ based on the confusion-free net shown in Fig. 9.*
$$\forall z \in \mathbb{N}^+ \, \forall j \in [1..z] \, (e_j \in E_j) \ \wedge \ \mu \in cmodel_{mc}(\mathrm{N4}) \ \wedge \ U_1^\mu = \{e_1, \ldots, e_z\}$$
$$\implies p(\mu) = p_{\mathrm{STD}}(M_{\mathrm{N4}}^{init}, \{e_1, \ldots, e_z\}).$$

*Proof.*
$p(\mu) = p(U_1^\mu)$  (by Definition 11 and definition of $\mu$)

$$= \frac{\prod\limits_{e \in U_1^\mu} w(e)}{\sum\limits_{d=1}^{|\widetilde{E}|} \prod\limits_{e \in U_{1,d}} w(e)} \qquad \text{(by definitions of } p(U_1) \text{ in Definition 11 and } \widetilde{E} \text{ in Definition 16)}$$

$$= \frac{\prod\limits_{e \in U_1^\mu} w(e)}{\prod\limits_{j=1}^{z} \sum\limits_{e \in E_j} w(e)} \qquad \text{(by combinatorics)}$$

$$= \prod_{j=1}^{z} \frac{w(e_j)}{\sum\limits_{e \in E_j} w(e)} \qquad \text{(by definition of } U_1^\mu \text{ and factorization)}$$

$$= p_{\mathrm{STD}}(M_{\mathrm{N4}}^{init}, \{e_1, \ldots, e_z\})$$
(by definition of standard probability in Definition 16).   $\Diamond$

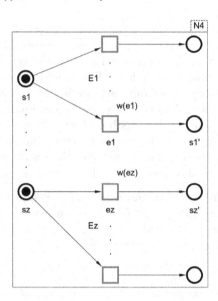

**Fig. 9.** Confusion-free well-formed acyclic net consisting of $z$ disjoint simple sequential acyclic nets with choice.

**Lemma 4.** *Let* $\forall z \in \mathbb{N}^+ \ \forall j \in [1..z] \ (a_j \in \mathbb{R}^+)$, *let* $perm(a_1, \ldots, a_z)$ *denote the set of permutations of* $(a_1, \ldots, a_z)$ *where* $a_1, \ldots, a_z$ *are not necessarily distinct, let* $\forall j \in [1..z] \ (((a_1, \ldots, a_z) \setminus a_j) \triangleq (a_1, \ldots, a_{j-1}, a_{j+1}, \ldots, a_z))$, *and let* $T(a_1, \ldots, a_z) \quad \triangleq \sum\limits_{\substack{(a_{i_z}, \ldots, a_{i_1}) \\ \in perm(a_1, \ldots, a_z)}} \dfrac{1}{a_{i_1} + \cdots + a_{i_z}} \times \dfrac{1}{a_{i_1} + \cdots + a_{i_{z-1}}} \times \cdots \times \dfrac{1}{a_{i_1}}$

*where* $i \in [1..|z|!]$ *is an index over the elements in* $perm(a_1, \ldots, a_z)$.
$T(a_1, \ldots, a_z) = \frac{1}{a_1 \ldots a_z}$

Proof by induction on $z$.
For $z \in \mathbb{N}^+$, let $Prop(z)$ be the proposition $T(a_1, \ldots, a_z) = \frac{1}{a_1 \ldots a_z}$.
Base Case: Proof of $Prop(1)$.
$T(a_1) = \sum\limits_{\substack{a_{i_1} \\ \in perm(a_1)}} \frac{1}{a_{i_1}}$ (by definition of $T(a_1)$)

$= \frac{1}{a_1}$ (by definition of $perm(a_1)$). $\qquad\qquad\qquad\qquad\qquad\qquad \diamondsuit$

Induction Step:
Proof of $\forall z \in \mathbb{N}^+ \ (Prop(z) \implies Prop(z+1))$.
For $z \in \mathbb{N}^+$, assume $Prop(z)$ holds (inductive hypothesis).
$T(a_1, \ldots, a_{z+1}) \quad = \sum\limits_{\substack{(a_{i_{z+1}}, \ldots, a_{i_1}) \\ \in perm(a_1, \ldots, a_{z+1})}} \dfrac{1}{a_{i_1} + \cdots + a_{i_{z+1}}} \times \dfrac{1}{a_{i_1} + \cdots + a_{i_z}} \times \cdots \times \dfrac{1}{a_{i_1}}$

(by definition of $T(a_1, \ldots, a_{z+1})$)
$= \dfrac{1}{a_1 + \cdots + a_{z+1}} \sum\limits_{\substack{(a_{i_{z+1}}, \ldots, a_{i_1}) \\ \in perm(a_1, \ldots, a_{z+1})}} \dfrac{1}{a_{i_1} + \cdots + a_{i_z}} \times \cdots \times \dfrac{1}{a_{i_1}}$

(by definition of $(a_{i_{z+1}}, \ldots, a_{i_1})$, commutativity of $+$, and factorization)

$$= \frac{1}{a_1 + \cdots + a_{z+1}} \sum_{a_j \in \{a_1, \ldots, a_{z+1}\}} \sum_{(a_{i_z}, \ldots, a_{i_1}) \in perm((a_1, \ldots, a_{z+1}) \setminus a_j)} \frac{1}{a_{i_1} + \cdots + a_{i_z}} \times \cdots \times \frac{1}{a_{i_1}} \quad \text{(by permutation algebra)}$$

$$= \frac{1}{a_1 + \cdots + a_{z+1}} \sum_{a_j \in \{a_1, \ldots, a_{z+1}\}} T((a_1, \ldots, a_{z+1}) \setminus a_j) \quad \text{(by definition of } T\text{)}$$

$$= \frac{1}{a_1 + \cdots + a_{z+1}} \sum_{j=1}^{z+1} \frac{1}{a_1 \ldots a_{j-1} \cdot a_{j+1} \ldots a_{z+1}} \quad \text{(by induction hypothesis)}$$

$$= \frac{1}{a_1 + \cdots + a_{z+1}} \sum_{j=1}^{z+1} \frac{a_j}{a_1 \ldots a_{z+1}} = \frac{1}{a_1 + \cdots + a_{z+1}} \frac{1}{a_1 \ldots a_{z+1}} (a_1 + \cdots + a_{z+1}) \quad \text{(by arithmetic)}$$

$$= \frac{1}{a_1 \ldots a_{z+1}} \quad \text{(by cancellation of factors)}.$$

$\therefore Prop(z+1)$ holds (by definition of $Prop(z+1)$).

$\therefore \forall z \in \mathbb{N}^+ \ (Prop(z) \Longrightarrow Prop(z+1)) \quad (\because z$ is arbitrary). $\qquad \Diamond$

$\therefore \forall z \in \mathbb{N}^+ \ (T(a_1, \ldots, a_z) = \frac{1}{a_1 \ldots a_z})$ (by induction). $\qquad \Diamond$

**Theorem 7.** *Let* $pacnet = (\text{N4}, cmodel_{ic}(\text{N4}), w)$ *be the probabilistic acyclic net with interleaving concurrency model* $cmodel_{ic}(\text{N4})$ *based on the confusion-free net shown in Fig. 9. Let* $E \triangleq \bigcup_{j \in [1..z]} E_j$.

$\forall z \in \mathbb{N}^+ \ \forall j \in [1..z] \ (e_j \in E_j) \ \wedge$

$S = \{\mu \mid \mu \in cmodel_{ic}(\text{N4}) \ \wedge \ \bigcup mixsseqsteps(\mu) = \{e_1, \ldots, e_z\}\}$

$\Longrightarrow \sum_{\mu \in S} p(\mu) = p_{\text{STD}}(M_{\text{N4}}^{init}, \{e_1, \ldots, e_z\}).$

*Proof.*

For $z \in \mathbb{N}^+$, let $\forall j \in [1..z] \ (a_j \triangleq \sum_{e \in E_j} w(e))$.

Let $perm(e_1, \ldots, e_z)$, $perm(E_1, \ldots, E_z)$, and $perm(a_1, \ldots, a_z)$ denote respectively the sets of permutations of $(e_1, \ldots, e_z)$, $(E_1, \ldots, E_z)$, and $(a_1, \ldots, a_z)$ indexed by $i \in [1..|z|!]$ where

$\forall i \in [1..|z|!] \ \forall k \in [1..z]$

$((e_{i_z}, \ldots, e_{i_k}, \ldots, e_{i_1}) \in perm(e_1, \ldots, e_z) \ \wedge$

$(E_{i_z}, \ldots, E_{i_k}, \ldots, E_{i_1}) \in perm(E_1, \ldots, E_z) \ \wedge$

$(a_{i_z}, \ldots, a_{i_k}, \ldots, a_{i_1}) \in perm(a_1, \ldots, a_z) \ \wedge \ e_{i_k} \in E_{i_k} \ \wedge \ a_{i_k} = \sum_{e \in E_{i_k}} w(e)).$

$\sum_{\mu \in S} p(\mu) = \sum_{\mu \in S} p(\sigma^\mu)$ (by Definition 11)

$$= \sum_{\substack{(e_{i_z}, \ldots, e_{i_1}) \\ \in perm(e_1, \ldots, e_z)}} \frac{w(e_{i_z})}{\sum_{e \in E} w(e)} \times \frac{w(e_{i_{z-1}})}{\sum_{E \setminus E_{i_z}} w(e)} \times \cdots \times \frac{w(e_{i_1})}{\sum_{e \in E_{i_1}} w(e)} \quad \text{(by definitions of } \mu \text{ and } p(\sigma^\mu))$$

$$= w(e_1) \ldots w(e_z) \sum_{\substack{(a_{i_z}, \ldots, a_{i_1}) \\ \in perm(a_1, \ldots, a_z)}} \frac{1}{a_{i_1} + \cdots + a_{i_z}} \times \frac{1}{a_{i_1} + \cdots + a_{i_{z-1}}} \times \cdots \times \frac{1}{a_{i_1}}$$

(by definitions of $a_{i_k}$ and $(e_{i_z}, \ldots, e_{i_1})$, commutativity of $\times$, and factorization)

$= w(e_1) \ldots w(e_z) \cdot \frac{1}{a_1 \ldots a_z}$ (by Lemma 4)

$$= \prod_{j=1}^{z} \frac{w(e_j)}{\sum_{e \in E_j} w(e)} \quad \text{(by definition of } a_j)$$

$= p_{\text{STD}}(M_{\text{N4}}^{init}, \{e_1, \ldots, e_z\})$

(by definition of $p_{\text{STD}}(M_{\text{N4}}^{init}, \{e_1, \ldots, e_z\})$, and $z$ is arbitrary). $\qquad \Diamond$

## 5    Concluding Remarks and Future Work

This paper has presented a solution to the issue of how to compute probabilities in nets with confusion. A confusion-tolerant framework has been developed based on execution traces (mixed step sequences) in a concurrency model of an acyclic net. A novel formula has been defined to compute the Bayesian probability of a step consisting of concurrent weighted events, which is used to calculate the probability of a trace in a concurrency model of a net. The probabilities of maximal traces are used to define the probabilities of the markings, steps, and nodes of the net. We have proved our framework satisfies generic probability requirements, and therefore can be used to calculate valid probabilities in nets with and without confusion. We have also proved that our formula for computing trace probability simplifies to the standard probability formula for independent concurrent events in the maximal and interleaving concurrency models of confusion-free well-formed disjoint simple sequential acyclic nets with choice.

Future work will continue development of the theory and its support tool. The framework will be extended to include structured acyclic nets with communicating subnets and subnets at different levels of abstraction. Theorems 6 and 7 will be generalized to be applicable to a wider class of confusion-free nets and to concurrency models other than maximal and interleaving concurrency. The basis for allocating weights to events will be investigated further. The theoretical developments will be implemented in the SONcraft tool.

**Acknowledgements.** This research has been partly funded by the EPSRC IAA – Complex Scenarios project. The authors acknowledge with thanks our discussions with other members of the SON Group at the School of Computing, especially with Brian Randell, whose insistence on explaining the formal framework through clear writing, examples, and diagrams definitely improved the readability of the paper. The authors also thank the reviewers for their helpful comments and suggestions.

## Appendix

**Theorem 2.** *For any probabilistic acyclic net*
*pacnet = (acnet, cmodel, w) the following hold:*

1.  $\bigcup\{\mathrm{mixsseqmarkings}(\mu') \mid \mu' \in cmodel \setminus S_{max}^{cmodel}\}$
    $\subset \bigcup\{\mathrm{mixsseqmarkings}(\mu) \mid \mu \in S_{max}^{cmodel}\}$
2.  $\bigcup\{\mathrm{mixsseqsteps}(\mu') \mid \mu' \in cmodel \setminus S_{max}^{cmodel}\}$
    $\subseteq \bigcup\{\mathrm{mixsseqsteps}(\mu) \mid \mu \in S_{max}^{cmodel}\}$

*Proof of Item 1.*
$cmodel \setminus S_{max}^{cmodel} = prfx(S_{max}^{cmodel})$ (by Theorem 1)
$\implies \bigcup\{\mathrm{mixsseqmarkings}(\mu') \mid \mu' \in cmodel \setminus S_{max}^{cmodel}\}$
$= \bigcup\{\mathrm{mixsseqmarkings}(\mu') \mid \exists \mu \in S_{max}^{cmodel} (\mu' < \mu)\}$
(by definition of $prfx(S_{max}^{cmodel})$)
$\implies \bigcup\{\mathrm{mixsseqmarkings}(\mu') \mid \mu' \in cmodel \setminus S_{max}^{cmodel}\}$ (by definition of $\mu' < \mu$).
$\subseteq \bigcup\{\mathrm{mixsseqmarkings}(\mu) \mid \mu \in S_{max}^{cmodel}\}$

To prove strong set inclusion,
let $\mathcal{M}' \triangleq \bigcup\{\text{mixsseqmarkings}(\mu') \mid \mu' \in cmodel \setminus S_{max}^{cmodel}\}$
and let $\mathcal{M} \triangleq \bigcup\{\text{mixsseqmarkings}(\mu) \mid \mu \in S_{max}^{cmodel}\}$.
$\mu \in S_{max}^{cmodel}$
$\implies M_{|\mu|}^{\mu} \in \mathcal{M}$     (by definitions of $\mu$, mixsseqmarkings$(\mu)$, and $\mathcal{M}$)     $\wedge$
$\neg\exists U M\,(\mu U M \in \text{mixsseq}(acnet))$
(by definitions of $S_{max}^{cmodel}$ and maxmixsseq$(acnet)$)
$\implies M_{|\mu|}^{\mu} \in \mathcal{M}' \vee M_{|\mu|}^{\mu} \in \mathcal{M} \setminus \mathcal{M}'$ $(\because \mathcal{M}' \subseteq \mathcal{M})$.
If $M_{|\mu|}^{\mu} \in \mathcal{M}'$ then $\exists \mu' \in cmodel \setminus S_{max}^{cmodel}\,(M_{|\mu|}^{\mu} \in \text{mixsseqmarkings}(\mu'))$
(by definition of $\mathcal{M}'$)
$\implies \exists \mu'' \in S_{max}^{cmodel}\,(\mu' < \mu'')$     (by Lemma 1)
$\implies M_{|\mu|}^{\mu} \in \text{mixsseqmarkings}(\mu'')$
(by definitions of $\mu' < \mu''$ and mixsseqmarkings$(\mu'')$).
Now $M_{|\mu''|}^{\mu''} = M_{|\mu|}^{\mu} \vee M_{|\mu''|}^{\mu''} \neq M_{|\mu|}^{\mu}$     (by first-order logic).
If $M_{|\mu''|}^{\mu''} = M_{|\mu|}^{\mu}$
then $\exists k \in \mathbb{N}\,(k < |\mu''| \wedge M_k^{\mu''} = M_{|\mu|}^{\mu} = M_{|\mu''|}^{\mu''})$
$(\because M_{|\mu|}^{\mu} \in \text{mixsseqmarkings}(\mu') \wedge \mu' < \mu'')$
$\implies acnet$ is not acyclic
(by definition of acyclic; which is a contradiction).
If $M_{|\mu''|}^{\mu''} \neq M_{|\mu|}^{\mu}$ then $\exists U M\,(\mu U M \in \text{mixsseq}(acnet))$
$(\because M_{|\mu|}^{\mu} \in \text{mixsseqmarkings}(\mu''))$; which is a contradiction).
$\therefore M_{|\mu|}^{\mu} \in \mathcal{M} \setminus \mathcal{M}'$ $(\because M_{|\mu|}^{\mu} \notin \mathcal{M}' \wedge M_{|\mu|}^{\mu} \in \mathcal{M} \wedge \mathcal{M}' \subseteq \mathcal{M})$
$\implies \bigcup\{\text{mixsseqmarkings}(\mu') \mid \mu' \in cmodel \setminus S_{max}^{cmodel}\}$
$\subset \bigcup\{\text{mixsseqmarkings}(\mu) \mid \mu \in S_{max}^{cmodel}\}$
(by definitions of $\mathcal{M}'$ and $\mathcal{M}$, and by set theory).     $\diamondsuit$

*Proof of Item 2.*
$cmodel \setminus S_{max}^{cmodel} = \text{prfx}(S_{max}^{cmodel})$     (by Theorem 1)
$\implies \bigcup\{\text{mixsseqsteps}(\mu') \mid \mu' \in cmodel \setminus S_{max}^{cmodel}\}$
$= \bigcup\{\text{mixsseqsteps}(\mu') \mid \exists \mu \in S_{max}^{cmodel}\,(\mu' < \mu)\}$
(by definition of prfx$(S_{max}^{cmodel})$)
$\implies \bigcup\{\text{mixsseqsteps}(\mu') \mid \mu' \in cmodel \setminus S_{max}^{cmodel}\}$
$\subseteq \bigcup\{\text{mixsseqsteps}(\mu) \mid \mu \in S_{max}^{cmodel}\}$ (by definition of $\mu' < \mu$).     $\diamondsuit$

**Theorem 3.** *For any probabilistic acyclic net*
$pacnet = (acnet, cmodel, w)$, $S_{max}^{cmodel} \in \text{maxexclusivetracesset}(cmodel)$.

*Proof.* $S_{max}^{cmodel} \in \text{maxexclusivetracesset}(cmodel)$
$\Longleftrightarrow S_{max}^{cmodel} \in \text{exclusivetracesset}(cmodel) \wedge$
$\quad \forall \mu \in cmodel \setminus S_{max}^{cmodel}\,(S_{max}^{cmodel} \cup \{\mu\} \notin \text{exclusivetracesset}(cmodel))$
(by definition of maxexclusivetracesset$(cmodel)$).
Proof of $S_{max}^{cmodel} \in \text{exclusivetracesset}(cmodel)$.
If $S_{max}^{cmodel} \notin \text{exclusivetracesset}(cmodel)$ then $\exists \mu, \mu' \in S_{max}^{cmodel}\,(\mu < \mu')$
(by definition of exclusivetracesset$(cmodel)$)

$\implies \mu \in prfx(S_{max}^{cmodel})$ (by definitions of $prfx(\mu')$ and $prfx(S_{max}^{cmodel})$)
$\implies \mu \notin S_{max}^{cmodel}$ (by Theorem 1; which is a contradiction).
$\therefore S_{max}^{cmodel} \in$ exclusivetracesset($cmodel$).
Proof of $\forall \mu \in cmodel \setminus S_{max}^{cmodel}$
$\qquad\qquad (S_{max}^{cmodel} \cup \{\mu\} \notin$ exclusivetracesset($cmodel$)).
$\mu \in cmodel \setminus S_{max}^{cmodel}$
$\implies \exists \mu' \in S_{max}^{cmodel} (\mu < \mu')$ (by Lemma 1)
$\implies S_{max}^{cmodel} \cup \{\mu\} \notin$ exclusivetracesset($cmodel$)
(by definition of exclusivetracesset($cmodel$))
$\implies \forall \mu \in cmodel \setminus S_{max}^{cmodel} (S_{max}^{cmodel} \cup \{\mu\} \notin$ exclusivetracesset($cmodel$))
($\because \mu \in cmodel \setminus S_{max}^{cmodel}$ is arbitrary).
$\therefore S_{max}^{cmodel} \in$ maxexclusivetracesset($cmodel$)
($\because S_{max}^{cmodel} \in$ exclusivetracesset($cmodel$)).          $\Diamond$

**Lemma 2.** *For any probabilistic acyclic net* $pacnet = (acnet, cmodel, w)$,
$\forall S \in$ maxexclusivetracesset($cmodel$) $\forall n \in [0..maxlen(S)]$
($Trunc(S, n) \in$ maxexclusivetracesset($cmodel$)).

*Proof.* Let $pacnet = (acnet, cmodel, w)$ be a probabilistic acyclic net, and let $S \in$ maxexclusivetracesset($cmodel$) be a maximum exclusive set of execution traces in $cmodel$.
Backward induction is used on the length $n$ of traces in $S$ and of their prefix traces.
For $n \in [0..maxlen(S)]$, let $Prop(n)$ be the proposition
$Trunc(S, n) \in$ maxexclusivetracesset($cmodel$).

Base Case: Proof of $Prop(maxlen(S))$.
$Trunc(S, maxlen(S)) = S$
(by definitions of $Trunc(S, maxlen(S))$ and $maxlen(S)$)
$\implies Trunc(S, maxlen(S)) \in$ maxexclusivetracesset($cmodel$)
(by definition of $S$).          $\Diamond$

Induction Step:
Proof of $\forall n \in [1..maxlen(S)] (Prop(n) \implies Prop(n-1))$.
For $n \in [1..maxlen(S)]$, assume $Prop(n)$ holds (inductive hypothesis).
$\neg Prop(n-1)$
iff $Trunc(S, n-1) \notin$ maxexclusivetracesset($cmodel$)
(by definition of $Prop(n-1)$)
$\iff Trunc(S, n-1) \notin$ exclusivetracesset($cmodel$) $\vee$
$\exists \mu \in cmodel \setminus Trunc(S, n-1)$
($Trunc(S, n-1) \cup \{\mu\} \in$ exclusivetracesset($cmodel$))
(by definition of maxexclusivetracesset($cmodel$)).
If $Trunc(S, n-1) \notin$ exclusivetracesset($cmodel$)
then $\exists \mu, \mu' \in Trunc(S, n-1) (\mu < \mu')$
(by definition of exclusivetracesset($cmodel$),
and because $Trunc(S, n-1) \neq \emptyset$)
$\implies \mu \in Trunc(S, n) \wedge \exists \mu'' \in Trunc(S, n) (\mu < \mu'')$

$(\because |\mu| < n - 1$, and by definitions of $\mu < \mu'$, $Trunc(S, n-1)$, and $Trunc(S, n)$, and (if relevant) by transitivity of $<$)

$\implies Trunc(S, n) \notin$ exclusivetracesset($cmodel$)

(by definition of exclusivetracesset($cmodel$))

$\implies Trunc(S, n) \notin$ maxexclusivetracesset($cmodel$)

(by definition of maxexclusivetracesset($cmodel$); which contradicts the inductive hypothesis).

$\therefore Trunc(S, n-1) \in$ exclusivetracesset($cmodel$).

If $\exists \mu \in cmodel \setminus Trunc(S, n-1)$

$\quad (Trunc(S, n-1) \cup \{\mu\} \in$ exclusivetracesset($cmodel$))

then $\forall \mu' \in Trunc(S, n-1) \, (\mu \not< \mu' \land \mu' \not< \mu)$

(by definition of exclusivetracesset($cmodel$))

$\implies \forall \mu'' \in Trunc(S, n) \, (\mu \not< \mu'' \land \mu'' \not< \mu) \, \land \, \mu \notin Trunc(S, n)$

(by definitions of $\mu$, $<$, $Trunc(S, n-1)$, and $Trunc(S, n)$)

$\implies \mu \in cmodel \setminus Trunc(S, n)$

$\qquad (Trunc(S, n) \cup \{\mu\} \in$ exclusivetracesset($cmodel$))

(by $Prop(n)$ and definitions of $\mu$ and exclusivetracesset($cmodel$))

$\implies Trunc(S, n) \notin$ maxexclusivetracesset($cmodel$)

(by definition of maxexclusivetracesset($cmodel$); which contradicts the inductive hypothesis).

$\therefore \forall \mu \in cmodel \setminus Trunc(S, n-1)$

$\quad (Trunc(S, n-1) \cup \{\mu\} \notin$ exclusivetracesset($cmodel$)).

$\therefore Trunc(S, n-1) \in$ maxexclusivetracesset($cmodel$)

$(\because Trunc(S, n-1) \in$ exclusivetracesset($cmodel$)).

$\therefore Prop(n-1)$ holds   (by first-order logic).

$\therefore \forall n \in [1..maxlen(S)] \, (Prop(n) \implies Prop(n-1))$   $(\because n$ is arbitrary).          $\diamond$

$\therefore \forall n \in [0..maxlen(S)] \, (Prop(n))$ holds   (by backward induction).

$\therefore \forall S \in$ maxexclusivetracesset($cmodel$) $\forall n \in [0..maxlen(S)]$

$(Trunc(S, n) \in$ maxexclusivetracesset($cmodel$))

(by definition of $Prop(n)$, and because $pacnet$ and

$S \in$ maxexclusivetracesset($cmodel$) are arbitrary).          $\diamond$

**Lemma 3.** *For any probabilistic acyclic net pacnet* $= (acnet, cmodel, w)$,
$\forall S \in$ *maxexclusivetracesset*($cmodel$) $\setminus \{\{M_{acnet}^{init}\}\} \forall n \in [1..maxlen(S)]$
$(\mu'' \in Trunc(S, n-1) \land \mu''UM \in Trunc(S, n)$
$\quad \implies (\mu''U'M' \in cmodel \implies \mu''U'M' \in Trunc(S, n)))$.

Proof by contradiction.

Let $pacnet = (acnet, cmodel, w)$ be a probabilistic acyclic net,
let $S \in$ maxexclusivetracesset($cmodel$) $\setminus \{\{M_{acnet}^{init}\}\}$ be a maximum exclusive set of execution traces in $cmodel$, and let $n \in [1..maxlen(S)]$.

$\neg(\mu'' \in Trunc(S, n-1) \land \mu''UM \in Trunc(S, n)$

$\qquad \implies (\mu''U'M' \in cmodel \implies \mu''U'M' \in Trunc(S, n)))$

$\implies \mu'' \in Trunc(S, n-1) \land \mu''UM \in Trunc(S, n) \land$

$\qquad \exists U'M' \, (\mu''U'M' \in cmodel \land \mu''U'M' \notin Trunc(S, n))$

$\implies Trunc(S, n) \cup \{\mu''U'M'\} \notin$ exclusivetracesset($cmodel$)

$(\because Trunc(S, n) \in maxexclusivetracesset(cmodel)$ (by Lemma 2))
$\implies \exists \mu \in Trunc(S, n) (\mu < \mu''U'M' \lor \mu''U'M' < \mu)$
$(\because Trunc(S, n) \in exclusivetracesset(cmodel)$
(by definition of $maxexclusivetracesset(cmodel)))$
$\implies \mu < \mu''U'M'$
$(\because |\mu''U'M'| = n$ (by definitions of $\mu''$, $Trunc(S, n-1)$, and $Trunc(S, n))$, and
by definitions of $<$ and $Trunc(S, n))$
$\implies \mu < \mu''UM$ (by definition of $<$)
$\implies Trunc(S, n) \notin exclusivetracesset(cmodel)$
$(\because \mu, \mu''UM \in Trunc(S, n)$, and by definition of $exclusivetracesset(cmodel)$; which
is a contradiction).
$\therefore \forall S \in maxexclusivetracesset(cmodel) \setminus \{\{M_{acnet}^{init}\}\} \forall n \in [1..maxlen(S)]$
$(\mu'' \in Trunc(S, n-1) \land \mu''UM \in Trunc(S, n)$
$\quad \implies (\mu''U'M' \in cmodel \implies \mu''U'M' \in Trunc(S, n)))$
$(\because pacnet, S \in maxexclusivetracesset(cmodel) \setminus \{\{M_{acnet}^{init}\}\}$, and
$n \in [1..maxlen(S)]$ are arbitrary).    $\diamondsuit$

**Theorem 4.** *For any probabilistic acyclic net* $pacnet = (acnet, cmodel, w)$ *the
following hold:*

1. $\forall \mu \in cmodel (p(\mu) \in [0..1])$
2. $\forall S \in maxexclusivetracesset(cmodel) (\sum\limits_{\mu \in S} p(\mu) = 1)$

*Proof.*
Let $pacnet = (acnet, cmodel, w)$ be a probabilistic acyclic net,
and let $\mu = M_{acnet}^{init}U_1^\mu M_1^\mu \ldots U_{|\mu|}^\mu M_{|\mu|}^\mu$ be an execution trace in $cmodel$.

*Proof of Item 1.*
$\mu \in cmodel \implies p(\mu) = \prod\limits_{i=1}^{|\mu|} p(U_i^\mu|\sigma_{i-1})$ (by Definitions 11 and 5).
$|\mu| = 0 \implies p(\mu) = p(M_{acnet}^{init}) = 1$ (by Definition 11).
$|\mu| \geq 1 \implies p(\mu) = p(U_1^\mu)...p(U_{|\mu|}^\mu|\sigma_{|\mu|-1})$ (by definition of $p(\mu)$) $\land$
$p(U_1^\mu), \ldots, p(U_{|\mu|}^\mu|\sigma_{|\mu|-1}) \in [0..1]$ (by definition of $p(U_i^\mu|\sigma_{i-1})$)
$\implies p(\mu) \in [0..1]$ (by arithmetic).
$\therefore$ Item 1 holds $(\because pacnet$ and $\mu \in cmodel$ are arbitrary).    $\diamondsuit$

*Proof of Item 2.*
Let $S \in maxexclusivetracesset(cmodel)$ be a maximum exclusive set of execution
traces in $cmodel$.
Backward induction is used on the length $n$ of traces in $S$ and of their prefix
traces.
For $n \in [0..maxlen(S)]$, let $Prop(n)$ be the proposition
$$\sum\limits_{\mu' \in Trunc(S,n)} p(\mu') = \sum\limits_{\mu \in S} p(\mu)$$

Base Case: Proof of $Prop(maxlen(S))$.
$$\sum\limits_{\mu' \in Trunc(S,n)} p(\mu')$$

$$= \sum_{\mu' \in \{trunc(\mu, maxlen(S)) \mid \mu \in S\}} p(\mu')$$

$(\because n = maxlen(S),$ and by definition of $Trunc(S, maxlen(S)))$

$$= \sum_{\mu \in S} p(\mu)$$

(by definitions of $trunc(\mu, maxlen(S))$ and $maxlen(S)$).                    ◇

Induction Step:

Proof of $\forall n \in [1..maxlen(S)]\,(Prop(n) \Longrightarrow Prop(n-1))$.

For $n \in [1..maxlen(S)]$, assume $Prop(n)$ holds (inductive hypothesis).

$$\sum_{\mu' \in Trunc(S, n)} p(\mu')$$

$$= \sum_{\mu' \in \{trunc(\mu, n) \mid \mu \in S\}} p(\mu') \quad \text{(by definition of } Trunc(S, n))$$

$$= \sum_{\mu' \in \{trunc(\mu, n) \mid \mu \in S \wedge |\mu| < n\}} p(\mu') \quad + \sum_{\mu' \in \{trunc(\mu, n) \mid \mu \in S \wedge |\mu| = n\}} p(\mu') \quad + \sum_{\mu' \in \{trunc(\mu, n) \mid \mu \in S \wedge |\mu| > n\}} p(\mu')$$

(by definition of $trunc(\mu, n)$)

$$= \sum_{\mu'' \in \{trunc(\mu, n-1) \mid \mu \in S \wedge |\mu| \leq n-1\}} p(\mu'') \quad + \sum_{\mu' \in \{trunc(\mu, n) \mid \mu \in S \wedge |\mu| \geq n\}} p(\mu')$$

(by definitions of $trunc(\mu, n-1)$ and $trunc(\mu, n)$).

Now $\forall \mu' \in \{trunc(\mu, n) \mid \mu \in S \wedge |\mu| \geq n\}$

$\exists! \mu'' \in \{trunc(\mu, n-1) \mid \mu \in S \wedge |\mu| > n-1\}\,(\mu' = \mu'' U_n^{\mu'} M_n^{\mu'})$

$\wedge$

$\forall \mu'' \in \{trunc(\mu, n-1) \mid \mu \in S \wedge |\mu| > n-1\}$

$\exists U_n^{\mu'} M_n^{\mu'}\,(\mu'' U_n^{\mu'} M_n^{\mu'} \in \{trunc(\mu, n) \mid \mu \in S \wedge |\mu| \geq n\})$

(by definitions of $trunc(\mu, n)$, $trunc(\mu, n-1)$, and $\mu$)

$$\Longrightarrow \sum_{\mu' \in \{trunc(\mu, n) \mid \mu \in S \wedge |\mu| \geq n\}} p(\mu')$$

$$= \sum_{\mu'', \mu'} p(\mu'' U_n^{\mu'} M_n^{\mu'})$$

where

$\mu'' \in \{trunc(\mu, n-1) \mid \mu \in S \wedge |\mu| > n-1\} \wedge$

$\mu' \in \{trunc(\mu, n) \mid \mu \in S \wedge |\mu| \geq n\} \wedge$

$\mu' = \mu'' U_n^{\mu'} M_n^{\mu'}$

(by substitution)

$$= \sum_{\mu'', \mu'} p(\mu'')\, p(U_n^{\mu'} \mid \sigma_{n-1}^{\mu''})$$

where

$\mu'' \in \{trunc(\mu, n-1) \mid \mu \in S \wedge |\mu| > n-1\} \wedge$

$\mu' \in \{trunc(\mu, n) \mid \mu \in S \wedge |\mu| \geq n\} \wedge$

$\mu' = \mu'' U_n^{\mu'} M_n^{\mu'} \wedge$

$\sigma_{n-1}^{\mu''}$ is the step sequence of $\mu''$

(by Definition 11 and arithmetic)

$$= \sum_{\mu'' \in \{trunc(\mu, n-1) \mid \mu \in S \wedge |\mu| > n-1\}} p(\mu'') \left( \sum_{d=1}^{|altsteps(\mu'')|} \frac{\prod_{e \in U_{n,d}} w(e)}{\sum_{d=1}^{|altsteps(\mu'')|} \prod_{e \in U_{n,d}} w(e)} \right)$$

where
$$\forall \mu'' \in \{trunc(\mu, n-1) \mid \mu \in S \wedge |\mu| > n-1\}$$
$$(altsteps(\mu'') \triangleq \{U \mid \mu'' U M \in cmodel\} \wedge$$
$$\forall d \in [1..|altsteps(\mu'')|] (U_{n,d} \in altsteps(\mu'')))$$
(by Lemma 3, Definition 11, and factorization using $p(\mu'')$)

$$= \sum_{\mu'' \in \{trunc(\mu, n-1) \mid \mu \in S \wedge |\mu| > n-1\}} p(\mu'') \quad \frac{1}{\sum_{d=1}^{|altsteps(\mu'')|} \prod_{e \in U_{n,d}} w(e)} \sum_{d=1}^{|altsteps(\mu'')|} \prod_{e \in U_{n,d}} w(e)$$

(by factorization)

$$= \sum_{\mu'' \in \{trunc(\mu, n-1) \mid \mu \in S \wedge |\mu| > n-1\}} p(\mu'') \quad \text{(by cancellation of factors).}$$

$$\therefore \sum_{\mu'' \in \{trunc(\mu, n-1) \mid \mu \in S \wedge |\mu| \le n-1\}} p(\mu'') \quad + \quad \sum_{\mu' \in \{trunc(\mu, n) \mid \mu \in S \wedge |\mu| \ge n\}} p(\mu')$$

$$= \sum_{\mu'' \in \{trunc(\mu, n-1) \mid \mu \in S \wedge |\mu| \le n-1\}} p(\mu'') \quad + \quad \sum_{\mu'' \in \{trunc(\mu, n-1) \mid \mu \in S \wedge |\mu| > n-1\}} p(\mu'') \quad \text{(by substitution)}$$

$$= \sum_{\mu'' \in \{trunc(\mu, n-1) \mid \mu \in S\}} p(\mu'') \quad \text{(by definition of } trunc(\mu, n-1))$$

$$= \sum_{\mu'' \in Trunc(S, n-1)} p(\mu'') \quad \text{(by definition of } Trunc(S, n-1))$$

$$\implies \sum_{\mu' \in Trunc(S, n)} p(\mu') \quad = \quad \sum_{\mu'' \in Trunc(S, n-1)} p(\mu'') \quad \text{(by substitution)}$$

$$\implies \sum_{\mu'' \in Trunc(S, n-1)} p(\mu'') \quad = \quad \sum_{\mu \in S} p(\mu) \quad \text{(by inductive hypothesis } Prop(n)).$$

$\therefore Prop(n-1)$ holds  (by definition of $Prop(n-1)$).
$\therefore \forall n \in [1..maxlen(S)] (Prop(n) \implies Prop(n-1))$  ($\because n$ is arbitrary).    $\diamondsuit$

$\therefore \forall n \in [0..maxlen(S)] (Prop(n))$ holds  (by backward induction)
$$\implies \sum_{\mu' \in Trunc(S,0)} p(\mu') \quad = \quad \sum_{\mu \in S} p(\mu) \quad \text{(by } Prop(0))$$
$$\implies \sum_{\mu \in S} p(\mu) = p(M_{acnet}^{init}) \quad \text{(by definitions of } Trunc(S,0) \text{ and } trunc(\mu,0))$$
$$\implies \sum_{\mu \in S} p(\mu) = 1 \quad (\because p(M_{acnet}^{init}) = 1 \text{ (by Definition 11)}).$$
$\therefore$ Item 2 holds
($\because$ pacnet and $S \in$ maxexclusivetracesset($cmodel$) are arbitrary).    $\diamondsuit$

**Theorem 5.** *For any probabilistic acyclic net pacnet* $= (acnet, cmodel, w)$ *the following hold:*

1. $\forall M \in cmmarkings(cmodel) (p(M) \in [0..1])$
2. $\forall \mathcal{M} \in maxexclusivemarkingsset(cmodel) (\sum_{M \in \mathcal{M}} p(M) = 1)$
3. $\forall U \in cmsteps(cmodel) (p(U) \in [0..1])$
4. $\forall \mathcal{U} \in maxexclusivestepsset(cmodel) (\sum_{U \in \mathcal{U}} p(U) = 1)$

*Proof of Item 1.*
$M \in cmmarkings(cmodel) \wedge$
$S_M = \{\mu \mid \mu \in S_{max}^{cmodel} \wedge M \in mixsseqmarkings(\mu)\}$
$\implies \forall \mu \in S_M (p(\mu) \in [0..1])$ (by definition of $S_{max}^{cmodel}$ and Theorem 4.1)
$\implies 0 \le \sum_{\mu \in S_M} p(\mu)$ (by arithmetic) $\wedge$

$$\sum_{\mu \in S_M} p(\mu) \leq 1 \quad (\because S_M \subseteq S_{max}^{cmodel} \text{ (by definition of } S_M)$$

and $S_{max}^{cmodel} \in \text{maxexclusivetracesset}(cmodel)$ (by Theorem 3),
and by Theorem 4.2 and arithmetic)
$\Longleftrightarrow p(M) \in [0..1]$  (by definition of marking probability)
$\Longrightarrow \forall M \in cmmarkings(cmodel) \, (p(M) \in [0..1])$
$(\because M \in cmmarkings(cmodel)$ is arbitrary).                    $\diamond$

*Proof of Item 2.*
Let $\mathcal{M} \in \text{maxexclusivemarkingsset}(cmodel)$
and $\forall M \in \mathcal{M} \, (S_M = \{\mu \mid \mu \in S_{max}^{cmodel} \wedge M \in \text{mixsseqmarkings}(\mu)\})$.
$\forall M \in \mathcal{M} \, (S_M \subseteq S_{max}^{cmodel} \wedge S_M = markingtraces(M, S_{max}^{cmodel}))$
(by definitions of $S_M$ and $markingtraces(M, S_{max}^{cmodel})$)
$\Longrightarrow \bigcup_{M \in \mathcal{M}} S_M = S_{max}^{cmodel} \wedge$
   $\forall M, M' \in \mathcal{M} \, (M \neq M' \Longrightarrow S_M \cap S_{M'} = \emptyset)$(by definition of $\mathcal{M}$)
$\Longrightarrow \sum_{M \in \mathcal{M}} \sum_{\mu \in S_M} p(\mu) = \sum_{\mu \in S_{max}^{cmodel}} p(\mu)$  (by set theory)
$\Longrightarrow \sum_{M \in \mathcal{M}} p(M) = 1$
(by definition of marking probability, Theorem 3, and Theorem 4.2)
$\Longrightarrow \forall \mathcal{M} \in \text{maxexclusivemarkingsset}(cmodel) \, (\sum_{M \in \mathcal{M}} p(M) = 1)$
$(\because \mathcal{M} \in \text{maxexclusivemarkingsset}(cmodel)$ is arbitrary).      $\diamond$

*Proof of Item 3.*
$U \in cmsteps(cmodel) \wedge$
$S_U = \{\mu \mid \mu \in S_{max}^{cmodel} \wedge U \in \text{mixsseqsteps}(\mu)\}$
$\Longrightarrow \forall \mu \in S_U \, (p(\mu) \in [0..1])$ (by definition of $S_{max}^{cmodel}$ and Theorem 4.1)
$\Longrightarrow 0 \leq \sum_{\mu \in S_U} p(\mu)$  (by arithmetic)  $\wedge$
   $\sum_{\mu \in S_U} p(\mu) \leq 1 \quad (\because S_U \subseteq S_{max}^{cmodel} \text{ (by definition of } S_U)$
and $S_{max}^{cmodel} \in \text{maxexclusivetracesset}(cmodel)$ (by Theorem 3),
and by Theorem 4.2 and arithmetic)
$\Longleftrightarrow p(U) \in [0..1]$  (by definition of step probability)
$\Longrightarrow \forall U \in cmsteps(cmodel) \, (p(U) \in [0..1])$
$(\because U \in cmsteps(cmodel)$ is arbitrary).                    $\diamond$

*Proof of Item 4.*
Let $\mathcal{U} \in \text{maxexclusivestepsset}(cmodel)$
and $\forall U \in \mathcal{U} \, (S_U = \{\mu \mid \mu \in S_{max}^{cmodel} \wedge U \in \text{mixsseqsteps}(\mu)\})$.
$\forall U \in \mathcal{U} \, (S_U \subseteq S_{max}^{cmodel} \wedge S_U = steptraces(U, S_{max}^{cmodel}))$
(by definitions of $S_U$ and $steptraces(U, S_{max}^{cmodel})$)
$\Longrightarrow \bigcup_{U \in \mathcal{U}} S_U = S_{max}^{cmodel} \wedge$
   $\forall U, U' \in \mathcal{U} \, (U \neq U' \Longrightarrow S_U \cap S_{U'} = \emptyset)$  (by definition of $\mathcal{U}$)
$\Longrightarrow \sum_{U \in \mathcal{U}} \sum_{\mu \in S_U} p(\mu) = \sum_{\mu \in S_{max}^{cmodel}} p(\mu)$  (by set theory)

$$\implies \sum_{U \in \mathcal{U}} p(U) = 1$$

(by definition of step probability, Theorem 3, and Theorem 4.2)

$$\implies \forall \mathcal{U} \in \text{maxexclusivestepsset}(cmodel) \ (\sum_{U \in \mathcal{U}} p(U) = 1)$$

($\because \mathcal{U} \in \text{maxexclusivestepsset}(cmodel)$ is arbitrary).                    $\Diamond$

# References

1. Abbes, S., Benveniste, A.: True-concurrency probabilistic models branching cells and distributed probabilities for event structures. Inf. Comput. **204**(2), 231–274 (2006)
2. Bhattacharyya, A., Li, B., Randell, B.: Time in structured occurrence nets. In: Proceedings of the International Workshop on Petri Nets and Software Engineering (PNSE 2016), pp. 35–55 (2016)
3. Bruni, R., Melgratti, H., Montanari, U.: Concurrency and probability: removing confusion, compositionally. In Proceedings of the 33rd Annual ACM/IEEE Symposium on Logic in Computer Science (LICS), pp. 195–204 (2018)
4. Burke, A., Leemans, S.J.J., Wynn, M.T.: Discovering stochastic process models by reduction and abstraction. In Proceedings of the 42nd International Conference on Applications and Theory of Petri Nets and Concurrency (PETRI NETS 2021), pp. 312–336 (2021)
5. Desel, J., Esparza, J.: Free Choice Petri Nets. Cambridge University Press (1995)
6. Feller, W.: An Introduction to Probability Theory and Its Applications, 3rd ed., vol. 1. Wiley (1968)
7. Haas, P.J.: Stochastic Petri Nets. SSOR, Springer, New York (2002). https://doi.org/10.1007/b97265
8. Karp, R.M.: Reducibility among combinatorial problems. In: Miller, R.E., Thatcher, J.W., Bohlinger, J.D. (eds.) Complexity of Computer Computations. The IBM Research Symposia Series, pp. 85–103. Springer, Boston, MA (1972). https://doi.org/10.1007/978-1-4684-2001-2_9
9. Katoen, J.-P., Peled, D.: Taming confusion for modeling and implementing probabilistic concurrent systems. In: Felleisen, M., Gardner, P. (eds.) ESOP 2013. LNCS, vol. 7792, pp. 411–430. Springer, Heidelberg (2013). https://doi.org/10.1007/978-3-642-37036-6_23
10. Koutny, M., Randell, B.: Structured occurrence nets: a formalism for aiding system failure prevention and analysis techniques. Fund. Inform. **97**(1–2), 41–91 (2009)
11. Kudlek, M.: Probability in Petri nets. Fund. Inform. **67**(1–3), 121–130 (2005)
12. Kwiatkowska, M., Norman, G., Parker, D., Santos, G.: PRISM-games 3.0: stochastic game verification with concurrency, equilibria and time. In: Lahiri, S.K., Wang, C. (eds.) CAV 2020. LNCS, vol. 12225, pp. 475–487. Springer, Cham (2020). https://doi.org/10.1007/978-3-030-53291-8_25
13. Li, B., Randell, B., Bhattacharyya, A., Alharbi, T., Koutny, M.: SONCraft: a tool for construction, simulation, and analysis of structured occurrence nets. In: Proceedings of the 18th International Conference on Application of Concurrency to System Design (ACSD 2018), pp. 70–74 (2018)
14. Marsan, M.A., Balbo, G., Chiola, G., Conte, G.: Generalized stochastic Petri nets revisited: random switches and priorities. In: Proceedings of the International Workshop on Petri Nets and Performance Models (PNPM 1987), pp. 44–53 (1987)

15. Varacca, D., Völzer, H., Winskel, G.: Probabilistic event structures and domains. Theoret. Comput. Sci. **358**(2–3), 173–199 (2006)
16. von der Linden, W., Dose, V., von Toussaint, U.: Bayesian Probability Theory: Applications in the Physical Sciences. Cambridge University Press (2014)

# An Efficient State Space Construction for a Class of Timed Automata

Johan Arcile[1]([✉]), Raymond Devillers[2], and Hanna Klaudel[3]

[1] LORIA, Campus Scientifique, BP 239, 54506 Vandoeuvre-lès-Nancy, France
arcile.johan@gmail.com
[2] ULB, Bruxelles, Belgium
rdevil@ulb.ac.be
[3] IBISC, Univ Evry, Université Paris-Saclay, 91025 Evry, France
hanna.klaudel@univ-evry.fr

**Abstract.** In this paper we propose a timed abstraction, called acceleration, for the analysis of NCTAs, a class of networks of timed automata tailored to model systems composed out of non-deterministic cyclic agents updating shared variables. The abstraction is based on "maximal action zones", easy to compute on the fly, which generally aggregate regions in a different way than classical zones do. The original and accelerated semantics are shown coherent in the sense that they both lead to the same untimed semantics, and satisfy the same class of positive reachability queries.

**Keywords:** timed automata · model checking · zone graph · abstraction

## 1 Introduction

This work proposes an original abstraction for a timed automata-like class of models, called MAPT [5], tailored for model-checking multi-agent systems composed of periodic communicating autonomous agents using a common memory. As an example, MAPT was successfully used to study the impact of latency and communication delays on the behaviour of communicating autonomous vehicles (CAVs [15]). Compared to state-of-the-art tools such as UPPAAL, it offers three important characteristics: (i) the possibility of handling arbitrarily nested CTL queries, (ii) the possibility to directly compute numerical characteristics of the models, and (iii) the access to classical programming language data types for variables and functions.

In this paper, we first define the class of timed automata corresponding to MAPT, called NCTA for *Network of Cyclic Timed Automata*, and then focus on the timed abstraction (referred to as *accelerated semantics* of MAPT), which was mentioned but not formalized in [5]. We improve and formalize this new abstraction and discuss its differences with conventional methods. The method is based on a concept of *action zones*, defined as maximum time intervals in which

© The Author(s), under exclusive license to Springer-Verlag GmbH, DE, part of Springer Nature 2024
M. Koutny et al. (Eds.): TPNOMCXVII, LNCS 14150, pp. 246–263, 2024.
https://doi.org/10.1007/978-3-662-68191-6_10

the same transitions are enabled from a given vector of locations. Thanks to the specific characteristics of the NCTA, it is possible to compute the *maximal action zones*, which aggregate regions in a different way than what is usually performed by classical zones [14]. We propose then an efficient algorithm allowing to compute the abstracted state space in a straightforward way.

We show that the proposed accelerated semantics supports numerical queries as well as all the *positive reachability* CTL queries (negations may only act on variables, not on temporal expressions). We also show that the original and accelerated semantics are coherent in the sense that they both lead to the same (untimed) abstract semantics. The formalism and tool are not restricted to integer variables as it is usually the case; this may seem anecdotal but it appeared to be crucial in modeling complex systems as it allows a better precision, more comfort and less error prone approximations.

Timed automata were introduced by Alur and Dill in [1] as models describing state spaces where states are uncountable, since the time aspect is measured by real value variables. The authors thus proposed to consider clock regions, an abstraction on clock values allowing to rely on countably many states. However, such an abstraction is not practical for actual model checking tools. In [13], Daws and Tripakis define a number of abstractions for which reachability properties are preserved. The most important one allows for a representation of symbolic states where clock values are relative to each other. The resulting "simulation graph" is the basis of the symbolic semantics used by UPPAAL [7], KRONOS [12], and many others tools. Another important abstraction from [13] is the extrapolation, which allows to cope with diverging clock values. This abstraction, which was thoroughly discussed in [8], is of no use in the context of NCTAs, where clocks never diverge due to syntactic constraints.

*Outline.* In the following, we start in Sect. 2 with the definition of the class of timed automata motivated by our application domains. Section 3 introduces our abstraction and proves its coherence with the original semantics. We also recall other techniques from [5] that may be used together with the accelerated semantics to reduce computation time. Section 4 briefly introduces elements of the query language and the related properties of the accelerated semantics. Then, in Sect. 5, we discuss its efficiency.

## 2   Models

We first define a class of timed automata called NCTA for *Network of Cyclic Timed Automata*, composed of $n$ automata updating a common memory represented here without loss of generality by a unique shared variable $V$. As mentioned above, NCTA are a timed automata version of MAPT [5] designed to model and study multi-agent real time systems comprising agents having a cyclic behaviour, such as autonomous vehicles, mobile robots completing cyclically tasks according to their own objectives, flying drone squadrons, etc.

Each automaton (representing an agent) is associated with a unique local clock and performs actions occurring in some given time intervals. There is no competition between agents in the sense that no agent will ever have to wait for another one's action in order to perform its own actions. That means that if, at some point, agent $A_1$ offers a transition $t_1$ and agent $A_2$ offers a transition $t_2$, neither the execution of $t_1$ disables $t_2$, nor $t_2$ disables $t_1$. However, the order of $t_1$ and $t_2$ may be visible in $V$ if the effects of these transitions on $V$ do not commute.

We may also have a choice between transitions and delays, and in that case the latter may disable some transitions and enable new ones (Fig. 1).

In the following, when considering a directed graph and a node $x$ of it, we shall classically denote by $x^\bullet$ the set of arcs originating from $x$, and by $^\bullet x$ the set of arcs leading to $x$.

**Definition 1 (NCTA).** *Let $V$ be a variable with values in some set $\mathcal{V}$ and $F$ a (finite) set of computable functions from $\mathcal{V}$ to $\mathcal{V}$. An NCTA is a tuple $(\{A_1, \ldots, A_n\}, \mathsf{Init})$ where each $A_i \stackrel{\mathrm{df}}{=} (L_i, C_i, T_i, E_i)$ is a timed automaton, such that*

- *$L_i$ is a set of locations denoted as a list $L_i \stackrel{\mathrm{df}}{=} (l_i^1, \ldots, l_i^{m_i})$, with $m_i > 1$, such that $\forall i \neq j,\ L_i \cap L_j = \emptyset$; $l_i^1$ is the first location, $l_i^{m_i}$ is the last location of $A_i$ and each location $l \in L_i$ is associated with an invariant $\mathrm{inv}(l)$;*
- *$C_i \in \mathbb{R}_{\geq 0}$ is the unique clock of agent $A_i$ (we assume $C_i \neq C_j$ if $i \neq j$, but they may have the same value);*
- *$T_i$ is a finite set of transitions, each of them being of the form $(l, f, G, R, l')$ where $l, l' \in L_i$ are the source and destination locations[1], $f \in F$ is a transformation function, $G \stackrel{\mathrm{df}}{=} [a, b]$ with $a, b \in \mathbb{N}$ and $a \leq b$, denotes the transition guard, i.e., the interval when the transition may occur, and $R \in \{\emptyset, C_i\}$ is the clock reset,*

*and $\mathsf{Init} = ((\mathsf{init}L_1, \cdots, \mathsf{init}L_n), (\mathsf{init}C_1, \cdots, \mathsf{init}C_n), \mathsf{init}_V)$, where $\forall i \in [1, n]$, $\mathsf{init}L_i \in L_i$, $\mathsf{init}C_i \in \mathrm{inv}(\mathsf{init}L_i) \cap \mathbb{N}$ and $\mathsf{init}_V \in \mathcal{V}$, is the initial state of the model.*

*Each agent $A_i$ of an NCTA satisfies the following constraints:*

1. *There is a unique transition $r_i = (l_i^{m_i}, f, [E_i, E_i], C_i, l_i^1)$ resetting clock $C_i$, $E_i \in \mathbb{N} \setminus \{0\}$ being the reset period of automaton $A_i$.*
2. *The other transitions (with no reset) form an acyclic graph and each of them is on a path between $l_i^1$ and $l_i^{m_i}$.*
3. *For each location $l \in L_i \setminus \{l_i^1, l_i^{m_i}\}$,*

$$\max\{b \mid (l', f, [a, b], \emptyset, l) \in {}^\bullet l\} \leq \min\{b' \mid (l, f', [a', b'], \emptyset, l'') \in l^\bullet\}.$$

4. *For $l_i^{m_i}$, $\max\{b \mid (l', f, [a, b], \emptyset, l_i^{m_i}) \in {}^\bullet l_i^{m_i}\} \leq E_i$.*

---

[1] Note that, since $L_i \cap L_j = \emptyset$ when $i \neq j$, $T_i \cap T_j = \emptyset$ too, so that each location or transition belongs to a single agent, avoiding confusions in the model.

5. *For each location $l \in L_i$ its invariant, specifying when one may enter it and must leave it, is* $\mathrm{inv}(l) \stackrel{df}{=} [a_l, b_l]$,

$$b_l = \begin{cases} E_i & \text{if } l = l_i^{m_i} \\ \max\{b \mid (l, f, [a, b], R, l') \in l^\bullet\} & \text{otherwise.} \end{cases}$$

*and*

$$a_l = \begin{cases} 0 & \text{if } l = l_i^1 \\ \min\{a \mid (l', f, [a, b], R, l) \in {}^\bullet l\} & \text{otherwise.} \end{cases}$$

◊

**Example 1** *Let us consider the NCTA with two non-deterministic agents, where*

- $\mathcal{V} = \mathbb{R} \times \mathbb{N}$, $F = \{f_1, f_2, f_3, f_4, f_5, f_6, f_7, id\}$ *with*

$$\begin{aligned} f_1(x, y) &\to (2x, y + 1) & f_2(x, y) &\to (x * 1.3, y) \\ f_3(x, y) &\to (x/2, y) & f_4(x, y) &\to (y - 2x, 2y) \\ id(x, y) &\to (x, y) & f_5(x, y) &= f_6(x, y) = f_7(x, y) \to ((x + y)/2, y + 2) \end{aligned}$$

- $A_1 = \{(L_1, C_1, T_1, E_1) \text{ and } A_2 = (L_2, C_2, T_2, E_2)\}$ *with*

$$L_1 = \{1, 2, 3\} \; T_1 = \begin{cases} t_1 = (1, f_1, [0, 2], \emptyset, 3), t_5 = (1, f_5, [5, 8], \emptyset, 3), \\ t_3 = (1, f_3, [1, 6], \emptyset, 2), t_7 = (2, f_7, [4, 10], \emptyset, 3), \\ r_1 = (3, id, [10, 10], C_1, 1) \end{cases}$$

$$L_2 = \{4, 5, 6\} \; T_2 = \begin{cases} t_4 = (4, f_4, [4, 9], \emptyset, 6), t_2 = (4, f_2, [0, 3], \emptyset, 5), \\ t_6 = (5, f_6, [5, 5], \emptyset, 6), r_2 = (6, id, [10, 10], C_2, 4) \end{cases}$$

- $\mathsf{Init} = ((1, 4), (0, 0), (0.5, 1))$.

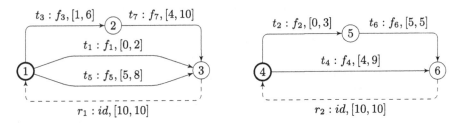

**Fig. 1.** Visual representation of the *NCTA* from Example 1. The reset transitions are represented by dashed arrows and the initial locations by rounds with thick borders.

Intuitively, each agent in the network cycles over a fixed (integer) period. Its unique clock is reset every $E_i$ time units (and never elsewhere). There can be several possible different cycles though, since a given location may be the source of several transitions, so that there may be several paths from $l_i^1$ to $l_i^{m_i}$.

The behaviour of the system is defined as usual as a transition system from the initial state. A state is a tuple $s = (\vec{l}, \vec{c}, v)$ with $\vec{l} = (l_1, \cdots, l_n)$ where $l_i \in L_i$ is the current location of agent $A_i$ $(i = 1, \ldots, n)$, $\vec{c} = (c_1, \cdots, c_n)$ where $c_i \in \mathbb{R}$ is the current value of clock $C_i$, and $v \in V$ is the current value of variable $V$. The state is said valid if, for each $i \in [1, \ldots, n]$, $c_i$ makes the invariant $\mathsf{inv}(l_i)$ true (note that, by definition, the initial state is valid).

In the following $\vec{c'} = \vec{c} + k$ with $k \in \mathbb{R}$ means that $\forall i \in [1, \ldots, n] : c_i' = c_i + k$.

**Definition 2 (Evolution of a NCTA).** *There are three possible kinds of state changes from a valid state $s = (\vec{l}, \vec{c}, v)$, namely a transition firing, a clock reset and a delay:*

- *A transition $(l, f, [a, b], \emptyset, l') \in T_i$ can be fired if $l_i = l$ and $c_i \in [a, b]$, which implies that $\mathsf{inv}(l')$ is true. Then, in the new state, $l_i \leftarrow l'$ and $V \leftarrow f(v)$ (the other components are left unchanged).*
- *The clock reset transition $r_i = (l_i^{m_i}, f, [E_i, E_i], C_i, l_i^1)$ of agent $A_i$ may be fired if $c_i = E_i$. Then, $C_i \leftarrow 0$ and $V \leftarrow f(v)$.*
- *A delay corresponds to a time increase by some $d \in \mathbb{R}_{>0}$ such that, in the "aged" state $s' = (\vec{l}, \vec{c} + d, v)$, with $\forall i \in [1, \ldots, n] : c_i' \in \mathsf{inv}(l_i)$.*

This means that sometimes we must perform a delay, and sometimes we may not wait before performing a transition or a reset. From the properties of NCTA models, the new state is always valid (*i.e.* deadlock is not possible). With respect to a former version [5] of our framework, two extensions are introduced here: resets may update the variable and time delays may be non-integer.

The transition system associated with a NCTA is driven by these state changes, from the initial state. It may be observed that there is a single shared element in such a system: variable $V$ (all the other ones are local to an agent). It is unique but its values may have the form of a vector, and an agent may modify several components of this vector through the functions of $F$ used in its transitions, thus emulating the presence of several shared variables. The values of $V$ are not restricted to the integer domain, but there is only a countable set of values that may be reached: the ones that may be obtained from $\mathsf{init}_V$ by a recursive application of functions from $F$ ($V$ is not modified by the delays). However this domain may be dense inside the reals, for instance. It may be objected that, on a concrete computer, variables are always equivalent to integers up to some factor. However, in the model, discretization leads to numerous renormalizations, some loss of precision, hence less comfort and more opportunities to make mistakes, as experimented in our previous framework VERIFCAR [4].

Time may increase indefinitely, but we shall usually consider a finite horizon, for instance because we are only interested by a portion of road used by vehicles, or because each agent is powered by a battery with a finite capacity (as in [16]).

The constraints on NCTAs ensure that whenever a location is entered, any (and not only some) transition originated from that location will have the possibility to occur in some future. In other words, each transition in $l^\bullet$ is enabled when entering $l$ or will (possibly) be enabled in the future (after possibly some delays in order to reach the lower bound $a$). NCTA semantics when considered in a naive way is prone to a state space explosion phenomena (in fact the state space is continuous). However, as we shall see in Sect. 3, the constraints we assumed allow for an optimised discretisation.

# 3   Accelerated and Untimed Semantics

In this section, we present first the accelerated semantics, which takes advantage of the particular constraints of our class of models, then the untimed one.

## 3.1   Accelerated Semantics

*Action Zones.* First, we may remark that, since we start from integer clock values in Init, and since any reset occurs at integer times, $\forall i, j : c_i \mod 1 = c_j \mod 1$ (*i.e.*, the non integer part is always identical for all clocks). For any $c_i$ et $c'_i$ belonging to the open interval $(\lfloor c_i \rfloor, \lceil c_i \rceil)$, the transitions enabled from state $(\vec{l}, \vec{c}, v)$ and $(\vec{l}, \vec{c'}, v)$ are the same. Hence, it is possible to replace the continuous state space by a discrete one such that each state $(\vec{l}, \vec{c}, v)$ is in one of two types of *regions* depending on the clock vector:

- the region denoted by $(\vec{l}, \vec{c}, v)$ if $\forall i \in [1, \dots, n] : c_i \in \mathbb{N}$ (*i.e.*, if all clocks are integer values) or
- the region denoted by $(\vec{l}, \overrightarrow{(\lfloor c \rfloor, \lceil c \rceil)}, v)$ if $\forall i \in [1, \dots, n] : c_i \notin \mathbb{N}$ belongs to the open interval $(\lfloor c \rfloor, \lceil c \rceil)$ (*i.e.*, if the clocks are not integer).

A delay from a region $(\vec{l}, \vec{c}, v)$ leads to a region $(\vec{l}, \overrightarrow{(\lfloor c \rfloor, \lceil c \rceil)}, v)$ while a delay from $(\vec{l}, \overrightarrow{(\lfloor c \rfloor, \lceil c \rceil)}, v)$ leads to $(\vec{l}, \vec{c} + 1, v)$, and so on, cf. Fig. 2.

Next, we may aggregate successive regions in each location and consider *action zones* (called just zones in the following), defined as maximum time intervals in which the same transitions (including resets) are enabled from a given vector of locations. The zone is left-closed iff this left extremity is the start of the interval of a transition from the considered locations (otherwise we may extend the zone to the left). Similarly the zone is right-closed iff this right extremity is the end of the interval of a transition from the considered locations (otherwise we may extend the zone to the right). A zone may be a single point, in particular, when a transition with interval $[a, a]$ is enabled, like it is the case for reset transitions, the zone has length 0, since before $a$ the corresponding transition is not enabled yet and after $a$ it is no longer enabled. Like for the regions, the action zones available at some location vector form a sequence. Instead of increasing time by a succession of real steps before performing a transition, we can then progress in one step from an action zone to the next one, until we decide to fire a transition (we must do so if no delay is allowed). This will again reduce the size of the transition system.

However, if we consider two states $s_1, s_2$ in such a zone and a (same) transition $t$ from them: $s_1 \xrightarrow{t} s'_1$ and $s_2 \xrightarrow{t} s'_2$, then it may happen that $s'_1$ and $s'_2$ does

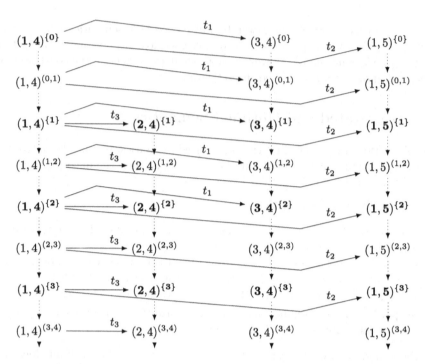

**Fig. 2.** Initial fragment of the graph of the region-based semantics of Ex 1. All (vertical) dotted transitions represent delays. The nodes have the form $\vec{l}^{\,I}$, where $I$ is the total elapsed time (either a singleton $\{k\}$ or an open interval $(k, k + 1)$ of length 1). The variable is omitted here.

not belong to the same action zone (in the new location). In our context however it does not harm because, from constraints 3 and 4 in Definition 1, when we jump into a new location, whatever the starting point in the zone, we shall never lose the possibility to perform a next transition. By progressing in time in the new state, we shall then be allowed to recover all the possible evolutions we want to check (queries do not rely on clocks and the variable do not change when we do not change location).

*Maximal Action Zones.* The previous remark leads to the observation that not all action zones reachable by delays from a given state need to be explored: we may neglect action zones which are *dominated* by connected ones, *i.e.*, for which the set of enabled transitions is included in the previous or next action zone. As an example, let us assume that the sets of enabled transitions are successively (from the current state): $\{t_1, t_2\} \to \{\mathbf{t_1}, \mathbf{t_2}, \mathbf{t_3}\} \to \{t_2, t_3\} \to \{t_3\} \to \{t_3, t_4\} \to \{\mathbf{t_3}, \mathbf{t_4}, \mathbf{t_5}\} \to \{t_4, t_5\} \dots$ (i.e., letting the time evolve, we first encounter $a_3$, then $b_1, b_2, a_4, a_5, b_3, \dots$). The maximal (non-dominated) action zones are indicated in bold. We may thus first jump (in time) to the end of the zone allowing $\{t_1, t_2, t_3\}$ (as we shall see the maximal zones are always closed to the right), then choose if we want to fire $t_1$ or $t_2$ or $t_3$, or jump to the end of the zone allowing $\{t_3, t_4, t_5\}$, where we can again decide to fire a transition or not (unless a firing is mandatory, *i.e.*, there is no further non-dominated action zone). The arcs in the graph of the maximal zones thus will have labels of the form $*$, meaning time passes to reach the end of the next maximal zone (if any), then $t$ to perform transition $t$ to go to a new location, or $t*$ to perform a transition and then let time pass to reach the end of the next maximal zone in the new location.

*Reaching the Next Maximal Action Zone.* In order to detail the analysis, let $s = (\vec{l}, \vec{c}, v)$ be the current state and, for each agent $A_i$ let

$$B_i \stackrel{\mathrm{df}}{=} \max\{b - c_i \mid (l_i, f, [a, b], l') \in l_i^{\bullet}\} \text{ (in particular, } B_i = E_i - c_i \text{ if } l_i = l_i^{m_i})$$
$$B \stackrel{\mathrm{df}}{=} \min\{B_i \mid i \in [1, n]\}$$

If the state is valid, each $B_i$, hence also $B$, is non-negative, and we may not let pass more than $B$ time units before choosing to fire a transition. In particular, if $B = 0$, increasing time would lead to a non-valid state and prevent any transition in some location to ever be enabled again: we must thus choose a transition to fire in this case. Note that, in such a case, we are positioned on one or more ends of enabling intervals, the only action zone from the current state has length 0, it is trivially non-dominated, and is right-closed.

When time evolves, if we reach $a$ (the lower bound of the guard of a transition) or $E$ (the period of a reset) the set of enabled transitions increases and if we overtake $b$ (the upper bound of the guard of a transition), this set shrinks. Note that $E$ plays the role of $a$ as well as $b$, and it cannot be overtaken.

Hence, if we are positioned on one or more ends of enabling intervals, $[0, 0]$ is trivially a (right-closed) non-dominated action zone reachable from the current state and we are positioned on its end.

To guarantee that we are positioned at the end of a maximal action zone, we must find the next $b$ or $E$, i.e., compute

$$\lambda \stackrel{\mathrm{df}}{=} \min\{b - c_i \mid \exists (l_i, f', [a, b], l') \in l_i^{\bullet} \text{ for some agent } A_i\}$$

and perform a time passing of $\lambda$ to reach the end of the current or next (right-closed) maximal action zone.

If we are already positioned at the end of a maximal action zone but instead of performing some transition we would like to go further to the next one (if any), we must thus find the first $b$ or $E$ preceded by at least one $a$. This may be done as follows: let

$$
\mathbf{a} \overset{\text{df}}{=}
\begin{cases}
\min(\alpha) & \text{if } \alpha \overset{\text{df}}{=} \{a - c_i \mid \exists\, (l_i, f, [a, b], l_i') \in T_i \text{ for some agent } A_i \\
& \text{and } c_i < a \le B\} \cup \{E_i - c_i \mid l_i = l_i^{m_i} \text{ for some agent } A_i \\
& \text{and } c_i < E_i \le B\} \neq \emptyset \\
0 & \text{otherwise}
\end{cases}
$$

$$
\delta \overset{\text{df}}{=}
\begin{cases}
\min(\beta) & \text{if } \beta \overset{\text{df}}{=} \{b - c_i \mid \exists\, (l_i, f', [a, b], l') \in l_i^{\bullet} \text{ for some agent } A_i \\
& \text{with } 0 < a \le b - c_i \le B\} \cup \{E_i - c_i \mid l_i = l_i^{m_i} \text{ for some} \\
& \text{agent } A_i \text{ with } E_i \le c_i + B\} \neq \emptyset \\
0 & \text{otherwise}
\end{cases}
$$

It may be observed that $\mathbf{a} > 0 \iff \alpha \neq \emptyset \iff \beta \neq \emptyset \iff \delta > 0$.

If $\mathbf{a} = 0$, there is no way to increase the set of enabled transitions in the future; there is thus no interest to let time evolve (and indeed $\delta = 0$) and we must choose now a transition to be fired (time will possibly be allowed to increase in the new location). Otherwise, we may fire a transition or perform a time jump of $\delta$ time units. Note that when a transition is fired, we need to recompute $B$; when a time shift (or jump) is performed, $\delta > 0$ and we need to adjust all the clocks and $B$: $\forall i : c_i \leftarrow c_i + \delta$ and $B \leftarrow B - \delta$.

We may remark that the initial state as well as the states reached after a firing are not necessarily at the end of a maximal zone. We may then force a time jump $\lambda$ as computed above to reach the end of the first maximal zone before wondering if we shall perform a firing.

Finally, we may observe that, when we perform a firing in some agent $A_i$, we are positioned before $B$, hence before $B_i$ by definition. From constraints 3 and 4 in Definition 1, whatever the time jumps performed in the previous state, the first maximal zone is the same, so that we do not miss a possible firing from the new current state. Note that we could also be positioned exactly on $B$, which would imply that no time jump can be performed from the current state.

*Examples.* Let us consider the example of acceleration illustrated in Fig. 3, with two agents $A_1$ and $A_2$ having aligned clocks $C_1$ and $C_2$ ($c_1 = c_2$), so that the time intervals of the transitions can be represented in the same space. The current state of the system can be described as follows: from the current location of agent $A_1$, the outgoing transitions $t_1$ and $t_2$ can be fired respectively in the intervals $[0, 3]$ and $[1, 5]$, while from the current location of agent $A_2$, the outgoing transitions $t_3$ and $t_4$ (thick interval in Fig. 3 a)) can be fired respectively in $[0, 6]$ and $[2, 4]$. For any transition $t_i$, its lower and upper bounds will be referred to as $a_i$ and $b_i$. Let us assume that we are currently at instant 1. In such a case, the current action zone is $[a_2, a_4)$ and it enables $t_1$, $t_2$ and $t_3$. The next action zone $[a_4, b_1]$ enables all four transitions (and is thus maximal). So, from the current action zone we may fire one of $t_1$, $t_2$ or $t_3$ or let the time pass. The (accelerated) delay should lead then to action zone $[a_4, b_1]$, for instance at $b_1$. That way, we would include all the possible sequences of transitions, including the firing of $t_4$ followed by $t_1$.

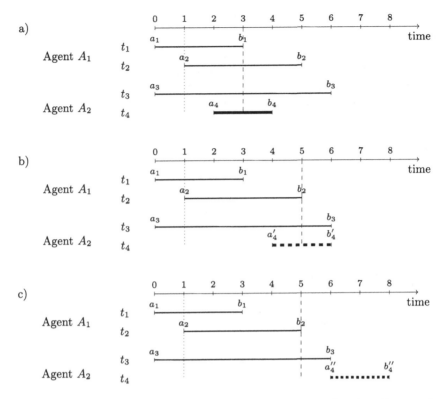

**Fig. 3.** Examples of time increase based on the action zone acceleration. Current time and the maximal possible time increase are indicated by vertical dotted and dashed lines, respectively.

Now let us consider a variant of the example, illustrated in Fig. 3 b), in which $t_4$ is replaced by $t_4'$, with a time interval of $[4, 6]$ (dashed in the figure). In that scenario, the current action zone is $[a_2, b_1]$ and it enables $t_1$, $t_2$ and $t_3$. The next zone is $(b_1, a4')$, which enables $t2$ and $t3$ only: since the enabled transitions are included in the current action zone, this zone is not interesting from a causality point of view. Finally, the zone $[a_4', b_2]$ enables $t_2$, $t_3$ and $t_4$, which is interesting because a new transition becomes enabled and the next delay should lead to the end of this zone. Hence, this state allows four possible actions: the firing of $t_1$, $t_2$ or $t_3$, or a time increase up to $b_2$.

Finally, let us consider another variant, in which $t_4$ is replaced by $t_4''$, with a time interval of $[6, 8]$ (dotted in the figure). In that scenario, the current action zone is still $[a_2, b_1]$, which enables $t_1$, $t_2$ and $t_3$. The next action zone $(b_1, b_2]$ enables $t2$ and $t3$ only. As before, the enabled transitions are included in the current action zone, which means that going to this zone is irrelevant. However, it is not possible to go further ahead since we reached $B$ (corresponding here to $b_2$). We must thus choose a transition to fire in the current zone. Transition $t_4''$

is presently not enabled; it may become enabled in the future however, after (at least) $t_1$ or $t_2$ is fired.

Note finally an interesting (but expected) feature of the accelerated semantics: if we change the granularity of the time and multiply all the timing constants by some factor, the size of the graph of time regions is inflated accordingly. On the contrary, the size (and structure) of the accelerated semantics remains the same.

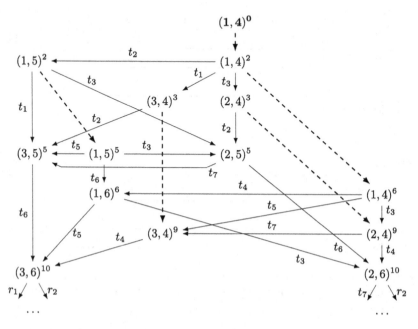

**Fig. 4.** Initial fragment of the graph of the accelerated semantics for the NCTA from Ex 1 (variable values are omitted). Unlabeled dashed arcs represent delays; labelled arcs represent a transition, possibly followed by a delay; nodes are of the form $\vec{l}^n$, where $n$ is the time elapsed since the start. For instance, initially, in location $(1,4)$, the ends of maximal zones occur after 2 time units (enabling $t_1, t_2, t_3$) and 6 time units (enabling $t_3, t_4, t_5$).

*Accelerated Semantics.* A formal definition of the accelerated semantics of an NCTA is then as follows.

**Definition 3 (Accelerated semantics of a NCTA).** *Let* $\lambda(\vec{l}, \vec{c})$ *be the value of* $\lambda$ *and* $\delta(\vec{l}, \vec{c})$ *the value of* $\delta$ *obtained from* $\vec{l}$ *and* $\vec{c}$, *using the definitions of* $\lambda$ *and* $\delta$. *There are three possible kinds of state changes from a valid state* $s = (\vec{l}, \vec{c}, v)$ *to its successor* $s'$, *namely a transition firing, a clock reset and a delay:*

- *A transition* $(l, f, [a, b], \emptyset, l') \in T_i$ *may be fired if* $l_i = l$ *and* $c_i \in [a, b]$, *which implies that* inv$(l')$ *is true. Then,* $s' = (\vec{l'}, \vec{c} + \lambda((\vec{l'}, \vec{c})), f(v))$ *with* $l_i \leftarrow l' \in \vec{l'}$ *(the other locations are left unchanged).*

- *The clock reset transition $r_i = (l_i^{m_i}, f, [E_i, E_i], C_i, l_i^1)$ of agent $A_i$ may be fired if $c_i = E_i$. Then, $s' = (\vec{l'}, \vec{c} + \lambda((\vec{l'}, \vec{c})), f(v))$ with $l_i \leftarrow l_i^1 \in \vec{l'}$ and $c_i \leftarrow 0 \in \vec{c'}$ (the other locations and clock values are left unchanged).*
- *A delay may be fired if $\delta(\vec{l}, \vec{c}) > 0$. Then, $s' = (\vec{l}, \vec{c} + \delta(\vec{l}, \vec{c}), v)$.*

## 3.2    Untimed Semantics

We are interested now by the causality features of our models, thus omitting all purely timed aspects. To this end, starting from any of the previous semantics, we shall consider the graph whose nodes are the projections of evolutions from the initial state on the set of transitions (including resets). Said differently, if we have a word on the alphabet composed of $+\delta$ (delay, of any size), $t_{i,j}$'s or $r_i$'s (transitions of agent $A_i$) representing a possible evolution of the system up to some point, by dropping all the $+\delta$'s we shall get its projection, and a node of the abstracted (from timing aspects) graph. The (labelled) arcs between those nodes will be defined by the following rule: if $\alpha$ and $\alpha t$ are two nodes, there is an arc labelled $t$ between them. This will define a (usually infinite, but as said earlier we shall often limit it to some finite horizon) labelled tree, untimed unfolding of the semantics (either original or time region-based or accelerated) of the considered system.

The initial node (corresponding to the empty evolution) will be labelled by the projection $(\overrightarrow{\text{init}L}, v)$ of the initial state $(\overrightarrow{\text{init}L}, \overrightarrow{\text{init}C}, v)$. This will automatically (recursively) determine the label of the other nodes: if $(\vec{l}; v)$ is the label of some node and there is an arc labelled $t = (l_i, f, [a, b], R, l_i')$ from it to another node, the latter will be labelled $(\vec{l'}; f(v))$, where $\vec{l'}$ is $\vec{l}$ with $l_i$ replaced by $l_i'$.

As an illustration consider the NCTA of Example 1, where we neglect the values of the variable to simplify a bit the presentation. The initial fragment of the untimed semantics corresponding to the accelerated one in Fig. 4 is represented in Fig. 5, assuming initially the clocks are both equal to 0, $A_1$ is in state 1 and $A_2$ is in state 3.

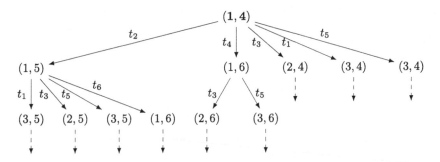

**Fig. 5.** Initial fragment of the corresponding abstract semantic tree. The nodes $\vec{l}$ indicate the reached location (variables are again omitted).

**Proposition 4.** *The original, the region-based and the accelerated semantics of an* NCTA *lead to the same untimed semantics.*

*Proof.* We only have to show that the sets of (untimed) projections of evolutions in each of these semantics are the same.

First, from the definitions, it is clear that the original and the region-based semantics are equivalent since any delay may be composed in a succession of small delays visiting the intermediate regions, and allowing to perform after that exactly the same transitions.

Next, we may observe that each evolution in the accelerated semantics is also an evolution in the original one: we simply restrict delays to the ones allowing to reach the end of the next maximal action zone (if any).

It thus remains to show that, if $\mathsf{word}(\omega)$ is the projection of some evolution $\omega$ of the original semantics, it is also the projection of some evolution $\omega'$ of the accelerated one. We shall proceed by induction on the length of $\omega$ and show more exactly that for each $\omega$ in the original semantics there is an accelerated evolution $\omega'$ such that $\mathsf{word}(\omega') = \mathsf{word}(\omega)$ and the set of enabled transitions after $\omega$ is included in the one after $\omega'$.

The property is trivially satisfied initially, when $\omega = \omega' = \varepsilon$, but also if the initial state is not at the end of a maximal zone and we choose the accelerated strategy only visiting the ends of maximal zones. Indeed, we know by definition that initially, either we are in a maximal zone but not at the end and it is possible to jump to this point while satisfying the inductive hypothesis, or we are not in a maximal zone but there is a succeeding one where we may jump at the end, satisfying again the inductive hypothesis.

We already observed (see the second paragraph in the present section) that, if $\mathsf{word}(\omega) = \mathsf{word}(\omega')$, the location vector and the variable are the same after $\omega$ and $\omega'$. Let $\Delta(\omega)$ be the time elapsed during the evolution described by $\omega$. We may observe that the clocks are determined by $\mathsf{word}(\omega)$ and $\Delta(\omega)$, independently on when the delays exactly occurred: for any agent $A_i$, $c_i = \mathsf{init}C_i + \Delta(\omega) - E_i \cdot \#_{r_i}(\omega)$, where $\#_{r_i}(\omega)$ is the number of resets of $A_i$ in $\mathsf{word}(\omega)$. We also have that we may not have a succession of delays yielding all together more than $\min_i\{E_i\}$ time units, since then we should have a reset occurring before.

We shall now assume that $\widetilde{\omega}$ extends $\omega$ by one event, that $\omega$ and $\omega'$ form an adequate pair, and show that it is then possible to build an adequate accelerated evolution $\widetilde{\omega}'$.

If $\widetilde{\omega} = \omega.\delta$, i.e., if $\widetilde{\omega}$ is obtained from $\omega$ by adding a delay of size $\delta$, the projection of $\widetilde{\omega}$ is the same as the one of $\omega$, hence of $\omega'$ by the induction hypothesis. If the enabled set after $\widetilde{\omega}$ is still included in the one after $\omega'$, the latter still satisfies the induction hypothesis. If the enabled set after $\widetilde{\omega}$ is no longer included in the one after $\omega'$, that means we reached one or more $a$'s which were not reached yet by $\omega'$, so that we may deduce that $\Delta(\omega') < \Delta(\widetilde{\omega})$. But then, going to the end of the next maximal action zone with the aid of one or more delays in the accelerated semantics, we shall reach those $a$'s (without trespassing $B$ since otherwise this would also occur for $\widetilde{\omega}$, forcing to first perform a transition or reset after $\omega$) and recover the induction hypothesis.

If the reset $r_i$ of some agent $A_i$ belongs to the set of transitions enabled after $\omega$ and $\widetilde{\omega} = \omega r_i$, we must have that $\mathsf{init}C_i + \Delta(\widetilde{\omega}) = \mathsf{init}C_i + \Delta(\omega) = k \cdot E_i$ for some factor $k$. But an action zone enabling a reset is an interval of length 0, and is maximal. Hence after $\omega'$ we have the same action zone and $\mathsf{init}C_i + \Delta(\omega') = k \cdot E_i$ (the same factor for $\omega'$ as for $\widetilde{\omega}$ since the delays between resets are limited). We may thus also perform $r_i$ after $\omega'$, the state after $\omega' r_i$ is the same as after $\widetilde{\omega}$, and the situation is the same as initially.

If $\widetilde{\omega} = \omega t$, for some non-reset transition $t$ of some agent $A_i$, by the induction hypothesis $t$ may also occur after $\omega'$ and $\mathsf{word}(\widetilde{\omega}) = \mathsf{word}(\omega' t)$. Any $t'$ enabled after $\omega$ in any $A_j$ for $j \neq i$ remains enabled after $\widetilde{\omega}$ as well as after $\omega' t$, by the induction hypothesis. For agent $A_i$, from constraint 3 of Definition 1, no transition at the new location has already reached its enabling end point in the original (after $\widetilde{\omega}$) and in the accelerated (after $\omega' t$) semantics. If $\Delta(\widetilde{\omega}) \leq \Delta(\omega' t) = \Delta(\omega')$, the clock $C_i$ of $A_i$ is not greater after $\widetilde{\omega}$ than after $\omega' t$ (see the formula above yielding $c_i$) so that all the enabled transitions of $A_i$ after $\widetilde{\omega}$ are also enabled after $\widetilde{\omega}' t$, and the induction hypothesis remains valid. On the contrary, if $\Delta(\widetilde{\omega}) > \Delta(\omega' t)$, it may happen that some $\widetilde{t}$ in $A_i$ is enabled after $\widetilde{\omega}$ but not after $\omega' t$. However, from $\omega' t$ it is then possible to let time pass during $\Delta(\widetilde{\omega}) - \Delta(\omega' t)$, which leads to the same state as after $\widetilde{\omega}$. It is then also possible to consider a maximal action zone after $\omega' t$ which encompasses all the transitions enabled after $\widetilde{\omega}$, to reach its end in the accelerated semantics, and the induction hypothesis remains valid. $\diamond$

## 4   Temporal and Numerical Queries

In order to analyse NCTA systems, we are interested in both temporal and numerical queries.

For the temporal queries, we shall restrict our attention to "positive reachability" formulas. This is a bit restrictive but is enough for the properties that are usually of interest for the kind of systems we are interested in.

Let $P$ be a set of Boolean propositions in $L \times V \to \{true, false\}$, where $L = \{\vec{l}\,\}$ is the space of locations of the model under consideration. For any $p \in P$, this allows one to associate a proposition $p(s) = p(\vec{l}, v)$ to any reachable state $s = (\vec{l}, \vec{c}, v)$. Note that the clock values are not considered in these evaluations, but elapsed time may be approximated through some variables. For instance, it is possible to count the number of resets for a given automaton.

We shall then consider the following fragment of $CTL$ [10] without the $X$ operator[2], based on the basic propositions:

$$\Phi{::} = p(s) \mid (\Phi \vee \Phi) \mid (\Phi \wedge \Phi) \mid (\mathbf{EF}\ \Phi) \mid (\mathbf{EG}\ \Phi) \mid \mathbf{E}(\Phi \mathbf{U} \Phi)$$

($\mathbf{EF}\ \Phi$ meaning that, from the present state, there exist a future finally leading to a state satisfying $\Phi$; $\mathbf{EG}\ \Phi$ meaning that, from the present state, there exist

---

[2] Operator $X$ is irrelevant here since there is no true "next" state when time may evolve continuously.

a future globally satisfying $\Phi$; $\mathbf{E}(\Phi_1 \mathbf{U} \Phi_2)$ meaning that, from the present state, there exist a future satisfying $\Phi_1$ until $\Phi_2$ becomes true).

Note that the queries about NCTAs do not rely on the exact moments where transitions (including resets) occur. It is then possible to check them on classic timed automata region/zone abstractions [9]. However, as we shall see, other state space abstractions may be considered here.

In addition to the temporal queries, we shall also consider numerical ones. Let $g$ be a (computable) indicator function of the form $L \times V \to W$, where $(W, \wedge)$ is some semilattice[3] [11]. As usual, $g$ will be extended to reachable states[4] by $g(\vec{l}, \vec{c}, v) = g(\vec{l}, v)$, i.e., the clock values are again not considered in these evaluations. A numerical query will then have the form $\wedge_\Phi(g)$ and the result will be the value $\wedge(\{g(s) \mid \Phi(s)\})$, i.e., the upper bound of all the values of $g$ computed on the set of the reachable states satisfying the formula $\Phi$.

*Termination.* The previous results only concern the finite evolutions. Problems could occur if some paths do not terminate. Hence the interest to enforce finiteness of trajectories in the state space. This can be achieved by considering a finite horizon upon which no transitions may be taken, and is here obtained by using $V$ to ensure acyclicity. Although agent $A_i$ has a cyclic behavior of period $E_i$, it is possible to lift $V$ into a partially ordered set $(V, <)$ such that, for some agent, each cycle induces a strictly increasing update of $V$. It then suffices to define a value for the ordered set upon which no transition becomes available, making finite any path in the state space. For instance, in the case of vehicles, the ordering may be based on the distances covered, elapsed timed, fuel consumption, etc.

**Corollary 5.** *Positive reachability formulas as well as numerical queries evaluate the same in the original, region-based and accelerated semantics.*

*Proof.* It may be observed that the evaluation of the positive reachability formulas we consider here is only defined by the projections of the possible evolutions of our semantics. Hence, from Proposition 4, our query formulas evaluate the same in the three (original, region-based and accelerated) semantics.

Similarly, the set of values of the variable that may be observed is determined by the sequences of transitions and resets that may occur. From Proposition 4 again, that means that numerical queries evaluate the same in all three semantics.                                                                        ◇

Curiously, if we add negative reachability formulas, i.e., if we add the possibility to use $\neg\Phi$ in the syntax of temporal queries, this preservation result is no longer true. Indeed, let us assume that we encode in $V$, through the functions in $F$, the sequence *visible_history* $\in T^*$ of transitions performed up to now, and consider the query $\mathbf{EF}(\textit{visible\_history}(V) = \varepsilon) \wedge \neg\mathbf{EF}(\textit{visible\_history}(V) = t_3)$.

---

[3] Typically, it will be $(\mathbb{R}, \sup)$ or $(\mathbb{R}, \inf)$.

[4] In particular, that means that $g(s) \wedge g(s) = g(s)$ and $\wedge g(S_1 \cup S_2) = (\wedge g(S_1)) \wedge (\wedge g(S_2))$ for any reachable state $s$ and state sets $S_1, S_2$.

In our running example, with the original semantics this formula is satisfied (consider the reachable location $(1,4)^7$), while it is not in the accelerated semantics (the location $(1,4)^6$ is the last one without any visible evolution), nor in the abstract one where there is a single state $(1,4)$.

This is due to the fact that some states may lose some future paths when time passes, which may be observed by those negative formulas. If we want to check all the reachability formulas, it is thus necessary to modify the accelerated semantics by only dropping the action zones with an enabled set included in a further one.

## 5    Efficiency of the Accelerated Semantics

The accelerated semantics has been exploited in a study comprising three models already used in [4], representing systems of communicating autonomous vehicles and featuring various state space sizes. Table 1 provides for each model the number of states in its state space in both semantics along with the number of states obtained when parsing them with UPPAAL. Results for a bounded version of the model depicted in Example 1 are given for reference. The algorithms for the exploration of the state space were implemented with ZINC [18], a compiler for high level Petri nets that generates a library of functions (in PYTHON) allowing to easily explore the state space. We use for that the translation from NCTA to high-level Petri nets detailed in [5]. Sources for the models and algorithms used in this case study are available in [2].

There are many reasons making the accelerated semantics appealing.

First, as expected, compared to the original one, it is more compact since it retains only one state for each maximal action zone. The size of the state space is very similar to the one of obtained with UPPAAL, and it is efficient to compute since from a given vector of localities, it only relies on the bounds of the outgoing transitions, resulting in a linear complexity for the computation of the next maximal zone. Also, it is quite straightforward to implement.

Second, when facing temporal or numerical queries, it is compatible with the framework [5], bringing some very useful improvements compared to UPPAAL. The framework supports in particular:

- Various programming language-like types of variables thus avoiding a potential loss in precision and realism in models, as well as mistakes in the translation;
- Positive reachability nested CTL queries. Note that although a small subset of nested CTL queries can be checked in UPPAAL by enriching models with Boolean variables (for example $\mathbf{EF}(p \wedge \mathbf{EF}q)$) this does not apply to most of the queries that can be expressed with the framework. Typically queries like $\mathbf{EF}(\mathbf{EF}p \wedge \mathbf{EF}q)$ or $\mathbf{EG}(p \vee \mathbf{EF}q)$ cannot be checked by those means;
- Analysis of numerical indicators in one run instead of the multiple passes necessary with UPPAAL through a dichotomy technique.

Finally, for queries that may also be handled by UPPAAL, the usage of this accelerated semantics, combined with the other techniques was shown in [5] to present similar execution times, with some gain for reachability properties where a target state exists. In the case of numerical queries, the gain may be more significant: for example, in Model 3, obtaining the range of values of a given set of indicators took 700 s with our framework against 3500 s with UPPAAL.

**Table 1.** Sizes of the state spaces.

|  | Model 1 | Model 2 | Model 3 | Example 1 |
|---|---|---|---|---|
| original semantics (regions) | 10340 | 81291 | 382282 | 31120 |
| accelerated semantics | 2686 | 22958 | 105268 | 4412 |
| UPPAAL | 2617 | 19766 | 94775 | 3666 |

## 6   Conclusion

This paper introduced a new kind of timed abstraction called accelerated semantics for a class of timed automata tailored for multi-agent systems, such as the CAVs, where each agent is described by a large set of variables updated in a regular timed schema upon which all possibles actions of the agent rely.

The accelerated semantics has been implemented as a part of a checking environment for NCTA [3] with the (open) academic tool ZINC [18]. It may be combined with other techniques such as stratification or various kinds of heuristics (details may be found in [5,6]).

For practitioners, often limited to use constrained integers for the variables of the model, it offers the advantage of supporting ordinary programming data types with good precision, e.g. float or long. It is not *stricto sensu* a gain of expressiveness because one can always represent a rational (real) number with two integers and achieve suitable precision, but we believe that modellers may appreciate not to have to work at such a low level, which may be particularly error prone [17], in particular when it is not possible to know beforehand the required precision.

It also offers the possibility of using nested positive CTL formulas and numerical queries expressed in a usual programming language. Compared to UPPAAL, the former effectively extends the expressiveness while maintaining comparable efficiency (the abstracted state spaces have similar sizes). The latter is also a valuable enhancement, which contributes to improve the overall quality of the work.

## References

1. Alur, R., Dill, D.L.: A theory of timed automata. Theor. Comput. Sci. **126**(2), 183–235 (1994)
2. Arcile, J.: Sources of the MAPTs models and exploration algorithms. https://forge.ibisc.univ-evry.fr/jarcile/MAPTs/. Accessed 11 Oct 2019

3. Arcile, J.: Conception, modélisation et vérification formelle d'un système temps-réel d'agents coopératifs: application aux véhicules autonomes communicants. PhD thesis, Université Paris-Saclay, France; préparée à l'Université d'Evry-Val-d'Essonne: https://www.biblio.univ-evry.fr/theses/2019/2019SACLE029.pdf (2019)

4. Arcile, J., Devillers, R., Klaudel, H.: VerifCar: a framework for modeling and model checking communicating autonomous vehicles. Auton. Agent. Multi-Agent Syst. **33**(3), 353–381 (2019). https://doi.org/10.1007/s10458-019-09409-x

5. Arcile, J., Devillers, R.R., Klaudel, H.: Dynamic exploration of multi-agent systems with periodic timed tasks. Fundam. Informaticae **175**(1–4), 59–95 (2020)

6. Arcile, J., Devillers, R., Klaudel, H.: Models for dynamic exploration of the state spaces of autonomous vehicles. In: Proceedings of the International Workshop on Petri Nets and Software Engineering co-located with 41st International Conference on Application and Theory of Petri Nets and Concurrency (PETRI NETS 2020), Paris, France, June 24, 2020 (due to COVID-19: virtual conference), pp. 29–48 (2020)

7. Behrmann, G., Bengtsson, J., David, A., Larsen, K.G., Pettersson, P., Yi, W.: UPPAAL implementation secrets. In: Damm, W., Olderog, E.-R. (eds.) FTRTFT 2002. LNCS, vol. 2469, pp. 3–22. Springer, Heidelberg (2002). https://doi.org/10.1007/3-540-45739-9_1

8. Behrmann, G., Bouyer, P., Larsen, K.G., Pelánek, R.: Lower and upper bounds in zone-based abstractions of timed automata. Int. J. Softw. Tools Technol. Transfer **8**(3), 204–215 (2006). https://doi.org/10.1007/s10009-005-0190-0

9. Bengtsson, J., Yi, W.: Timed automata: semantics, algorithms and tools. In: Desel, J., Reisig, W., Rozenberg, G. (eds.) ACPN 2003. LNCS, vol. 3098, pp. 87–124. Springer, Heidelberg (2004). https://doi.org/10.1007/978-3-540-27755-2_3

10. Clarke, E.M., Grumberg, O., Peled, D.: Model Checking. MIT Press (2001)

11. Davey, B.A., Priestley, H.A.: Introduction to Lattices and Order, 2nd edn. Cambridge University Press, Cambridge (2002)

12. Daws, C., Olivero, A., Tripakis, S., Yovine, S.: The tool KRONOS. In: Alur, R., Henzinger, T.A., Sontag, E.D. (eds.) HS 1995. LNCS, vol. 1066, pp. 208–219. Springer, Heidelberg (1996). https://doi.org/10.1007/BFb0020947

13. Daws, C., Tripakis, S.: Model checking of real-time reachability properties using abstractions. In: Steffen, B. (ed.) TACAS 1998. LNCS, vol. 1384, pp. 313–329. Springer, Heidelberg (1998). https://doi.org/10.1007/BFb0054180

14. Dill, D.L.: Timing assumptions and verification of finite-state concurrent systems. In: Sifakis, J. (ed.) CAV 1989. LNCS, vol. 407, pp. 197–212. Springer, Heidelberg (1990). https://doi.org/10.1007/3-540-52148-8_17

15. Elliott, D., Keen, W., Miao, L.: Recent advances in connected and automated vehicles. J. Traffic Transp. Eng. (English Edition) **6**(2), 109–131 (2019)

16. Jamroga, W., Konikowska, B., Kurpiewski, D., Penczek, W.: Multi-valued verification of strategic ability. Fundam. Informaticae **175**(1–4), 207–251 (2020)

17. Moler, C.: Pentium division bug documents. MATLAB Central File Exchange (2021)

18. Pommereau, F.: ZINC: a compiler for "any language"-coloured Petri nets. IBISC, university of Evry/Paris-Saclay, Technical report (2018)

# Compositional Techniques for Boolean Networks and Attractor Analysis

Hanin Abdulrahman[1,2] and Jason Steggles[2(✉)]

[1] Faculty of Computer and Information Sciences,
Princess Nourah Bint Abdulrahman University, Riyadh, Saudi Arabia
[2] School of Computing, Newcastle University, Newcastle upon Tyne, UK
{H.Y.I.Abdulrahman2,Jason.Steggles}@ncl.ac.uk

**Abstract.** Recently a new compositional framework for constructing and analysing Boolean networks was presented based on merging entities using Boolean connectives. While this framework provides a good basis for engineering Boolean networks, its practical application is limited by the restricted composition structures allowed and the lack of support for attractor analysis. In this paper we significantly extend this compositional framework by developing a new general structure for compositions and by providing new techniques for compositionally identifying the attractors of a Boolean network. The results presented are important as they support ongoing work to use the framework for engineering biological systems and also provide a new basis for analysing Boolean networks which helps to address the practical limitations imposed by the state space explosion problem.

## 1 Introduction

Qualitative modelling techniques have been shown to be a vital tool for understanding and engineering biological systems [7,8]. *Boolean networks* [18,19] are an important qualitative modelling approach that are widely used in biological modelling. The idea is to model regulatory entities as Boolean states and to capture their dynamic behaviour using next-state Boolean functions. The resulting model can be analysed by identifying its *attractors* (i.e. key cyclic behaviour) which can provide important biological insights [17,27]. Boolean networks have been successfully applied to a wide range of biological regulatory systems (for example, see [2,15,20,24]).

The practical application of Boolean networks is limited by the well-known *state space explosion problem* where the exponential growth of the state space severely limits the size of models that can be considered. To address this researchers have considered applying compositional and decompositional analysis techniques to Boolean networks (for example, see [12,22,33,35]). One recent novel approach focused on composing Boolean networks by merging entities using Boolean operators like conjunction [3–5]. The aim of this work was to develop a compositional framework to support the construction and analysis of Boolean

M. Koutny et al. (Eds.): TPNOMCXVII, LNCS 14150, pp. 264–294, 2024.
https://doi.org/10.1007/978-3-662-68191-6_11

networks and so aid the engineering of biological systems. The framework also provides a foundation for analysing existing Boolean networks by allowing their decomposition to be considered. While the initial results for this compositional framework are very promising, more work is now needed to facilitate its practical application. In particular, the form of compositions currently allowed is too restrictive and needs to be generalised. Another important limitation is that the existing analysis techniques focus only on behaviour preservation of the underlying subnetworks in the composition and no support for compositionally identifying the attractors of a composed model is currently available.

In this paper we address the limitations highlighted above by significantly extending the existing compositional framework with new techniques and tools. We begin by generalising the definition of a composition to allow arbitrary compositions based on an underlying graph structure. The resulting new general structure for a composition allows multiple Boolean networks to be composed over multiple entities. We then consider developing new techniques for identifying the attractors of a composed model which use its underlying compositional structure. The approach we take is based on analysing the *interference state graph* [4], a state graph that extends a Boolean network's normal behaviour with the additional dynamics that can occur due to interference from a composition. We identify the *strongly connected components (SCCs)* [21] associated with the interference state graphs for the underlying Boolean networks and then selectively merge their cyclic behaviour using an important new property called *interference alignment*. We formally show our approach is correct by proving that it is *sound* and *complete* for attractor identification.

In order to facilitate the practical application and evaluation of our techniques we develop a new support tool. We begin by using our new theoretical results as the basis to develop an algorithm for compositionally identifying attractors. The approach we take uses a new notion of a *aligned state tuples*, that is, a collection of states for the underlying Boolean networks in the composition which are consistent with each other and which are realisable in practice. We consider carefully how to efficiently generate such aligned state tuples to ensure the algorithm developed is practical. This algorithm is then used as the basis for a prototype support tool which is implemented using *Python* and the *NetworkX* package [13].

We investigate the practical performance of our attractor analysis approach by carrying out two performance test studies on our prototype tool using a series of compositional test models that range in size from 54 to 233 entities. In order to evaluate the performance of our tool we compare our results to those for three existing attractor identification tools in the literature: *BoolNet* [23], *BNS* [10] and *BoolSim* [11]. The results of these studies indicate that our approach performs very well compared to existing mature tools in this field and helped identify areas for future development.

This paper is organised as follows. In Sect. 2 we briefly introduce Boolean networks and the compositional framework for Boolean networks that forms the starting point for this paper. We also briefly review related work. In Sect. 3

we present a new definition of a composition that significantly generalises the existing definition. In Sect. 4 we develop a new theoretical approach for compositionally identifying attractors and in Sect. 5 we develop tool support for these techniques. In Sect. 6 we evaluate our new techniques and tools by performing a range of performance tests. Finally, in Sect. 7 we make some concluding remarks.

## 2   Boolean Networks and Composition

In this section we recall the background definitions and results needed in the sequel. We begin with some basic definitions for Boolean networks and then give a brief overview of the compositional framework presented in [4]. We then review a range of related work on compositional attractor analysis.

### 2.1   Boolean Networks

A Boolean network [1,19] is a qualitative model that consists of a set of regulatory entities which have a binary state, where 1 represents that an entity is active and 0 represents that an entity is inactive. The behaviour of each entity is regulated by other entities in the model and the set of these entities is referred to as the *neighbourhood* of an entity (where an entity may or may not be a member of its own neighbourhood). Each entity has an associated *next–state function* and this is applied to the current states of the entities in its neighbourhood to determine its next state.

More formally, we can define a Boolean network as follows.

**Definition 1.** *A Boolean Network $\mathcal{BN}$ is a tuple $\mathcal{BN} = (G, N, F)$ where:*

i) *$G = \{g_1, \ldots, g_n\}$ is a non-empty, finite set of entities;*
ii) *$N = (N(g_1), \ldots, N(g_n))$ is a tuple of neighbourhoods, such that $N(g_i) \subseteq G$ is the neighbourhood of $g_i$; and*
iii) *$F = (F(g_1), \ldots, F(g_n))$ is a tuple of next-state functions, such that the function $F(g_i) : \mathbb{B}^{|N(g_i)|} \to \mathbb{B}$ defines the next state of $g_i$.*

A Boolean network $\mathcal{BN} = (G, N, F)$ consisting of $n \geq 1$ entities $G = \{g_1, \ldots, g_n\}$ has a *global state* $(s_1, \ldots, s_n)$, where $s_i$ is a Boolean value representing the state of entity $g_i$. As a notational convenience we often use $s_1 \ldots s_n$ to represent a global state $(s_1, \ldots, s_n)$. The state space $S_{\mathcal{BN}} = \mathbb{B}^{|G|}$ of a Boolean network $\mathcal{BN}$ is defined to be the set of all possible global states.

The global state of a Boolean network is normally updated either *synchronously* [19,32], where the state of all entities is updated simultaneously in a single update step, or *asynchronously* [14], where entities update their state independently. A range of other update semantics, such as sequential and block-sequential asynchronous, have also been considered in the literature [6]. We focus on the synchronous update semantics here which has been well studied and appears to have practical biological relevance [28]. We let $S_1 \xrightarrow{\mathcal{BN}} S_2$ represent a *(synchronous) update step* where $S_2$ is the global state that results from simultaneously updating the state of each entity $g_i$ by applying its associated update function $F(g_i)$ to the appropriate neighbourhood of states from $S_1$. Note that for any global state there is only one possible next state under the synchronous update semantics.

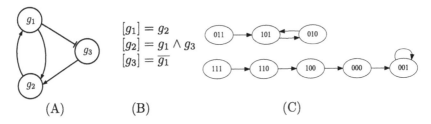

(A)               (B)                           (C)

**Fig. 1.** Example of a Boolean network $\mathcal{BN}_{Ex}$ consisting of: (A) interaction graph; (B) next–state functions; and (C) state graph.

As an illustrative example, consider the Boolean network $\mathcal{BN}_{Ex}$ defined in Fig. 1. It consists of entities $G_{Ex} = \{g_1, g_2, g_3\}$ and these have neighbourhoods (see Fig. 1.(A)) $N_{Ex}(g_1) = \{g_2\}$, $N_{Ex}(g_2) = \{g_1, g_3\}$, and $N_{Ex}(g_3) = \{g_1\}$. The next-state functions $F_{Ex}$ are defined equational in Fig. 1.(B), where we use $[g_i]$ to represent the next state of an entity $g_i$. Given a global state such as 101 (denoting that entity $g_1 = 1$, $g_2 = 0$, and $g_3 = 1$) we can apply the next–state functions to make a synchronous update step $101 \xrightarrow{\mathcal{BN}_{Ex}} 010$.

The complete synchronous behaviour of a Boolean network $\mathcal{BN}$ can be concisely represented as a *state graph* $SG(\mathcal{BN}) = (S_{\mathcal{BN}}, \xrightarrow{\mathcal{BN}})$. An example of a state graph is given in Fig. 1.(C) for the Boolean network $\mathcal{BN}_{Ex}$. A *path* (often also referred to as a *trace*) for a Boolean network is an infinite sequence of global states

$$\langle S_0, S_1, S_2, \ldots \rangle$$

such that $S_i \in S_{\mathcal{BN}}$ and $S_i \xrightarrow{\mathcal{BN}} S_{i+1}$, for $i \in \mathbb{N}$. We let $Path(SG(\mathcal{BN}))$ represent the set of all such (infinite) paths. Since the global state space for a Boolean network is finite, such paths must ultimately enter a cycle which we refer to as an *attractor cycle* [19,31]. In the example Boolean network $\mathcal{BN}_{Ex}$ (see Fig. 1) we have a path $\langle 110, 100, 000, 001, 001, \ldots \rangle$ which ends in the point attractor $[001, 001]$. By looking at this Boolean network's state graph we can see that it has one other attractor $[101, 010, 101]$.

Attractor cycles can be seen to capture key underlying behaviour of a Boolean network and are therefore very important in biological modelling where they can be associated with biological phenomenon (such as different cellular types [17]).

## 2.2    A Compositional Framework

The compositional framework developed by *Alkhudhayr* and *Steggles* [3–5] is based on composing Boolean networks by merging entities using (idempotent) Boolean connectives such as conjunction. The idea is that given two Boolean networks to compose $\mathcal{BN}_1$ and $\mathcal{BN}_2$ we take an entity from each, say $g_1^1$ and $g_1^2$ respectively, and then merge their next state functions using, for example, conjunction to create a new entity $g^c$ (see Fig. 2). The resulting composed model is denoted by $\mathcal{C}(\mathcal{BN}_1, \mathcal{BN}_2, g_1^1, g_1^2)$.

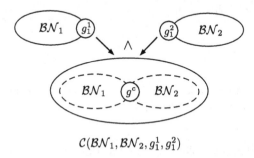

$$\mathcal{C}(\mathcal{BN}_1, \mathcal{BN}_2, g_1^1, g_1^2)$$

**Fig. 2.** Pictorial representation of composing two Boolean networks $\mathcal{BN}_1$ and $\mathcal{BN}_2$ to form a new Boolean network $\mathcal{C}(\mathcal{BN}_1, \mathcal{BN}_2, g_1^1, g_1^2)$ by using conjunction to merge entities $g_1^1$ and $g_1^2$ to form a new entity $g^c$.

To illustrate the idea, consider composing the Boolean networks $\mathcal{BN}_{Ex1}$ and $\mathcal{BN}_{Ex2}$ given in Fig. 3. The two Boolean networks are composed by merging entities $g_1^1$ and $g_1^2$ using conjunction. The result is a new Boolean network $\mathcal{C}(\mathcal{BN}_{Ex1}, \mathcal{BN}_{Ex2}, g_1^1, g_1^2)$ in which the entities $g_1^1$ and $g_1^2$ have been replaced by a single composed entity $g^c$ whose next state function is defined by merging $F(\mathcal{BN}_{Ex1})(g_1^1)$ and $F(\mathcal{BN}_{Ex2})(g_1^2)$ as follows

$$[g^c] = (\overline{g^c} \vee \overline{g_2^1}) \wedge \overline{g_2^2}$$

The results and tools developed for this compositional framework [3,4] focused on the preservation of the behaviour of the underlying models used in the composition. One important aspect of this work is that Boolean networks used in a composition can interfere with each other to produce new behaviour in the composed model. For example, consider $\mathcal{C}(\mathcal{BN}_{Ex1}, \mathcal{BN}_{Ex2}, g_1^1, g_1^2)$ (see Fig. 4) and suppose the composed model is in global state 001. Then the underlying Boolean networks will want to make the following transitions: $00 \xrightarrow{\mathcal{BN}_{Ex1}} 10$ and $01 \xrightarrow{\mathcal{BN}_{Ex2}} 01$. This means that entity $g_1^1$ in $\mathcal{BN}_{Ex1}$ would like to transition from state 0 to state 1 but entity $g_1^2$ in $\mathcal{BN}_{Ex2}$ would like to transition from 0 to 0. The merged entity $g^c$ will therefore transition to $0 \wedge 1 = 0$ meaning that the underlying behaviour of $\mathcal{BN}_{Ex1}$ has been interfered with. This shows that when using conjunction for composition interference will occur to the underlying

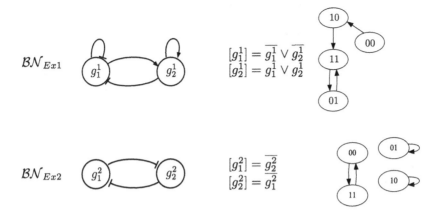

**Fig. 3.** The interaction graphs, next–state functions and the state graphs for two example Boolean Networks $\mathcal{BN}_{Ex1}$ and $\mathcal{BN}_{Ex2}$.

behaviour of a merged entity whenever it wants to transition to 1 but its merged counterpart wants to transition to 0.

In order to formalise the possible *interference* that can occur between composed Boolean networks we extend a Boolean network's state graph with additional edges representing the behaviour that could result from interference. The idea (based on using conjunction) is that whenever the entity to be merged transitions to 1 then we add another edge to the state graph to represent that the transition could instead go to 0 due to interference. We refer to the resulting state graph as the *interference state graph* [4]. We give an updated formal definition for the interference state graph and a range of examples in Sect. 3.

## 2.3   Related Work

Given the practical limitations imposed by the state space explosion problem there has been a range of work looking at compositional/decompositional techniques for identifying attractors. We briefly review some relevant examples from the literature below and relate them to the new approach we present.

A compositional approach for computing the attractors of large random Boolean networks is considered in [9] based on identifying independent subnetworks of a Boolean network whose composed behaviour can infer attractors. In [35] an interesting attractor identification approach based on decomposing a synchronous Boolean network into a set of *Boolean control networks* is developed. The idea is that Boolean control networks are subnetworks that contain input entities duplicated from other subnetworks. An approach for aggregating the *input-state cycles* of these control networks is used to calculate the attractors of the original Boolean network. The approach considers using the *strongly connected components (SCCs)* of a Boolean network's interaction graph to optimise the decomposition. This approach is further developed in [22,33,34] by refining

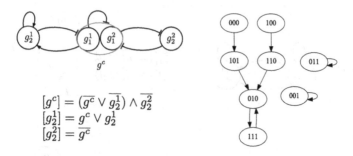

$$[g^c] = (\overline{g^c} \vee \overline{g_2^1}) \wedge \overline{g_2^2}$$
$$[g_2^1] = g^c \vee g_2^1$$
$$[g_2^2] = \overline{g^c}$$

**Fig. 4.** Composed model $C(\mathcal{BN}_{Ex1}, \mathcal{BN}_{Ex2}, g_1^1, g_1^2)$ resulting from composing $\mathcal{BN}_{Ex1}$ with $\mathcal{BN}_{Ex2}$ on $g_1^1$ and $g_1^2$ using conjunction.

the SCC decomposition of a Boolean network into blocks and then iteratively recombining blocks to calculate attractors.

A similar approach for decomposing a Boolean network into subnetworks is developed in [12] where the underlying attractor identification technique is based on a SAT-based approach and a parallel version of their attractor identification algorithm is considered. A key issue with this approach is that it becomes inefficient for Boolean networks with high in-degree. This issue is considered in [16] where they investigate techniques for finding the smallest optimal partition for decompositionally applying a SAT solver and introduce the concept of a *minimum essential block*.

In [25] a compositional/decompositional theoretical approach for *Boolean Automata Networks (BANs)* is developed based on adding external inputs to models and then allowing these to be wired together. Interesting initial theoretical work on developing attractor analysis techniques for this framework is presented in [26] but the complexity of the approach appears to be an issue for its practical application.

While the approaches above have basic similarities to the techniques developed here there are some significant differences. The techniques we develop are based on the novel idea of merging entities by using logical operators [4] and this is very different to the approach of using control networks with input places that is currently used in the related work above. In particular, our work focuses on the behavioural interference generated when subnetworks are composed using the notion of an *interference state graph*. Also our approach is based around a compositional framework which is primarily concerned with the compositional construction of Boolean network models and so we are able to use the resulting compositional structure directly to compositional identify attractors without the need for decomposition (though developing decomposition techniques using our framework is an interesting area for further work). The use of SCCs is also significantly different since we use them to identify potential cyclic behaviour in subnetworks rather than as a basis for decomposing a Boolean network's structure.

## 3   Generalising a Composition

An important practical limitation of the current compositional framework [3,4] is that the compositional structures allowed are too restrictive. In this section we address this by reformulating the definition of a composition in terms of a graph structure. The underlying idea of merging entities using Boolean connectives remains the same but the new definition allows for arbitrary compositional structures involving multiple Boolean networks and multiple entities.

We note that in the sequel we focus on using conjunction to merge the behaviour of entities in a composition. However, it should be noted that all the definitions and results presented can be straightforwardly adapted to the use of disjunction.

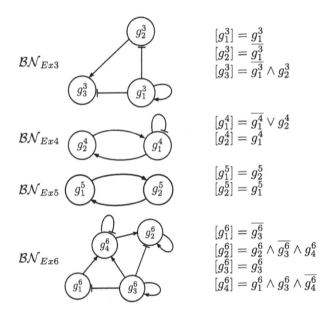

**Fig. 5.** Four further example Boolean networks $\mathcal{BN}_{Ex3}$, $\mathcal{BN}_{Ex4}$, $\mathcal{BN}_{Ex5}$ and $\mathcal{BN}_{Ex6}$ which we use in our composition examples.

To illustrate the idea behind the new graph based compositional structure consider the composition presented in Fig. 6 in which the Boolean networks $\mathcal{BN}_{Ex1}, \ldots, \mathcal{BN}_{Ex6}$ (defined in Fig. 3 and Fig. 5) are composed. The composition of two Boolean networks is specified by naming the pair of entities that are merged between them. For example, the composition of $\mathcal{BN}_{Ex1}$ and $\mathcal{BN}_{Ex3}$ shown in Fig. 6 is specified by the pair $\{g_1^1, g_2^3\}$ and the composition of $\mathcal{BN}_{Ex2}$ and $\mathcal{BN}_{Ex6}$ by $\{g_1^2, g_1^6\}$.

This idea leads to the following new general definition of a composition that significantly extends the original definition [4].

**Definition 2.** *(Composition) A composition* $\Sigma$ *is defined to be a pair* $\Sigma = (M, E)$, *where* $M = \{\mathcal{BN}_1, \ldots, \mathcal{BN}_n\}$ *is a set of Boolean networks for some* $n \in \mathbb{N}$, $n > 1$, *and*

$$E \subseteq \{\{g_1, g_2\} \mid \mathcal{BN}_i, \mathcal{BN}_j \in M, \ \mathcal{BN}_i \neq \mathcal{BN}_j \text{ and } g_1 \in \mathcal{BN}_i, \ g_2 \in \mathcal{BN}_j\}$$

*is a set defining the entities merged which satsifies the following condition: for each* $\mathcal{BN}_i \in M$ *there must exist an entity* $g_1 \in \mathcal{BN}_i$ *such that* $\{g_1, g_2\} \in E$, *for some* $\mathcal{BN}_j \in M$, $\mathcal{BN}_i \neq \mathcal{BN}_j$ *and* $g_2 \in \mathcal{BN}_j$.

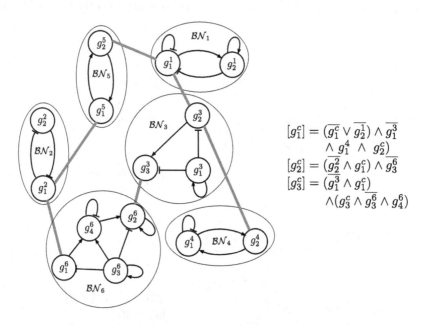

$$[g_1^c] = (\overline{g_1^c} \vee \overline{g_1^1}) \wedge \overline{g_1^3}$$
$$\wedge \ g_1^4 \ \wedge \ g_2^c)$$
$$[g_2^c] = (\overline{g_2^2} \wedge g_1^c) \wedge g_3^6$$
$$[g_3^c] = (\overline{g_1^3} \wedge g_1^c)$$
$$\wedge (g_3^c \wedge g_3^6 \wedge g_4^6)$$

**Fig. 6.** An example composition $\Sigma_{Ex}$ in which the six Boolean networks $\mathcal{BN}_{Ex1}, \ldots, \mathcal{BN}_{Ex6}$ are composed (where the thick blue edges represent entity composition) resulting in the composed entities $g_1^c = \{g_1^1, g_2^3, g_2^4, g_2^5\}$, $g_2^c = \{g_1^2, g_1^5, g_1^6\}$, $g_3^c = \{g_3^3, g_2^6\}$.

The composition depicted in Fig. 6 can be formally specified by the composition $\Sigma_{Ex} = (M_{Ex}, E_{Ex})$, where $M_{Ex} = \{\mathcal{BN}_{Ex1}, \ldots, \mathcal{BN}_{Ex6}\}$ and

$$E_{Ex} = \{\{g_1^1, g_2^3\}, \{g_1^1, g_2^5\}, \{g_2^3, g_2^4\}, \{g_1^2, g_1^5\}, \{g_1^2, g_1^6\}, \{g_3^3, g_2^6\}\}$$

It is worth noting that an entity can be used in more than one composition as is the case for our example where entity $g_1^2$ is used to compose $\mathcal{BN}_{Ex2}$ with $\mathcal{BN}_{Ex5}$ and $\mathcal{BN}_{Ex6}$.

In order to facilitate the theoretical results developed in this paper we use the following alternative approach of representing global states based on functions instead of tuples. For any Boolean network $\mathcal{BN} = (G, N, F)$ we define a global state to be a function $S : G \to \mathbb{B}$ and let $S(g)$ represent the state of entity $g \in G$ in global state $S$. As normal we let $S_{\mathcal{BN}} = [G \to \mathbb{B}]$ represent the set of all global states. It should be clear that representing global states using tuples or as functions is equivalent and we move between the two approaches as required to support our formal development.

Given a non-empty subset $X \subseteq G$ we let $S[X] : X \to \mathbb{B}$ represent the global state $S \in S_{\mathcal{BN}}$ projected over $X$, where $S[X](g) = S(g)$, for any $g \in X$. Given a path $\alpha = \langle S_1, S_2, \ldots \rangle \in Path(SG(\mathcal{BN}))$ we let $\alpha[X] = \langle S_1[X], S_2[X], \ldots \rangle$.

In the sequel we let $\mathcal{BN}_i = (G_i, N_i, F_i)$ be an arbitrary Boolean network, for some $n \in \mathbb{N}$, $n > 1$, and for $i = 1, \ldots, n$. We assume that the sets of entities $G_1, \ldots, G_n$ are disjoint. We let $\Sigma = (M, E)$ be an arbitrary composition with $M = \{\mathcal{BN}_1, \ldots, \mathcal{BN}_n\}$.

We introduce the following important definitions and notation for reasoning about a given composition $\Sigma = (M, E)$.

We let $gc(\Sigma, \mathcal{BN}_i)$ be the set of all entities from $\mathcal{BN}_i \in M$ involved in the composition $\Sigma$ defined by

$$gc(\Sigma, \mathcal{BN}_i) = \{g \mid g \in \mathcal{BN}_i \text{ and } \{g, g'\} \in E\}$$

We let $gc(\Sigma) = gc(\Sigma, \mathcal{BN}_i) \cup \ldots \cup gc(\Sigma, \mathcal{BN}_n)$ be the set of all entities used in the composition.

We define $\lambda(g)$ to be the index of the Boolean network entity $g$ belongs to, i.e. if $g \in G_i$, for some $i \in \{1, \ldots, n\}$, then $\lambda(g) = i$.

For any $g \in gc(\Sigma)$ we define $\Delta(g)$ to be the set of entities that entity $g$ is composed with (i.e. the entities that can interfere with the behaviour of $g$). This set is important since an entity can be used in more than one composition. We will see later that it is useful to include $g$ itself in this set. We define $\Delta(g)$ formally by

$$\Delta(g) = \left( \bigcup_{i \in \mathbb{N}} H_i(g) \right) \cup \{g\}$$

where $H_i(g)$ is defined recursively as follows:

1) **Base Case:** $H_0(g) = \{g' \mid \{g, g'\} \in E\}$
2) **Recursive case:** let $i \in \mathbb{N}$ and define

$$H_{i+1}(g) = \{g'' \mid g' \in H_i(g), \{g', g''\} \in E\}$$

For any entity $g \in gc(\Sigma)$ we use $\Delta(g)$ as the name of the composed entity in the Boolean network $BN(\Sigma)$ that results from the composition. Given an entity $g \in (G_1 \cup \ldots \cup G_n)$ we define

$$\Sigma(g) = \begin{cases} g, & \text{if } g \notin gc(\Sigma); \\ \Delta(g), & \text{otherwise} \end{cases}$$

Given a set of entities $X \subseteq (G_1 \cup \ldots \cup G_n)$ we define $\Sigma(X) = \{\Sigma(g) \mid g \in X\}$.

We let $BN(\Sigma)$ be the the Boolean network that results from a composition $\Sigma$. We can define $BN(\Sigma)$ formally as follows.

**Definition 3.** *(Composed Model) Let $\Sigma = (M, E)$ be a composition. Then we define the Boolean network $BN(\Sigma) = (G(\Sigma), N(\Sigma), F(\Sigma))$ that results from $\Sigma$ as follows.*
**1. Entities:** $G(\Sigma) = \Sigma(G_1 \cup \ldots \cup G_n)$.
**2. Neighbourhood:** *for any entity $h \in G(\Sigma)$, the neighbourhood $N(\Sigma)(h)$ is defined by*

$$N(\Sigma)(h) = \begin{cases} \bigcup_{g \in h} \Sigma(N_{\lambda(g)}(g)), & \text{if } h = \Delta(g'), \text{ for some } g' \in gc(\Sigma); \\ \Sigma(N_{\lambda(h)}(h)), & \text{otherwise} \end{cases}$$

**3. Functions:** *For any $g \in G(\Sigma)$ we define the next–state function $F(\Sigma)(g)$ on any $S \in S_{BN(\Sigma)}$ by*

$$F(\Sigma)(g)(S[N(\Sigma)(g)]) =$$

$$\begin{cases} \bigwedge_{h \in \Delta(g')} F_{\lambda(h)}(h)(S[\Sigma(N_{\lambda(h)}(h))]), & \text{if } g = \Delta(g'), \text{ for some } g' \in gc(\Sigma); \\ F_{\lambda(g)}(g)(S[\Sigma(N_{\lambda(g)}(g))]), & \text{otherwise} \end{cases}$$

This definition is illustrated by the example shown in Fig. 6 where the Boolean network $BN(\Sigma_{Ex})$ results from the composition $\Sigma_{Ex}$.

The *interference state graph* for a Boolean network was introduced in [4] in order to formalise the possible *interference* that can occur between Boolean networks in a composition. The idea is to extend a Boolean network's state graph with additional edges representing the behaviour that could result from interference caused by a composition. In particular, whenever an entity used in the composition transitions to 1 then we add another edge to the state graph to represent that the transition could instead go to 0 due to interference (this assumes conjunction is being used in the composition). Since any given Boolean network can have a number of entities involved in the composition we need to define the set of all possible next states that can occur based on the possibility of interference as follows.

Let $BN = (G, N, F)$ be a Boolean network and $S \in S_{BN}$. For any entity $g \in G$ and $b \in \mathbb{B}$ we define $S[g \to b]$ to represent an update to state $S$ so that $g$ now has state $b$. More formally, for any $h \in G$ define

$$S[g \to b](h) = \begin{cases} b, & \text{if } g = h; \\ S(h), & \text{otherwise} \end{cases}$$

Let $v : \mathbb{B} \to \mathcal{P}(\mathbb{B})$ be defined by $v(0) = \{0\}$ and $v(1) = \{0, 1\}$. Let $X = \{g_1, \ldots, g_k\} \subseteq G$ be a non–empty subset of entities. Then we define $\Upsilon_X : S_{BN} \to \mathcal{P}(S_{BN})$ for any $S \in S_{BN}$ by

$$\Upsilon_X(S) = \{S[g_1 \to b_1] \cdots [g_k \to b_k] \mid b_1 \in v(S(g_1)), \ldots, b_k \in v(S(g_k))\}$$

We can now define the interference state graph (based on [3]).

**Definition 4.** *(Interference State Graph)* *Let* $\mathcal{BN} = (G, N, F)$ *be a Boolean network and let* $X \subseteq G$. *Then we define the interference state graph* $SG_X(\mathcal{BN})$ *by*

$$SG_X(\mathcal{BN}) = (S_{\mathcal{BN}}, \xrightarrow[X]{\mathcal{BN}})$$

*The extended edge relation* $\xrightarrow[X]{\mathcal{BN}}$ *is defined by* $\xrightarrow[X]{\mathcal{BN}} = \xrightarrow{\mathcal{BN}} \cup \,\mathcal{E}$, *where*

$$\mathcal{E} = \{S_1 \xrightarrow[X]{\mathcal{BN}} T \mid S_1, S_2 \in S_{\mathcal{BN}}, \; S_1 \xrightarrow{\mathcal{BN}} S_2, \; T \in \Upsilon_X(S_2)\}$$

As illustrative examples, consider the interference state graphs depicted in Fig. 7 for the Boolean networks $\mathcal{BN}_{Ex1}$, $\mathcal{BN}_{Ex2}$ and $\mathcal{BN}_{Ex3}$ introduced previously (see Fig. 3 and Fig. 5).

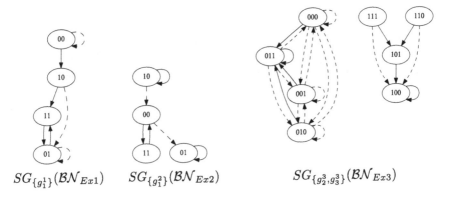

$SG_{\{g_1^1\}}(\mathcal{BN}_{Ex1})$    $SG_{\{g_1^2\}}(\mathcal{BN}_{Ex2})$    $SG_{\{g_2^3, g_3^3\}}(\mathcal{BN}_{Ex3})$

**Fig. 7.** The interference state graphs for $\mathcal{BN}_{Ex1}$ on $\{g_1^1\}$, $\mathcal{BN}_{Ex2}$ on $\{g_1^2\}$ and $\mathcal{BN}_{Ex3}$ on $\{g_2^3, g_3^3\}$.

In the sequel, let $I_i$ represent the interference state graph $SG_{gc(\Sigma, \mathcal{BN}_i)}(\mathcal{BN}_i)$ when $\Sigma$ and $\mathcal{BN}_i$ are clear from the context.

The following is an important result which shows that an interference state graph captures all the possible behaviour that can result for a Boolean network if it is used in a composition $\Sigma$. (Note this is an updated version of the theorem presented in [3,4].)

**Theorem 1.** *Let* $\beta \in Path(SG(BN(\Sigma)))$. *Then for* $i = 1, \ldots, n$ *we have*

$$\beta[\Sigma(G_i)] \in Path(I_i)$$

*Proof.* Let $\beta = \langle S_0, S_1, \ldots \rangle \in Path(SG(BN(\Sigma)))$. Then it suffices to show that for any $i \in \{1, \ldots, n\}$ and any $k \in \mathbb{N}$ we have

$$S_k[\Sigma(G_i)] \xrightarrow[gc(\Sigma, \mathcal{BN}_i)]{\mathcal{BN}_i} S_{k+1}[\Sigma(G_i)] \tag{1}$$

Let $S_k[\Sigma(G_i)] \xrightarrow{B\mathcal{N}_i} T$, for some $T \in S_{B\mathcal{N}_i}$. Clearly, for any $g \in G_i$, $g \notin gc(\Sigma, B\mathcal{N}_i)$ we have by the definition of $BN(\Sigma)$ (Definition 3) that

$$T(g) = S_{k+1}[\Sigma(G_i)](g)$$

For any $g \in gc(\Sigma, B\mathcal{N}_i)$ we know by the definition of $BN(\Sigma)$ (Definition 3) that $S_{k+1}(\Sigma(g)) \in v(T(g))$ and so it follows that

$$S_{k+1}[\Sigma(G_i)] \in \Upsilon_{gc(\Sigma,B\mathcal{N}_i)}(T)$$

Then by the definition of the interference state graph (Definition 4) it follows that (1) must hold. □

## 4   Compositionally Identifying Attractors

In this section we build on the general composition framework introduced in the previous section by developing techniques for compositionally identifying the attractors in a Boolean network. The approach is based on using the *strongly connected components* [21] associated with the interference state graphs for the underlying Boolean networks in the composition and then merging their behaviour where possible based on a new property called *interference alignment*. We present an algorithm for performing attractor analysis based on this new compositional approach and show formally that it is sound and complete for attractor identification.

### 4.1   A Basis for Compositional Attractor Analysis

Recall that a *strongly connected component (SCC)* [21] in a graph is a maximal set of vertices such that any two vertices are mutually reachable. SCCs in a Boolean network's interference state graph represent potential cyclic behaviour in a composed model and therefore provide a basis for determining attractor cycles.

We define formally what we mean by an SCC for an interference state graph as follows.

**Definition 5.** *(Strongly Connected Component) Let* $B\mathcal{N} = (G, N, E)$ *be a Boolean network and let* $X \subseteq G$ *be a non–empty subset of entities. Let* $\varphi = (S_\varphi, \xrightarrow{\varphi})$ *be a non-empty subgraph of* $SG_X(B\mathcal{N})$ *(i.e.* $S_\varphi \subseteq S_{B\mathcal{N}}$ *is a non-empty set of global states and* $\xrightarrow{\varphi} \subseteq \xrightarrow[X]{BN}$ *is a non-empty edge relation). Then* $\varphi$ *is a Strongly Connected Component (SCC) for* $SG_X(B\mathcal{N})$ *iff the following holds:*

*i) for any two states* $S, T \in S_\varphi$ *there is a directed path from* $S$ *to* $T$; *and*
*ii)* $\varphi$ *is maximal (adding any further nodes or edges from* $SG_X(B\mathcal{N})$ *to* $\varphi$ *breaks the above connectivity property).*

*We let* $SCC(SG_X(B\mathcal{N}))$ *denote the set of all SCCs for an interference state graph* $SG_X(B\mathcal{N})$.

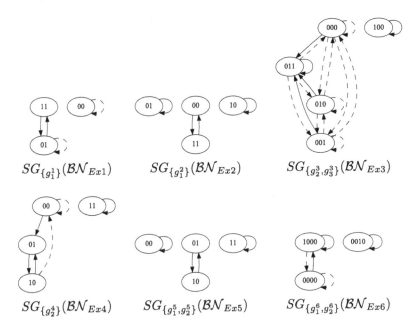

**Fig. 8.** The SCCs that arise for the example composition $\Sigma_{Ex}$.

As an illustrative example, consider the SCCs depicted in Fig. 8 for the interference state graphs that result for the example composition $\Sigma_{Ex}$.

Let $X \subseteq G$, $\varphi \in SCC(SG_X(\mathcal{BN}))$ and let $\alpha \in Path(\varphi)$ be an infinite path over $\varphi$. Then we say that $\alpha$ is a *cyclic path* iff there exists $k \in \mathbb{N}$ and $S_1, \ldots, S_k \in \mathcal{S}_\varphi$ such that

$$\alpha = \langle S_1, \ldots, S_k, S_1, \ldots, S_k, \ldots \rangle$$

We let $CPaths(\varphi)$ denote the set of all cyclic paths for an SCC $\varphi$ and let $CPaths(SG_X(\mathcal{BN}))$ denote the set of cyclic paths that can be generated from all SCCs in the interference state graph $SG_X(\mathcal{BN})$.

Given the SCCs for the Boolean networks that are to be composed we can consider merging the cyclic paths the SCCs generate to identify attractors in the composed model. In order to facilitate this process we introduce a new property called *interference alignment* that indicates when potential paths from submodels can be merged to produce paths in the composed model.

We begin by formalising when a state step does or does not rely on interference.

**Definition 6.** *Let $\mathcal{BN} = (G, N, F)$ be a Boolean network, let $g \in G$ and let $X \subseteq G$. Suppose $S_i \xrightarrow{\mathcal{BN}} S_{i+1}$ and $S_i \xrightarrow[X]{\mathcal{BN}} S'_{i+1}$, for some $S_i, S_{i+1}, S'_{i+1} \in \mathcal{S}_{\mathcal{BN}}$. We say $S_i \xrightarrow[X]{\mathcal{BN}} S'_{i+1}$ is a normal step for $g$ iff $S_{i+1}(g) = S'_{i+1}(g)$. We say $S_i \xrightarrow[X]{\mathcal{BN}} S'_{i+1}$ is an interference step for $g$ iff it is not a normal step for $g$.*

Next we define how states and paths can be merged in the context of a composition $\Sigma$.

**Definition 7.** *(Merging States and Paths)* *Let* $S_i \in S_{\mathcal{BN}_i}$, *for* $i = 1, \ldots, n$. *We define* $\wedge_\Sigma(S_1, \ldots, S_n) \in S_{BN(\Sigma)}$ *to be the composed state where for any* $g \in G(\Sigma)$ *we have*

$$\wedge_\Sigma(S_1, \ldots, S_n)(g) = \begin{cases} \wedge_{h \in \Delta(g')} S_{\lambda(h)}(h), & \text{if } g = \Delta(g'), \text{ for some } g' \in gc(\Sigma); \\ S_{\lambda(g)}(g), & \text{otherwise} \end{cases}$$

*Let* $\alpha_i = \langle S_0^i, S_1^i, \ldots \rangle \in Path(I_i)$, *for* $i = 1, \ldots, n$. *We define* $\wedge_\Sigma(\alpha_1, \ldots, \alpha_n)$ *to be the composed path defined by*

$$\wedge_\Sigma(\alpha_1, \ldots, \alpha_n) = \langle \wedge_\Sigma(S_0^1, \ldots, S_0^n), \wedge_\Sigma(S_1^1, \ldots, S_1^n), \ldots \rangle$$

We now give the important definition of *interference alignment* on paths involved in a composition.

**Definition 8.** *(Interference Alignment)* *Let* $\alpha_i = \langle S_0^i, S_1^i, \ldots \rangle \in Path(I_i)$, *for* $i = 1, \ldots, n$. *We say* $\alpha_1, \ldots, \alpha_n$ *interference align* *(for the composition* $\Sigma$*) iff for each* $g \in gc(\Sigma)$ *and each* $k \in \mathbb{N}$ *the following hold:*

1) $S_k^{\lambda(g)}(g) = S_k^{\lambda(h)}(h)$, *for all* $h \in \Delta(g)$;

2) *There exists* $h \in \Delta(g)$, *such that* $S_k^{\lambda(h)} \xrightarrow[gc(\Sigma, \mathcal{BN}_{\lambda(h)})]{\mathcal{BN}_{\lambda(h)}} S_{k+1}^{\lambda(h)}$ *is a normal step for* $h$.

The idea behind interference alignment is that it captures when paths from the Boolean networks involved in a composition can be merged to create a path in the resulting composed model. It does this by checking to make sure that interference actually occurs at the points required in each path. This is formally shown by the following result.

**Lemma 2.** *Let* $\alpha_1 \in Path(I_1), \ldots, \alpha_n \in Path(I_n)$. *Then if* $\alpha_1, \ldots, \alpha_n$ *interference align then*

$$\wedge_\Sigma(\alpha_1, \ldots, \alpha_n) \in Path(SG(BN(\Sigma)))$$

*Proof.* Let $\alpha_i = \langle S_0^i, S_1^i, \ldots \rangle \in Path(I_i)$, for $i = 1, \ldots, n$, such that $\alpha_1, \ldots, \alpha_n$ interference align. To show $\wedge_\Sigma(\alpha_1, \ldots, \alpha_n) \in Path(SG(BN(\Sigma)))$ it suffices by the definition of merging paths (Definition 7) to show for any $k \in \mathbb{N}$ that

$$\wedge_\Sigma(S_k^1, \ldots, S_k^n) \xrightarrow{BN(\Sigma)} \wedge_\Sigma(S_{k+1}^1, \ldots, S_{k+1}^n) \tag{1}$$

By Definition 3, to prove (1) we need to show that for any $g \in G(\Sigma)$ we have

$$\wedge_\Sigma(S_{k+1}^1, \ldots, S_{k+1}^n)(g) = F(\Sigma)(g)(\wedge_\Sigma(S_k^1, \ldots, S_k^n)[N(\Sigma)(g)]) \tag{2}$$

Note that by inteference alignment, the definition of merging states (Definition 7) and idempotency of conjunction it follows for any $p \in \{1, \ldots, n\}$ and any non-empty subset $X \subseteq G_p$ we know

$$\wedge_\Sigma (S_m^1, \ldots, S_m^n)[\Sigma(X)] = S_m^p[X] \tag{3}$$

for any $m \in \mathbb{N}$. To show (2) there are two cases to consider for each $g \in G(\Sigma)$ depending on whether or not $g$ is a composed entity.

**Case 1:** Suppose $g \in (G_1 \cup \ldots \cup G_n) \setminus gc(\Sigma)$ (i.e. $g$ is not used in the composition). Then we show each side of (2) reduces to $S_{k+1}^{\lambda(g)}(g)$. By (3) we know

$$\wedge_\Sigma (S_{k+1}^1, \ldots, S_{k+1}^n)(g) = S_{k+1}^{\lambda(g)}(g)$$

By definition of $BN(\Sigma)$ (Definition 3), assumption that $g$ is not used in the composition and (3) it follows

$$F(\Sigma)(g)(\wedge_\Sigma (S_k^1, \ldots, S_k^n)[N(\Sigma)(g)]) = F_{\lambda(g)}(g)(S_k^{\lambda(g)}[N_{\lambda(g)}(g)])$$

Then by assumptions that $\alpha_{\lambda(g)} \in Path(I_{\lambda(g)})$ and $g$ is not used in the composition, and by definition of the interference state graph (Definition 4) we have

$$F_{\lambda(g)}(g)(S_k^{\lambda(g)}[N_{\lambda(g)}(g)]) = S_{k+1}^{\lambda(g)}(g)$$

**Case 2:** Suppose $g = \Delta(g')$, for some $g' \in gc(\Sigma)$ (i.e. $g$ is a composed entity). Then by the definition of merging states (Definition 7) we have

$$\wedge_\Sigma (S_{k+1}^1, \ldots, S_{k+1}^n)(g) = \bigwedge_{h \in g} S_{k+1}^{\lambda(h)}(h)$$

By definition of $BN(\Sigma)$ (Definition 3) and (3) it follows

$$F(\Sigma)(g)(\wedge_\Sigma (S_k^1, \ldots, S_k^n)[N(\Sigma)(g)]) = \bigwedge_{h \in g} F_{\lambda(h)}(h)(S_k^{\lambda(h)}[N_{\lambda(h)}(h)])$$

It now remains to show that

$$\bigwedge_{h \in g} S_{k+1}^{\lambda(h)}(h) = \bigwedge_{h \in g} F_{\lambda(h)}(h)(S_k^{\lambda(h)}[N_{\lambda(h)}(h)])$$

There are two cases to consider:

**Case 2.1.** Suppose $\bigwedge_{h \in g} F_{\lambda(h)}(h)(S_k^{\lambda(h)}[N_{\lambda(h)}(h)]) = 1$. Then by conjunction it follows that for any $h \in g$ we have

$$F_{\lambda(h)}(h)(S_k^{\lambda(h)}[N_{\lambda(h)}(h)]) = 1$$

It then follows by interference alignment (Definition 8) that there must exist a normal step for some $h' \in g$ resulting in

$$S_{k+1}^{\lambda(h')}(h') = 1$$

Then by interference alignment (Definition 8) it follows that for all $h \in g$ we have

$$S_{k+1}^{\lambda(h)}(h) = 1$$

and so by conjunction it follows that

$$\bigwedge_{h \in g} S_{k+1}^{\lambda(h)}(h) = 1$$

**Case 2.2.** Suppose $\bigwedge_{h \in g} F_{\lambda(h)}(h)(S_k^{\lambda(h)}[N_{\lambda(h)}(h)]) = 0$. Then by conjunction there must exist $h \in g$ such that

$$F_{\lambda(h)}(h)(S_k^{\lambda(h)}[N_{\lambda(h)}(h)]) = 0$$

Then since $\alpha_{\lambda(h)} \in Path(I_{\lambda(h)})$ and by definition of the interference state graph (Definition 4) we must have

$$S_{k+1}^{\lambda(h)}(h) = 0$$

and so by definition of conjunction we have

$$\bigwedge_{h \in g} S_{k+1}^{\lambda(h)}(h) = 0$$

$\square$

Combining the formal definitions and results above provides a basis for compositionally identifying attractors in a composed Boolean network model. Suppose we have SCCs $\varphi_i \in SCC(I_i)$ and cyclic paths $\alpha_i \in CPaths(\varphi_i)$, for $i = 1, \ldots, n$. Then if these cyclic paths interference align then they can be merged to create a cyclic path $\wedge_\Sigma(\alpha_1, \ldots, \alpha_n)$ that must represent an attractor in the composed model $BN(\Sigma)$.

To illustrate this idea consider the following cyclic paths that result from the SCCs associated with the composition $\Sigma_{Ex}$ (see Fig. 8):

$$\langle 11, 01, 11, \ldots \rangle \in CPaths(SG_{\{g_1^1\}}(\mathcal{BN}_{Ex1})),$$

$$\langle 00, 11, 00, \ldots \rangle \in CPaths(SG_{\{g_1^2\}}(\mathcal{BN}_{Ex2})),$$

$$\langle 010, 000, 010, \ldots \rangle \in CPaths(SG_{\{g_2^3, g_3^3\}}(\mathcal{BN}_{Ex3})),$$

$$\langle 01, 10, 01, \ldots \rangle \in CPaths(SG_{\{g_2^4\}}(\mathcal{BN}_{Ex4})),$$

$$\langle 01, 10, 01, \ldots \rangle \in CPaths(SG_{\{g_1^5, g_2^5\}}(\mathcal{BN}_{Ex5})),$$

$$\langle 0000, 1000, 0000, \ldots \rangle \in CPaths(SG_{\{g_1^6, g_2^6\}}(\mathcal{BN}_{Ex6})).$$

These cyclic paths inteference align (for $\Sigma_{Ex}$) and when merged produce the cyclic path $\langle 100100000, 010110100, 100100000, \ldots \rangle$. It follows by Lemma 2 that this path is in $Path(SG(BN(\Sigma_{Ex})))$ and therefore that

$$[100100000, 010110100, 100100000]$$

is an attractor for $BN(\Sigma_{Ex})$.

We now formally prove the approach above for compositionally identifying attractors is correct by showing it is: *sound* - all attractors found are present in the composed model; and *complete* - every attractor in the composed model is found using the approach.

**Theorem 3.** *(Soundness)* *Let* $\varphi_i \in SCC(I_i)$ *and let* $\alpha_i \in CPaths(\varphi_i)$, *for* $i = 1, \ldots, n$. *Then if the cyclic paths* $\alpha_1, \ldots, \alpha_n$ *interference align then the path* $\wedge_\Sigma(\alpha_1, \ldots, \alpha_n)$ *represents an attractor in the composed model* $BN(\Sigma)$.

*Proof.* Let $\varphi_i \in SCC(I_i)$ and let $\alpha_i \in CPaths(\varphi_i)$, for $i = 1, \ldots, n$. Suppose that the cyclic paths $\alpha_1, \ldots, \alpha_n$ interference align. Then by the above assumptions and Lemma 2 it follows

$$\wedge_\Sigma(\alpha_1, \ldots, \alpha_n) \in Path(SG(BN(\Sigma)))$$

By the definition of cyclic paths we know that for each $i = 1, \ldots, n$ there must exist a minimal $k_i \in \mathbb{N}$ and states $S_1^i, \ldots, S_{k_i}^i \in S_{BN_i}$ such that

$$\alpha_i = \langle S_1^i, \ldots, S_{k_i}^i, S_1^i, \ldots, S_{k_i}^i, \ldots \rangle,$$

Let $LCM(k_1, \ldots, k_n)$ represent the lowest common multiple of $k_1, \ldots, k_n$. Then it follows that the first $LCM(k_1, \ldots, k_n) + 1$ states of $\wedge_\Sigma(\alpha_1, \ldots, \alpha_n)$ must represent an attractor in $BN(\Sigma)$. □

Next we consider showing the proposed approach is *complete* and begin with some necessary preliminary results about projecting and merging paths in a composed model. The first of these results shows that the composition of projected paths in the composed model must result in the original path.

**Lemma 4.** *Let* $\beta \in Path(SG(BN(\Sigma)))$. *Then*

$$\wedge_\Sigma(\beta[\Sigma(G_1)], \ldots, \beta[\Sigma(G_n)]) = \beta$$

*Proof.* Let $\beta = \langle T_0, T_1, \ldots \rangle \in Path(SG(BN(\Sigma)))$. Then it suffices to show that

$$T_i(g) = \wedge_\Sigma(T_i[\Sigma(G_1)], \ldots, T_i[\Sigma(G_n)])(g)$$

for any $i \in \mathbb{N}$ and any $g \in G(\Sigma)$. We do this using the following two cases.

**Case 1:** Suppose $g \in (G_1 \cup \ldots \cup G_n) \setminus gc(\Sigma)$ (i.e. $g$ is not used in the composition). Then by definition of state projection we know

$$T_i(g) = T_i[\Sigma(G_{\lambda(g)})](g)$$

and so by definition of merging states (Definition 7) we have

$$T_i[\Sigma(G_{\lambda(g)})](g) = \wedge_\Sigma(T_i[\Sigma(G_1)], \ldots, T_i[\Sigma(G_n)])(g)$$

**Case 2:** Suppose $g = \Delta(g')$, for some $g' \in gc(\Sigma)$ (i.e. $g$ is a composed entity). By the definition of merging states (Definition 7) we have

$$\wedge_\Sigma(T_i[\Sigma(G_1)], \ldots, T_i[\Sigma(G_n)])(g) = \bigwedge_{h \in \Delta(g')} T_i[\Sigma(G_{\lambda(h)})](h) \qquad (I)$$

Also by the definition of state projection we have

$$T_i[\Sigma(G_{\lambda(g')})](g') = T_i[\Sigma(G_{\lambda(h)})](h)$$

for all $h \in \Delta(g')$ and so it follows from (I) and the idempotency of conjunction that

$$\wedge_\Sigma(T_i[\Sigma(G_1)], \ldots, T_i[\Sigma(G_n)])(g) = T_i[\Sigma(G_{\lambda(g')})](g')$$

Then by definition of projection we have

$$T_i[\Sigma(G_{\lambda(g')})](g') = T_i(g)$$

$\square$

We now show that any path in the composed model projected over the entities of an underlying Boolean network will be a valid path in the interference state graph for that Boolean network.

**Lemma 5.** *Let $\beta \in Path(SG(BN(\Sigma)))$. Then for any $i \in \mathbb{N}$ we have*

$$\beta[\Sigma(G_i)] \in Path(I_i)$$

*Proof.* Let $\beta = \langle T_0, T_1, \ldots \rangle \in Path(SG(BN(\Sigma)))$. Then it suffices to show that for any $i \in \{1, \ldots, n\}$ and any $k \in \mathbb{N}$ we have

$$T_k[\Sigma(G_i)] \xrightarrow[gc(\Sigma, \mathcal{BN}_i)]{\mathcal{BN}_i} T_{k+1}[\Sigma(G_i)] \qquad (I)$$

Suppose $T_k[\Sigma(G_i)] \xrightarrow{\mathcal{BN}_i} S$, for some $S \in \mathcal{S}_{\mathcal{BN}_i}$. Then by definition of the interference state graph $I_i$ (Definition 4) to show (I) we need to prove

$$T_{k+1}[\Sigma(G_i)] \in \Upsilon_{gc(\Sigma, \mathcal{BN}_i)}(S)$$

We do this by showing that for each $g \in gc(\Sigma, \mathcal{BN}_i)$ we have

$$T_{k+1}[\Sigma(G_i)](g) \in \upsilon(S(g))$$

using the following two cases.

**Case 1:** Suppose $S(g) = 1$. Then $\upsilon(S(g)) = \{0,1\}$ and so it follows that

$$T_{k+1}[\Sigma(G_i)](g) \in \upsilon(S(g))$$

**Case 2:** Suppose $S(g) = 0$. Then by the definition of $BN(\Sigma)$ and conjunction we must have

$$T_{k+1}[\Sigma(G_i)](g) = 0$$

Since $\upsilon(S(g)) = \{0\}$ it then follows that

$$T_{k+1}[\Sigma(G_i)](g) \in \upsilon(S(g))$$

$\square$

We can now prove the completeness of the proposed compositional attractor identification approach.

**Theorem 6.** *(Completeness) Let $\psi$ be an attractor for the composed Boolean network $BN(\Sigma)$. Then there must exist $\varphi_i \in SCC(I_i)$ and cyclic paths $\alpha_i \in CPaths(\varphi_i)$, for $i = 1, \ldots, n$, such that the cyclic paths $\alpha_1, \ldots, \alpha_n$ interference align and $\wedge_\Sigma(\alpha_1, \ldots, \alpha_n)$ results in the attractor $\psi$.*

*Proof.* Let $\psi = [T_1, T_2, \ldots T_k, T_1]$ be an arbitrary attractor in the composed model $BN(\Sigma)$. Then $\psi$ can be viewed as representing the infinite cyclic path $\overline{\psi} = \langle T_1, \ldots T_k, T_1, \ldots T_k, \ldots \rangle$. It follows by Lemma 5 that for $i = 1, \ldots, n$ we have

$$\overline{\psi}[\Sigma(G_i)] \in Path(I_i)$$

Furthermore, it is clear that each path $\overline{\psi}[\Sigma(G_i)]$ must be a cyclic path and thus results from an SCC $\varphi_i$ in the interference state graph $I_i$. By Lemma 4 it follows that

$$\wedge_\Sigma(\overline{\psi}[\Sigma(G_1)], \ldots, \overline{\psi}[\Sigma(G_n)]) = \overline{\psi}$$

Given the above, it remains to show that $\overline{\psi}[\Sigma(G_1)], \ldots, \overline{\psi}[\Sigma(G_n)]$ interference align. To do this, first note that for any $g \in gc(\Sigma)$ we clearly have by the definition of projection that

$$\overline{\psi}[G_{\lambda(g)}](g) = \overline{\psi}[G_{\lambda(h)}](h),$$

for all $h \in \Delta(g)$. It remains to show that for any state transition $T \xrightarrow{BN(\Sigma)} T'$ in the path $\overline{\psi}$ and any $g \in gc(\Sigma)$ there exists $h \in \Delta(g)$ such that

$$T[\Sigma(G_{\lambda(h)})] \xrightarrow[gc(\Sigma, \mathcal{BN}_{\lambda(h)})]{\mathcal{BN}_{\lambda(h)}} T'[\Sigma(G_{\lambda(h)})]$$

is a normal step for $h$. This must hold by the definition of $F(\Sigma)$ in the composed model $BN(\Sigma)$ (Definition 3) since it composes normal steps together using conjunction and this means at least one normal step cannot be interfered with. $\square$

## 5   Developing an Algorithmic Approach

In this section we develop an algorithmic approach for the theoretical results so far developed and then use this to develop a prototype tool for the practical application and evaluation of our new compositional attractor analysis techniques.

## 5.1   Algorithm for Compositionally Analysing Attractors

The theoretical results for compositionally identifying attractors presented in the previous section are based on identifying cyclic paths over the SCCs in the subneworks' interference state graphs. We develop an algorithmic approach based on compositionally constructing these cyclic paths one step at a time till a repetition occurs. To do this we consider tuples of states over the SCCs which *align* (i.e. the states of entities to be merged are the same) and provide an approach to transition from one aligned tuple of states to the next which ensures that well-defined interference aligned cyclic paths are constructed.

More formally, let $\Sigma = (M, E)$ be an arbitrary composition with subnetworks $M = \{\mathcal{BN}_1, \dots, \mathcal{BN}_n\}$. Then we say that a state tuple $(S_1, \dots, S_n)$, for $S_1 \in S_{\mathcal{BN}_1}, \dots, S_n \in S_{\mathcal{BN}_n}$ is an *aligned state tuple (for $\Sigma$)* iff for each $g \in gc(\Sigma)$ we have $S_{\lambda(g)}(g) = S_{\lambda(h)}(h)$, for all $h \in \Delta(g)$.

When making a transition step to a new aligned state tuple we need at least one normal step to occur for each composed entity to ensure the step is realizable in practice. This leads to the following definition of an *interference aligned next state tuple* which adapts the definition of interference alignment on paths (see Definition 8).

**Definition 9.** *Suppose* $S_i \xrightarrow[gc(\Sigma, \mathcal{BN}_i)]{\mathcal{BN}_i} S_i'$, *for* $i = 1, \dots, n$ *and some* $S_i, S_i' \in S_{\mathcal{BN}_i}$. *Then we say* $(S_1', \dots, S_n')$ *is an interference aligned next state tuple for* $(S_1, \dots, S_n)$ *iff we have*

1) $(S_1', \dots, S_n')$ *is an aligned state tuple; and*
2) *For every* $g \in gc(\Sigma)$ *there exists* $h \in \Delta(g)$ *such that* $S_{\lambda(h)} \xrightarrow{\mathcal{BN}_{\lambda(h)}} S_{\lambda(h)}'$ *(i.e. a normal step).*

Clearly, an interference aligned next state tuple may not exist for a given state tuple. Interestingly, it can be shown that for any state tuple there is at most only one interference aligned next state tuple.

To identify the SCCs in each interference state graph we can use standard linear time algorithms based on depth-first search, such as *Kosaraju's algorithm* [29] and *Tarjan's algorithm* [30]. In order to efficiently deal with these SCCs we create a data structure $\Phi_\Sigma$ and for each $\mathcal{BN}_i$, we store in $\Phi_\Sigma[i]$ all the possible states that appear in its SCCs along with their set of next states.

We can now formulate an algorithm for a function *findAtt* which takes the SCC data structure $\Phi_\Sigma$ (for $\Sigma$) and then returns all the attractors in the resulting composed model $BN(\Sigma)$. The algorithm works by iterating through the set of all *aligned state tuples* over $\Phi_\Sigma$. For each one it attempts to generate a sequence of *interference aligned next state tuples* till a repeated aligned state tuple is reached indicating that a set of interference aligned cyclic paths have been found. If at any point we have an aligned state tuple that has previously been processed then we skip the current state tuple sequence since it has already been considered. The pseudo code for *findAtt* is given in Algorithm 1 and makes use of the following functions:

$alignSet(\Phi_\Sigma)$ returns the set of all aligned state tuples generated by the SCC information in $\Phi_\Sigma$.

$doStep((S_1, \ldots, S_n), \Phi_\Sigma)$ which returns the interference aligned next state tuple for $(S_1, \ldots, S_n)$ based on the SCC information in $\Phi_\Sigma$. If no interference aligned next state tuple exists then it returns a *Null* value.

$extCP(lstST)$ which merges the list of state tuples $lstST$ into a path (straightforward as the algorithm ensures states align) and extracts the attractor the path must end in.

---

**Algorithm 1:** $findAtt(\Phi_\Sigma)$

---

|  | **Input**     | : $\Phi_\Sigma$ : *SCC Data Structure* |
|--|--|--|
|  | **Output**    | : $attSet$ : *Set of Attractors* |
|  | **Variables** | : $ST, ST'$ : *StateTuple*; $lstST$ : *List of StateTuples*; |
|  |  | $seen$ : *Set of StateTuples* |

1 **Begin**
2     $attSet := \{\}$
3     $seen := \{\}$
4     **foreach** $ST \in alignSet(\Phi_\Sigma)$ **do**
5         $lstST := [\,]$
6         **Loop**
7             **if** $ST \in seen$ **then**
8                 **Exit Loop**
9             **else**
10                 $seen := seen \cup \{ST\}$
11                 $ST' := doStep(ST, \Phi_\Sigma)$
12                 **if** $ST' = Null$ **then**
13                     **Exit Loop**
14                 **else**
15                     $lstST := lstST + +[ST]$
16                     **if** $ST' \in lstST$ **then**
17                         $attSet := attSet \cup \{extCP(lstST + +[ST'])\}$
18                         **Exit Loop**
19                     **else**
20                         $ST := ST'$
21                     **end**
22                 **end**
23             **end**
24         **EndLoop**
25     **end**
26     **return** $attSet$
27 **End**

---

To illustrate how the algorithm works consider applying it to the example composition $\Sigma_{Ex}$ given in Fig. 6. The SCCs for $\Sigma_{Ex}$ result in 2880 possible state tuples but only 60 of these align. Suppose the algorithm for *findAtt* has selected the aligned state tuple $ST = (01, 11, 000, 00, 10, 1000)$. Then the following list of interference aligned next state tuples is generated:

$$lstST = [(01, 11, 000, 00, 10, 1000), (11, 00, 010, 01, 01, 0000),$$
$$(01, 11, 000, 10, 10, 1000), (11, 00, 010, 01, 01, 0000)]$$

Applying *extCP* returns the attractor $[100100000, 010110100, 100100000]$. It can be verified that the algorithm for *findAtt* does correctly identify all nine attractors in the composed model $BN(\Sigma_{Ex})$.

The performance of the algorithm is linked to the number of subnetworks in a composition, and the number and complexity of the associated SCCs. The algorithm should perform well in practice if a good compositional structure is used and we explore this experimentally in Sect. 6.

A key part of the above algorithm is generating the set of all *aligned state tuples* and deriving *interference aligned next state tuples*. Given the large state space that can be involved it is important these tasks are done efficiently and we consider algorithmic solutions to this in the subsections that follow.

## 5.2   Set of Aligned State Tuples

The algorithm for *findAtt* iterates through the set of all aligned state tuples $alignSet(\Phi_\Sigma)$ over $\Phi_\Sigma$. Since the number of aligned state tuples is normally much smaller than the set of all state tuples (for example, for $\Sigma_{Ex}$ there were 2880 state tuples but only 60 aligned state tuples) it is essential to consider how to efficiently generate the set $alignSet(\Phi_\Sigma)$.

We begin by observing that only entities involved in the composition need to be considered when checking tuple alignment. For each Boolean network $\mathcal{BN}_i$ we refer to its composed entities $gc(\Sigma, \mathcal{BN}_i)$ as its *key*. Since a key state normally forms part of many SCC states we can reduce the number of combinations to check by focusing on key states when computing aligned state tuples.

The SSC data structure $\Phi_\Sigma$ can straightforwardly be extended to include key states. We can then use this to generate the set of all aligned state tuples by recursively iterating through the Boolean networks and their key states, incrementally assigning values to keys that preserve the current state alignment. The order in which the Boolean networks are considered can impact the efficiency of this approach and we propose using the following greedy heuristic to order the Boolean networks: place the Boolean networks in descending order of the number of composed entities they influence. More formally, for each Boolean network $\mathcal{BN}_i$ we calculate its *impact factor* using the following formula:

$$\Sigma_{gc \in \{\Delta(g) \mid g \in gc(\Sigma, \mathcal{BN}_i)\}} |gc|$$

We select the Boolean network with the highest impact factor to be the first one to be considered (if there is more than one with the same impact factor then we simply randomly choose one). We then update the remaining impact factors by subtracting the composed entities now covered. We repeatedly apply the above process on the remaining Boolean networks to generate the processing order.

## 5.3 Computing Interference Aligned Next State Tuples

The algorithm for *findAtt* identifies interference aligned cyclic paths by generating a sequence of interference aligned next state tuples using *doStep* until a repeated state tuple occurs. Each subnetwork's state in an aligned state tuple must have one or more next states in its associated SCC but there is at most one interference aligned next state tuple as previously noted. It is therefore important to carefully develop an efficient approach for implementing $doStep(ST, \Phi_\Sigma)$.

The approach we take uses the observation that each composed entity $g \in gc(\Sigma, \mathcal{BN}_i)$ in a subnetwork $\mathcal{BN}_i$ has only four possible update situations:

1. The state of $g$ will be updated to 0 using a *normal step*.
2. The state of $g$ will be updated to 1 using a *normal step* and *interference is not possible*.
3. The state of $g$ is updated to 1 using a *normal step* or it can be updated to 0 using an *interference step*.
4. The state of $g$ will be updated to 0 using an *interference step* and *no normal step is possible*.

Our approach pre-processes the states in each subnetwork's SCCs, recording for each state which of the four cases above applies. We then use this information when determining the next state of a particular composed entity. Let $\Delta(\Sigma) = \{\Delta(g) \mid g \in gc(\Sigma)\}$ be the set of all composed entities in a composition. Given a composed entity $gc \in \Delta(\Sigma)$ the idea is to count the occurrences of each of the four cases in the entities that are merged in $gc$ (note that the Case 3 occurrence count turns out not to be needed). Given a current aligned state tuple $ST$ we let $cnt(gc, ST)[k]$ represent the number of occurrences of each case $k \in \{1, \ldots, 4\}$ for composed entity $gc$ given $ST$. We can then use these case counts to determine the state of the composed entity $gc$ in the interference aligned next state tuple that results from $ST$ as follows:

- If $cnt(gc, ST)[1] > 0$ and $cnt(gc, ST)[2] = 0$, then the next state for $g$ must be 0.
- If $cnt(gc, ST)[1] > 0$ and $cnt(gc, ST)[2] > 0$, then there is an inconsistent situation and no interference aligned next state tuple exists for $ST$.
- If $cnt(gc, ST)[1] = 0$ and $cnt(gc, ST)[4] = 0$, then the next state value of $gc$ must be 1 since no interference is possible.
- If $cnt(gc, ST)[1] = 0$ and $cnt(gc, ST)[4] > 0$, then there is an inconsistent situation and no interference aligned next state tuple exists for $ST$.

Note that in some cases the interference aligned next state tuple generated using this approach will not be realisable due to inconsistent constraints imposed by different composed entities on next states. To take account of this, we need to perform a simple final check on the interaction between entities.

## 5.4   A Prototype Support Tool

The algorithmic approach presented above has been used to develop a prototype tool for compositionally identifying attractors in a composed model. The tool was implemented in Python and makes use of the *NetworkX package* [13], which has tools to represent and manipulate network structures. The prototype tool reads in state graphs for the subnetworks, the merged entities of each submodel, and the set of all composed entities. It then implements the above algorithmic approach to identify the composed model's attractors using the processing steps given in Fig. 9.

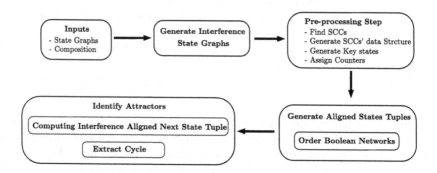

**Fig. 9.** Processing steps implemented in prototype tool.

## 6   Performance Evaluation

In this section, we evaluate the practical performance of our developed techniques for compositional attractor identification by undertaking two performance test studies on the developed prototype tool. Each study is based on identifying the attractors for a series of models which increase in size and which are formed by composing a set of seven underlying Boolean networks[1]. To help evaluate the performance of our tool we compare our results to those for three existing attractor identification tools in the literature: *BoolNet* [23], *BNS* [10] and *BoolSim* [11]. The first performance test study looks at the general performance of the tool while the second study considers how the performance is impacted by using models with more complex behaviour designed to stress the tool. The run-times are recorded in seconds and include all processing steps in Fig. 9 except generating the interference state graphs (these are assumed to have already been generated). All the experiments are performed on a laptop that contains an Intel(R) Core(TM) i7-8650U 1.90 GHz processor and 16.0 GB of memory.

---

[1] The models used in the tests are available by contacting the authors.

## 6.1  Performance Test Study One

In the first performance study we applied our tool to a series of 16 test models to see how its performance scaled as the model size increased. The results for this performance study are presented in Table 1 and in Fig. 10.

**Table 1.** Test results for Performance Study One based on a series of 16 compositional models constructed from seven submodels.

| No | Ents | Atts x Len | Aligned tuples | SCC states | $findAtt$ | $BoolNet$ | $BNS$ | $BoolSim$ |
|----|------|------------|----------------|------------|-----------|-----------|-------|-----------|
| 1  | 54   | 12 × 2     | 1460           | 74         | 0.037     | 0.154     | 0.166 | 0.162     |
| 2  | 62   | 6 × 2      | 1400           | 95         | 0.044     | 0.208     | 0.106 | 0.187     |
| 3  | 70   | 14 × 2     | 1224           | 97         | 0.080     | 0.361     | 0.180 | 0.260     |
| 4  | 80   | 12 × 2     | 3100           | 110        | 0.094     | 0.571     | 0.183 | 0.211     |
| 5  | 90   | 16 × 2     | 8100           | 138        | 0.182     | 1.088     | 0.319 | 0.329     |
| 6  | 102  | 24 × 2     | 15600          | 151        | 0.361     | 1.313     | 0.553 | 0.402     |
| 7  | 112  | 24 × 2     | 18840          | 176        | 0.438     | 1.700     | 0.628 | 0.556     |
| 8  | 122  | 28 × 2     | 21744          | 233        | 0.575     | 2.231     | 0.693 | 0.919     |
| 9  | 130  | 32 × 2     | 14576          | 267        | 0.740     | 2.451     | 0.794 | 1.100     |
| 10 | 142  | 48 × 2     | 30288          | 285        | 1.330     | 2.766     | 0.954 | 1.150     |
| 11 | 152  | 96 × 2     | 51480          | 388        | 1.594     | 3.610     | 1.480 | 2.170     |
| 12 | 167  | 32 × 2     | 70560          | 388        | 2.488     | 4.243     | 0.963 | 1.74      |
| 13 | 182  | 32 × 2     | 93600          | 544        | 3.702     | 5.317     | 1.2   | 1.76      |
| 14 | 197  | 32 × 2     | 108000         | 691        | 5.592     | 5.942     | 1.12  | 4.32      |
| 15 | 215  | 24 × 2     | 129600         | 848        | 6.682     | 7.605     | 0.983 | 6.23      |
| 16 | 233  | 24 × 2     | 172800         | 984        | 9.230     | 6.991     | 0.547 | 5.39      |

The results in Table 1 show that overall our prototype tool has performed very well compared to the other existing tools and is generally better or inline with the other tools (with the exception of *BNS* in the later tests). In particular, in the first nine tests the prototype tool has the best performance out of the tools. As the model size increases above 130 entities the performance continues to be good but the best tool is now *BNS*. It seems likely that the increase in the number of aligned tuples is playing a key role here in impacting the tools performance (see the second performance study below). This can be seen in Tests 11 and 12 which have the same number of SCC states but differ in the number of aligned tuples. This negatively impacts the resulting run-time for Test 12 even though Test 11 has considerably more attractors. Overall, the *BNS* tool appears to perform best in this set of tests.

## 6.2  Performance Test Study Two

In the second performance test study we set out to investigate the limitations of the tool by developing more complex test cases. Using the insights gained from the first performance study, we focused on generating composed models that had significantly more aligned state tuples and attractors. In particular, we introduced a new submodel with more complex behaviour and then constructed 11 new test models, focusing on increasing the complexity of the compositional structure. The results for the second performance test study are presented in Table 2 and in Fig. 10.

**Table 2.** Test results for Performance Test Study Two based on a series of 11 compositional models designed to stress test the prototype tool.

| No | Ents | Atts x Len | Aligned tuples | SCC states | $findAtt$ | $BoolNet$ | $BNS$ | $BoolSim$ |
|----|------|------------|----------------|------------|-----------|-----------|-------|-----------|
| 1  | 56   | 69 × 2     | 5248           | 86         | 0.112     | 0.214     | 0.471 | 0.477     |
| 2  | 64   | 28 × 2, 2 × 4 | 36480       | 105        | 0.472     | 0.312     | 1.33  | 0.323     |
| 3  | 74   | 32 × 2     | 64000          | 119        | 0.897     | 0.559     | 0.387 | 0.375     |
| 4  | 86   | 112 × 2    | 66520          | 126        | 1.099     | 1.015     | 1.48  | 1.14      |
| 5  | 92   | 192 × 2    | 85000          | 133        | 2.026     | 1.203     | 2.55  | 2.00      |
| 6  | 104  | 192 × 2    | 170000         | 156        | 3.849     | 1.891     | 2.73  | 2.34      |
| 7  | 118  | 192 × 2    | 312000         | 194        | 7.022     | 2.657     | 3.04  | 2.17      |
| 8  | 126  | 256 × 2    | 396000         | 240        | 9.684     | 3.328     | 3.63  | 2.94      |
| 9  | 136  | 256 × 2    | 504000         | 254        | 12.742    | 3.578     | 4.01  | 2.34      |
| 10 | 144  | 256 × 2    | 504000         | 295        | 14.238    | 4.502     | 4.36  | 3.49      |
| 11 | 156  | 576 × 2    | 540000         | 334        | 16.734    | 4.861     | 8.72  | 8.39      |

The results for the prototype tool in the second performance study are clearly worse than in the first test (see Fig. 10) and it is clear it has been impacted by the increase in complexity in these tests. In particular, it can be seen that from Test 6 onwards the prototype tools performance is worse than the other tools. Specifically, this seems to be connected to the larege increase in the number of aligned state tuples that occurs at this point and so this highlights an area that needs further developing in the tool. Interestingly, we can see that $BNS$ is also being impacted by the increased complexity of the models and now generally performs worse than $BoolNet$ and $BoolSim$.

Overall the results appear to show that our tool compares well with the other tools, especially given that it is a prototype tool developed in a short time to evaluate our techniques. More work is now needed to further refine the underlying algorithm used in our tool and to improve the efficiency of the prototype tool especially with respect to handling aligned set tuples.

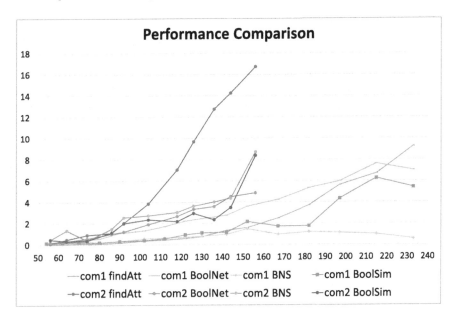

**Fig. 10.** Graph summarising the performance study results (where the lines beginning com1 represent results from Table 1 and those beginning com2 represent results from Table 2.

## 7   Conclusions

In this paper we have developed new techniques and tools that significantly enhance a recently proposed compositional framework for constructing and analysing Boolean networks [3,4]. This work is important as Boolean networks are extensively used for analysing and engineering biological systems but their practical application remains limited by the state space explosion problem. This paper makes the following important contributions:

1) We have formulated a new general definition for the compositional construction of Boolean networks based on using a graph based structure to allow the arbitrary composition of multiple Boolean networks over multiple entities. Importantly, this simplifies the presentation of key definitions and results for the compositional framework.
2) We have formally developed a new compositional approach for identifying the attractors of a Boolean network. This was based on using the SCCs in the subnetwork's interference state graphs to identify potential cyclic behaviour and then using a new property, *interference alignment*, that indicates when cyclic paths generated by SCCs can be composed to form attractors.
3) Using the definitions and results developed in 2) we formulated an algorithmic approach for compositional identifying attractors, considering a range of interesting problems related to efficiently computing aligned state tuples and used this to develop a prototype tool.

4) We investigated the practical performance of the developed techniques by undertaking a range of performance tests on the developed prototype tool (see Sect. 6). The results show that the developed techniques have the potential to work very well (see Sect. 6.1). However, they also indicate that work is needed to further develop our initial prototype tool to allow it to cope more efficiently as the underlying complexity of the composed models increases (see Sect. 6.2).

Work has now begun on extending our compositional techniques and results to asynchronous Boolean networks. We also plan in future work to undertake a large case study of applying our techniques to a realistic biological example to allow us to further evaluate their practical applicability and performance.

**Acknowledgments.** We would like to thank Hanadi Alkhudhayr for many interesting discussions on Boolean network composition. We gratefully acknowledge the financial support provided for this work by the Faculty of Computer and Information Sciences, Princess Nourah Bint Abdulrahman University.

# References

1. Akutsu, T., Miyano, S., Kuhara, S., et al.: Identification of genetic networks from a small number of gene expression patterns under the Boolean network model. Pac. Symp. Biocomput. **4**, 17–28 (1999)
2. Albert, R., Othmer, H.: The topology of the regulatory interactions predicts the expression pattern of the segment polarity genes in drosophila melanogaster. J. Theor. Biol. **223**(1), 1–18 (2003)
3. Alkhudhayr, H.: Developing a compositional framework for the construction and analysis of boolean networks. PhD thesis, School of Computing, Newcastle University (2020)
4. Alkhudhayr, H., Steggles, J.: A compositional framework for Boolean networks. Biosystems **186**, 103960 (2019)
5. Alkhudhayr, H., Steggles, J.: A formal framework for composing qualitative models of biological systems. In: Martín-Vide, C., Neruda, R., Vega-Rodríguez, M.A. (eds.) TPNC 2017. LNCS, vol. 10687, pp. 25–36. Springer, Cham (2017). https://doi.org/10.1007/978-3-319-71069-3_2
6. Aracena, J., Goles, E., Moreira, A., Salinas, L.: On the robustness of update schedules in Boolean networks. Biosystems **97**(1), 1–8 (2009)
7. Barbuti, R., Gori, R., Milazzo, P., Nasti, L.: A survey of gene regulatory networks modelling methods: from differential equations, to Boolean and qualitative bioinspired models. J. Membr. Comput. **2**, 207–226 (2020)
8. de Jong, H.: Modeling and simulation of genetic regulatory systems: a literature review. J. Comput. Biol. **9**, 67–103 (2002)
9. Dubrova, E., Teslenko, M.: Compositional properties of random Boolean networks. Phys. Rev. E **71**(5), 056116 (2005)
10. Dubrova, E., Teslenko, M.: A sat-based algorithm for finding attractors in synchronous Boolean networks. IEEE/ACM Trans. Comput. Biol. Bioinf. **8**(5), 1393–1399 (2011)

11. Garg, A., Di Cara, A., Xenarios, I., Mendoza, L., De Micheli, G.: Synchronous versus asynchronous modeling of gene regulatory networks. Bioinformatics **24**(17), 1917–1925 (2008)
12. Guo, W., Yang, G., Wei, W., He, L., Sun, M.: A parallel attractor finding algorithm based on Boolean satisfiability for genetic regulatory networks. PLoS ONE **9**(4), e94258 (2014)
13. Hagberg, A., Swart, P., Chult, D.S.: Exploring network structure, dynamics, and function using NetworkX. Technical report, Los Alamos National Lab. (LANL), Los Alamos, NM (United States) (2008)
14. Harvey, I., Bossomaier, T.: Time out of joint: attractors in asynchronous random Boolean networks. In: Proceedings of the Fourth European Conference on Artificial Life, pp. 67–75. MIT Press, Cambridge (1997)
15. Helikar, T., Konvalina, J., Heidel, J., Rogers, J.A.: Emergent decision-making in biological signal transduction networks. Proc. Natl. Acad. Sci. **105**(6), 1913–1918 (2008)
16. Hong, C., Hwang, J., Cho, K.-H., Shin, I.: An efficient steady-state analysis method for large Boolean networks with high maximum node connectivity. PLoS ONE **10**(12), e0145734 (2015)
17. Huang, S., Ingber, D.E.: Shape-dependent control of cell growth, differentiation, and apoptosis: switching between attractors in cell regulatory networks. Exper. Cell Res. **261**(1), 91–103 (2000)
18. Kauffman, S.A.: Metabolic stability and epigenesis in randomly constructed genetic nets. J. Theor. Biol. **22**(3), 437–467 (1969)
19. Kauffman, S.A.: The Origins of Order: Self Organization and Selection in Evolution. Oxford University Press, Oxford, USA (1993)
20. Li, F., Long, T., Lu, Y., Ouyang, Q., Tang, C.: The yeast cell-cycle network is robustly designed. Proc. Natl. Acad. Sci. **101**(14), 4781–4786 (2004)
21. Miller, B.W., Ranum, D.L.: Problem Solving with Algorithms and Data Structures Using Python, 2nd edn. Franklin, Beedle and Associates Inc, Portland (2011)
22. Mizera, A., Pang, J., Qu, H., Yuan, Q.: A new decomposition method for attractor detection in large synchronous Boolean networks. In: Larsen, K.G., Sokolsky, O., Wang, J. (eds.) SETTA 2017. LNCS, vol. 10606, pp. 232–249. Springer, Cham (2017). https://doi.org/10.1007/978-3-319-69483-2_14
23. Müssel, C., Hopfensitz, M., Kestler, H.A.: BoolNet-an R package for generation, reconstruction and analysis of Boolean networks. Bioinformatics **26**(10), 1378–1380 (2010)
24. Pandey, S., et al.: Boolean modeling of transcriptome data reveals novel modes of heterotrimeric g-protein action. Mol. Syst. Biol. **6**(1), 2375–2387 (2010)
25. Perrot, K., Perrotin, P., Sené, S.: A framework for (de)composing with Boolean automata networks. In: Durand-Lose, J., Verlan, S. (eds.) MCU 2018. LNCS, vol. 10881, pp. 121–136. Springer, Cham (2018). https://doi.org/10.1007/978-3-319-92402-1_7
26. Perrot, K., Perrotin, P., Sené, S.: Optimising attractor computation in Boolean automata networks. In: Leporati, A., Martín-Vide, C., Shapira, D., Zandron, C. (eds.) LATA 2021. LNCS, vol. 12638, pp. 68–80. Springer, Cham (2021). https://doi.org/10.1007/978-3-030-68195-1_6
27. Saadatpour, A., et al.: Dynamical and structural analysis of a t cell survival network identifies novel candidate therapeutic targets for large granular lymphocyte leukemia. PLoS Comput. Biol. **7**(11), e1002267 (2011)

28. Schwab, J.D., Kühlwein, S.D., Ikonomi, N., Kühl, M., Kestler, H.A.: Concepts in Boolean network modeling: what do they all mean? Comput. Struct. Biotechnol. J. **18**, 571–582 (2020)
29. Sharir, M.: A strong-connectivity algorithm and its applications in data flow analysis. Comput. Math. Appl. **7**(1), 67–72 (1981)
30. Tarjan, R.: Depth-first search and linear graph algorithms. SIAM J. Comput. **1**(2), 146–160 (1972)
31. Thieffry, D., Thomas, R.: Dynamical behaviour of biological regulatory networks-II Immunity control in bacteriophage lambda. Bull. Math. Biol. **57**(2), 277–297 (1995)
32. Wuensche, A.: Aggregation algorithm towards large-scale Boolean network analysis. In: Schlosser, G., Wagner, G.P., editors, Modularity in Development and Evolution, chapter 13, pp. 288–311. University of Chicago Press (2004)
33. Yuan, Q., Mizera, A., Pang, J., Hongyang, Q.: A new decomposition-based method for detecting attractors in synchronous Boolean networks. Sci. Comput. Program. **180**, 18–35 (2019)
34. Yuan, Q., Hongyang, Q., Pang, J., Mizera, A.: Improving BDD-based attractor detection for synchronous Boolean networks. Sci. China Inf. Sci. **59**(8), 1–16 (2016). https://doi.org/10.1007/s11432-016-5594-9
35. Zhao, Y., Kim, J., Filippone, M.: Aggregation algorithm towards large-scale Boolean network analysis. IEEE Trans. Autom. Control **58**(8), 1976–1985 (2013)

# Author Index

Printed in the United States
by Baker & Taylor Publisher Services